drew / hardy noir

THE DEATH OF NANCY DREW®

writer
Anthony Del Col

artist
Joe Eisma

letterers
ISSUES 1-3, 5-6
Crank!
ISSUE 4
Taylor Esposito

colorist
Salvatore Aiala

editor
Matt Idelson

collection cover
Joe Eisma

collection design
Cathleen Heard

creative assistants
Sasha Fraze
Keith WTS Morris
Toyin Oluwole

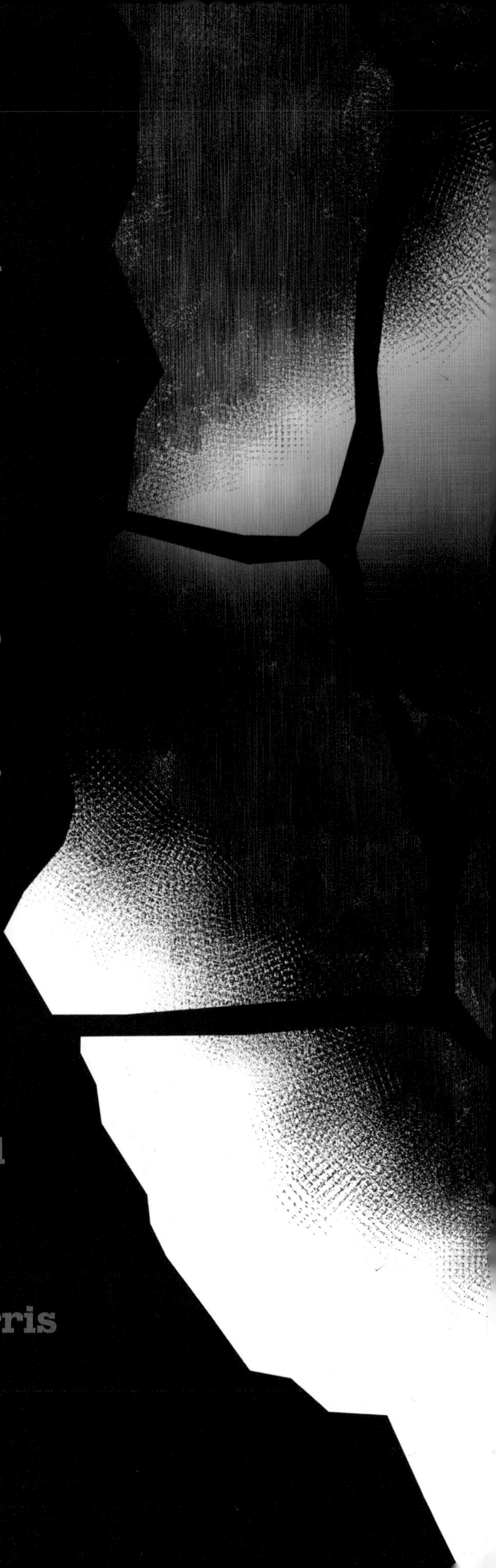

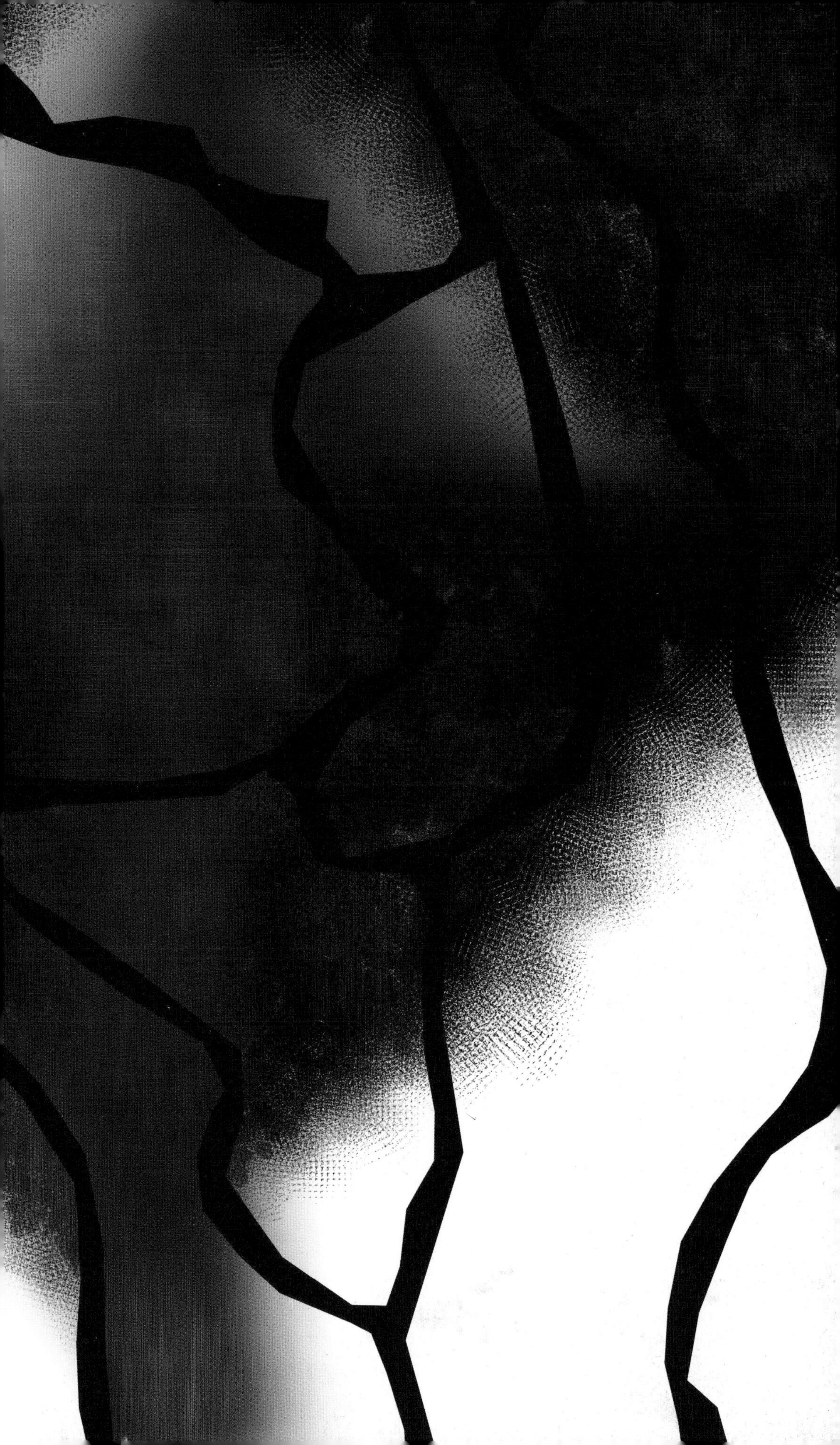

DYNAMITE®

Nick Barrucci, CEO / Publisher
Juan Collado, President / COO
Brandon Dante Primavera, V.P. of IT and Operations
Jim "Ski" Sokolowski, V.P., Associate Publisher

Joe Rybandt, Executive Editor
Matt Idelson, Senior Editor

Alexis Persson, Creative Director
Rachel Kilbury, Digital Multimedia Associate
Katie Hidalgo, Graphic Designer
Nick Pentz, Graphic Designer

Alan Payne, V.P. of Sales and Marketing
Vince Letterio, Director of Direct Market Sales
Rex Wang, Director of Sales and Branding
Vincent Faust, Marketing Coordinator

Jim Kuhoric, Vice President of Product Development
Jay Spence, Director of Product Development
Mariano Nicieza, Director of Research & Development

Online at www.dynamite.com
On Facebook /dynamitecomics
On Instagram /dynamitecomics
On Twitter @dynamitecomics

ISBN 13: 978-1-5241-1914-0
First Printing 10 9 8 7 6 5 4 3 2 1

For information regarding press, media rights, foreign rights, licensing, promotions, and advertising e-mail: marketing@dynamite.com.

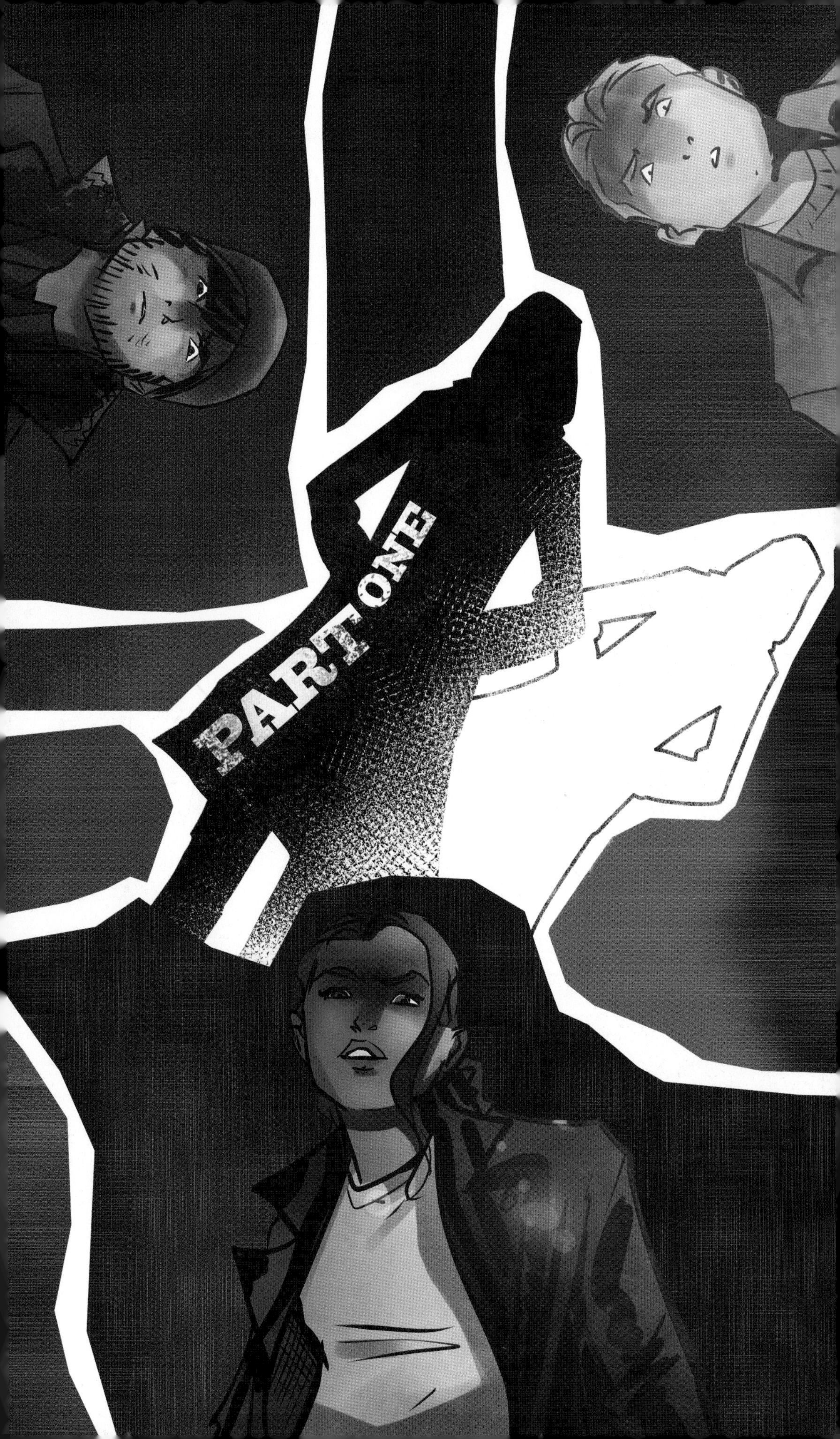
PART ONE

PART ONE COVER ART BY **JOE EISMA**

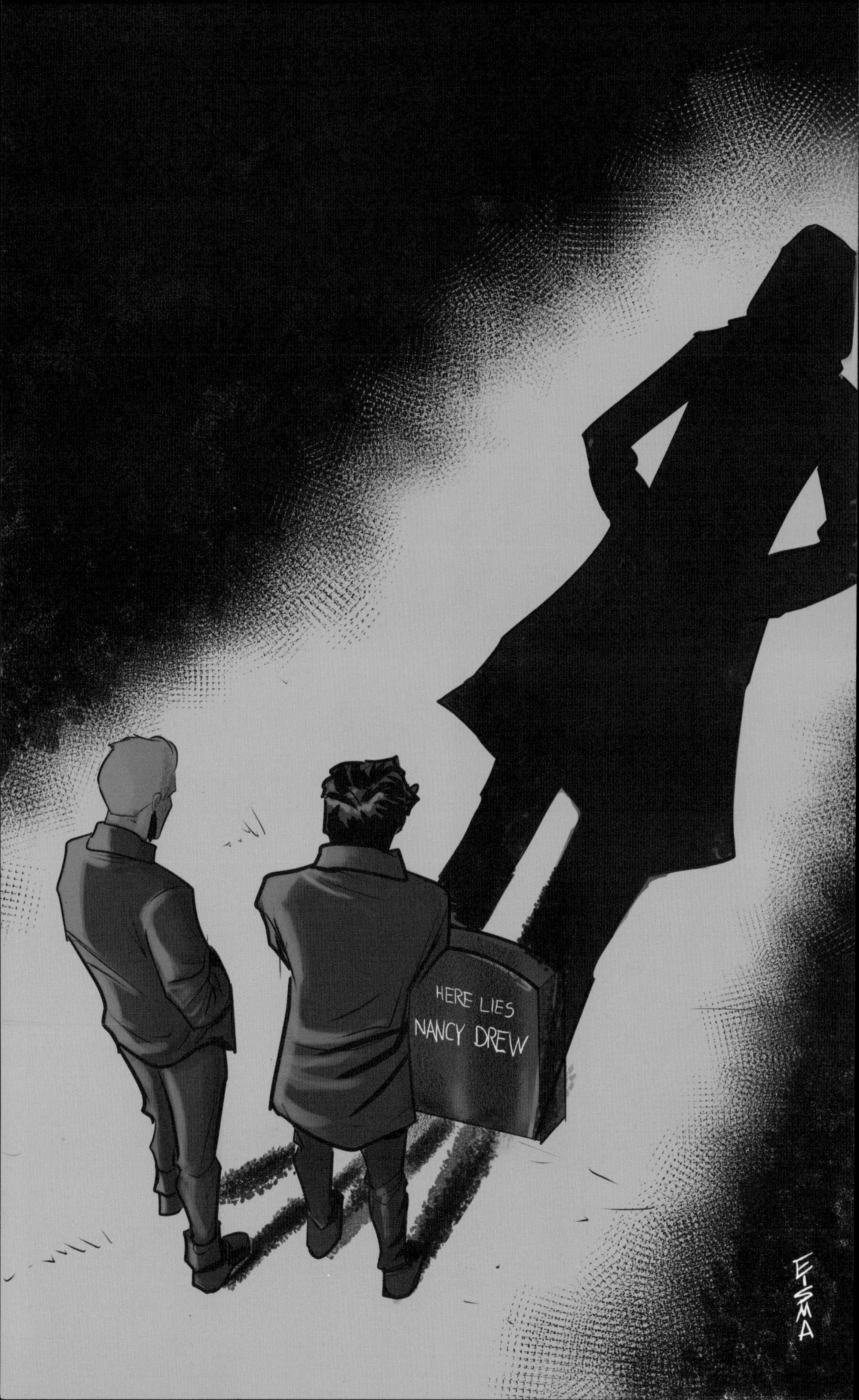

HERE LIES
NANCY DREW
EISMA

TWELVE YEARS AGO.

Who is Nancy Drew?

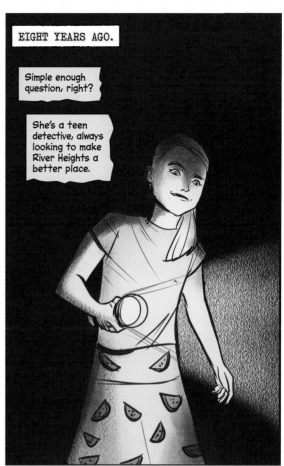

EIGHT YEARS AGO.

Simple enough question, right?

She's a teen detective, always looking to make River Heights a better place.

FOUR YEARS AGO.

She's a good daughter, a good student, a good friend.

Boring, some would say.

SIX MONTHS AGO.

They're wrong. Well, the question's wrong.

It should be...

...who *was* Nancy Drew?
TODAY. RIVER HEIGHTS.
I knew her for most of my life. Loved her for most of my life.
NANCY S. DREW
2000 - 2019
Beloved daughter
and friend
CATHERINE A. D
1970 - 201
Beloved mothe
and wife

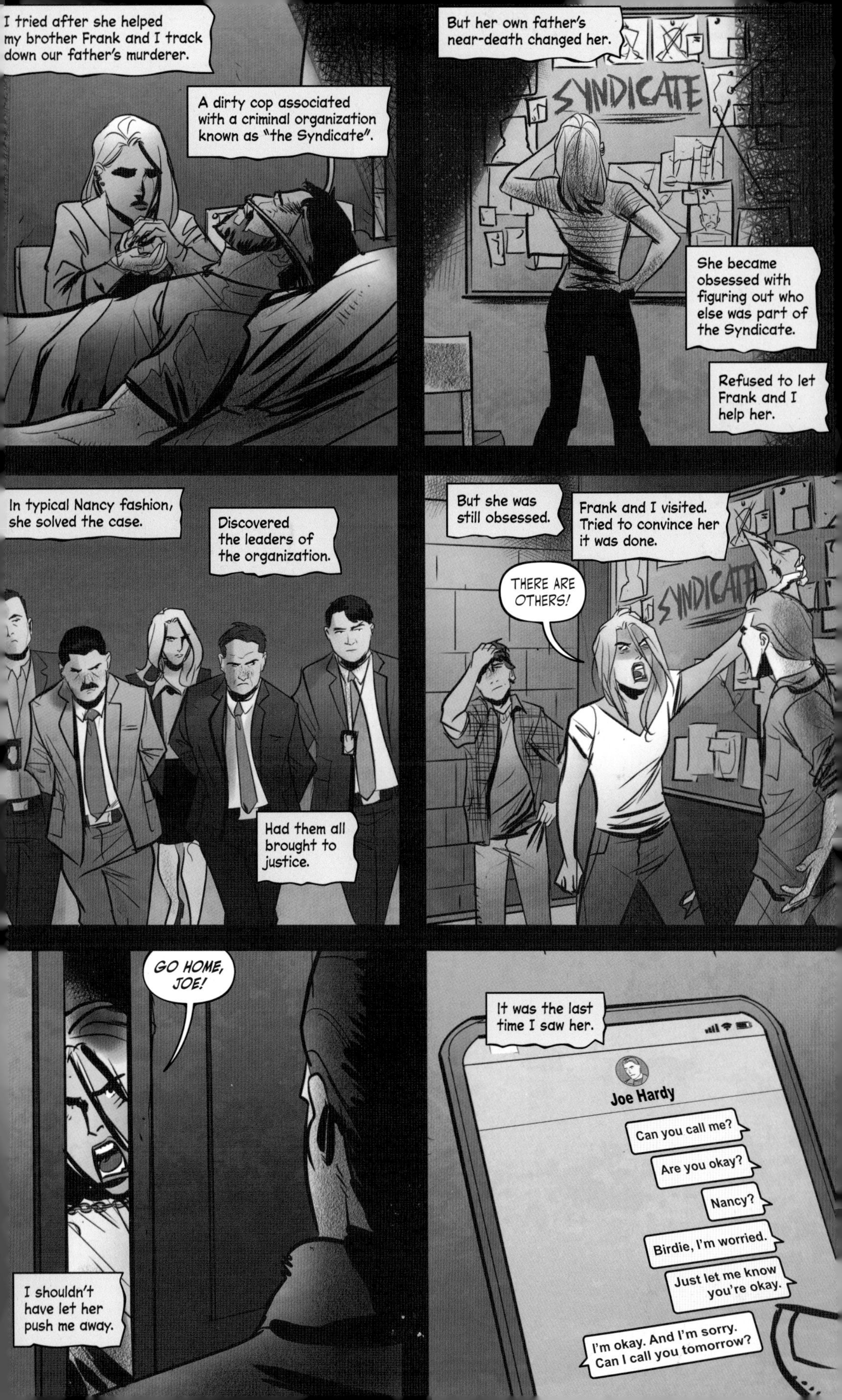

I tried after she helped my brother Frank and I track down our father's murderer.
A dirty cop associated with a criminal organization known as "the Syndicate".
But her own father's near-death changed her.
SYNDICATE
She became obsessed with figuring out who else was part of the Syndicate.
Refused to let Frank and I help her.
In typical Nancy fashion, she solved the case.
Discovered the leaders of the organization.
Had them all brought to justice.
But she was still obsessed.
Frank and I visited. Tried to convince her it was done.
THERE ARE OTHERS!
SYNDICATE
GO HOME, JOE!
I shouldn't have let her push me away.
It was the last time I saw her.
Joe Hardy
Can you call me?
Are you okay?
Nancy?
Birdie, I'm worried.
Just let me know you're okay.
I'm okay. And I'm sorry. Can I call you tomorrow?

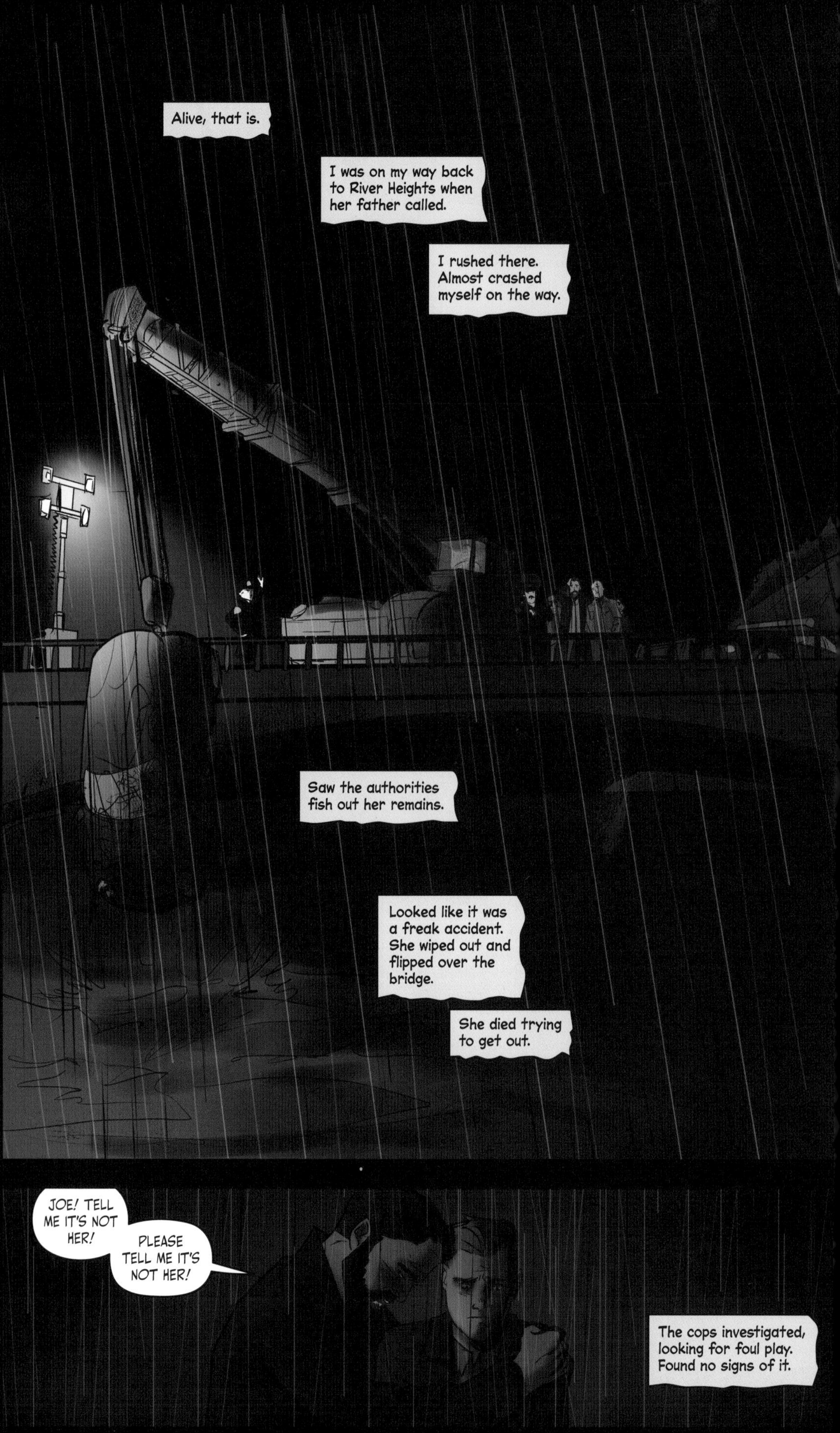
Alive, that is.
I was on my way back to River Heights when her father called.
I rushed there. Almost crashed myself on the way.
Saw the authorities fish out her remains.
Looked like it was a freak accident. She wiped out and flipped over the bridge.
She died trying to get out.
JOE! TELL ME IT'S NOT HER!
PLEASE TELL ME IT'S NOT HER!
The cops investigated, looking for foul play. Found no signs of it.

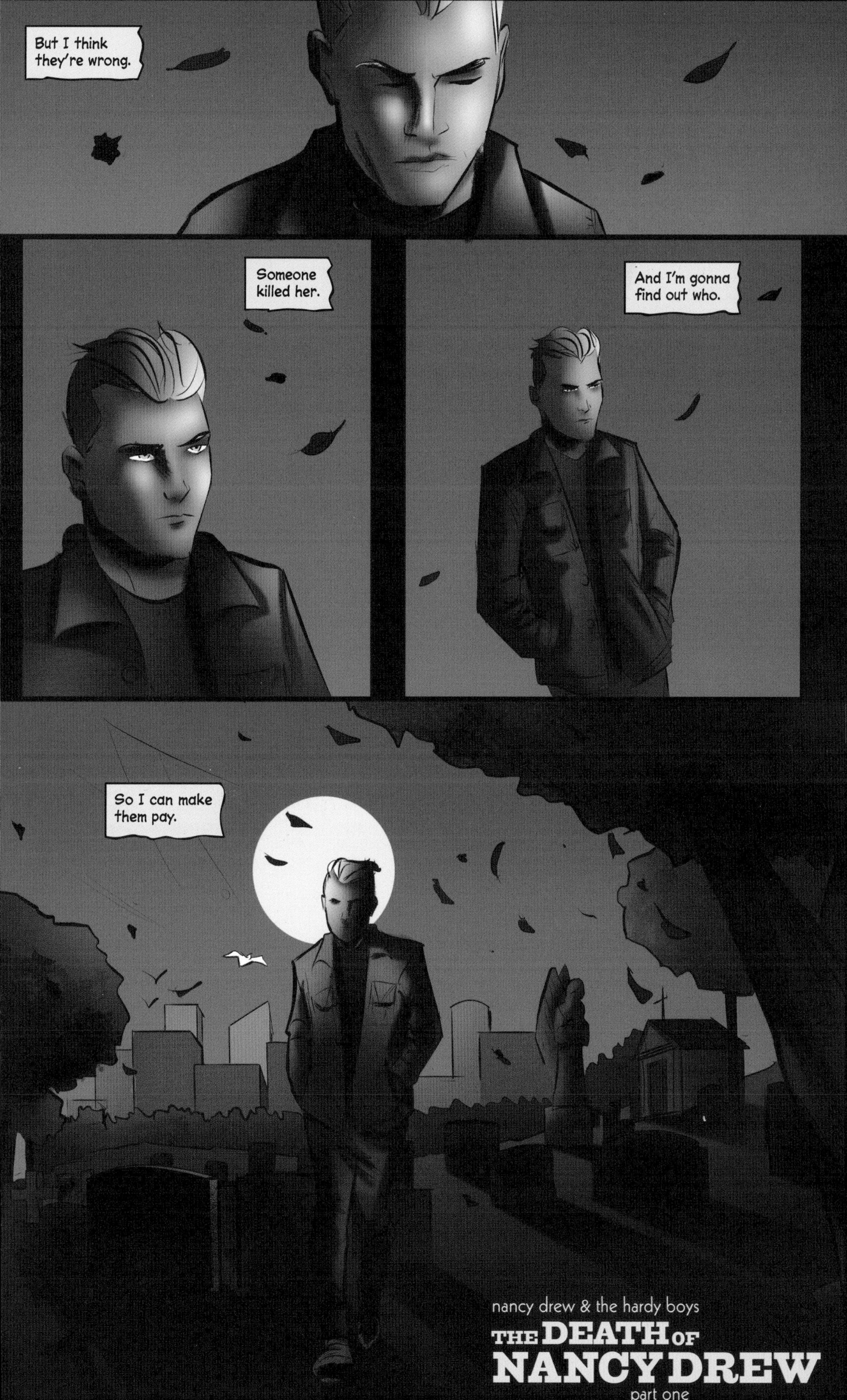

But I think they're wrong.
Someone killed her.
And I'm gonna find out who.
So I can make them pay.
nancy drew & the hardy boys
THE DEATH OF NANCY DREW
part one

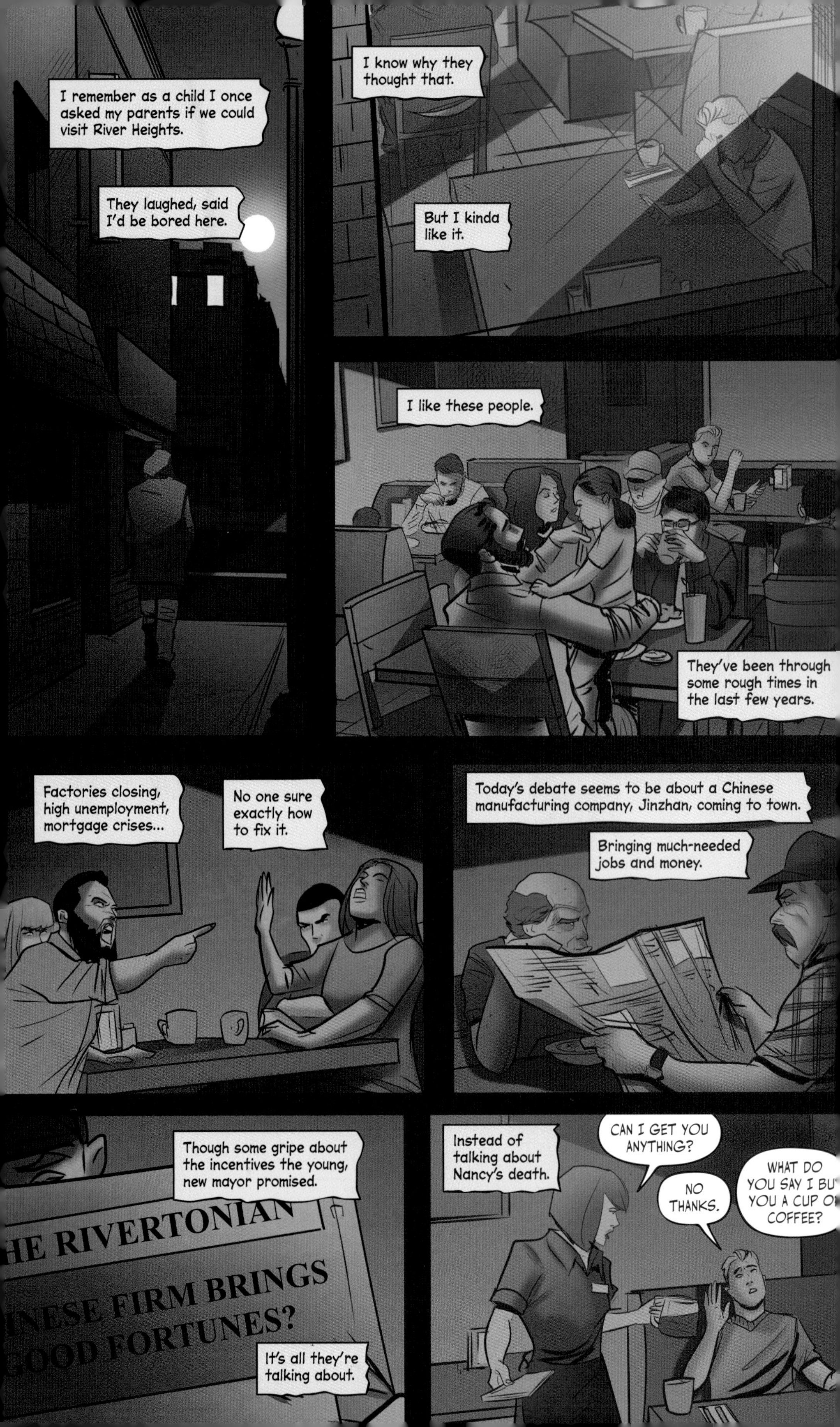

I remember as a child I once asked my parents if we could visit River Heights.
They laughed, said I'd be bored here.
I know why they thought that.
But I kinda like it.
I like these people.
They've been through some rough times in the last few years.
Factories closing, high unemployment, mortgage crises...
No one sure exactly how to fix it.
Today's debate seems to be about a Chinese manufacturing company, Jinzhan, coming to town.
Bringing much-needed jobs and money.
Though some gripe about the incentives the young, new mayor promised.
HE RIVERTONIAN
INESE FIRM BRINGS
GOOD FORTUNES?
It's all they're talking about.
Instead of talking about Nancy's death.
CAN I GET YOU ANYTHING?
NO THANKS.
WHAT DO YOU SAY I BU
YOU A CUP O
COFFEE?

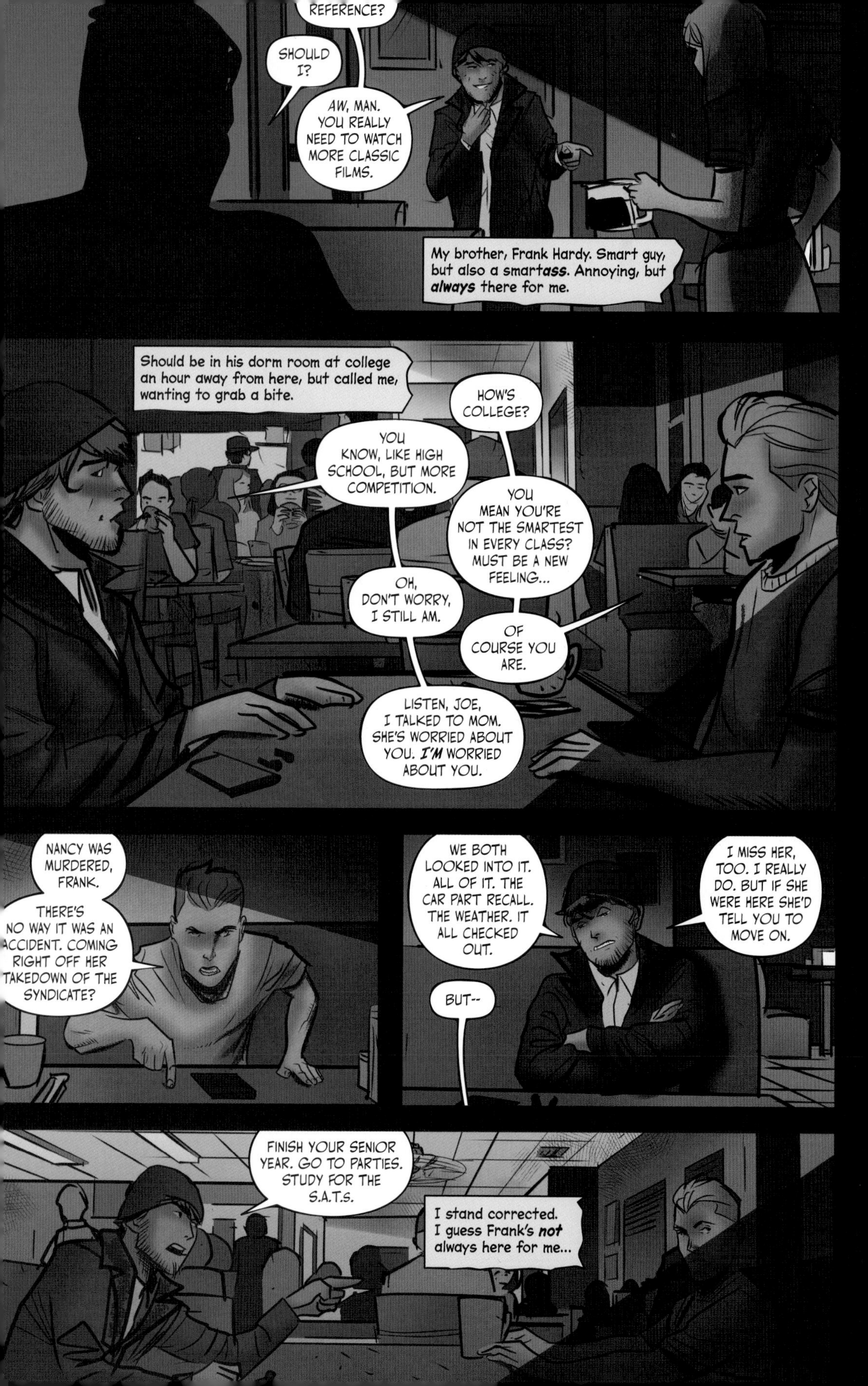
REFERENCE?
SHOULD I?
AW, MAN. YOU REALLY NEED TO WATCH MORE CLASSIC FILMS.
My brother, Frank Hardy. Smart guy, but also a smart*ass*. Annoying, but ***always*** there for me.
Should be in his dorm room at college an hour away from here, but called me, wanting to grab a bite.
HOW'S COLLEGE?
YOU KNOW, LIKE HIGH SCHOOL, BUT MORE COMPETITION.
YOU MEAN YOU'RE NOT THE SMARTEST IN EVERY CLASS? MUST BE A NEW FEELING...
OH, DON'T WORRY, I STILL AM.
OF COURSE YOU ARE.
LISTEN, JOE, I TALKED TO MOM. SHE'S WORRIED ABOUT YOU. ***I'M*** WORRIED ABOUT YOU.
NANCY WAS MURDERED, FRANK.
THERE'S NO WAY IT WAS AN ACCIDENT. COMING RIGHT OFF HER TAKEDOWN OF THE SYNDICATE?
WE BOTH LOOKED INTO IT. ALL OF IT. THE CAR PART RECALL. THE WEATHER. IT ALL CHECKED OUT.
BUT--
I MISS HER, TOO. I REALLY DO. BUT IF SHE WERE HERE SHE'D TELL YOU TO MOVE ON.
FINISH YOUR SENIOR YEAR. GO TO PARTIES. STUDY FOR THE S.A.T.S.
I stand corrected. I guess Frank's ***not*** always here for me...

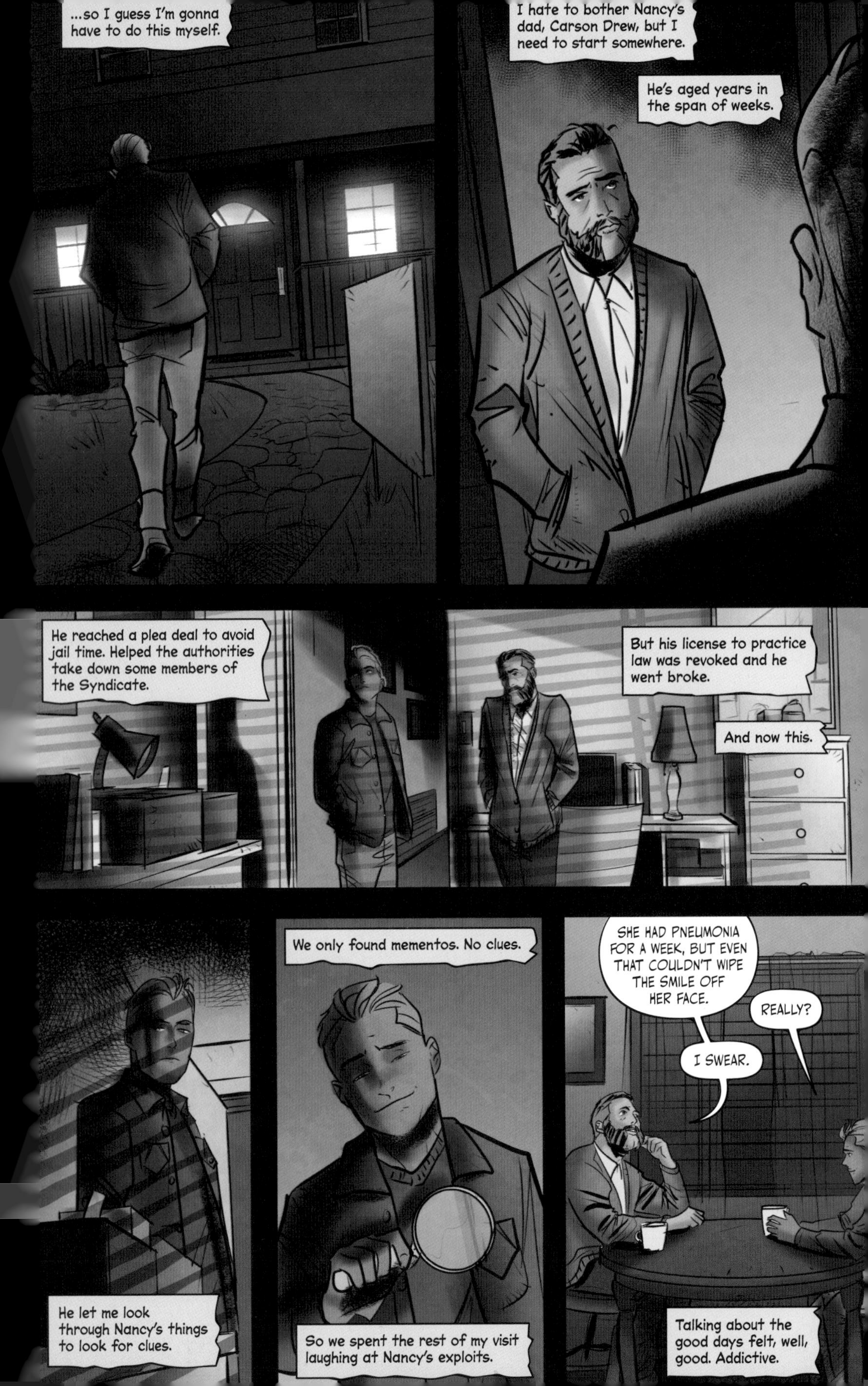
...so I guess I'm gonna have to do this myself.
I hate to bother Nancy's dad, Carson Drew, but I need to start somewhere.
He's aged years in the span of weeks.
He reached a plea deal to avoid jail time. Helped the authorities take down some members of the Syndicate.
But his license to practice law was revoked and he went broke.
And now this.
He let me look through Nancy's things to look for clues.
We only found mementos. No clues.
So we spent the rest of my visit laughing at Nancy's exploits.
SHE HAD PNEUMONIA FOR A WEEK, BUT EVEN THAT COULDN'T WIPE THE SMILE OFF HER FACE.
REALLY?
I SWEAR.
Talking about the good days felt, well, good. Addictive.

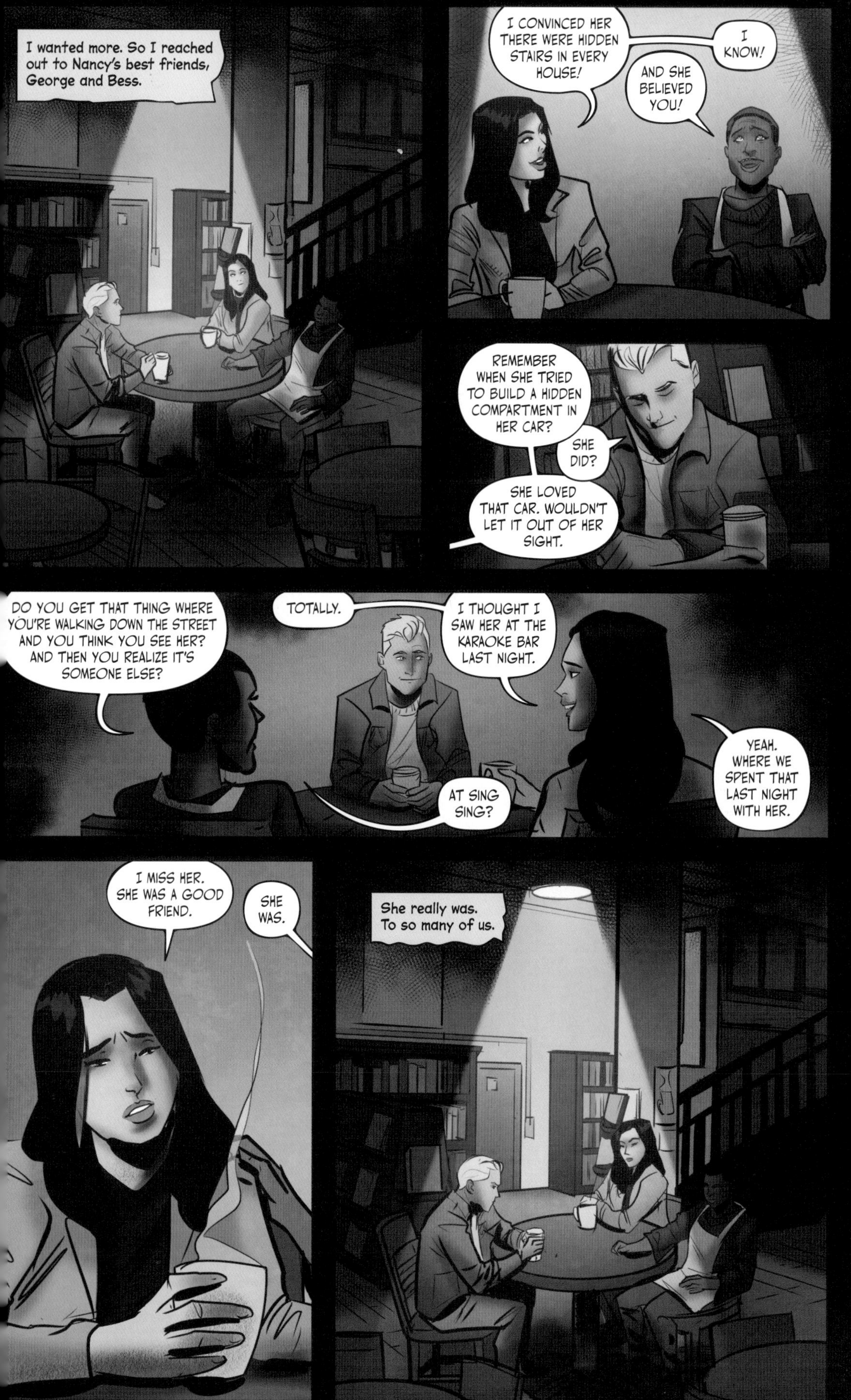
I wanted more. So I reached out to Nancy's best friends, George and Bess.
I CONVINCED HER THERE WERE HIDDEN STAIRS IN EVERY HOUSE!
I KNOW!
AND SHE BELIEVED YOU!
REMEMBER WHEN SHE TRIED TO BUILD A HIDDEN COMPARTMENT IN HER CAR?
SHE DID?
SHE LOVED THAT CAR. WOULDN'T LET IT OUT OF HER SIGHT.
DO YOU GET THAT THING WHERE YOU'RE WALKING DOWN THE STREET AND YOU THINK YOU SEE HER? AND THEN YOU REALIZE IT'S SOMEONE ELSE?
TOTALLY.
I THOUGHT I SAW HER AT THE KARAOKE BAR LAST NIGHT.
AT SING SING?
YEAH. WHERE WE SPENT THAT LAST NIGHT WITH HER.
I MISS HER. SHE WAS A GOOD FRIEND.
SHE WAS.
She really was. To so many of us.

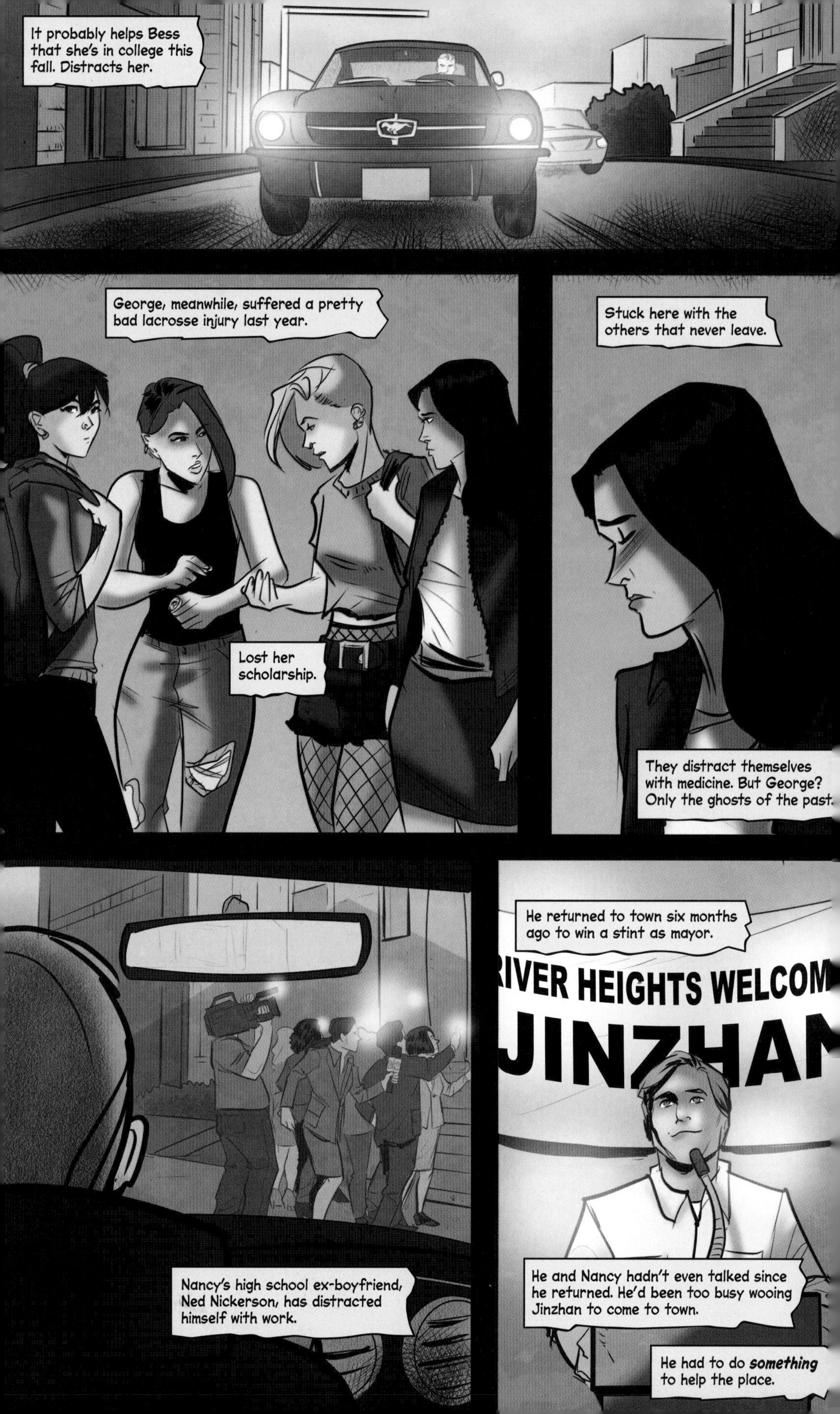
It probably helps Bess that she's in college this fall. Distracts her.
George, meanwhile, suffered a pretty bad lacrosse injury last year.
Lost her scholarship.
Stuck here with the others that never leave.
They distract themselves with medicine. But George? Only the ghosts of the past.
Nancy's high school ex-boyfriend, Ned Nickerson, has distracted himself with work.
He returned to town six months ago to win a stint as mayor.
RIVER HEIGHTS WELCOM
JINZHAN
He and Nancy hadn't even talked since he returned. He'd been too busy wooing Jinzhan to come to town.
He had to do *something* to help the place.

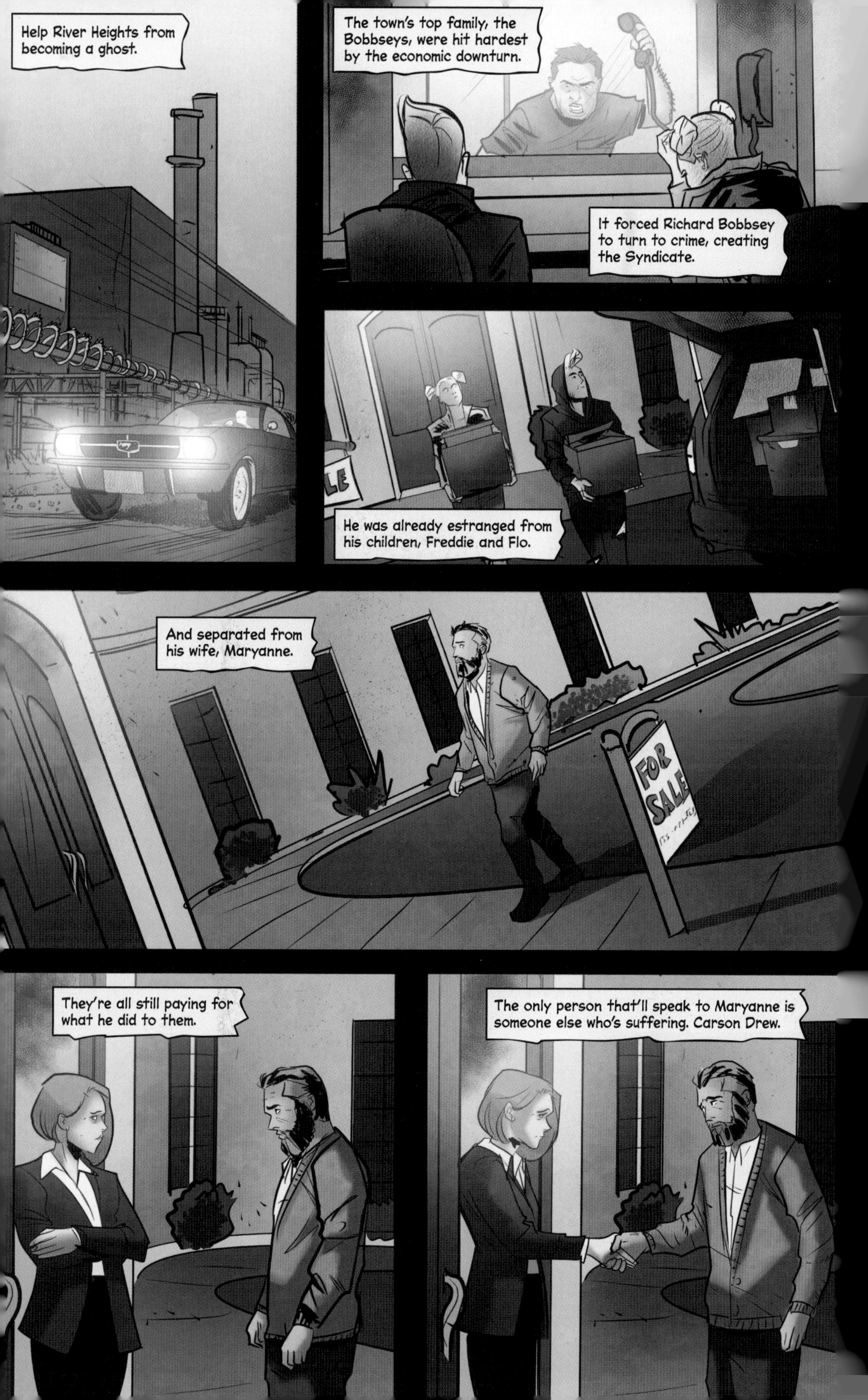

Help River Heights from becoming a ghost.
The town's top family, the Bobbseys, were hit hardest by the economic downturn.
It forced Richard Bobbsey to turn to crime, creating the Syndicate.
He was already estranged from his children, Freddie and Flo.
And separated from his wife, Maryanne.
FOR SALE
They're all still paying for what he did to them.
The only person that'll speak to Maryanne is someone else who's suffering. Carson Drew.

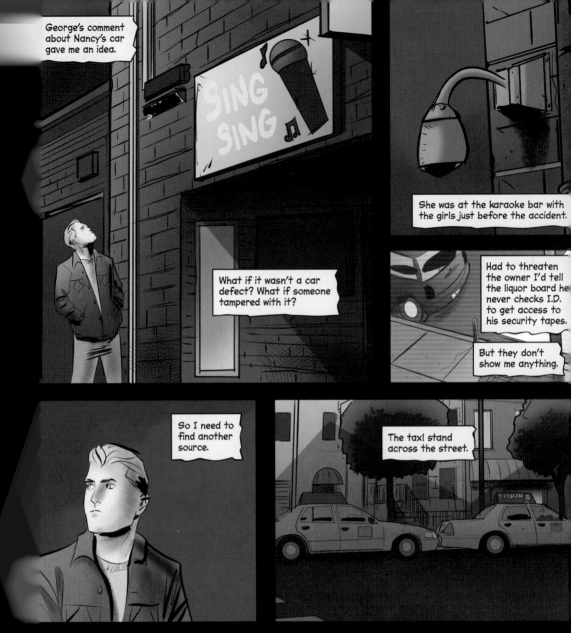

George's comment about Nancy's car gave me an idea.

SING SING

What if it wasn't a car defect? What if someone tampered with it?

She was at the karaoke bar with the girls just before the accident.

Had to threaten the owner I'd tell the liquor board he never checks I.D. to get access to his security tapes.

But they don't show me anything.

So I need to find another source.

The taxi stand across the street.

LAYMAN

Took a while to find out which cab was there that night.

Got his dash cam footage.

Bingo.

The bar's owner identified him as Lonnie Sadler.

A former employee.

Asked me to pass on a message to him

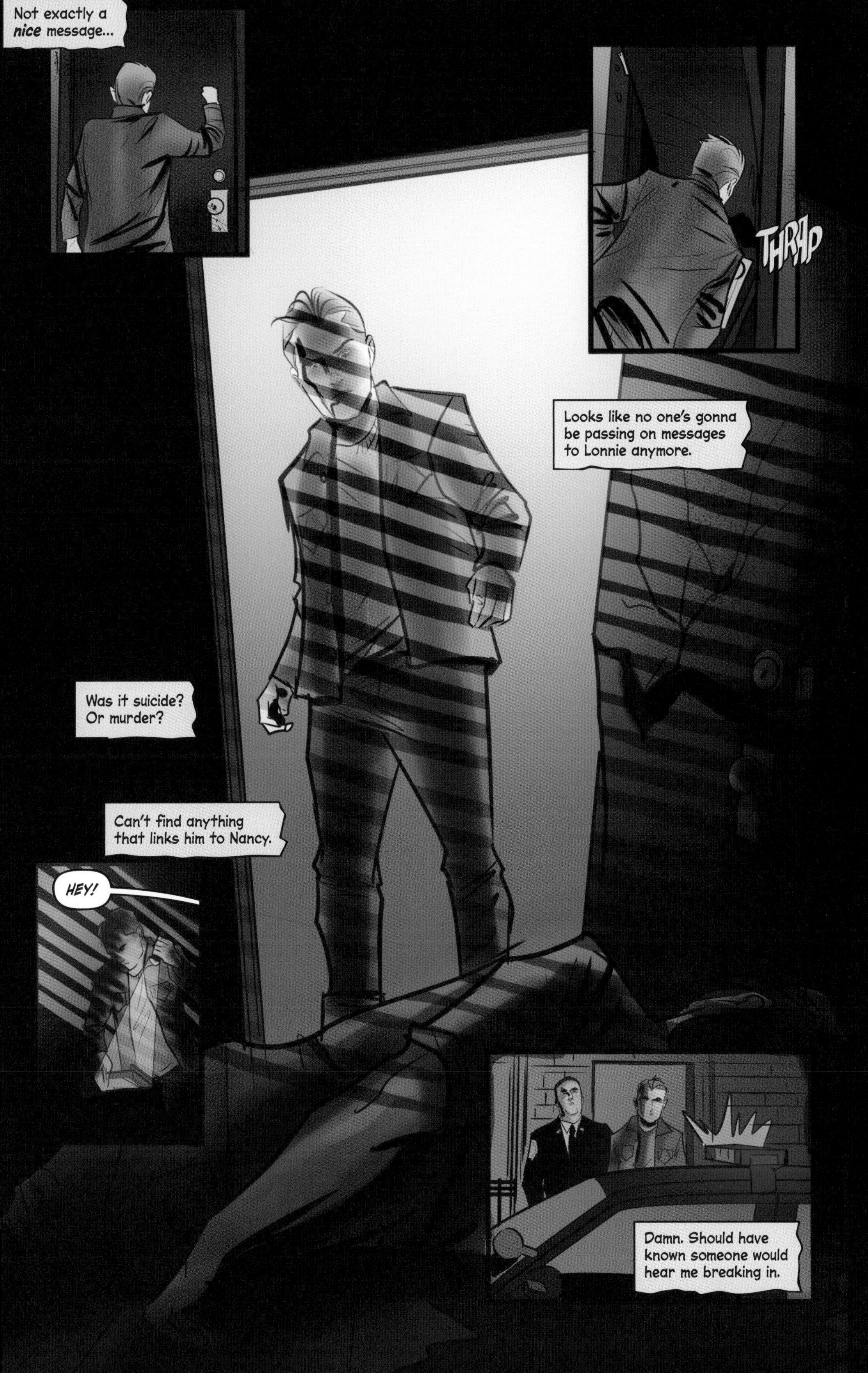
Not exactly a *nice* message...
THRAP
Looks like no one's gonna be passing on messages to Lonnie anymore.
Was it suicide? Or murder?
Can't find anything that links him to Nancy.
HEY!
Damn. Should have known someone would hear me breaking in.

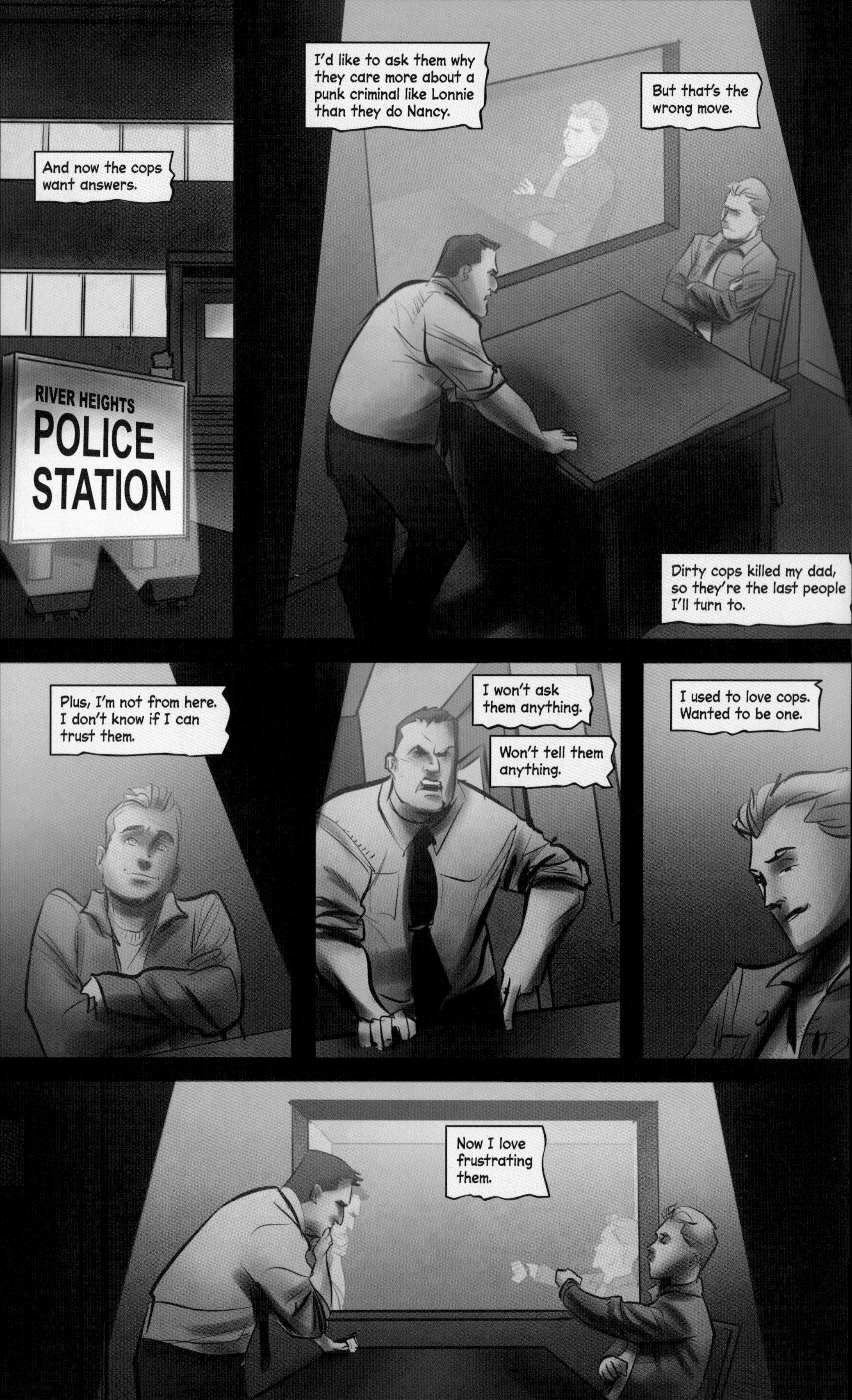
And now the cops want answers.
RIVER HEIGHTS POLICE STATION
I'd like to ask them why they care more about a punk criminal like Lonnie than they do Nancy.
But that's the wrong move.
Dirty cops killed my dad, so they're the last people I'll turn to.
Plus, I'm not from here. I don't know if I can trust them.
I won't ask them anything.
Won't tell them anything.
I used to love cops. Wanted to be one.
Now I love frustrating them.

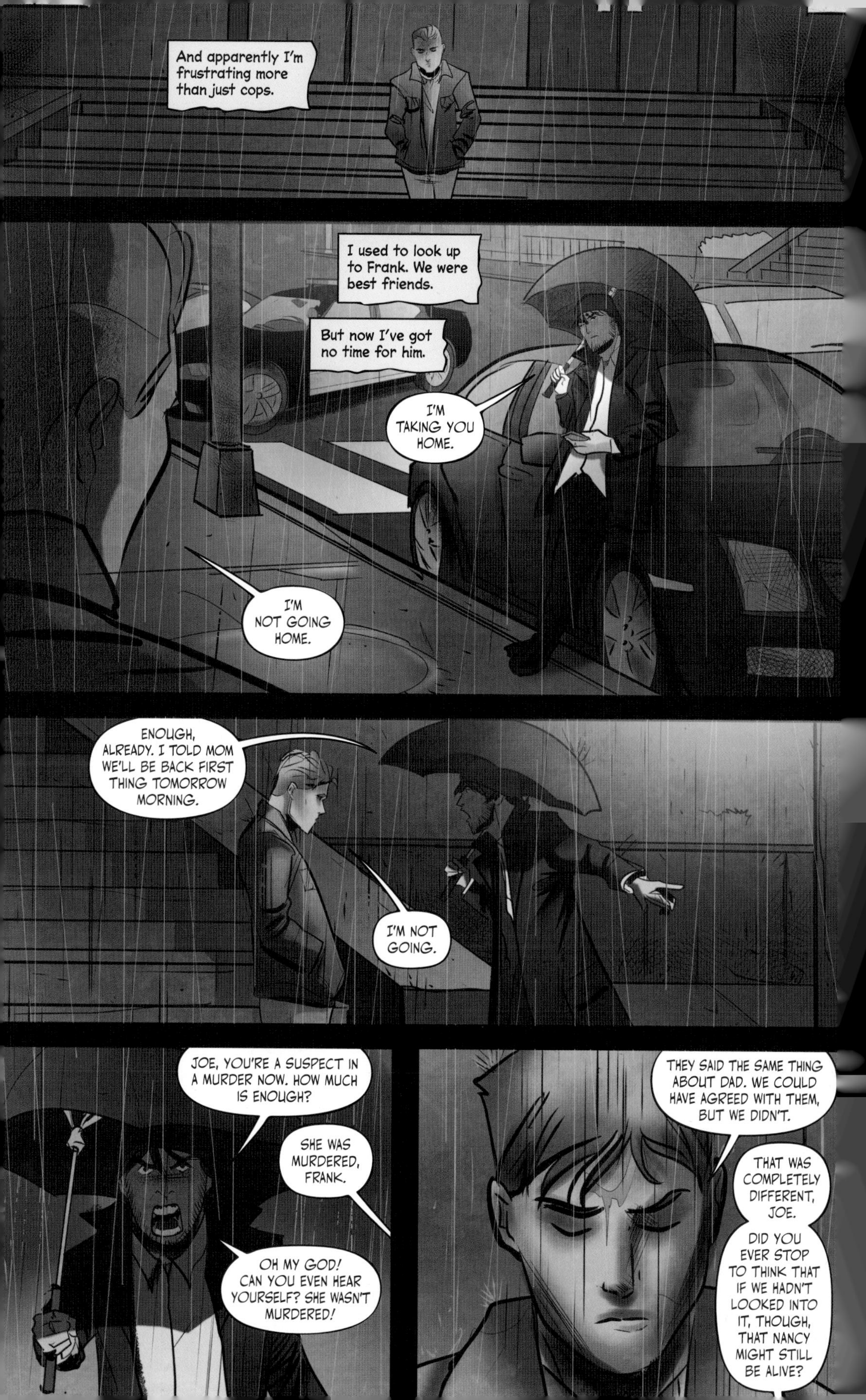
And apparently I'm frustrating more than just cops.
I used to look up to Frank. We were best friends.
But now I've got no time for him.
I'M TAKING YOU HOME.
I'M NOT GOING HOME.
ENOUGH, ALREADY. I TOLD MOM WE'LL BE BACK FIRST THING TOMORROW MORNING.
I'M NOT GOING.
JOE, YOU'RE A SUSPECT IN A MURDER NOW. HOW MUCH IS ENOUGH?
SHE WAS MURDERED, FRANK.
OH MY GOD! CAN YOU EVEN HEAR YOURSELF? SHE WASN'T MURDERED!
THEY SAID THE SAME THING ABOUT DAD. WE COULD HAVE AGREED WITH THEM, BUT WE DIDN'T.
THAT WAS COMPLETELY DIFFERENT, JOE.
DID YOU EVER STOP TO THINK THAT IF WE HADN'T LOOKED INTO IT, THOUGH, THAT NANCY MIGHT STILL BE ALIVE?

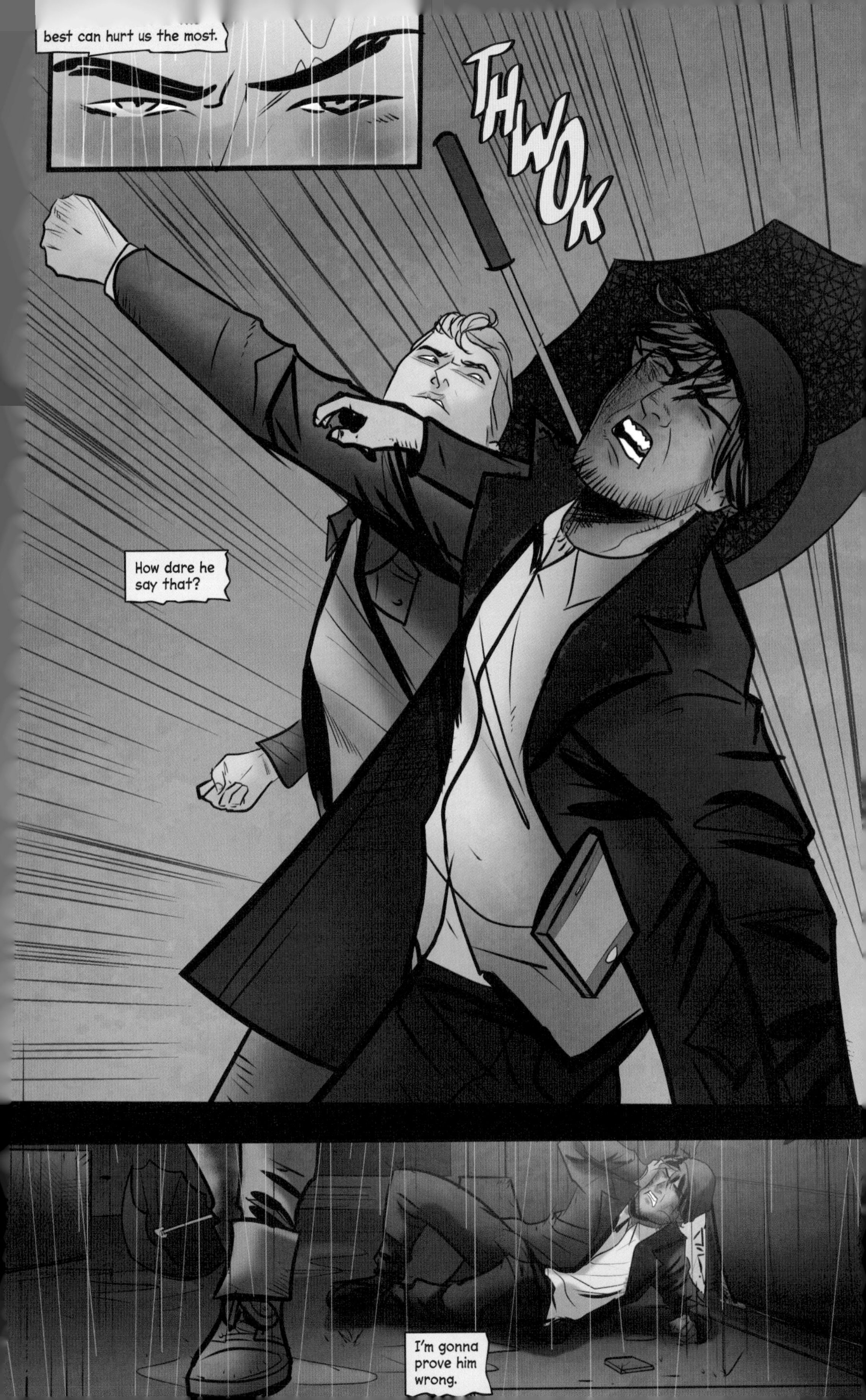
best can hurt us the most.
THWOK
How dare he say that?
I'm gonna prove him wrong.

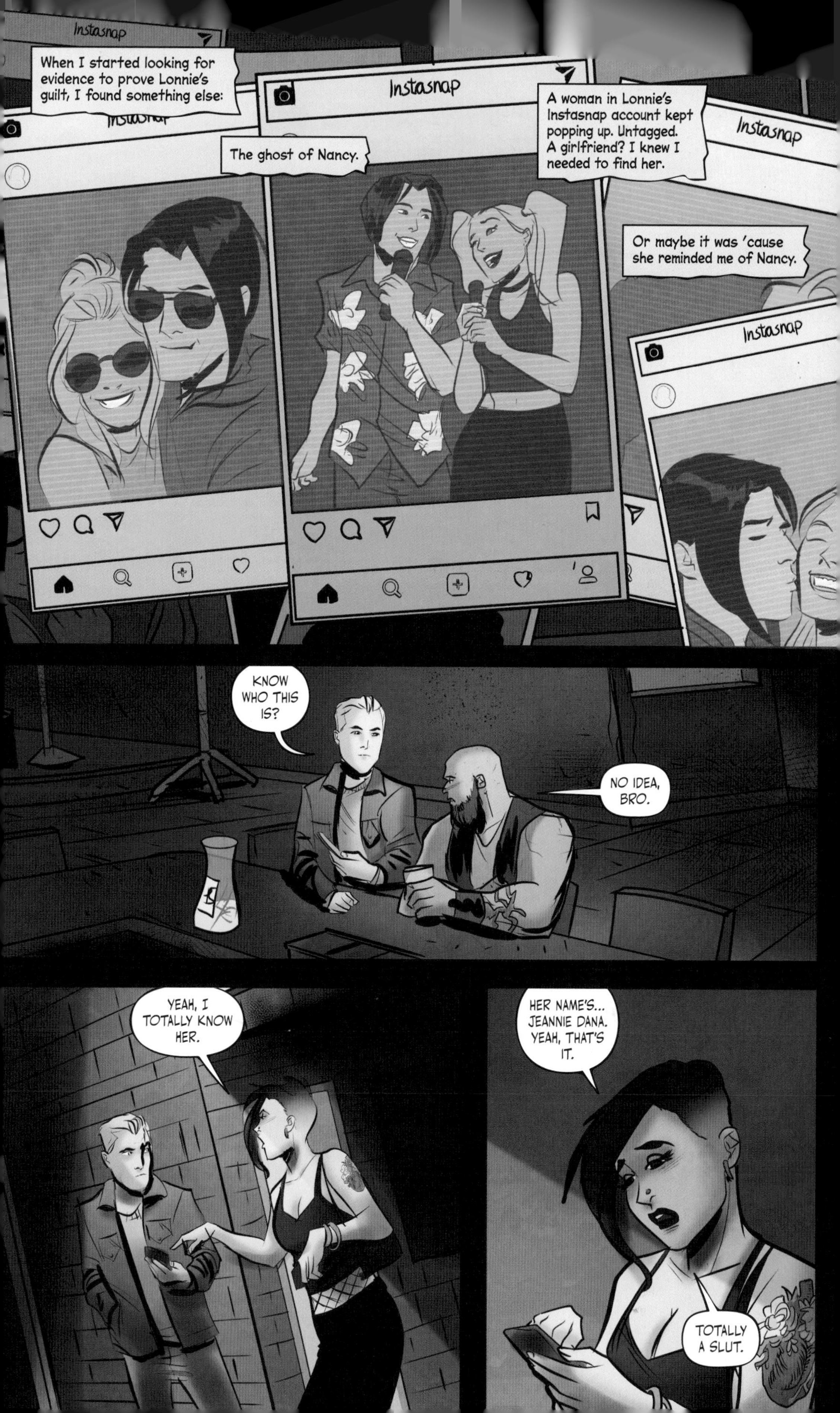
Instasnap
When I started looking for evidence to prove Lonnie's guilt, I found something else:
Instasnap
The ghost of Nancy.
A woman in Lonnie's Instasnap account kept popping up. Untagged. A girlfriend? I knew I needed to find her.
Instasnap
Or maybe it was 'cause she reminded me of Nancy.
Instasnap
KNOW WHO THIS IS?
NO IDEA, BRO.
YEAH, I TOTALLY KNOW HER.
HER NAME'S... JEANNIE DANA. YEAH, THAT'S IT.
TOTALLY A SLUT.

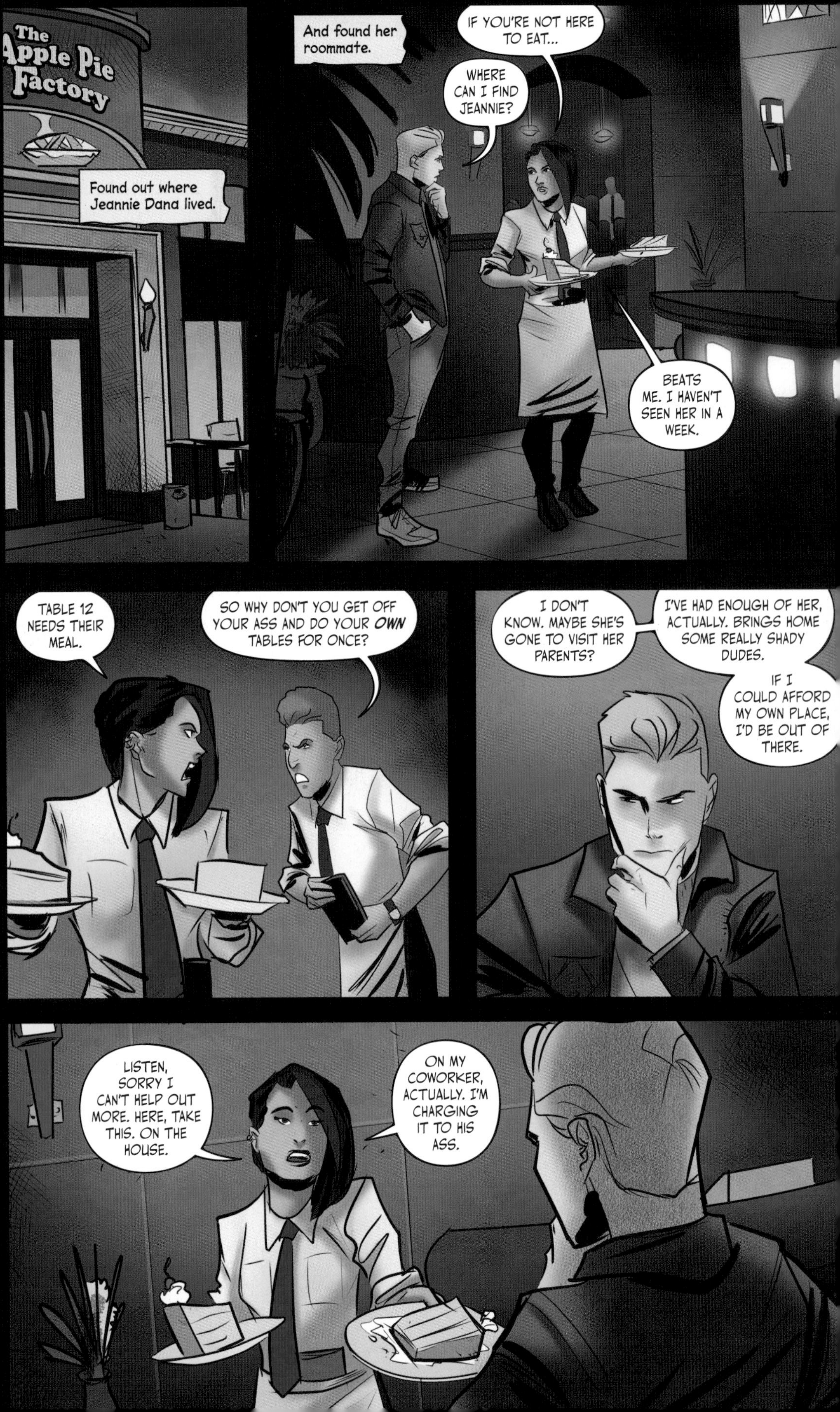
The Apple Pie Factory
Found out where Jeannie Dana lived.
And found her roommate.
WHERE CAN I FIND JEANNIE?
IF YOU'RE NOT HERE TO EAT...
BEATS ME. I HAVEN'T SEEN HER IN A WEEK.
TABLE 12 NEEDS THEIR MEAL.
SO WHY DON'T YOU GET OFF YOUR ASS AND DO YOUR *OWN* TABLES FOR ONCE?
I DON'T KNOW. MAYBE SHE'S GONE TO VISIT HER PARENTS?
I'VE HAD ENOUGH OF HER, ACTUALLY. BRINGS HOME SOME REALLY SHADY DUDES.
IF I COULD AFFORD MY OWN PLACE, I'D BE OUT OF THERE.
LISTEN, SORRY I CAN'T HELP OUT MORE. HERE, TAKE THIS. ON THE HOUSE.
ON MY COWORKER, ACTUALLY. I'M CHARGING IT TO HIS ASS.

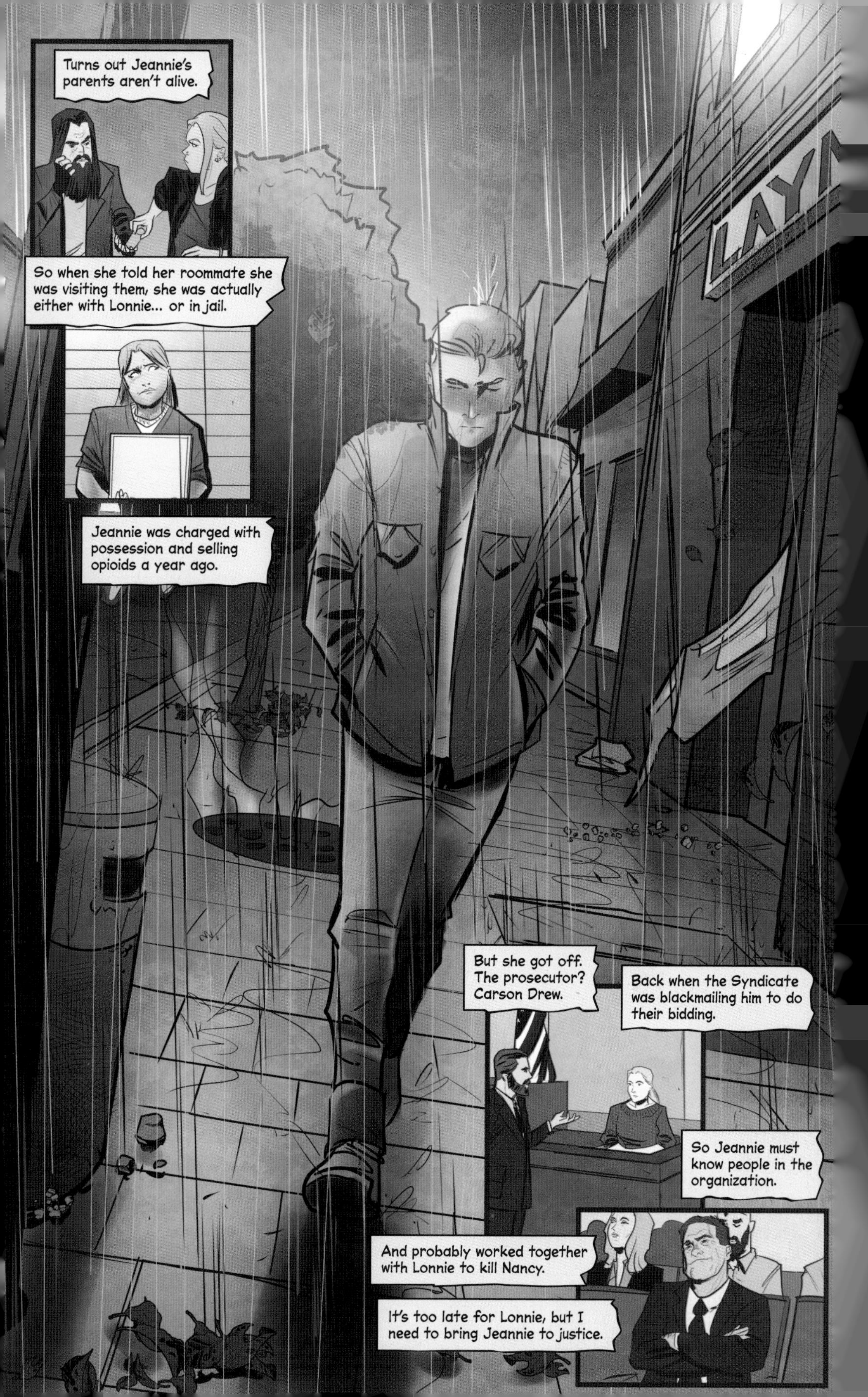
Turns out Jeannie's parents aren't alive.
So when she told her roommate she was visiting them, she was actually either with Lonnie... or in jail.
Jeannie was charged with possession and selling opioids a year ago.
But she got off. The prosecutor? Carson Drew.
Back when the Syndicate was blackmailing him to do their bidding.
So Jeannie must know people in the organization.
And probably worked together with Lonnie to kill Nancy.
It's too late for Lonnie, but I need to bring Jeannie to justice.

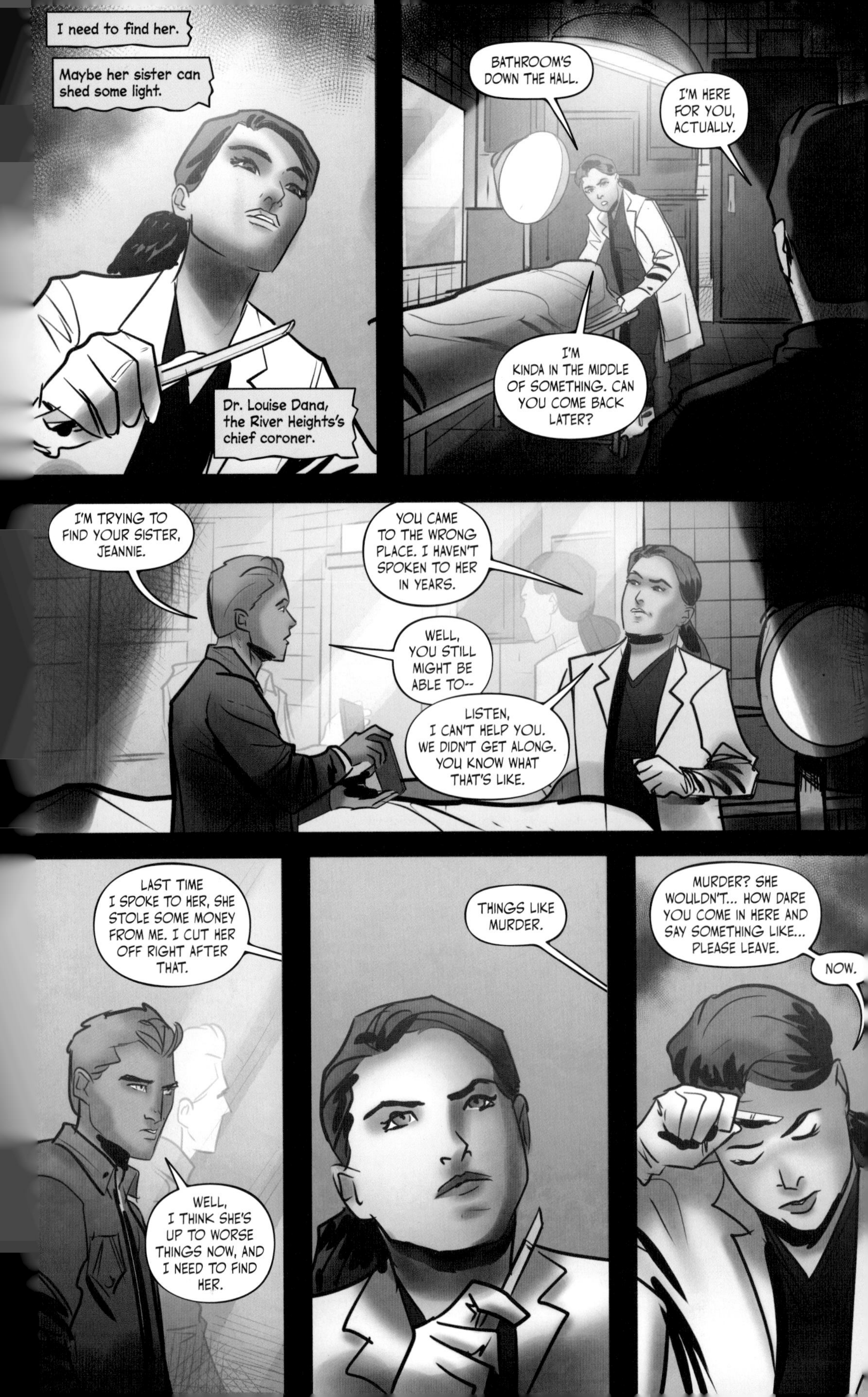
I need to find her.
Maybe her sister can shed some light.
Dr. Louise Dana, the River Heights's chief coroner.
BATHROOM'S DOWN THE HALL.
I'M HERE FOR YOU, ACTUALLY.
I'M KINDA IN THE MIDDLE OF SOMETHING. CAN YOU COME BACK LATER?
I'M TRYING TO FIND YOUR SISTER, JEANNIE.
YOU CAME TO THE WRONG PLACE. I HAVEN'T SPOKEN TO HER IN YEARS.
WELL, YOU STILL MIGHT BE ABLE TO--
LISTEN, I CAN'T HELP YOU. WE DIDN'T GET ALONG. YOU KNOW WHAT THAT'S LIKE.
LAST TIME I SPOKE TO HER, SHE STOLE SOME MONEY FROM ME. I CUT HER OFF RIGHT AFTER THAT.
WELL, I THINK SHE'S UP TO WORSE THINGS NOW, AND I NEED TO FIND HER.
THINGS LIKE MURDER.
MURDER? SHE WOULDN'T... HOW DARE YOU COME IN HERE AND SAY SOMETHING LIKE... PLEASE LEAVE.
NOW.

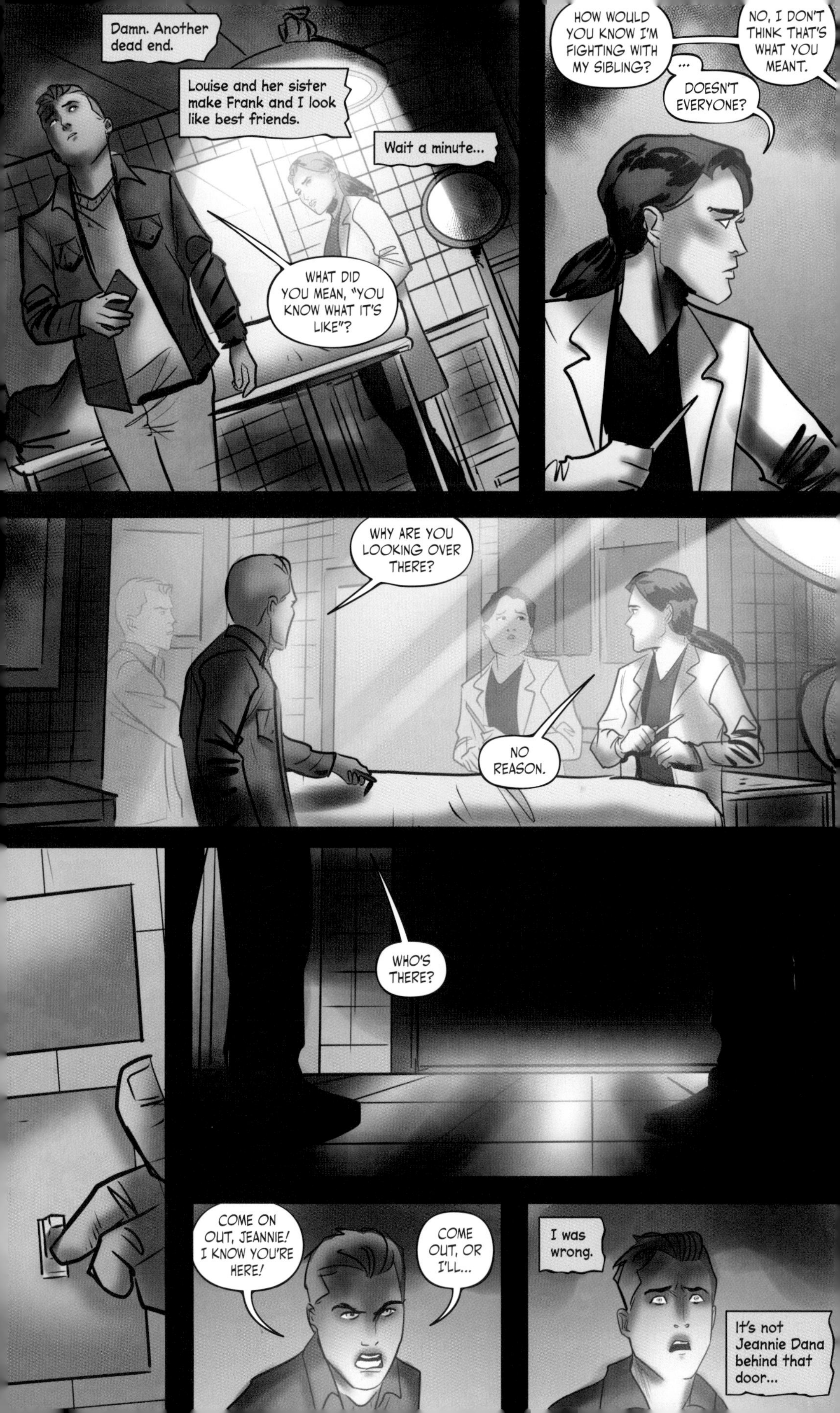
Damn. Another dead end.
Louise and her sister make Frank and I look like best friends.
Wait a minute...
WHAT DID YOU MEAN, "YOU KNOW WHAT IT'S LIKE"?
HOW WOULD YOU KNOW I'M FIGHTING WITH MY SIBLING?
...
DOESN'T EVERYONE?
NO, I DON'T THINK THAT'S WHAT YOU MEANT.
WHY ARE YOU LOOKING OVER THERE?
NO REASON.
WHO'S THERE?
COME ON OUT, JEANNIE! I KNOW YOU'RE HERE!
COME OUT, OR I'LL...
I was wrong.
It's not Jeannie Dana behind that door...

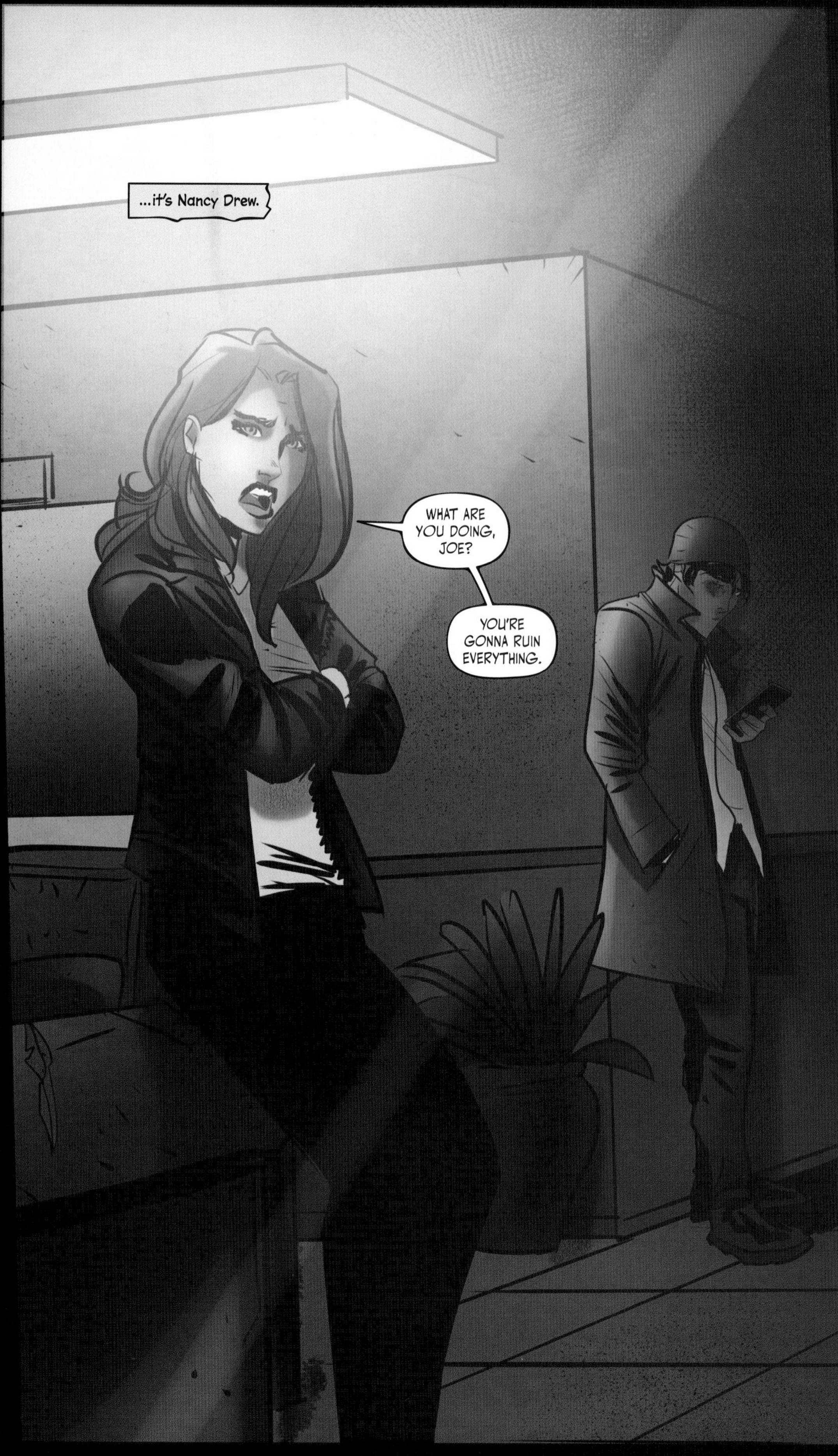
...it's Nancy Drew.
WHAT ARE YOU DOING, JOE?
YOU'RE GONNA RUIN EVERYTHING.

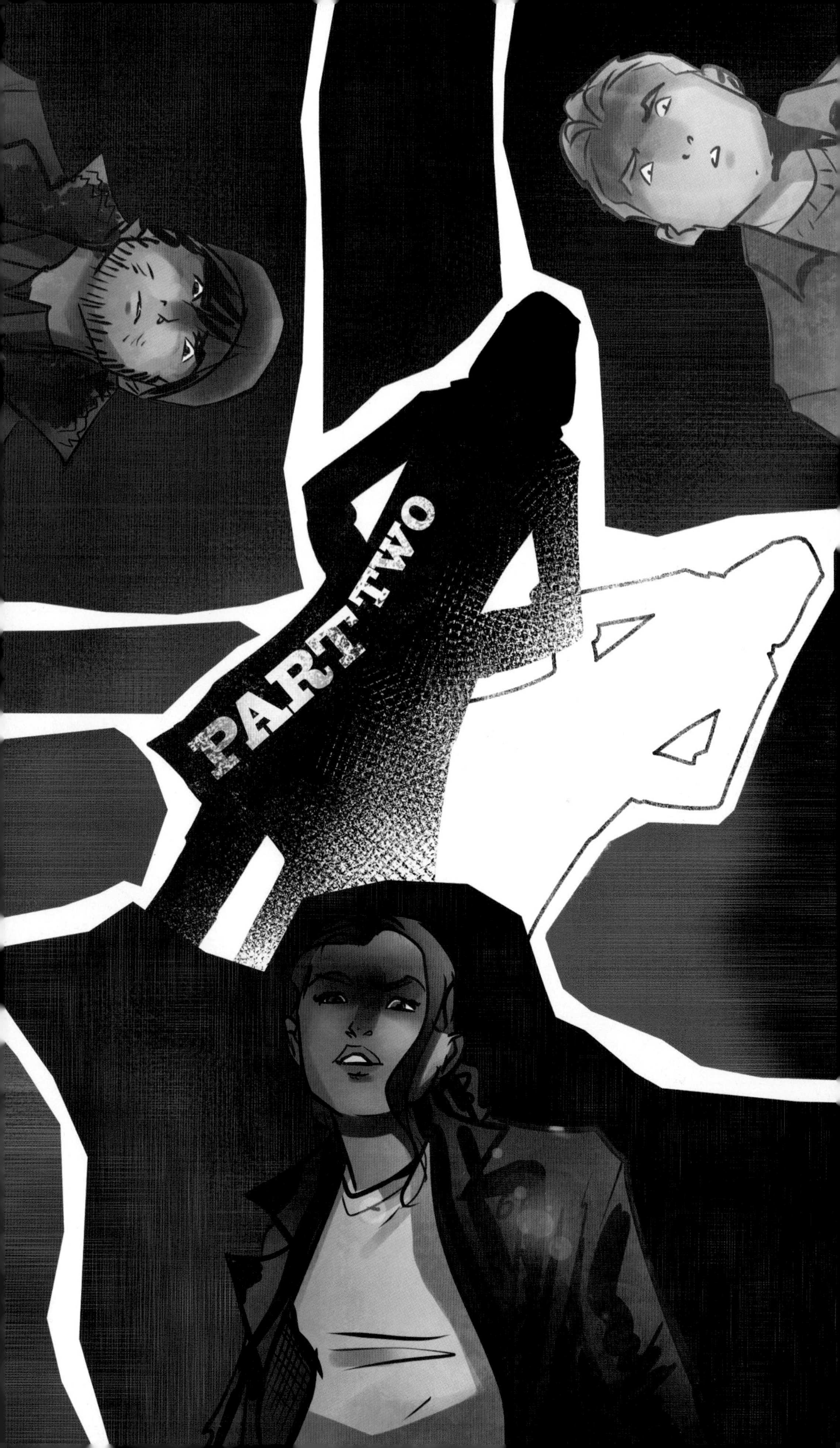
PART TWO

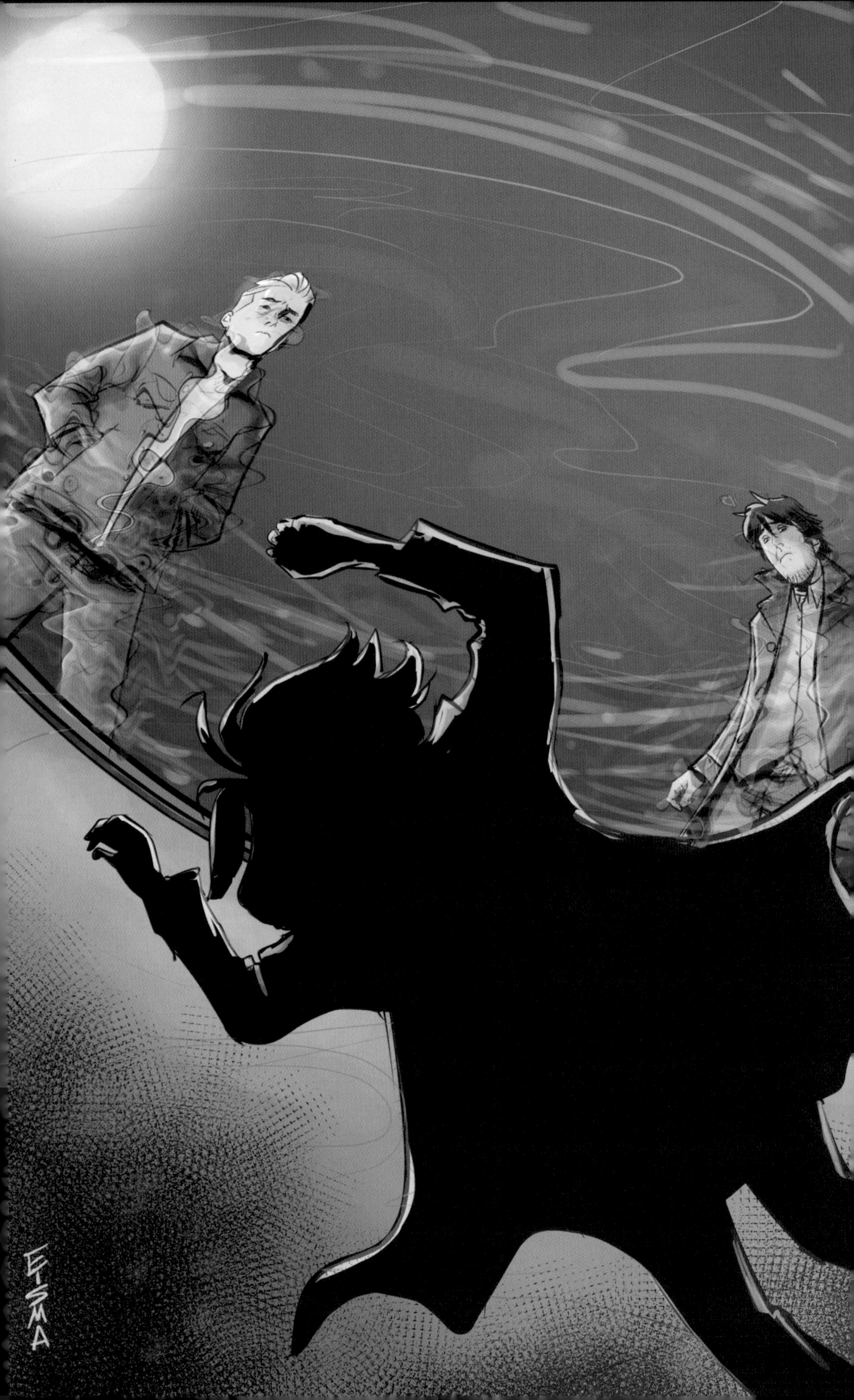
EISMA

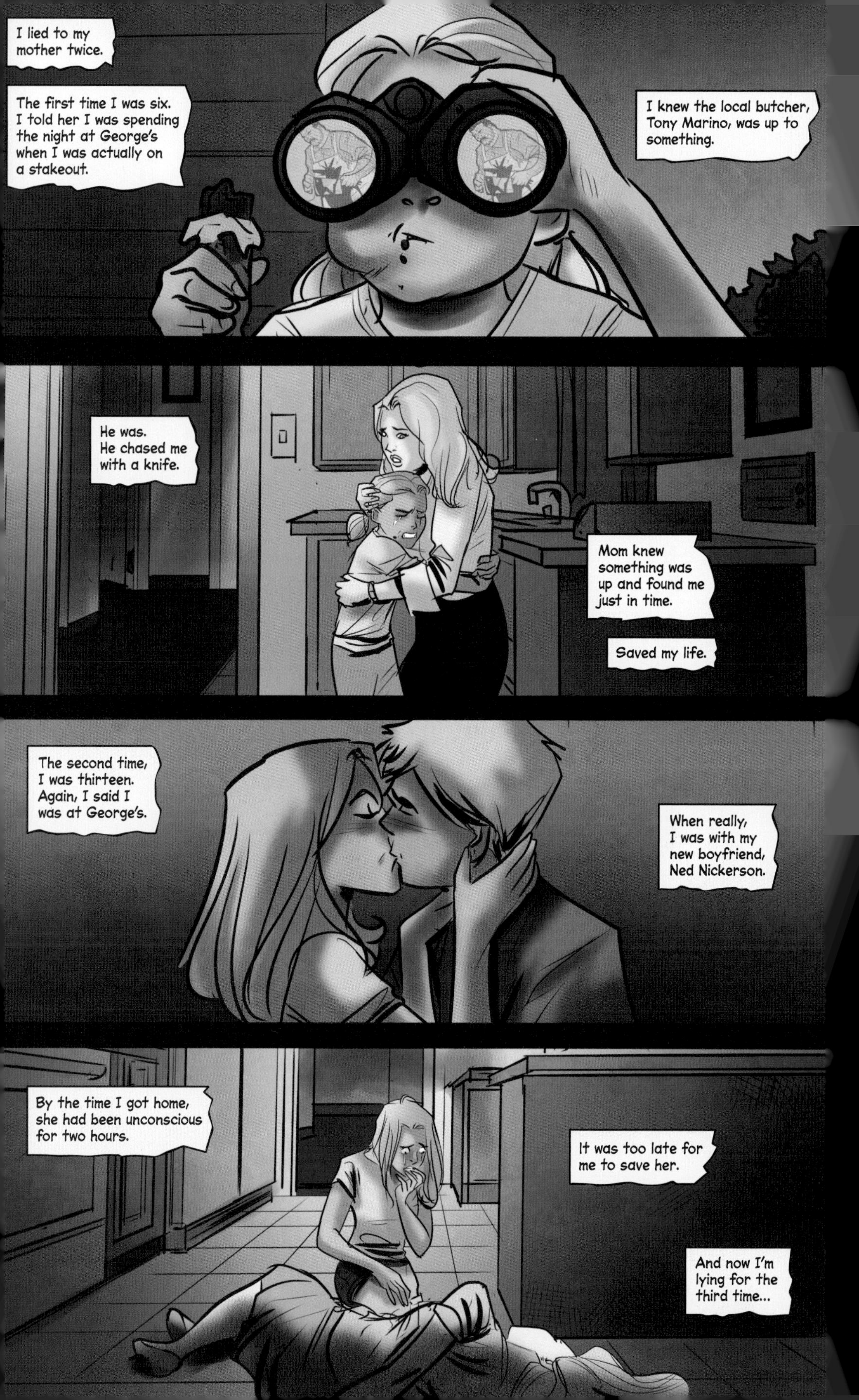
I lied to my mother twice.
The first time I was six. I told her I was spending the night at George's when I was actually on a stakeout.
I knew the local butcher, Tony Marino, was up to something.
He was. He chased me with a knife.
Mom knew something was up and found me just in time.
Saved my life.
The second time, I was thirteen. Again, I said I was at George's.
When really, I was with my new boyfriend, Ned Nickerson.
By the time I got home, she had been unconscious for two hours.
It was too late for me to save her.
And now I'm lying for the third time...

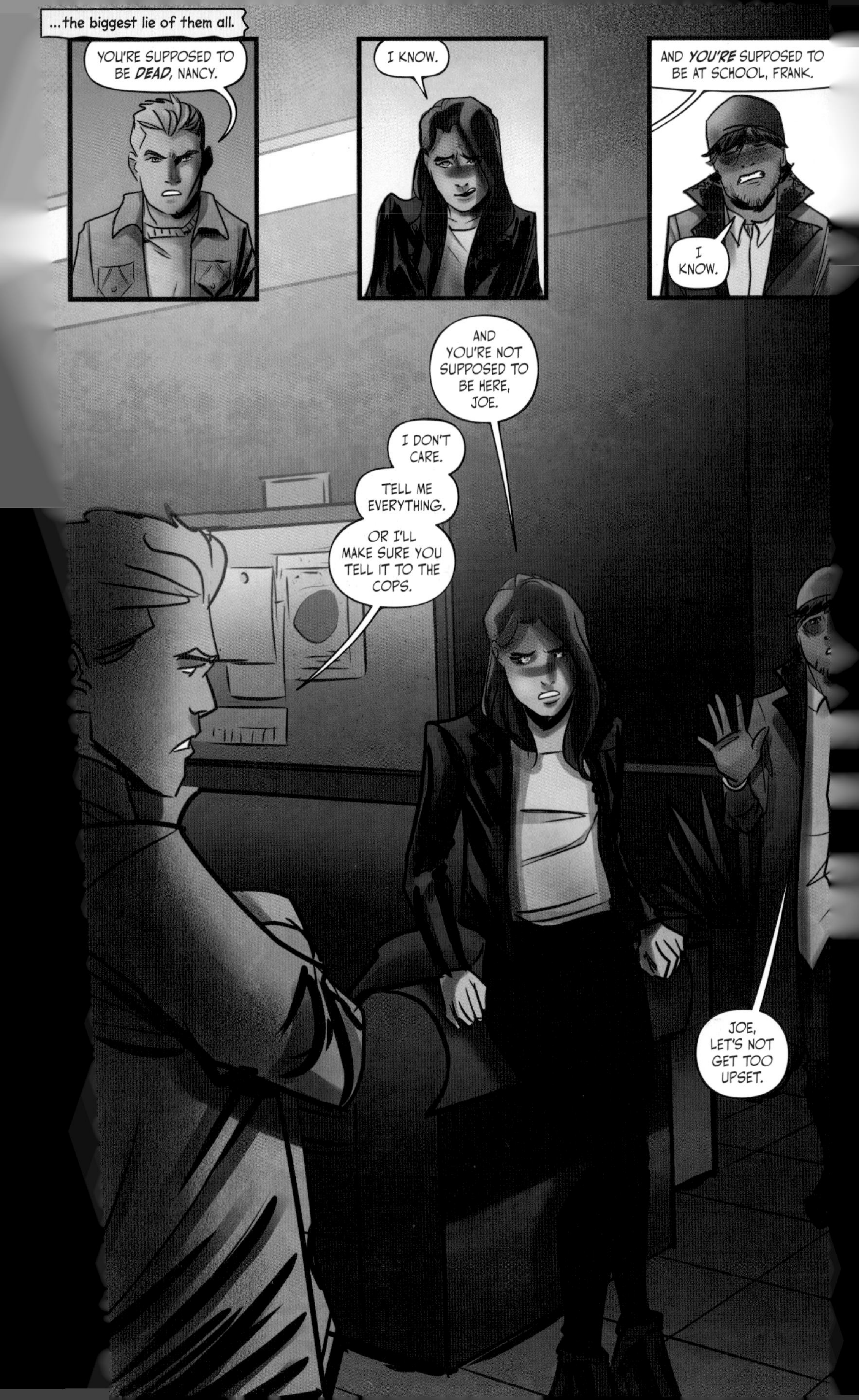
...the biggest lie of them all.
YOU'RE SUPPOSED TO BE DEAD, NANCY.
I KNOW.
AND YOU'RE SUPPOSED TO BE AT SCHOOL, FRANK.
I KNOW.
AND YOU'RE NOT SUPPOSED TO BE HERE, JOE.
I DON'T CARE.
TELL ME EVERYTHING.
OR I'LL MAKE SURE YOU TELL IT TO THE COPS.
JOE, LET'S NOT GET TOO UPSET.

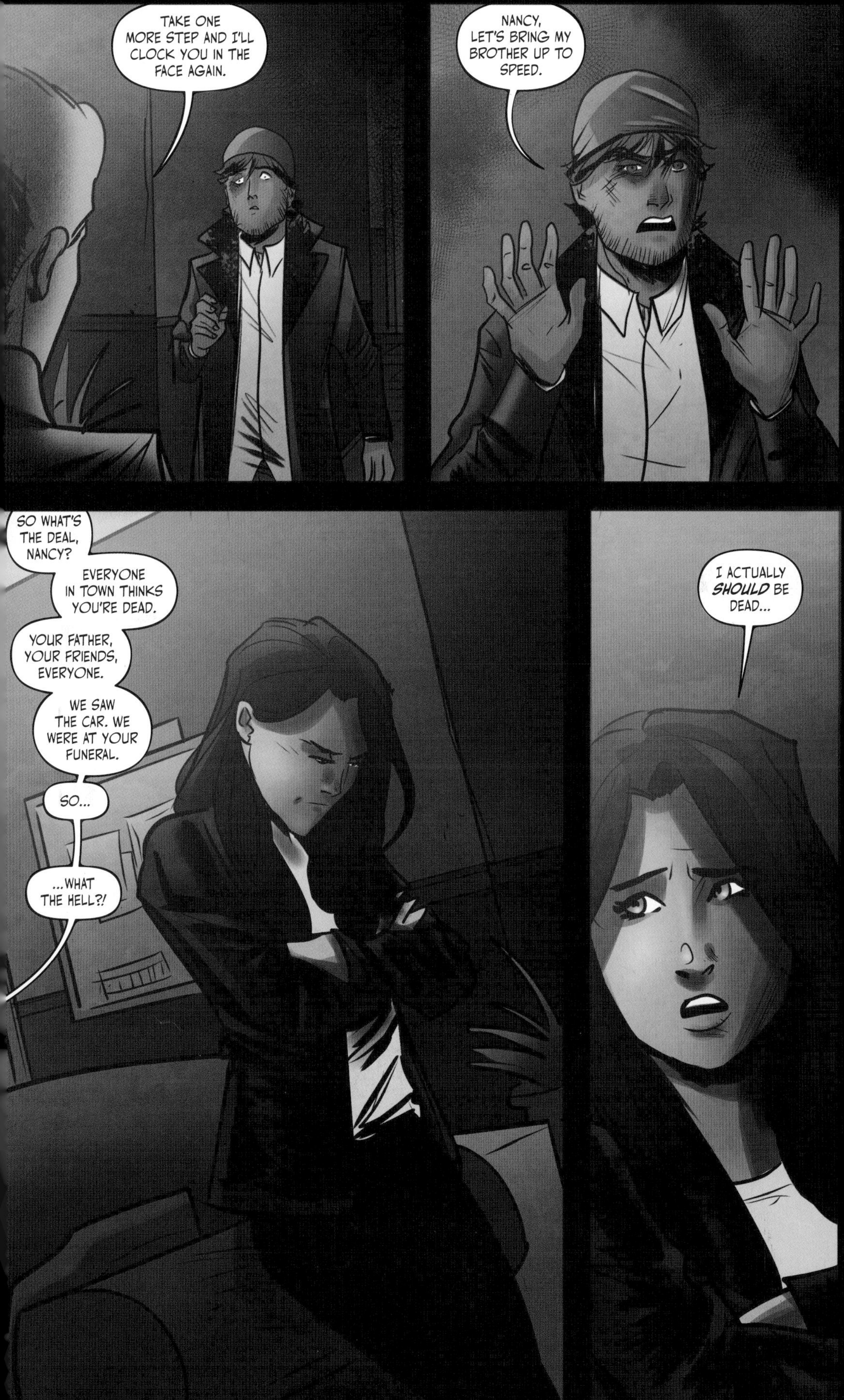
TAKE ONE MORE STEP AND I'LL CLOCK YOU IN THE FACE AGAIN.
NANCY, LET'S BRING MY BROTHER UP TO SPEED.
SO WHAT'S THE DEAL, NANCY?
EVERYONE IN TOWN THINKS YOU'RE DEAD.
YOUR FATHER, YOUR FRIENDS, EVERYONE.
WE SAW THE CAR. WE WERE AT YOUR FUNERAL.
SO...
...WHAT THE HELL?!
I ACTUALLY *SHOULD* BE DEAD...

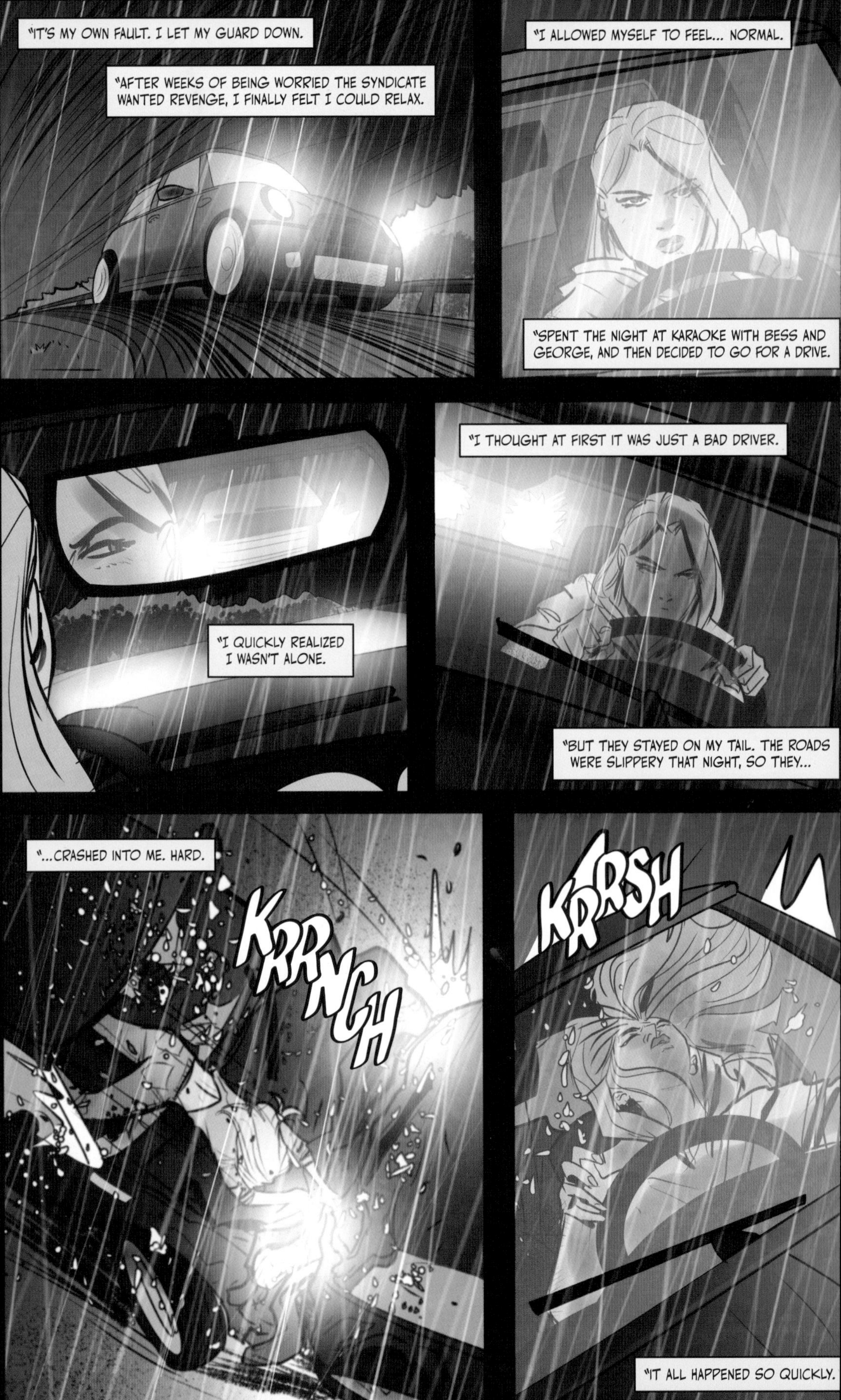
"IT'S MY OWN FAULT. I LET MY GUARD DOWN.
"AFTER WEEKS OF BEING WORRIED THE SYNDICATE WANTED REVENGE, I FINALLY FELT I COULD RELAX.
"I ALLOWED MYSELF TO FEEL... NORMAL.
"SPENT THE NIGHT AT KARAOKE WITH BESS AND GEORGE, AND THEN DECIDED TO GO FOR A DRIVE.
"I QUICKLY REALIZED I WASN'T ALONE.
"I THOUGHT AT FIRST IT WAS JUST A BAD DRIVER.
"BUT THEY STAYED ON MY TAIL. THE ROADS WERE SLIPPERY THAT NIGHT, SO THEY...
"...CRASHED INTO ME. HARD.
KRRNCH
KRRRSH
"IT ALL HAPPENED SO QUICKLY.

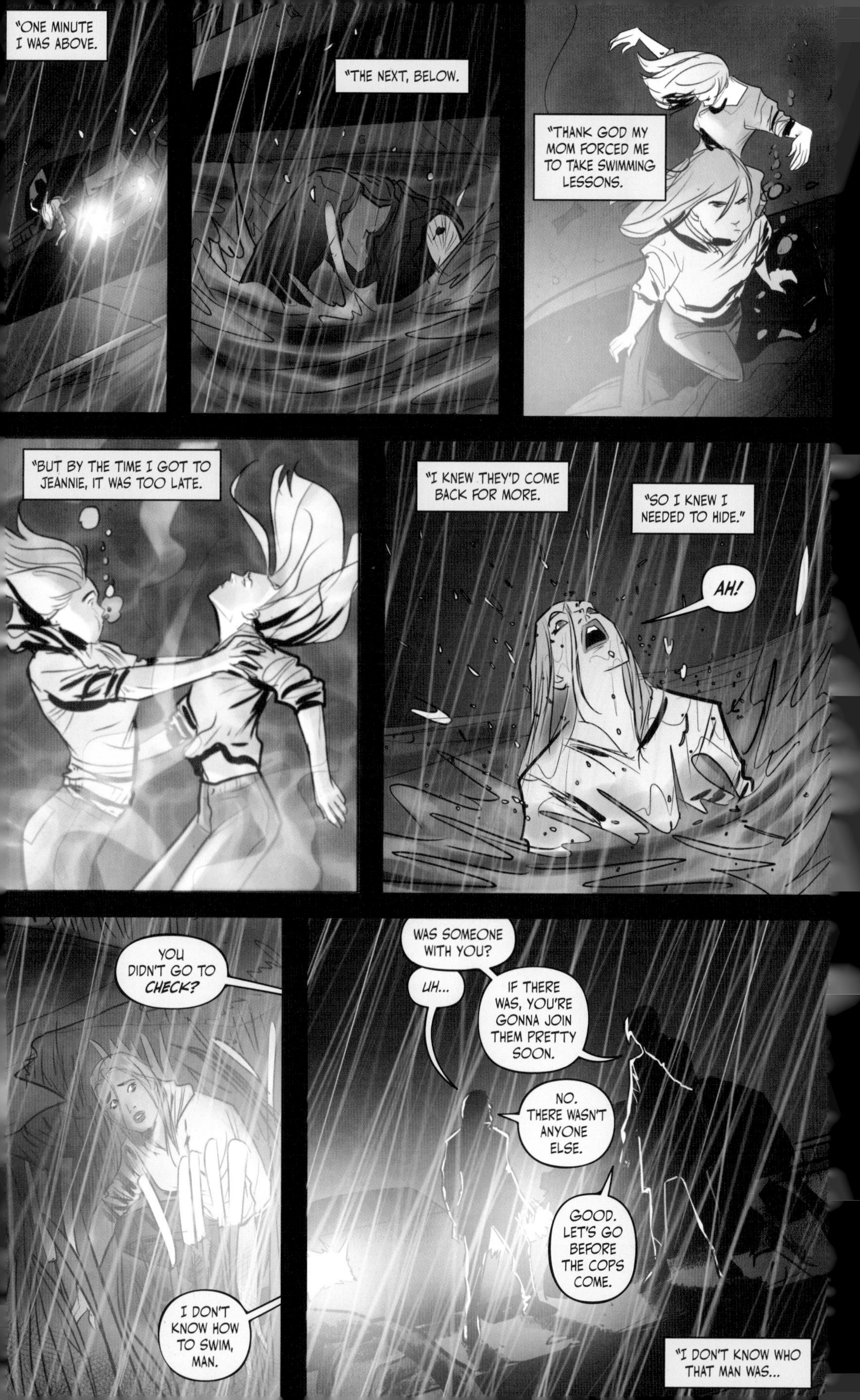
"ONE MINUTE I WAS ABOVE.
"THE NEXT, BELOW.
"THANK GOD MY MOM FORCED ME TO TAKE SWIMMING LESSONS.
"BUT BY THE TIME I GOT TO JEANNIE, IT WAS TOO LATE.
"I KNEW THEY'D COME BACK FOR MORE.
"SO I KNEW I NEEDED TO HIDE."
AH!
YOU DIDN'T GO TO CHECK?
I DON'T KNOW HOW TO SWIM, MAN.
WAS SOMEONE WITH YOU?
UH...
IF THERE WAS, YOU'RE GONNA JOIN THEM PRETTY SOON.
NO. THERE WASN'T ANYONE ELSE.
GOOD. LET'S GO BEFORE THE COPS COME.
"I DON'T KNOW WHO THAT MAN WAS...

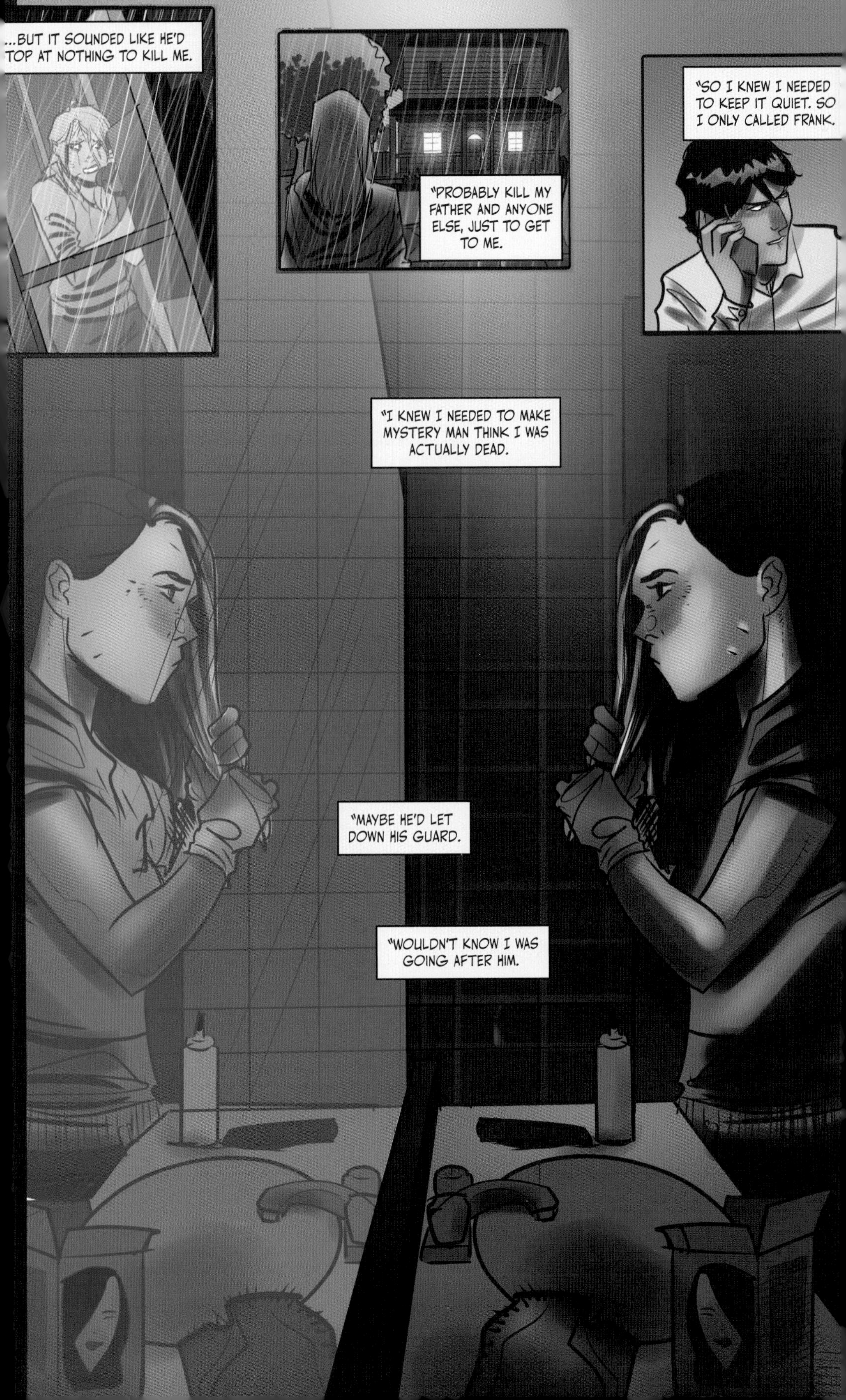
...BUT IT SOUNDED LIKE HE'D
TOP AT NOTHING TO KILL ME.
"PROBABLY KILL MY FATHER AND ANYONE ELSE, JUST TO GET TO ME.
"SO I KNEW I NEEDED TO KEEP IT QUIET. SO I ONLY CALLED FRANK.
"I KNEW I NEEDED TO MAKE MYSTERY MAN THINK I WAS ACTUALLY DEAD.
"MAYBE HE'D LET DOWN HIS GUARD.
"WOULDN'T KNOW I WAS GOING AFTER HIM.

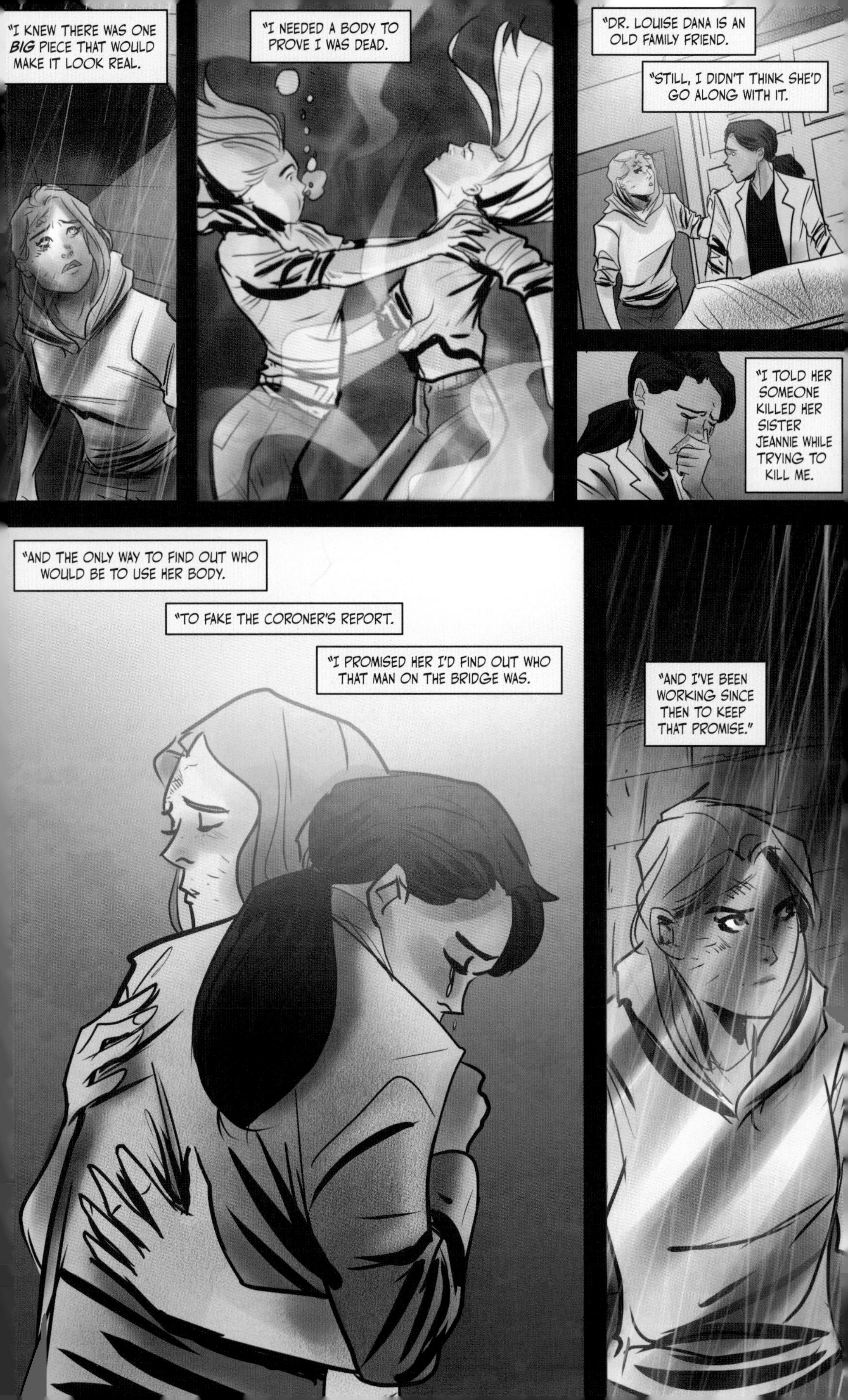
"I KNEW THERE WAS ONE BIG PIECE THAT WOULD MAKE IT LOOK REAL.
"I NEEDED A BODY TO PROVE I WAS DEAD.
"DR. LOUISE DANA IS AN OLD FAMILY FRIEND.
"STILL, I DIDN'T THINK SHE'D GO ALONG WITH IT.
"I TOLD HER SOMEONE KILLED HER SISTER JEANNIE WHILE TRYING TO KILL ME.
"AND THE ONLY WAY TO FIND OUT WHO WOULD BE TO USE HER BODY.
"TO FAKE THE CORONER'S REPORT.
"I PROMISED HER I'D FIND OUT WHO THAT MAN ON THE BRIDGE WAS.
"AND I'VE BEEN WORKING SINCE THEN TO KEEP THAT PROMISE."

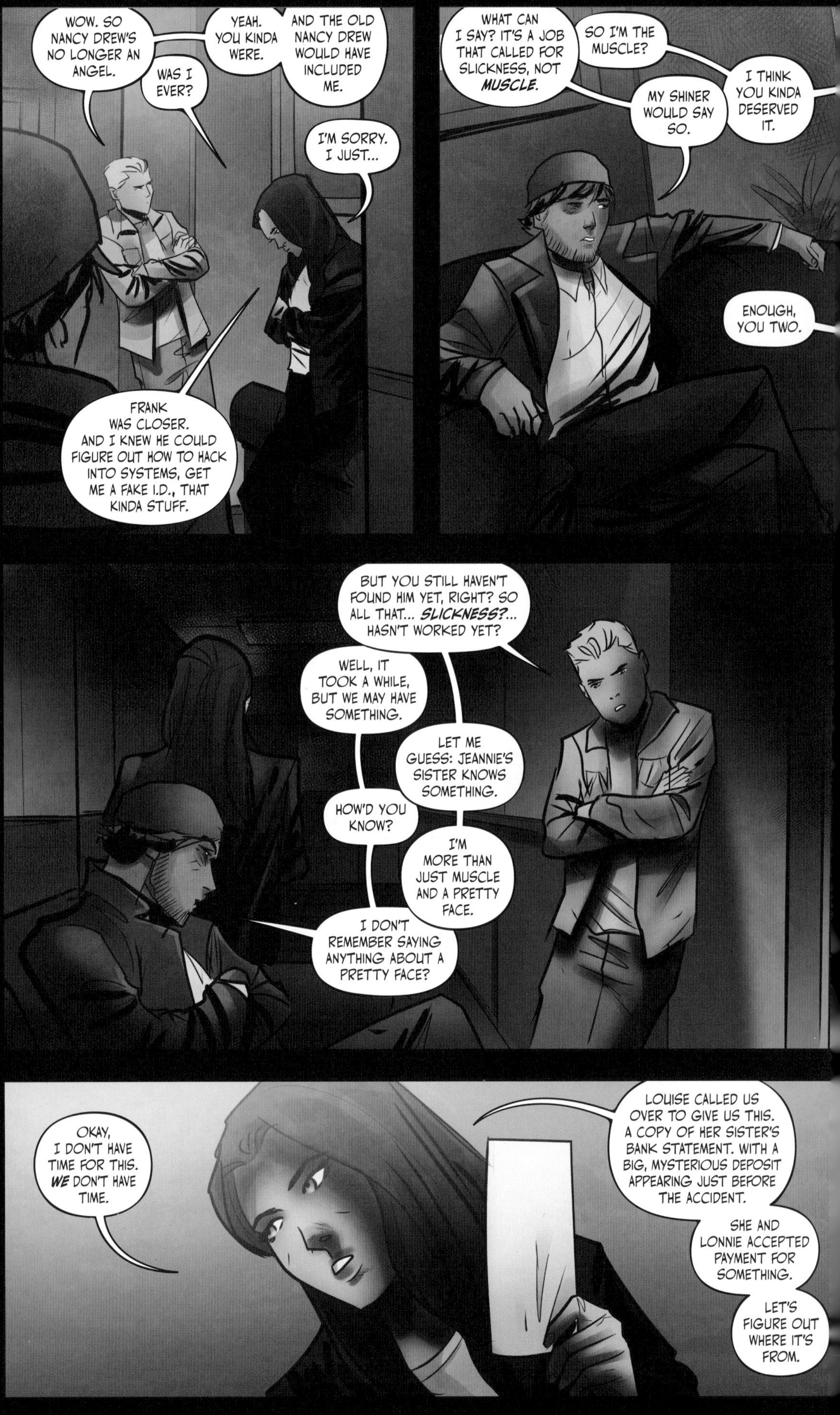
WOW. SO NANCY DREW'S NO LONGER AN ANGEL.
WAS I EVER?
YEAH. YOU KINDA WERE.
AND THE OLD NANCY DREW WOULD HAVE INCLUDED ME.
I'M SORRY. I JUST...
FRANK WAS CLOSER. AND I KNEW HE COULD FIGURE OUT HOW TO HACK INTO SYSTEMS, GET ME A FAKE I.D., THAT KINDA STUFF.
WHAT CAN I SAY? IT'S A JOB THAT CALLED FOR SLICKNESS, NOT *MUSCLE*.
SO I'M THE MUSCLE?
MY SHINER WOULD SAY SO.
I THINK YOU KINDA DESERVED IT.
ENOUGH, YOU TWO.
BUT YOU STILL HAVEN'T FOUND HIM YET, RIGHT? SO ALL THAT... *SLICKNESS?*... HASN'T WORKED YET?
WELL, IT TOOK A WHILE, BUT WE MAY HAVE SOMETHING.
LET ME GUESS: JEANNIE'S SISTER KNOWS SOMETHING.
HOW'D YOU KNOW?
I'M MORE THAN JUST MUSCLE AND A PRETTY FACE.
I DON'T REMEMBER SAYING ANYTHING ABOUT A PRETTY FACE?
OKAY, I DON'T HAVE TIME FOR THIS. *WE* DON'T HAVE TIME.
LOUISE CALLED US OVER TO GIVE US THIS. A COPY OF HER SISTER'S BANK STATEMENT. WITH A BIG, MYSTERIOUS DEPOSIT APPEARING JUST BEFORE THE ACCIDENT.
SHE AND LONNIE ACCEPTED PAYMENT FOR SOMETHING.
LET'S FIGURE OUT WHERE IT'S FROM.

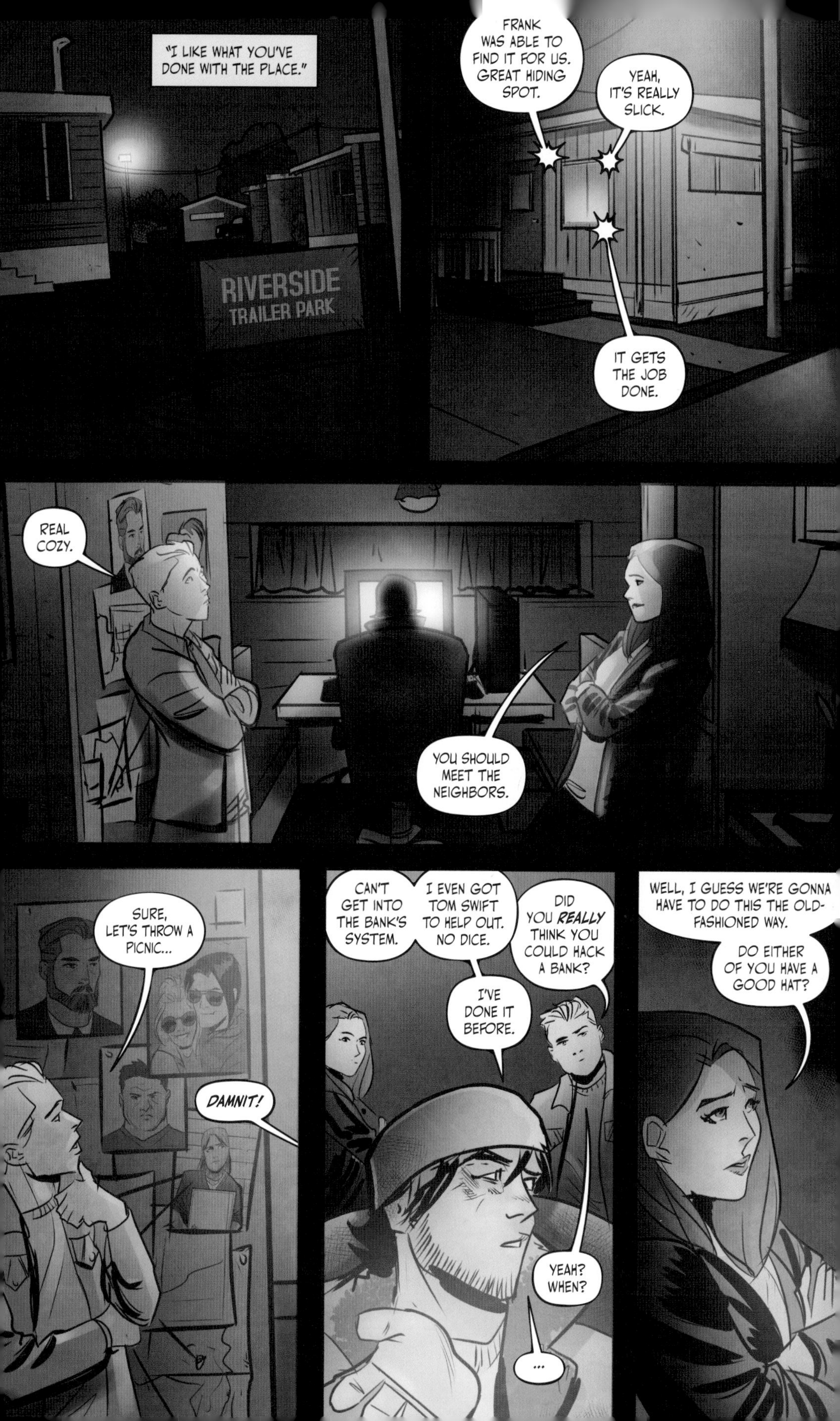
"I LIKE WHAT YOU'VE DONE WITH THE PLACE."
RIVERSIDE TRAILER PARK
FRANK WAS ABLE TO FIND IT FOR US. GREAT HIDING SPOT.
YEAH, IT'S REALLY SLICK.
IT GETS THE JOB DONE.
REAL COZY.
YOU SHOULD MEET THE NEIGHBORS.
SURE, LET'S THROW A PICNIC...
DAMNIT!
CAN'T GET INTO THE BANK'S SYSTEM.
I EVEN GOT TOM SWIFT TO HELP OUT. NO DICE.
DID YOU REALLY THINK YOU COULD HACK A BANK?
I'VE DONE IT BEFORE.
YEAH? WHEN?
...
WELL, I GUESS WE'RE GONNA HAVE TO DO THIS THE OLD-FASHIONED WAY.
DO EITHER OF YOU HAVE A GOOD HAT?

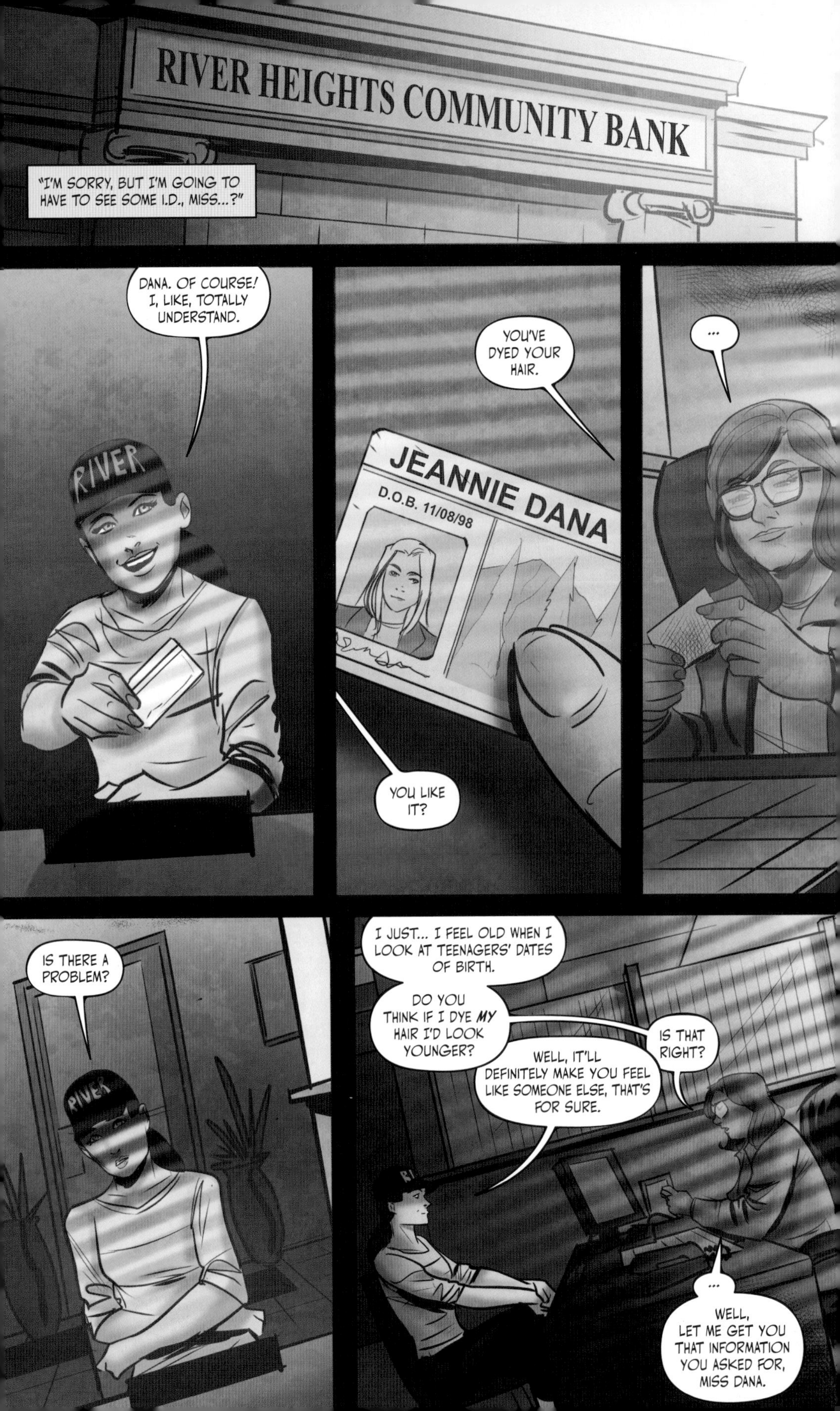
RIVER HEIGHTS COMMUNITY BANK
"I'M SORRY, BUT I'M GOING TO HAVE TO SEE SOME I.D., MISS...?"
DANA. OF COURSE! I, LIKE, TOTALLY UNDERSTAND.
RIVER
YOU'VE DYED YOUR HAIR.
JEANNIE DANA
D.O.B. 11/08/98
YOU LIKE IT?
...
IS THERE A PROBLEM?
RIVER
I JUST... I FEEL OLD WHEN I LOOK AT TEENAGERS' DATES OF BIRTH.
DO YOU THINK IF I DYE *MY* HAIR I'D LOOK YOUNGER?
IS THAT RIGHT?
WELL, IT'LL DEFINITELY MAKE YOU FEEL LIKE SOMEONE ELSE, THAT'S FOR SURE.
...
WELL, LET ME GET YOU THAT INFORMATION YOU ASKED FOR, MISS DANA.

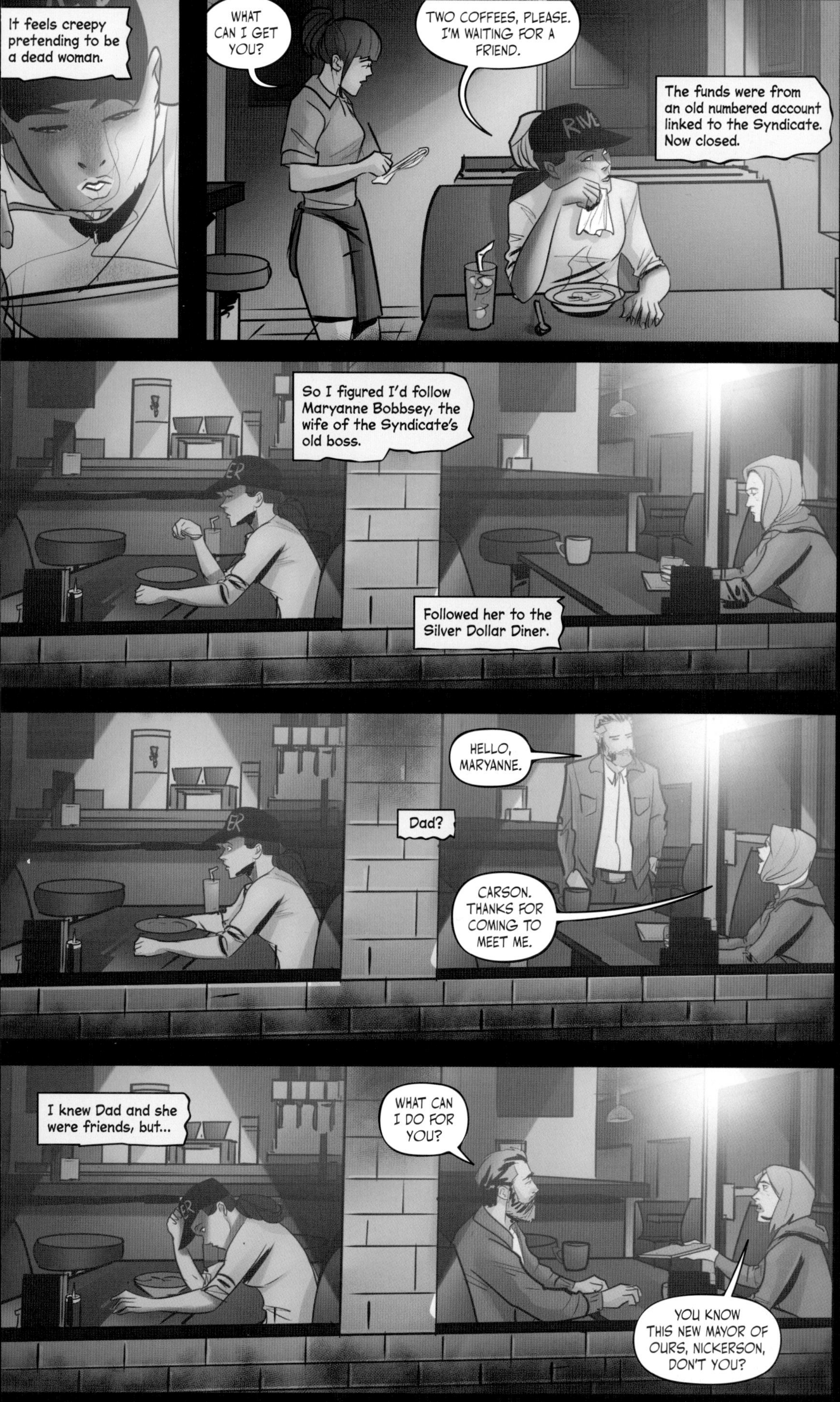

It feels creepy pretending to be a dead woman.
WHAT CAN I GET YOU?
TWO COFFEES, PLEASE. I'M WAITING FOR A FRIEND.
The funds were from an old numbered account linked to the Syndicate. Now closed.
RIVE
So I figured I'd follow Maryanne Bobbsey, the wife of the Syndicate's old boss.
Followed her to the Silver Dollar Diner.
HELLO, MARYANNE.
Dad?
CARSON. THANKS FOR COMING TO MEET ME.
I knew Dad and she were friends, but...
WHAT CAN I DO FOR YOU?
YOU KNOW THIS NEW MAYOR OF OURS, NICKERSON, DON'T YOU?

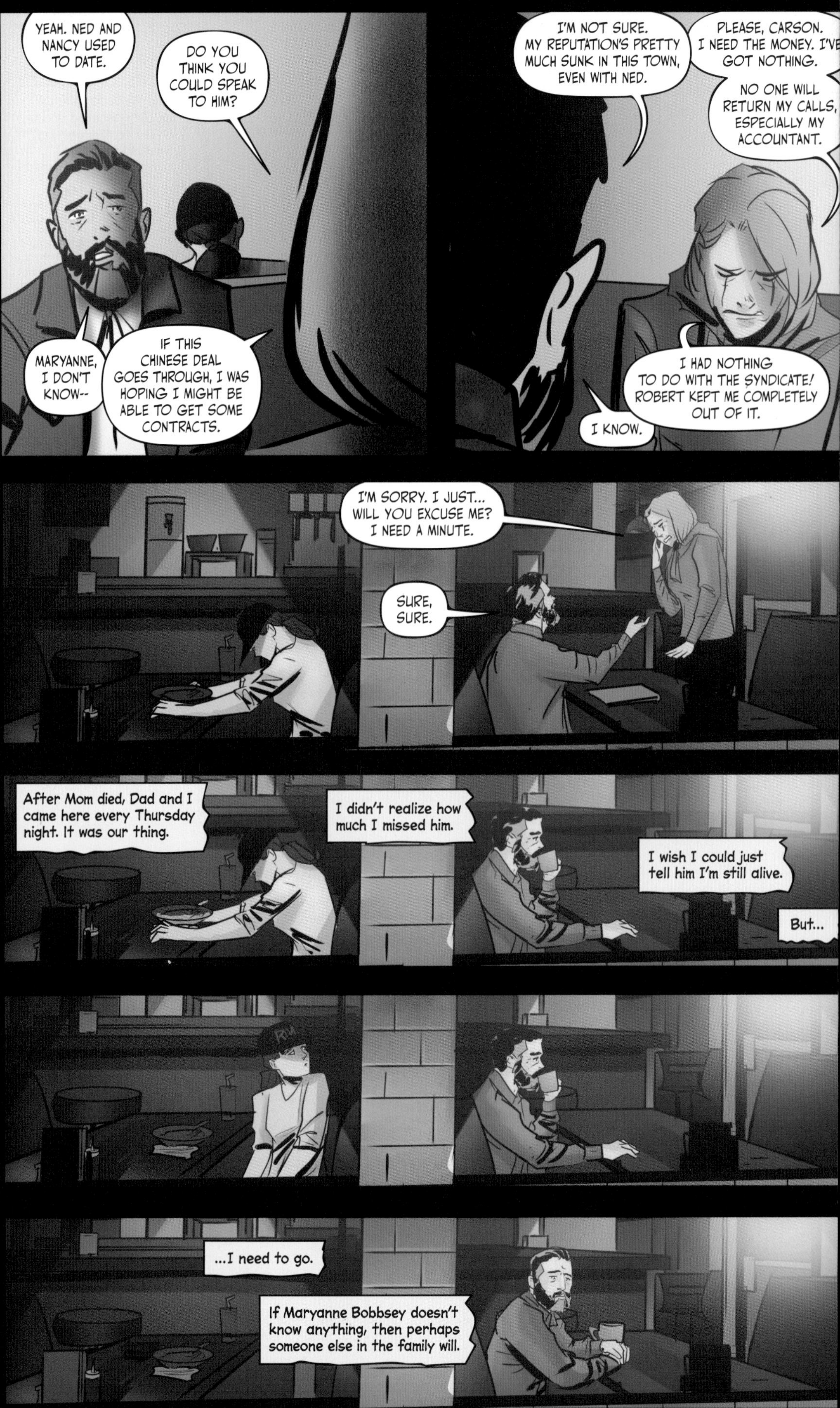
YEAH. NED AND NANCY USED TO DATE.
DO YOU THINK YOU COULD SPEAK TO HIM?
MARYANNE, I DON'T KNOW--
IF THIS CHINESE DEAL GOES THROUGH, I WAS HOPING I MIGHT BE ABLE TO GET SOME CONTRACTS.
I'M NOT SURE. MY REPUTATION'S PRETTY MUCH SUNK IN THIS TOWN, EVEN WITH NED.
PLEASE, CARSON. I NEED THE MONEY. I'VE GOT NOTHING.
NO ONE WILL RETURN MY CALLS, ESPECIALLY MY ACCOUNTANT.
I HAD NOTHING TO DO WITH THE SYNDICATE! ROBERT KEPT ME COMPLETELY OUT OF IT.
I KNOW.
I'M SORRY. I JUST... WILL YOU EXCUSE ME? I NEED A MINUTE.
SURE, SURE.
After Mom died, Dad and I came here every Thursday night. It was our thing.
I didn't realize how much I missed him.
I wish I could just tell him I'm still alive.
But...
...I need to go.
If Maryanne Bobbsey doesn't know anything, then perhaps someone else in the family will.

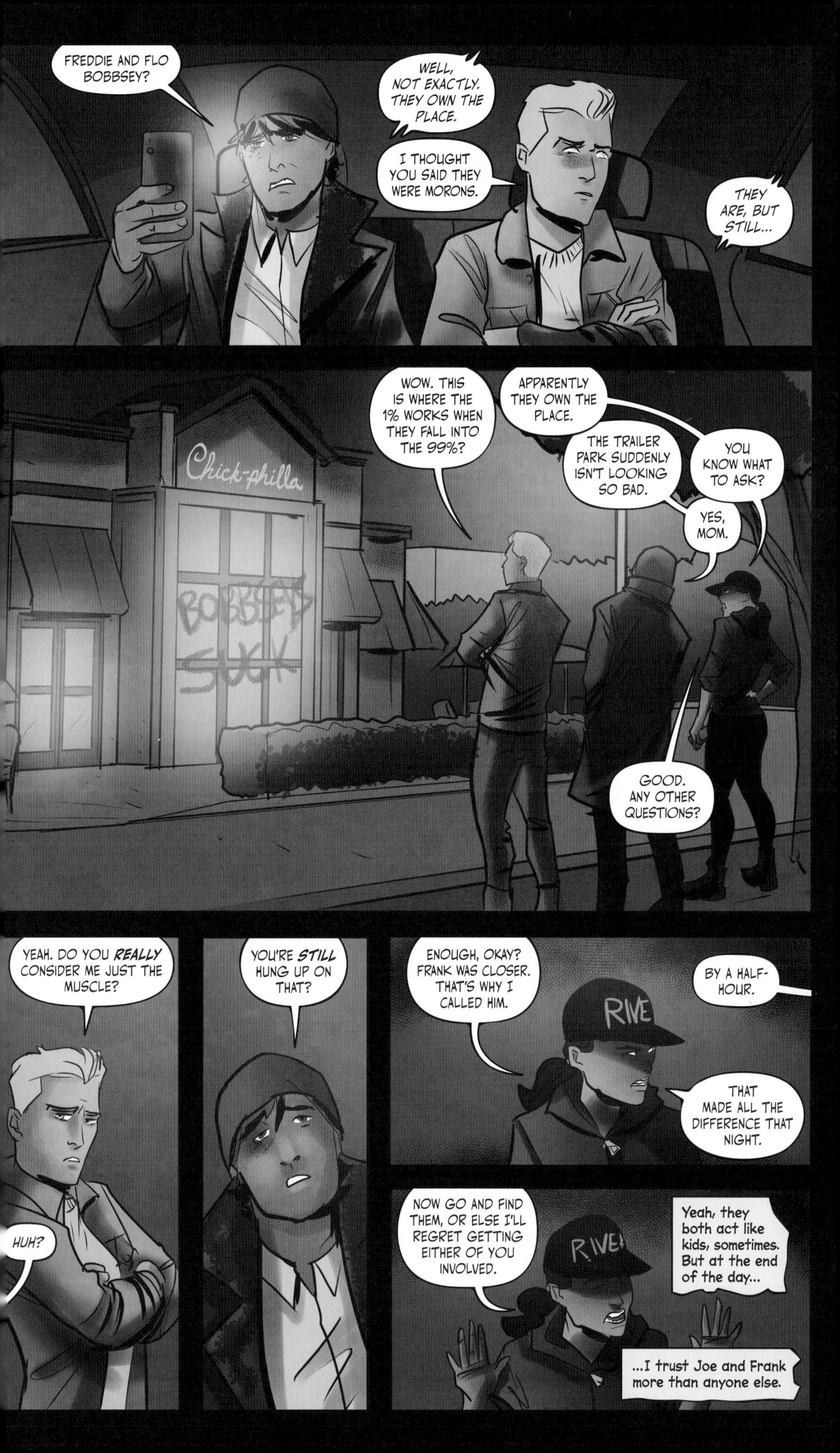
FREDDIE AND FLO BOBBSEY?
WELL, NOT EXACTLY. THEY OWN THE PLACE.
I THOUGHT YOU SAID THEY WERE MORONS.
THEY ARE, BUT STILL...
Chick-philla
BOBBSEYS SUCK
WOW. THIS IS WHERE THE 1% WORKS WHEN THEY FALL INTO THE 99%?
APPARENTLY THEY OWN THE PLACE.
THE TRAILER PARK SUDDENLY ISN'T LOOKING SO BAD.
YOU KNOW WHAT TO ASK?
YES, MOM.
GOOD. ANY OTHER QUESTIONS?
YEAH. DO YOU REALLY CONSIDER ME JUST THE MUSCLE?
HUH?
YOU'RE STILL HUNG UP ON THAT?
ENOUGH, OKAY? FRANK WAS CLOSER. THAT'S WHY I CALLED HIM.
BY A HALF-HOUR.
THAT MADE ALL THE DIFFERENCE THAT NIGHT.
NOW GO AND FIND THEM, OR ELSE I'LL REGRET GETTING EITHER OF YOU INVOLVED.
Yeah, they both act like kids, sometimes. But at the end of the day...
...I trust Joe and Frank more than anyone else.

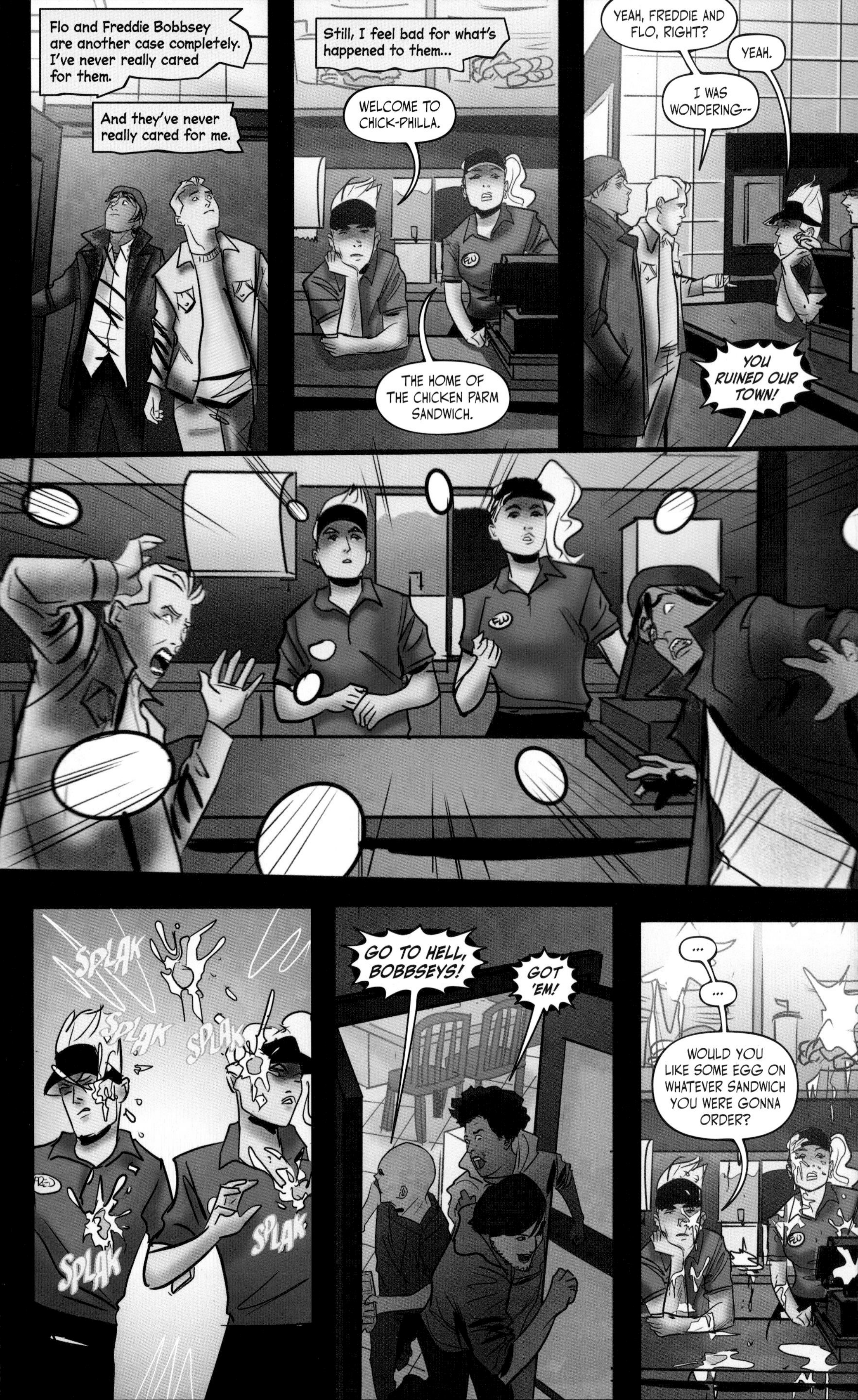

Flo and Freddie Bobbsey are another case completely. I've never really cared for them.
And they've never really cared for me.
Still, I feel bad for what's happened to them...
WELCOME TO CHICK-PHILLA.
THE HOME OF THE CHICKEN PARM SANDWICH.
YEAH, FREDDIE AND FLO, RIGHT?
YEAH.
I WAS WONDERING--
YOU RUINED OUR TOWN!
SPLAK
SPLAK
SPLAK
SPLAK
SPLAK
GO TO HELL, BOBBSEYS!
GOT 'EM!
...
...
WOULD YOU LIKE SOME EGG ON WHATEVER SANDWICH YOU WERE GONNA ORDER?

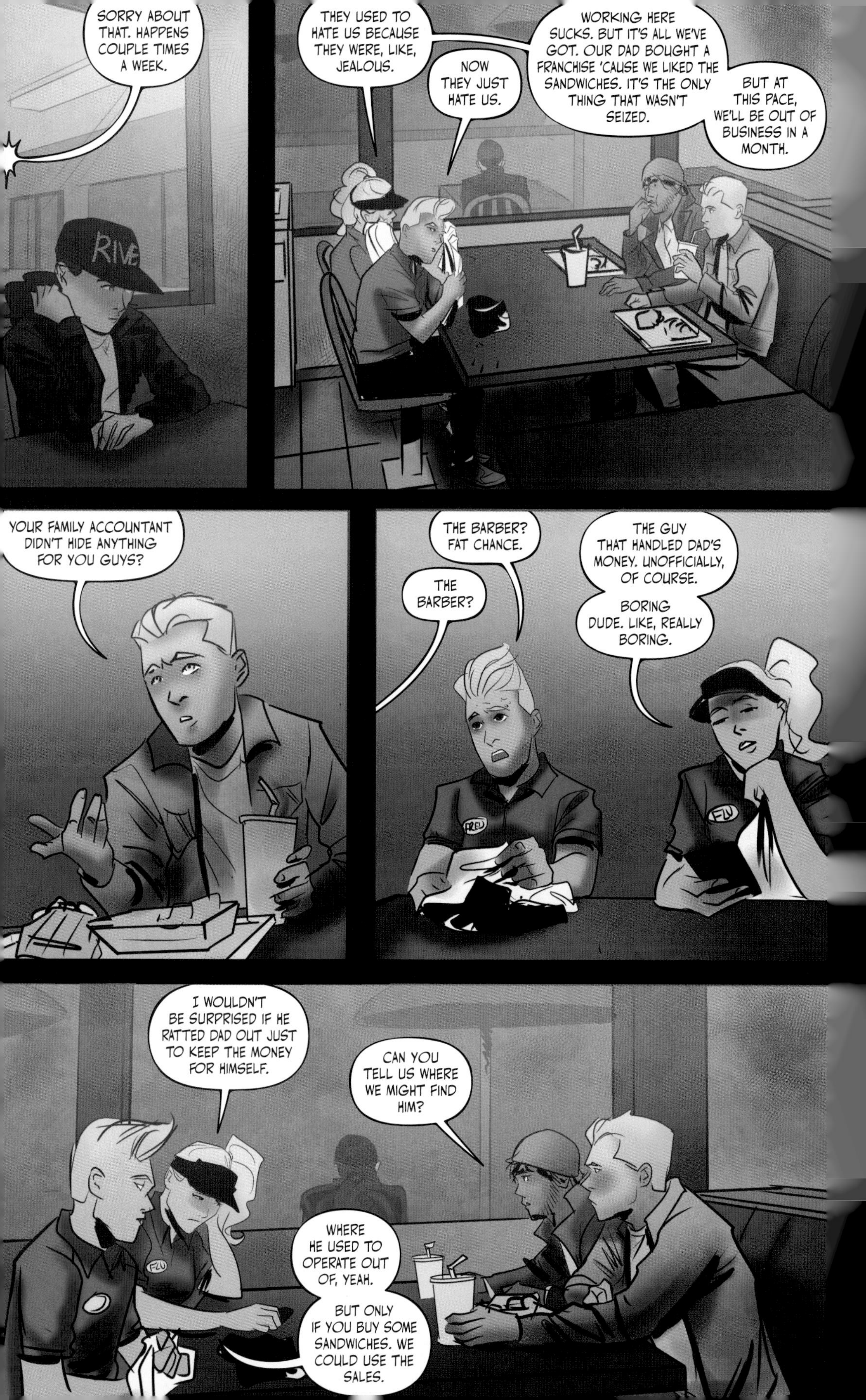
SORRY ABOUT THAT. HAPPENS COUPLE TIMES A WEEK.
THEY USED TO HATE US BECAUSE THEY WERE, LIKE, JEALOUS.
NOW THEY JUST HATE US.
WORKING HERE SUCKS. BUT IT'S ALL WE'VE GOT. OUR DAD BOUGHT A FRANCHISE 'CAUSE WE LIKED THE SANDWICHES. IT'S THE ONLY THING THAT WASN'T SEIZED.
BUT AT THIS PACE, WE'LL BE OUT OF BUSINESS IN A MONTH.
YOUR FAMILY ACCOUNTANT DIDN'T HIDE ANYTHING FOR YOU GUYS?
THE BARBER? FAT CHANCE.
THE BARBER?
THE GUY THAT HANDLED DAD'S MONEY. UNOFFICIALLY, OF COURSE.
BORING DUDE. LIKE, REALLY BORING.
I WOULDN'T BE SURPRISED IF HE RATTED DAD OUT JUST TO KEEP THE MONEY FOR HIMSELF.
CAN YOU TELL US WHERE WE MIGHT FIND HIM?
WHERE HE USED TO OPERATE OUT OF, YEAH.
BUT ONLY IF YOU BUY SOME SANDWICHES. WE COULD USE THE SALES.

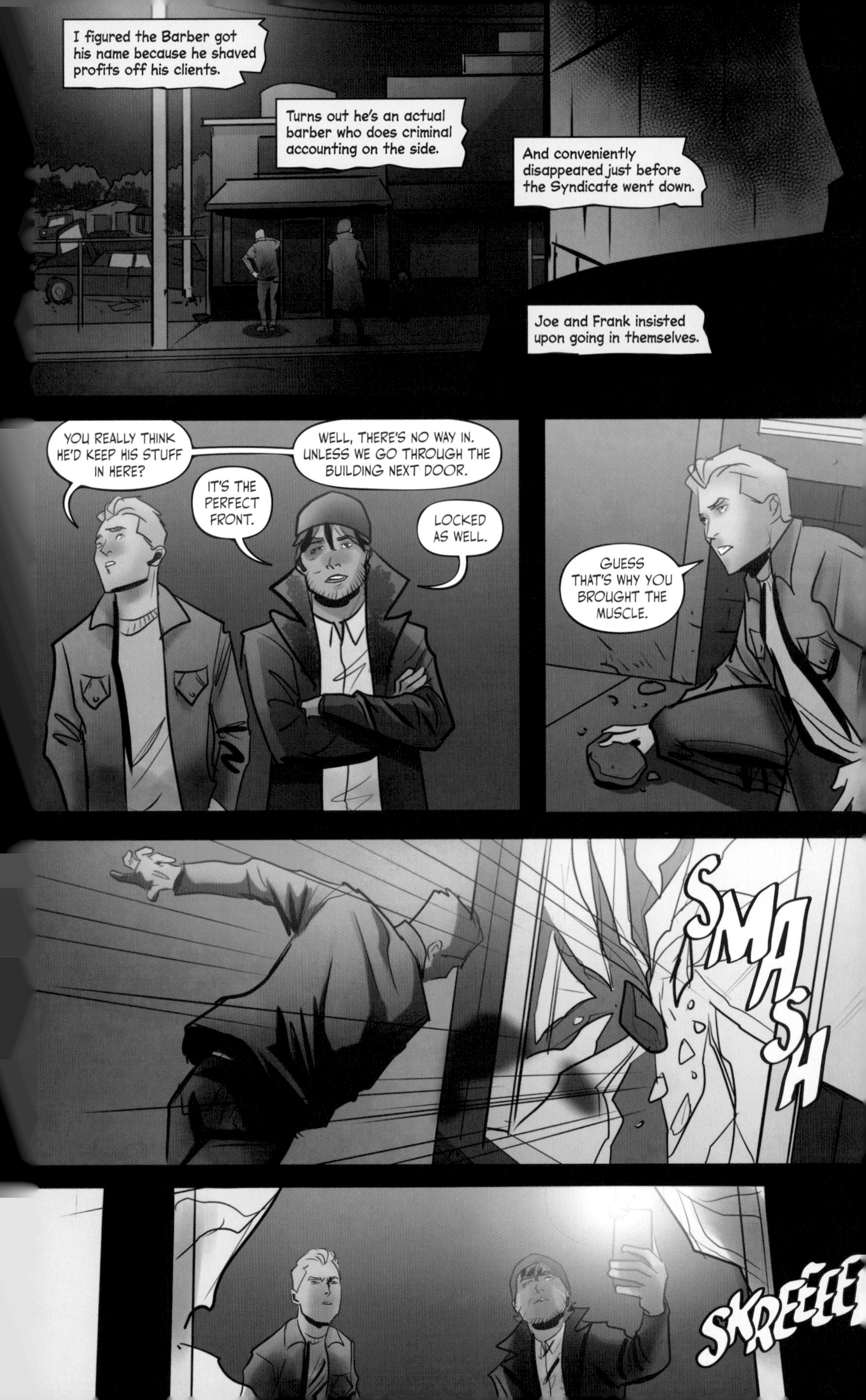
I figured the Barber got his name because he shaved profits off his clients.
Turns out he's an actual barber who does criminal accounting on the side.
And conveniently disappeared just before the Syndicate went down.
Joe and Frank insisted upon going in themselves.
YOU REALLY THINK HE'D KEEP HIS STUFF IN HERE?
IT'S THE PERFECT FRONT.
WELL, THERE'S NO WAY IN. UNLESS WE GO THROUGH THE BUILDING NEXT DOOR.
LOCKED AS WELL.
GUESS THAT'S WHY YOU BROUGHT THE MUSCLE.
SMASH
SKREEEE

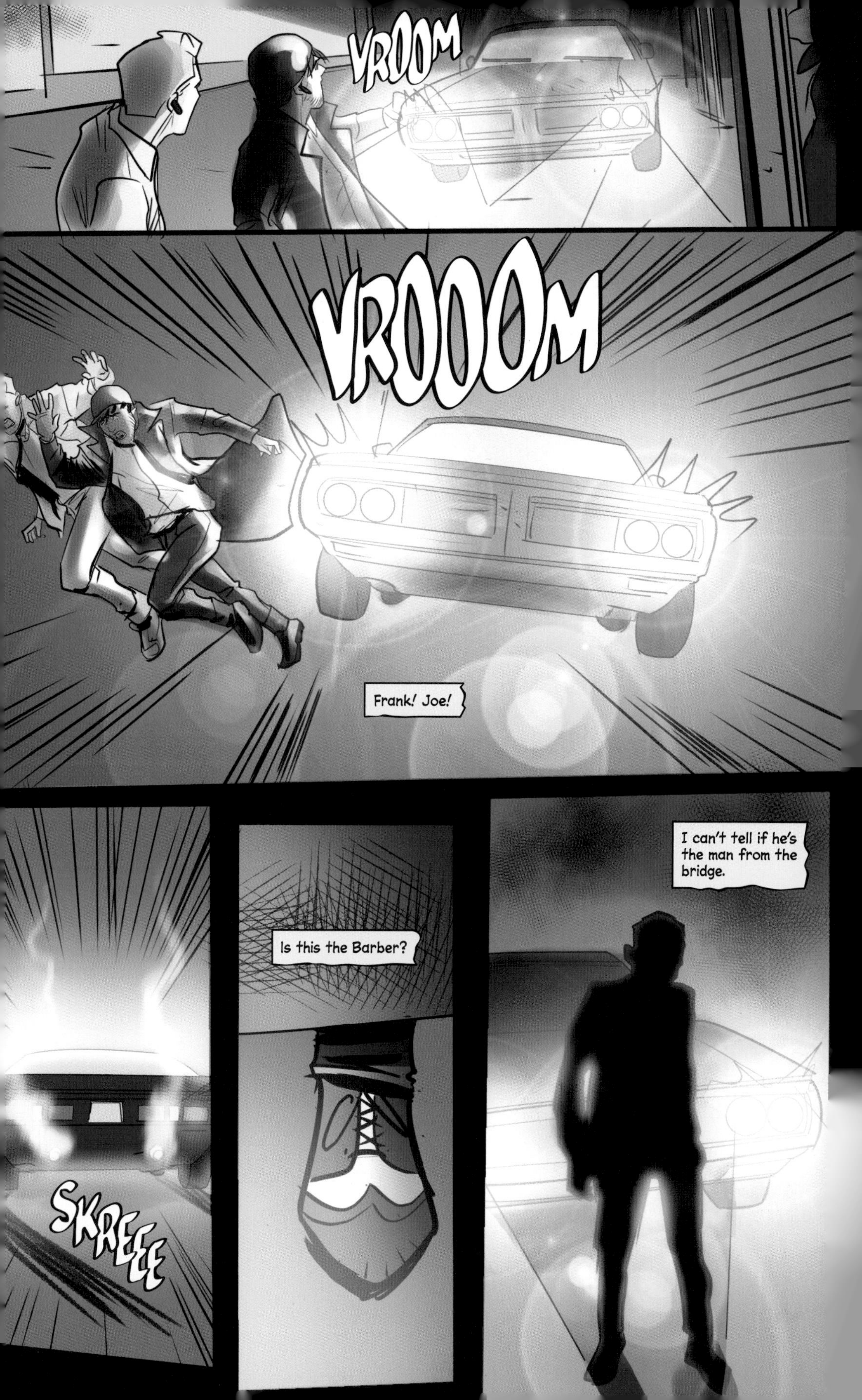
VROOM
VROOOM
Frank! Joe!
SKREEEE
Is this the Barber?
I can't tell if he's the man from the bridge.

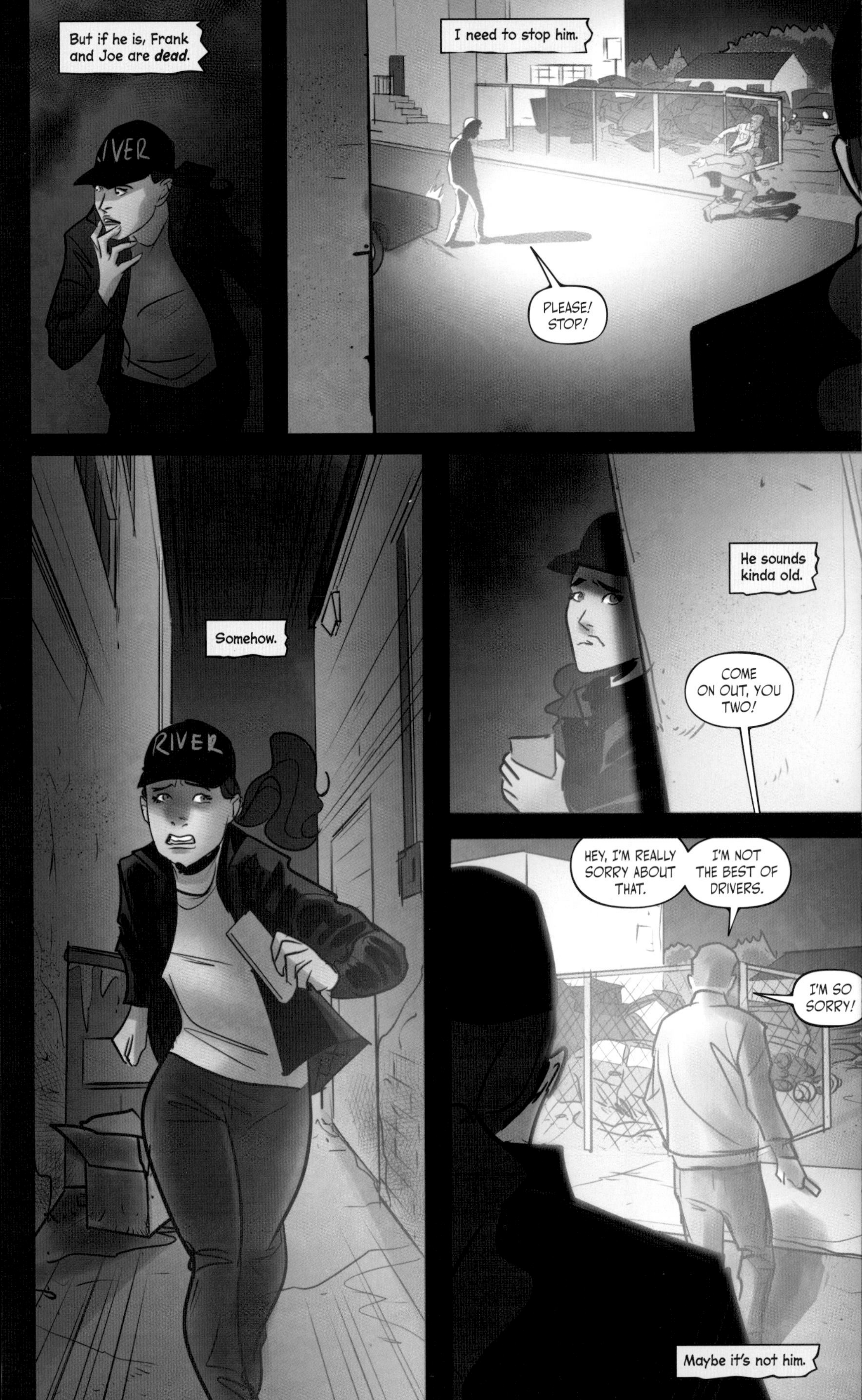
But if he is, Frank and Joe are ***dead***.
I need to stop him.
PLEASE! STOP!
Somehow.
He sounds kinda old.
COME ON OUT, YOU TWO!
HEY, I'M REALLY SORRY ABOUT THAT.
I'M NOT THE BEST OF DRIVERS.
I'M SO SORRY!
Maybe it's not him.

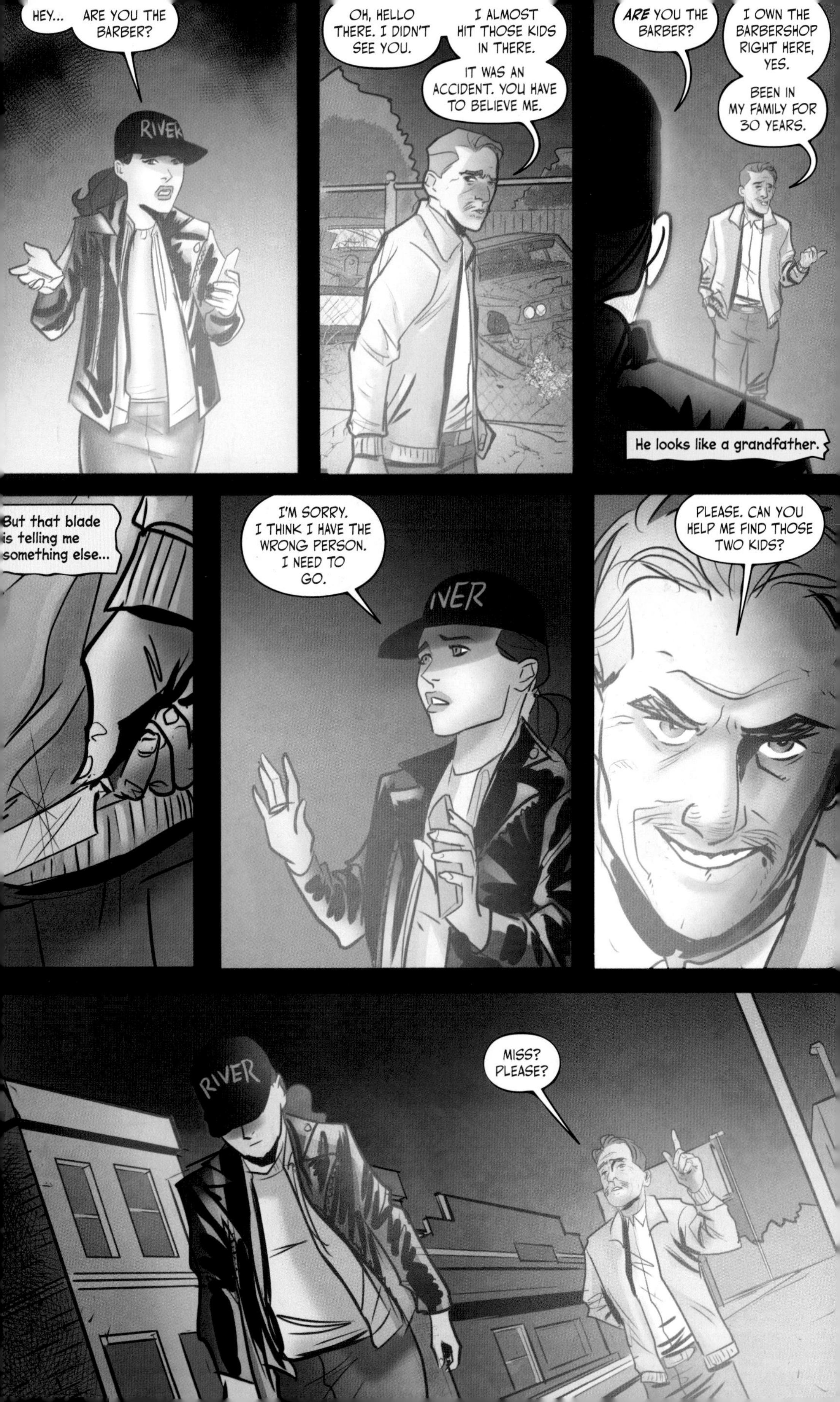

HEY...
ARE YOU THE BARBER?
RIVER
OH, HELLO THERE. I DIDN'T SEE YOU.
I ALMOST HIT THOSE KIDS IN THERE.
IT WAS AN ACCIDENT. YOU HAVE TO BELIEVE ME.
ARE YOU THE BARBER?
I OWN THE BARBERSHOP RIGHT HERE, YES.
BEEN IN MY FAMILY FOR 30 YEARS.
He looks like a grandfather.
But that blade is telling me something else...
I'M SORRY. I THINK I HAVE THE WRONG PERSON. I NEED TO GO.
IVER
PLEASE. CAN YOU HELP ME FIND THOSE TWO KIDS?
RIVER
MISS? PLEASE?

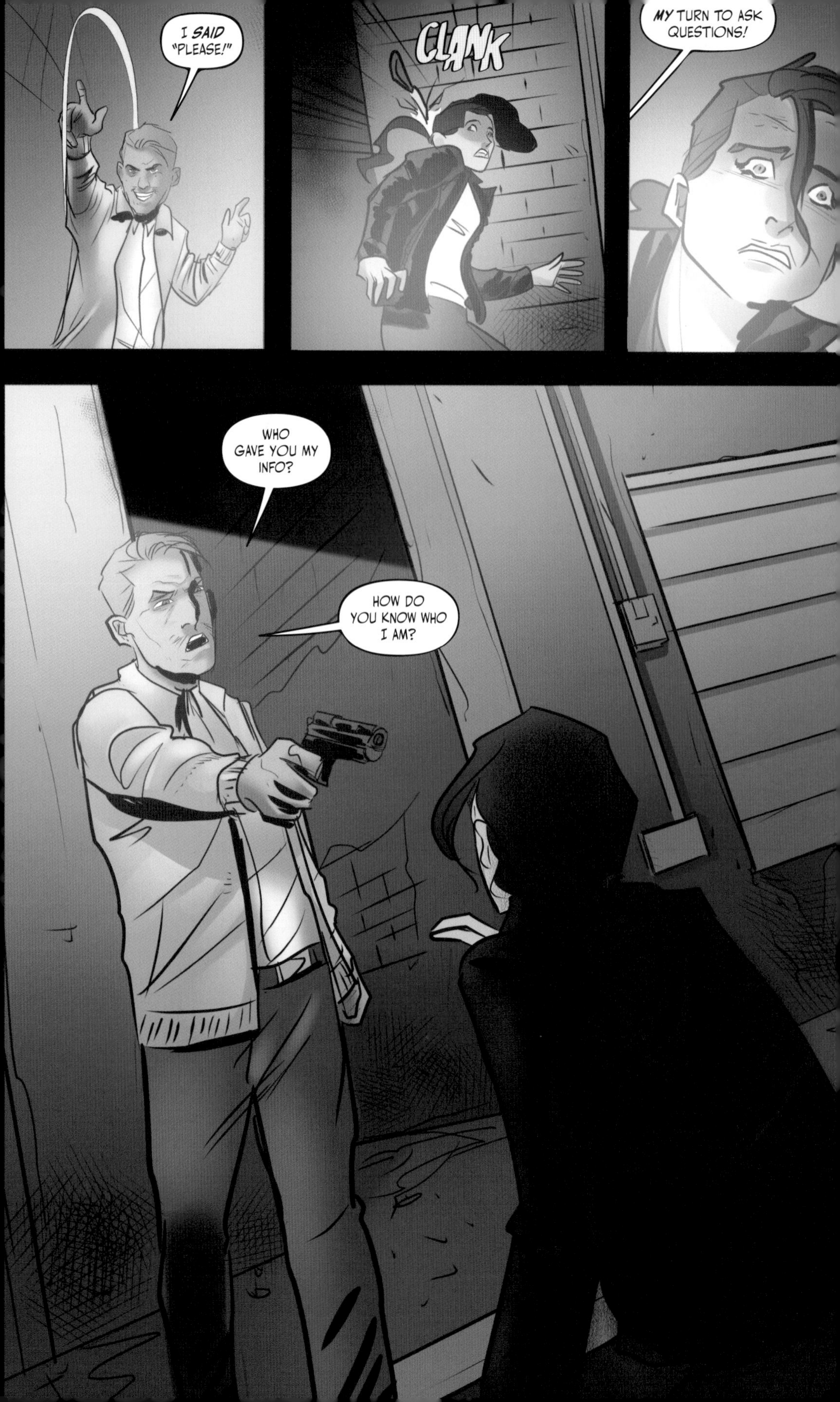
I SAID "PLEASE!"
CLANK
MY TURN TO ASK QUESTIONS!
WHO GAVE YOU MY INFO?
HOW DO YOU KNOW WHO I AM?

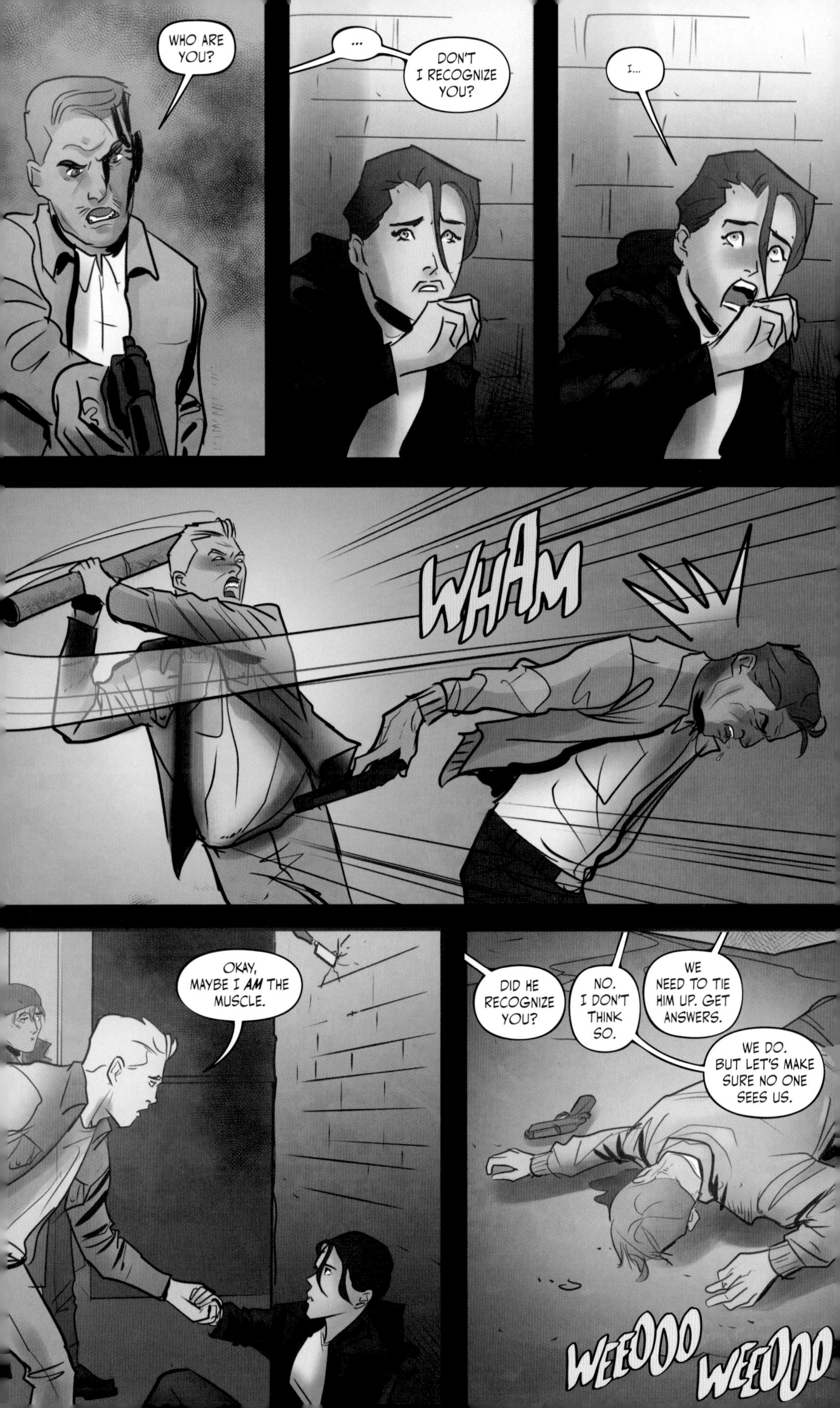
WHO ARE YOU?
...
DON'T I RECOGNIZE YOU?
I...
WHAM
OKAY, MAYBE I *AM* THE MUSCLE.
DID HE RECOGNIZE YOU?
NO. I DON'T THINK SO.
WE NEED TO TIE HIM UP. GET ANSWERS.
WE DO. BUT LET'S MAKE SURE NO ONE SEES US.
WEEOOO WEEOOO

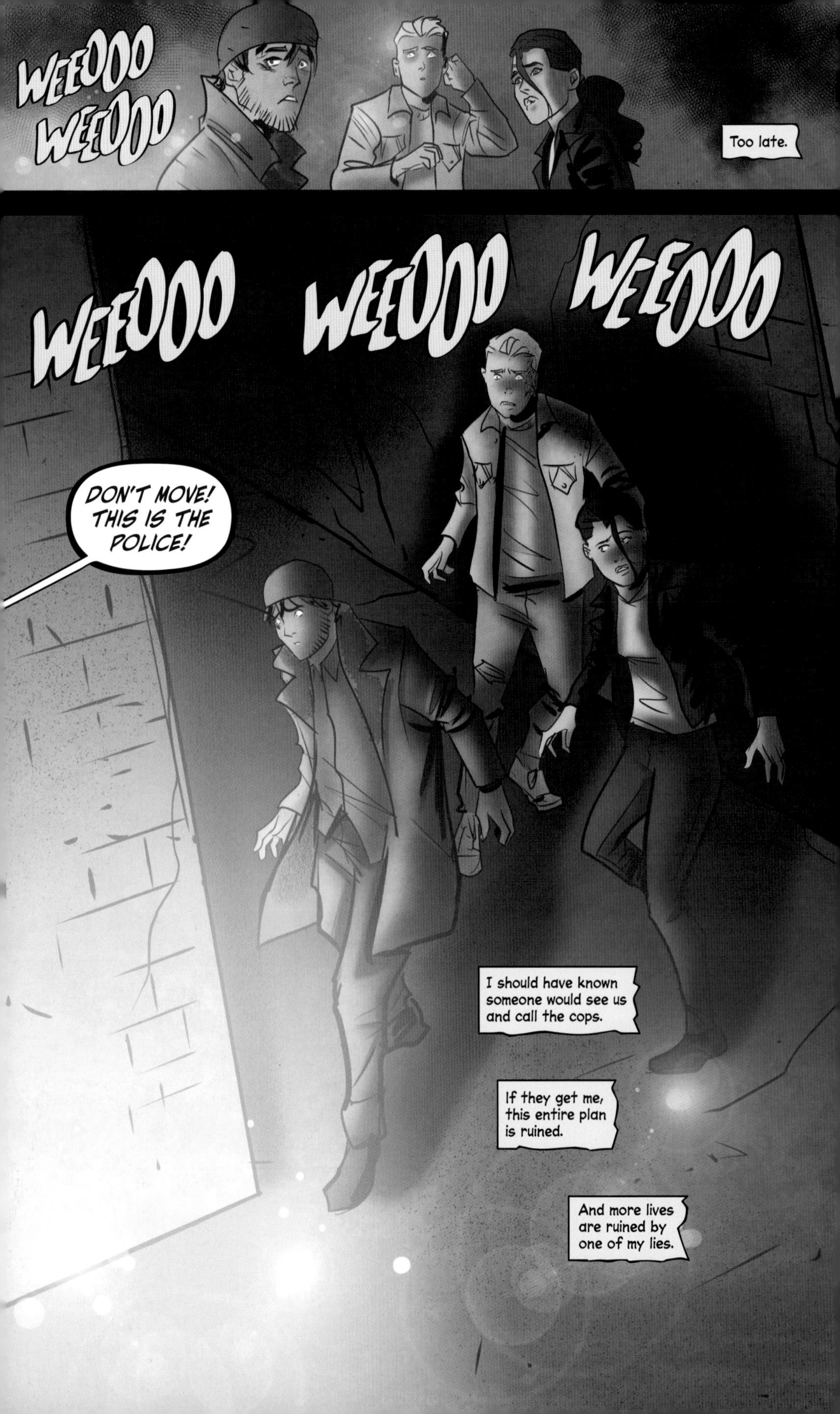
WEEOOO
WEEOOO
Too late.
WEEOOO
WEEOOO
WEEOOO
DON'T MOVE! THIS IS THE POLICE!
I should have known someone would see us and call the cops.
If they get me, this entire plan is ruined.
And more lives are ruined by one of my lies.

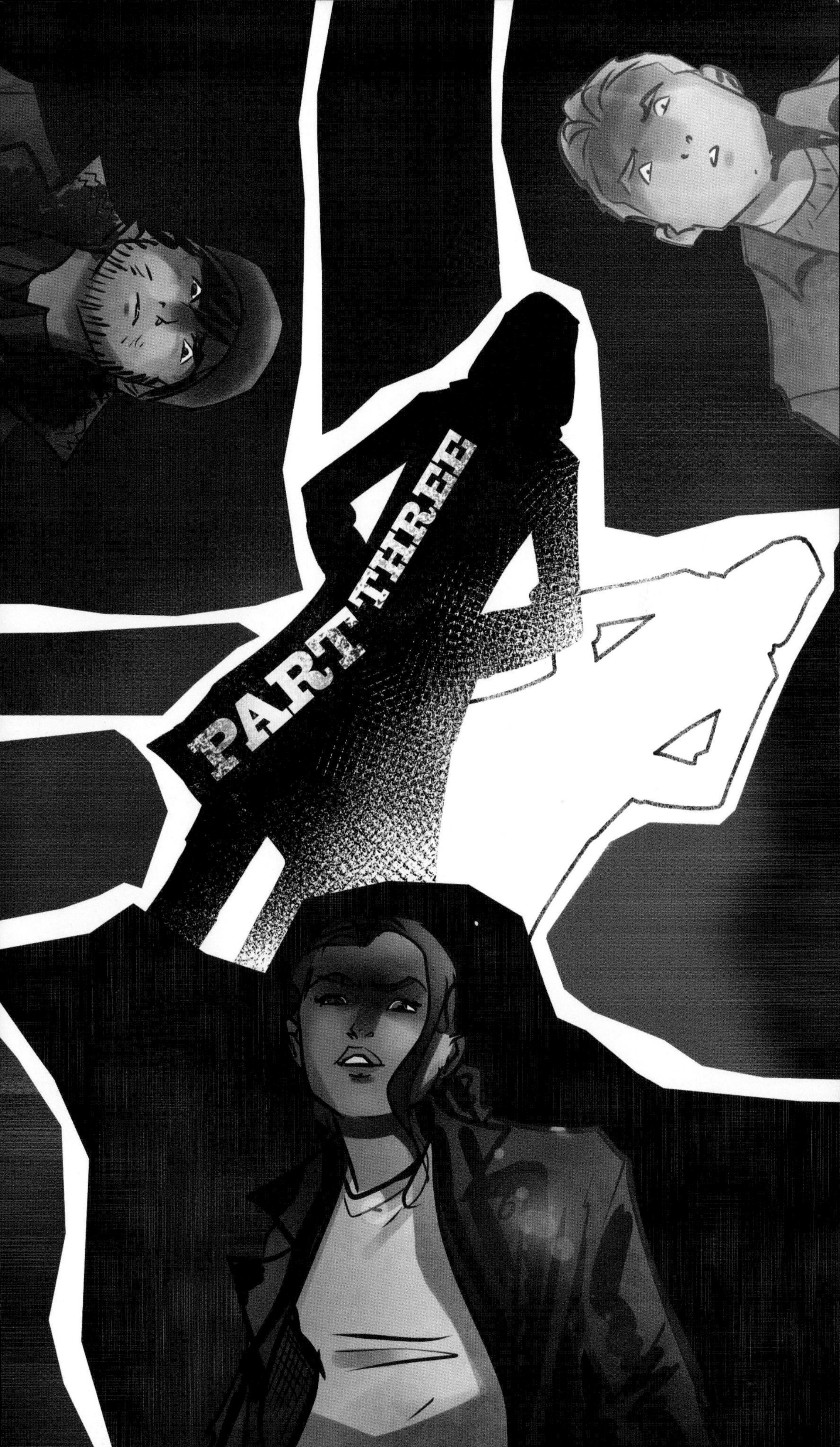
PART THREE

PART THREE COVER ART BY **JOE EISMA**

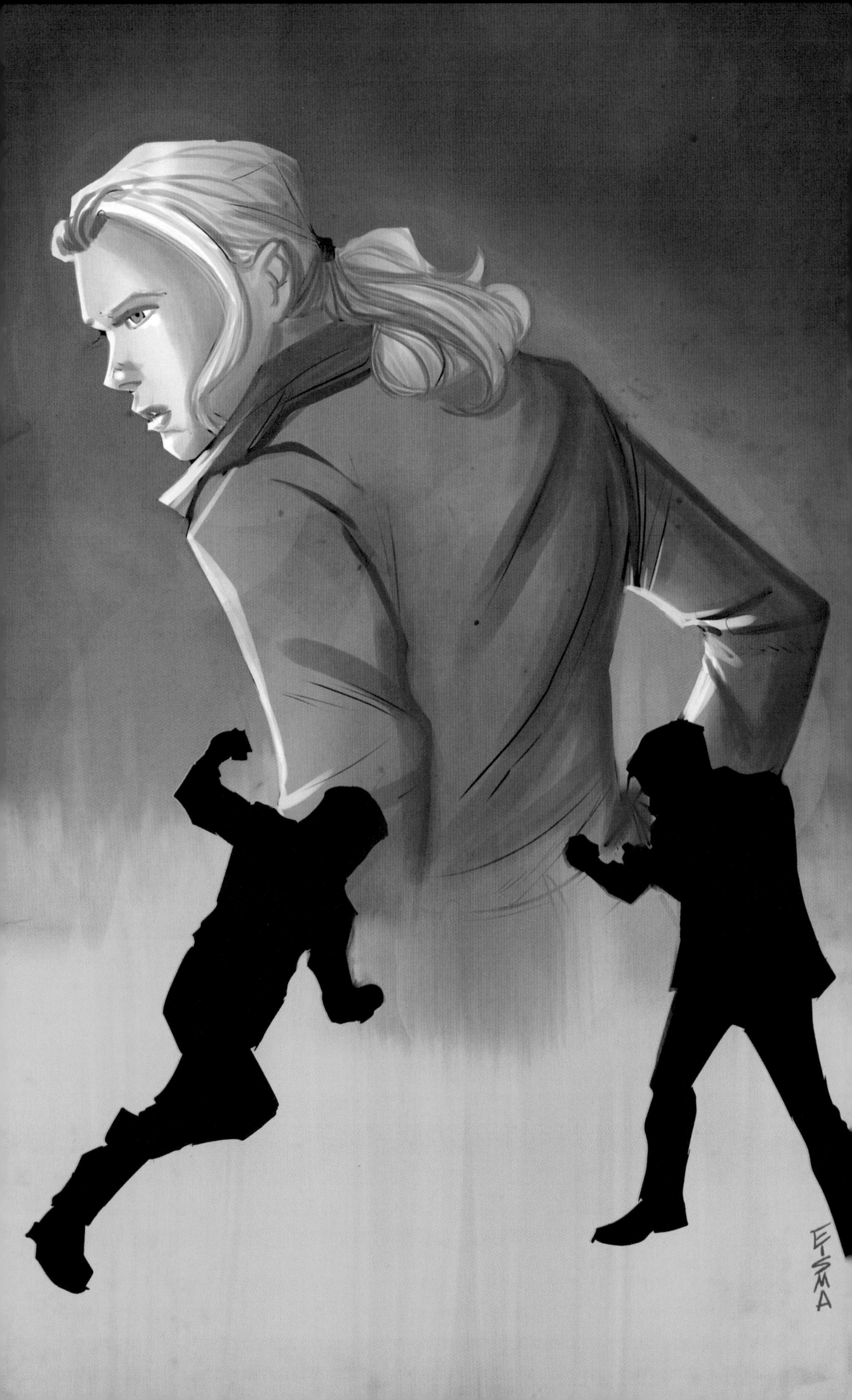

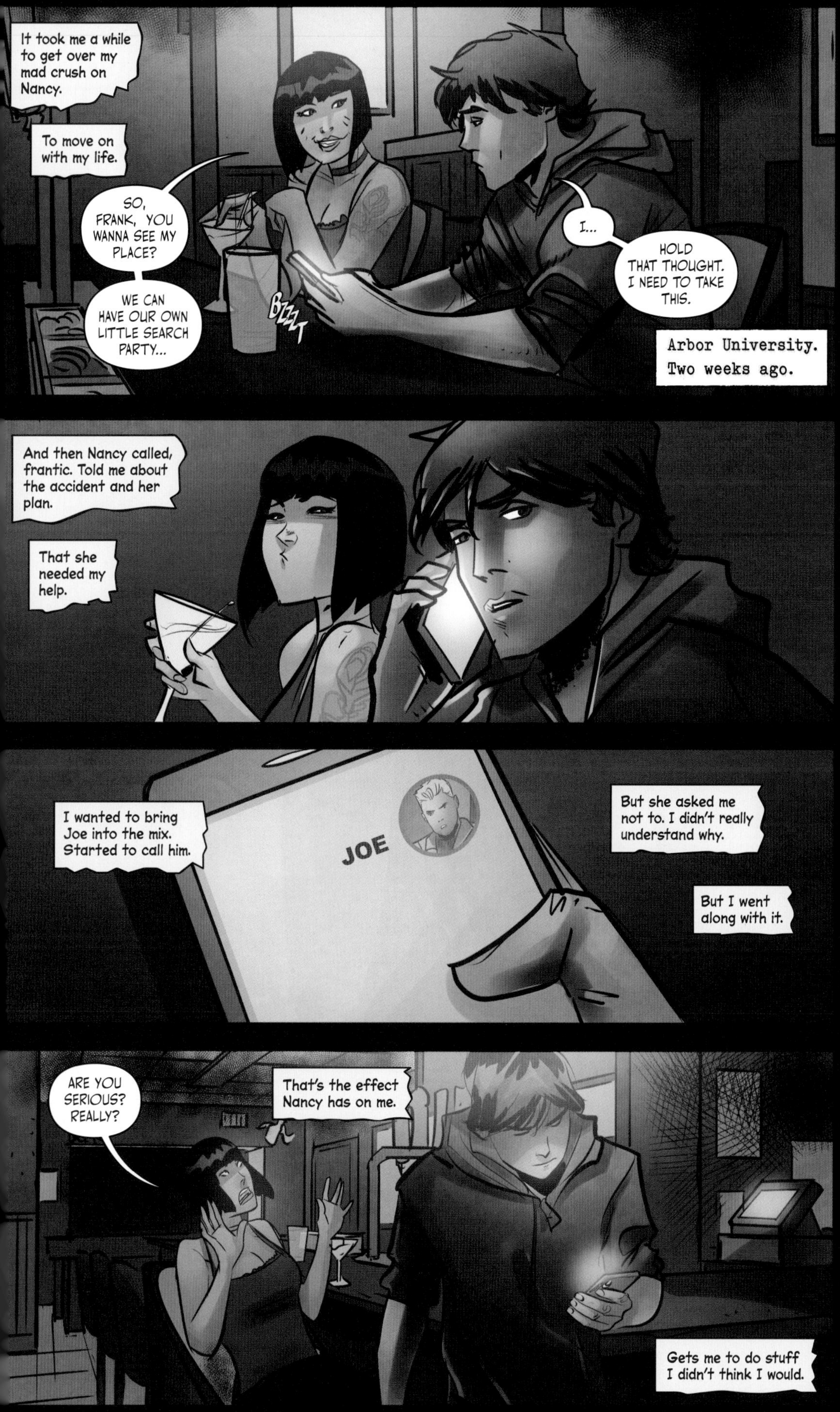
It took me a while to get over my mad crush on Nancy.
To move on with my life.
SO, FRANK, YOU WANNA SEE MY PLACE?
WE CAN HAVE OUR OWN LITTLE SEARCH PARTY...
BZZZT
I...
HOLD THAT THOUGHT. I NEED TO TAKE THIS.
Arbor University. Two weeks ago.
And then Nancy called, frantic. Told me about the accident and her plan.
That she needed my help.
I wanted to bring Joe into the mix. Started to call him.
JOE
But she asked me not to. I didn't really understand why.
But I went along with it.
ARE YOU SERIOUS? REALLY?
That's the effect Nancy has on me.
Gets me to do stuff I didn't think I would.

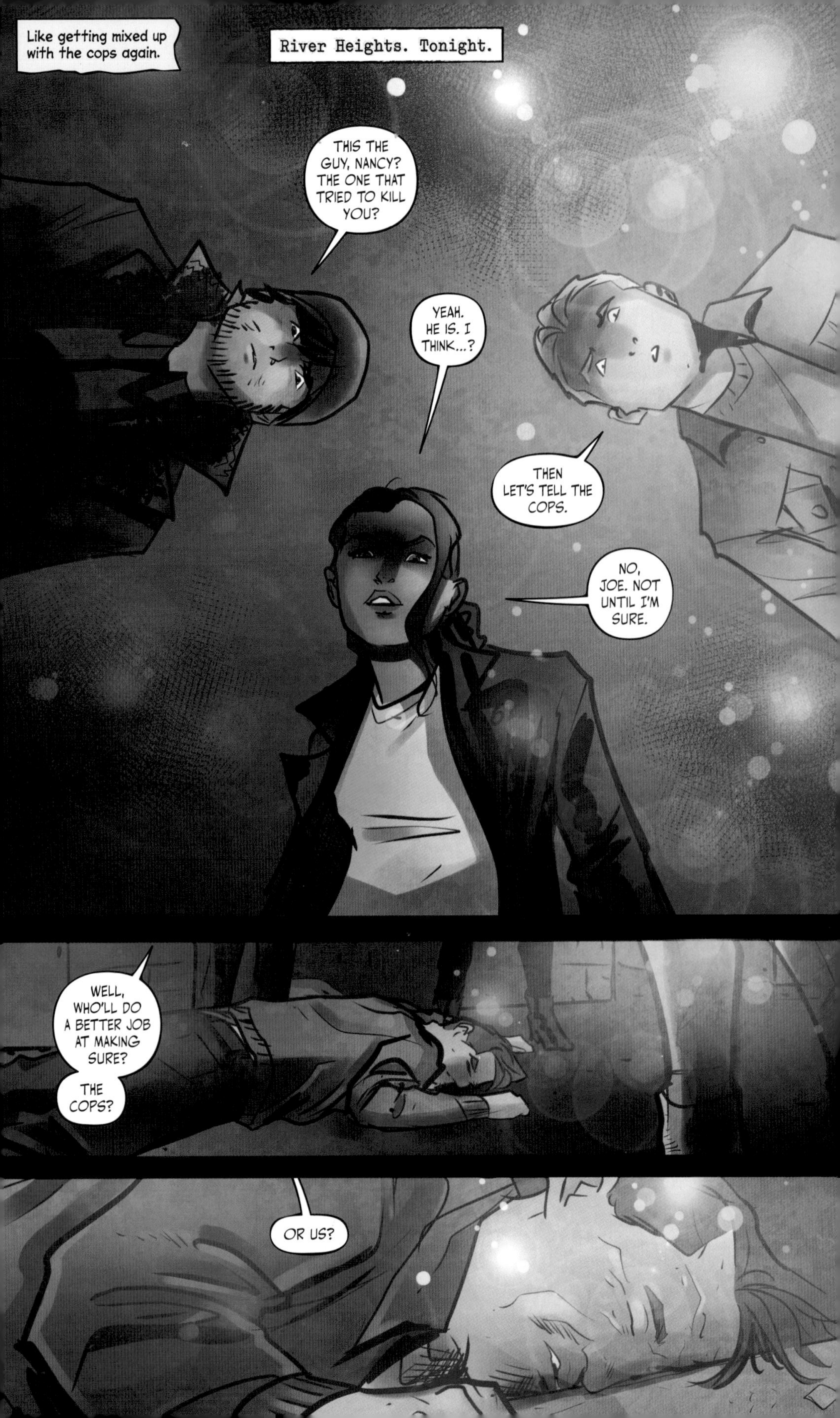

Like getting mixed up with the cops again.
River Heights. Tonight.
THIS THE GUY, NANCY? THE ONE THAT TRIED TO KILL YOU?
YEAH. HE IS. I THINK...?
THEN LET'S TELL THE COPS.
NO, JOE. NOT UNTIL I'M SURE.
WELL, WHO'LL DO A BETTER JOB AT MAKING SURE?
THE COPS?
OR US?

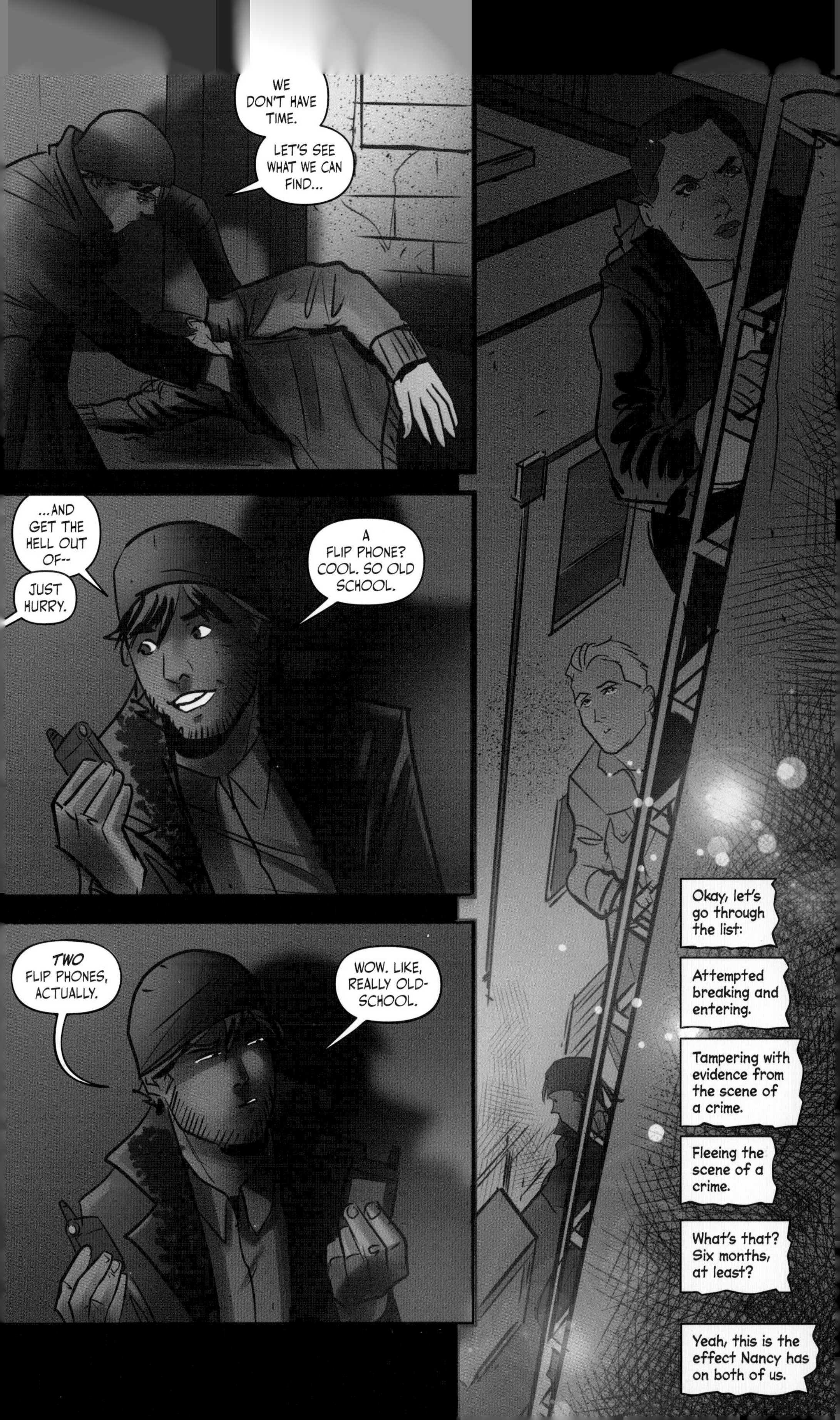
WE DON'T HAVE TIME.
LET'S SEE WHAT WE CAN FIND...
...AND GET THE HELL OUT OF--
JUST HURRY.
A FLIP PHONE? COOL. SO OLD SCHOOL.
TWO FLIP PHONES, ACTUALLY.
WOW. LIKE, REALLY OLD-SCHOOL.
Okay, let's go through the list:
Attempted breaking and entering.
Tampering with evidence from the scene of a crime.
Fleeing the scene of a crime.
What's that? Six months, at least?
Yeah, this is the effect Nancy has on both of us.

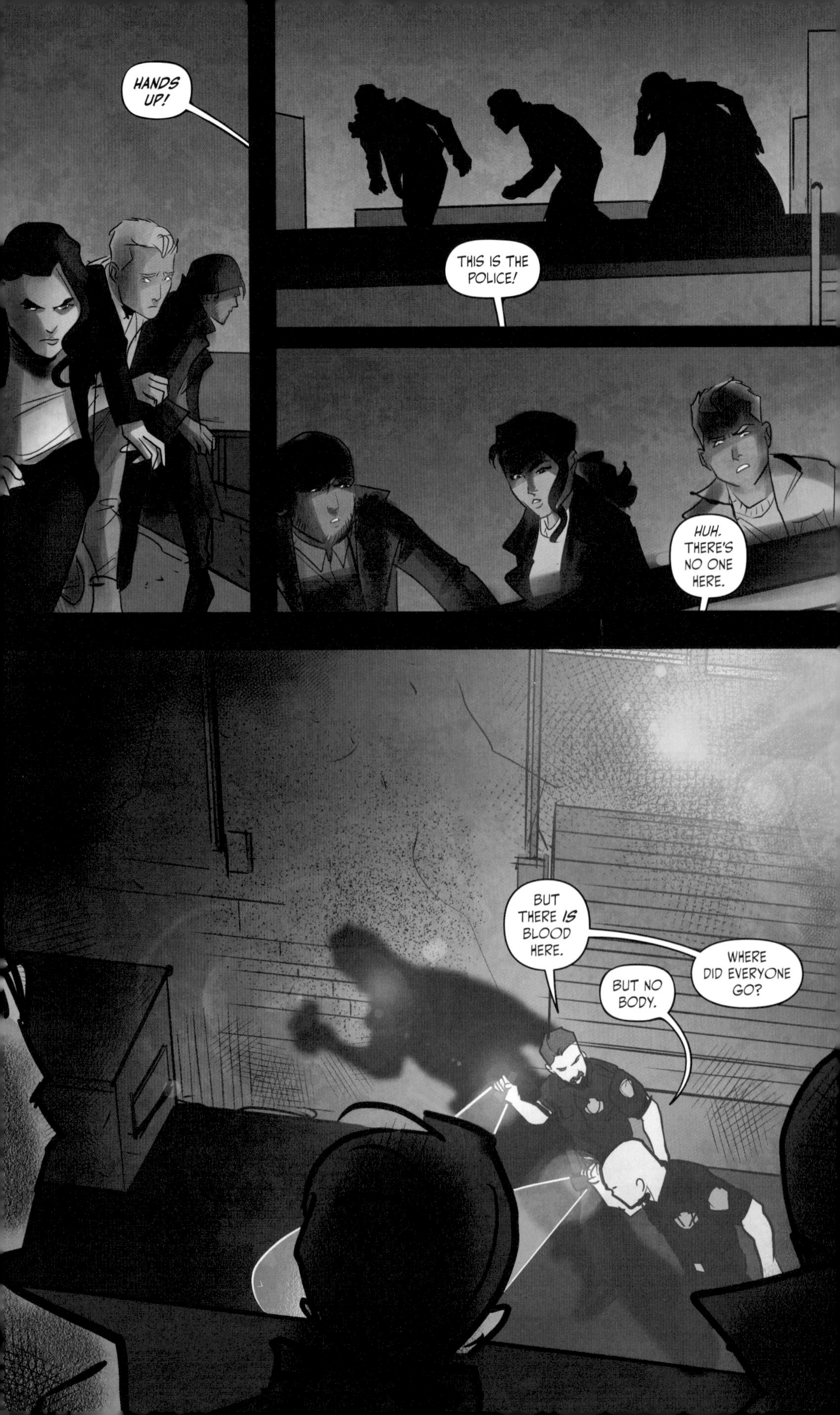
HANDS UP!
THIS IS THE POLICE!
HUH. THERE'S NO ONE HERE.
BUT THERE IS BLOOD HERE.
WHERE DID EVERYONE GO?
BUT NO BODY.

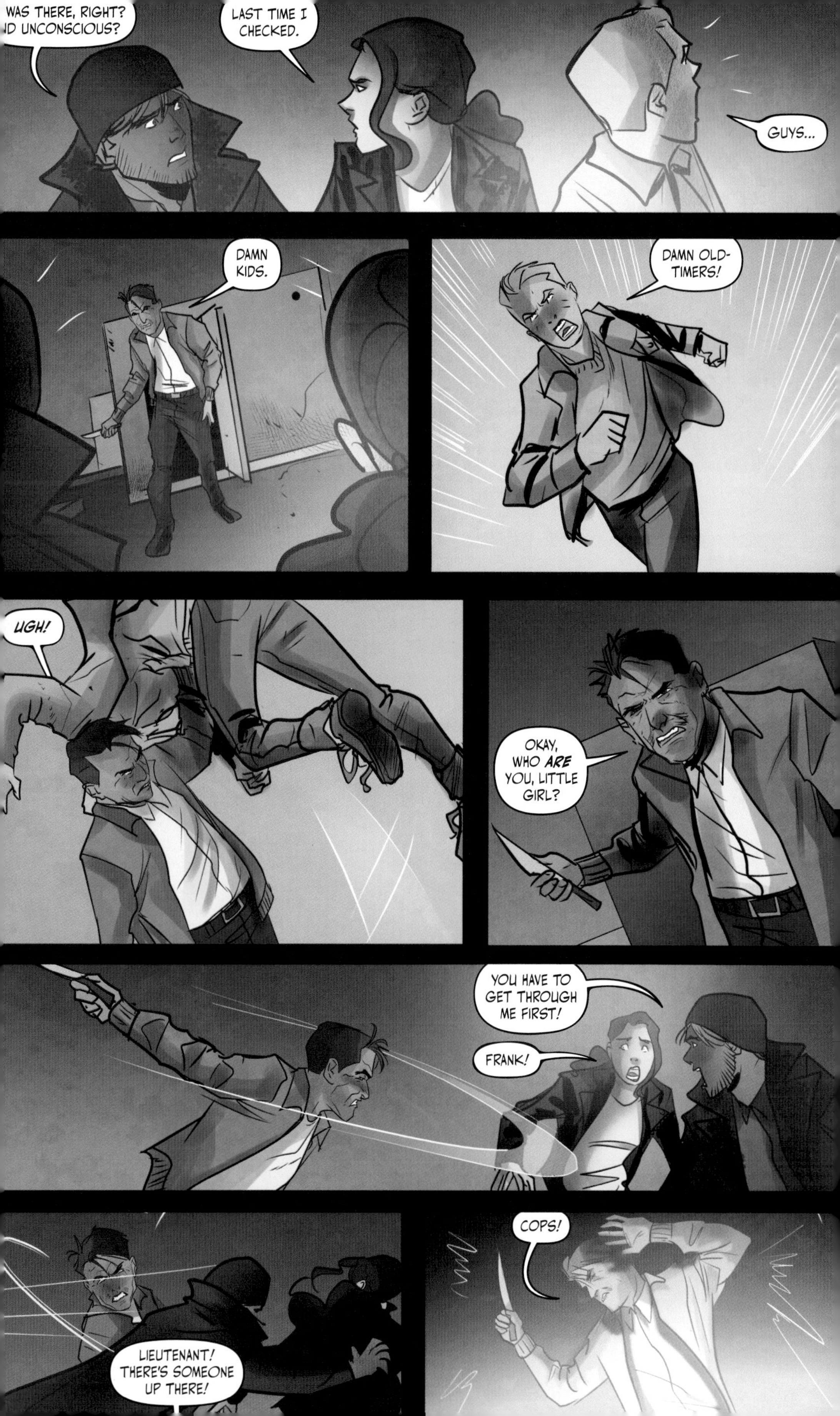
WAS THERE, RIGHT?
ID UNCONSCIOUS?
LAST TIME I CHECKED.
GUYS...
DAMN KIDS.
DAMN OLD-TIMERS!
UGH!
OKAY, WHO ARE YOU, LITTLE GIRL?
YOU HAVE TO GET THROUGH ME FIRST!
FRANK!
LIEUTENANT! THERE'S SOMEONE UP THERE!
COPS!

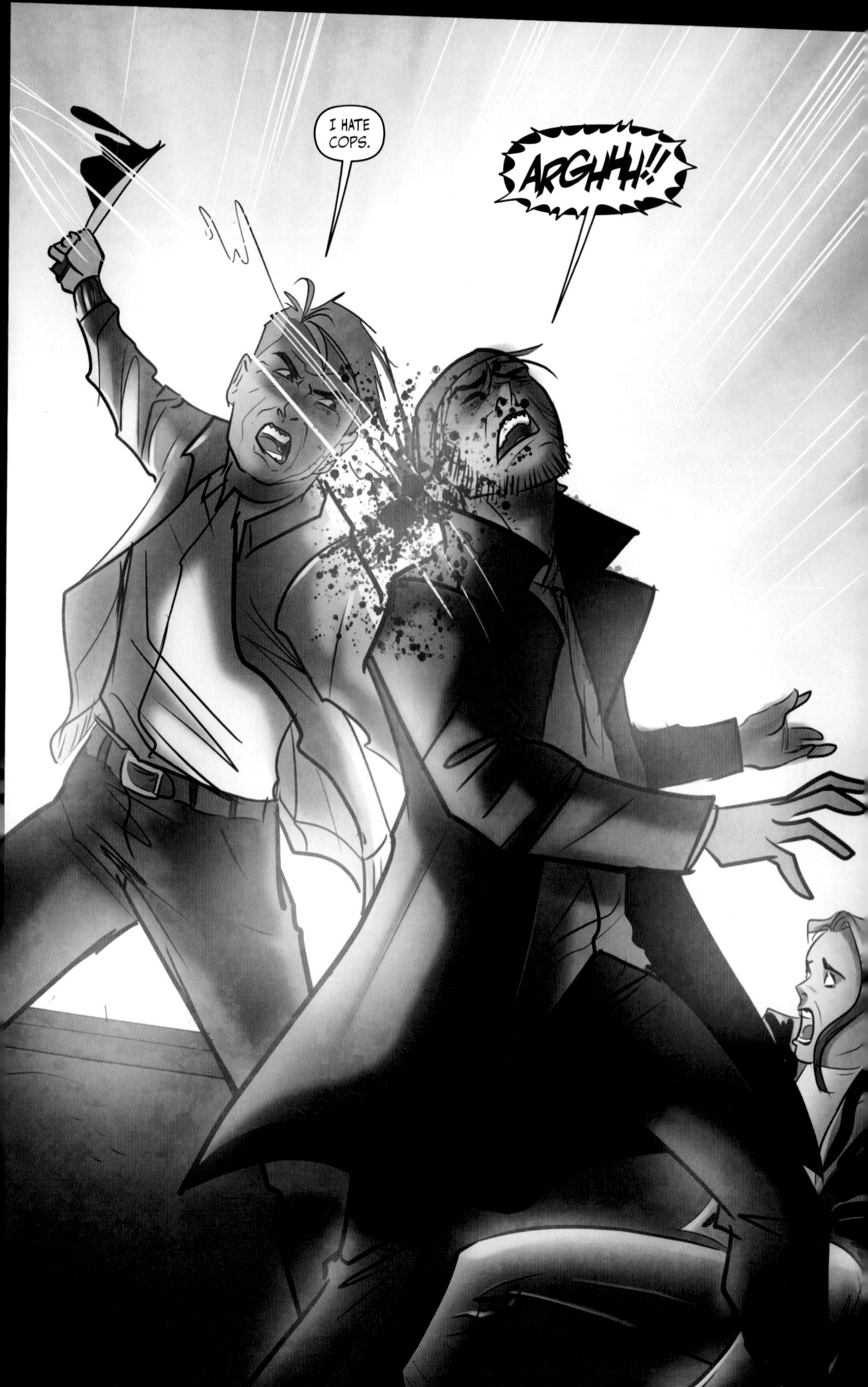
I HATE COPS.
ARGHHH!!

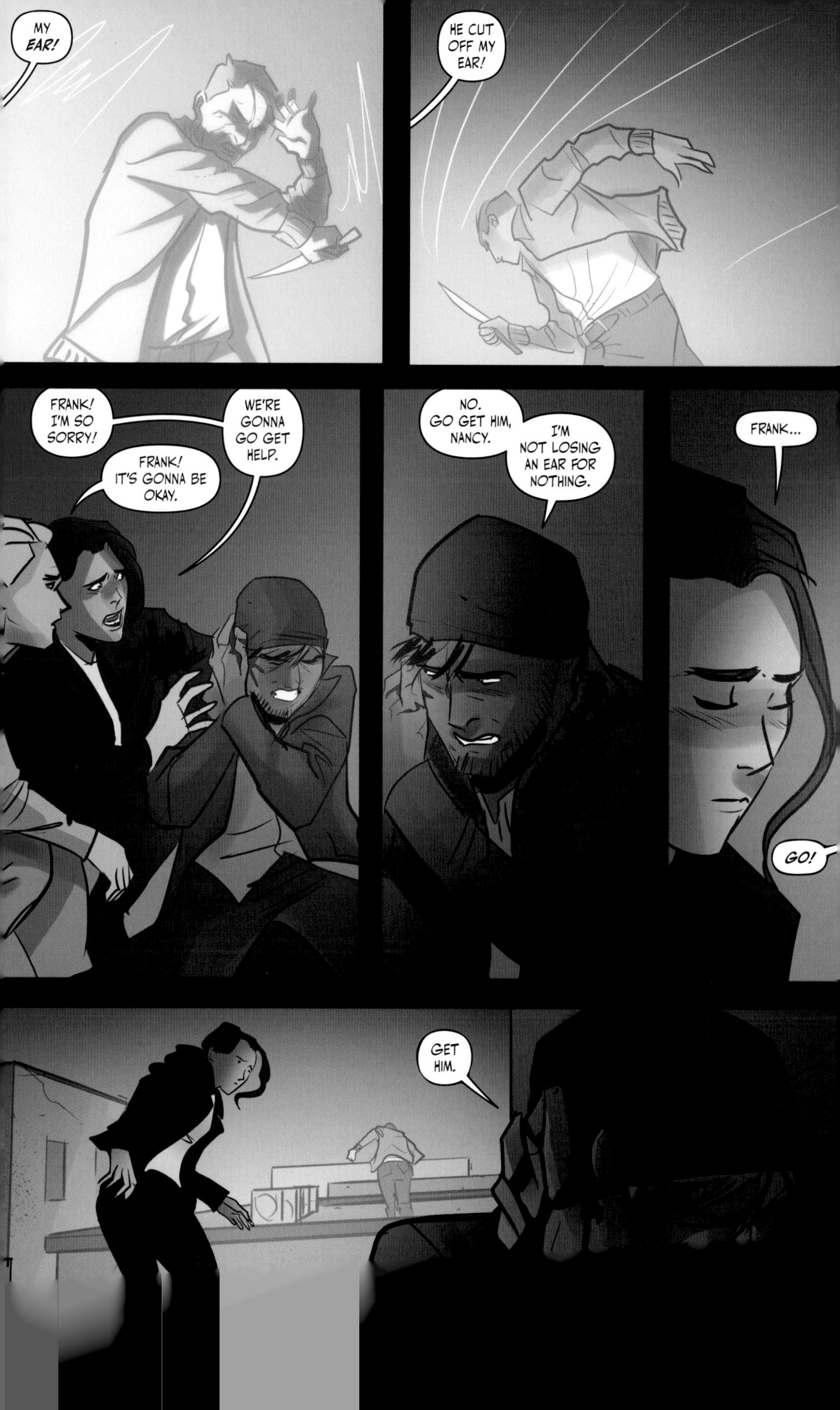
MY EAR!
HE CUT OFF MY EAR!
FRANK! I'M SO SORRY!
FRANK! IT'S GONNA BE OKAY.
WE'RE GONNA GO GET HELP.
NO. GO GET HIM, NANCY.
I'M NOT LOSING AN EAR FOR NOTHING.
FRANK...
GO!
GET HIM.

"ANESTHESIA, NOW!"

BOBBSEY WEST PLAZA

RIVER HEIGHTS HOSPITAL

YOU NEED TO FIX IT! PUT IT BACK TOGETHER!

WE'LL DO THE BEST WE CAN.

ANESTHESIA ADMINISTERED, DOCTOR.

COUNT BACKWARD FROM TE... FRANK.

TEN... NINE... EIGHT...

THAT'S NOT GONNA WORK. IT NEVER...

...WORKS...

IS HE GONNA BE ABLE TO HEAR AGAIN?

THE INJURYS NOT THAT BAD.

I'M SO SORRY, FRANK. I SHOULD HAVE STOPPED--

SHHHH...

NANCY, IF I DIE FOR SOME REASON, I WANT YOU TO KNOW...

I LOVE...

...

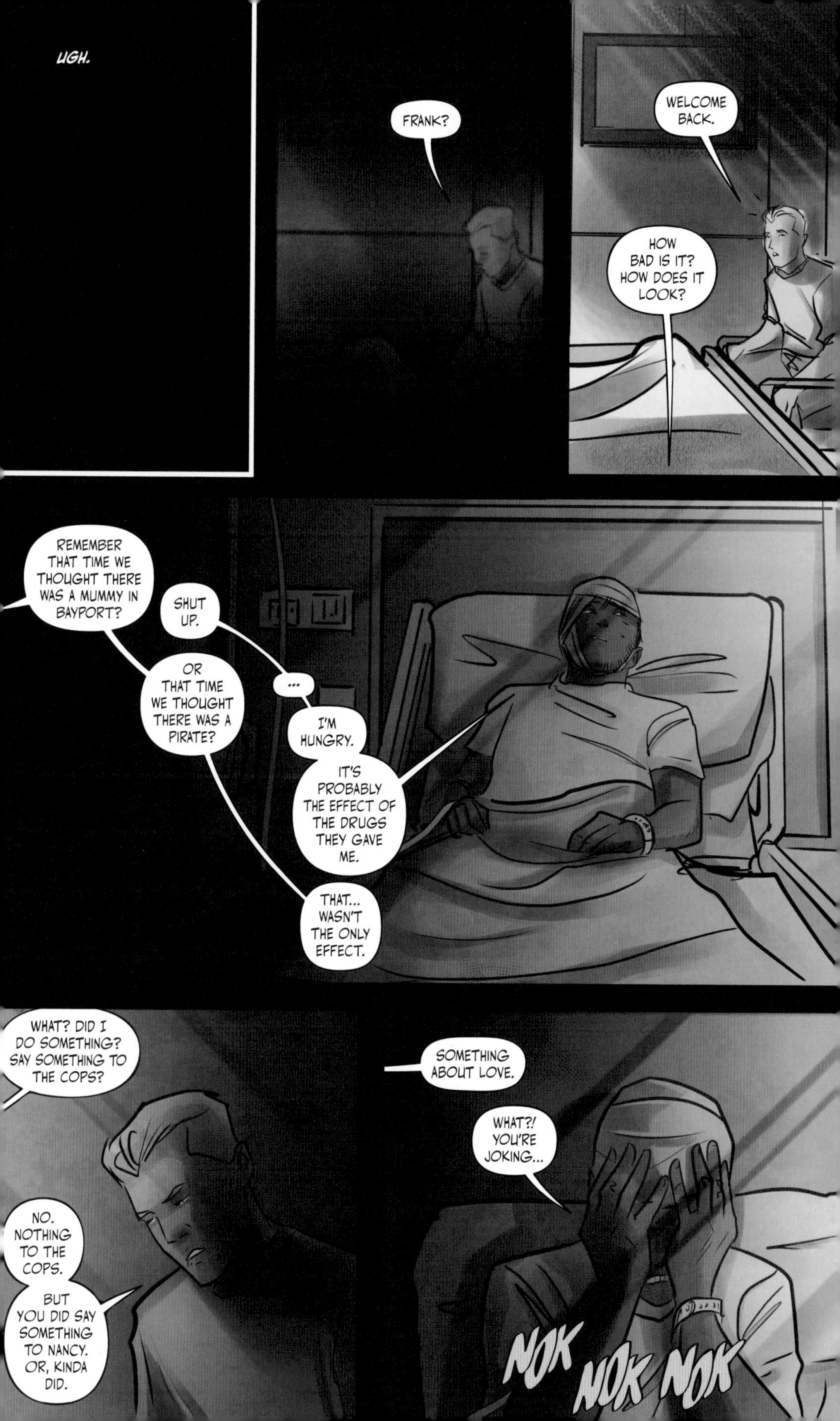
UGH.
FRANK?
WELCOME BACK.
HOW BAD IS IT? HOW DOES IT LOOK?
REMEMBER THAT TIME WE THOUGHT THERE WAS A MUMMY IN BAYPORT?
SHUT UP.
OR THAT TIME WE THOUGHT THERE WAS A PIRATE?
...
I'M HUNGRY.
IT'S PROBABLY THE EFFECT OF THE DRUGS THEY GAVE ME.
THAT... WASN'T THE ONLY EFFECT.
WHAT? DID I DO SOMETHING? SAY SOMETHING TO THE COPS?
SOMETHING ABOUT LOVE.
NO. NOTHING TO THE COPS.
BUT YOU DID SAY SOMETHING TO NANCY. OR, KINDA DID.
WHAT?! YOU'RE JOKING...
NOK NOK NOK

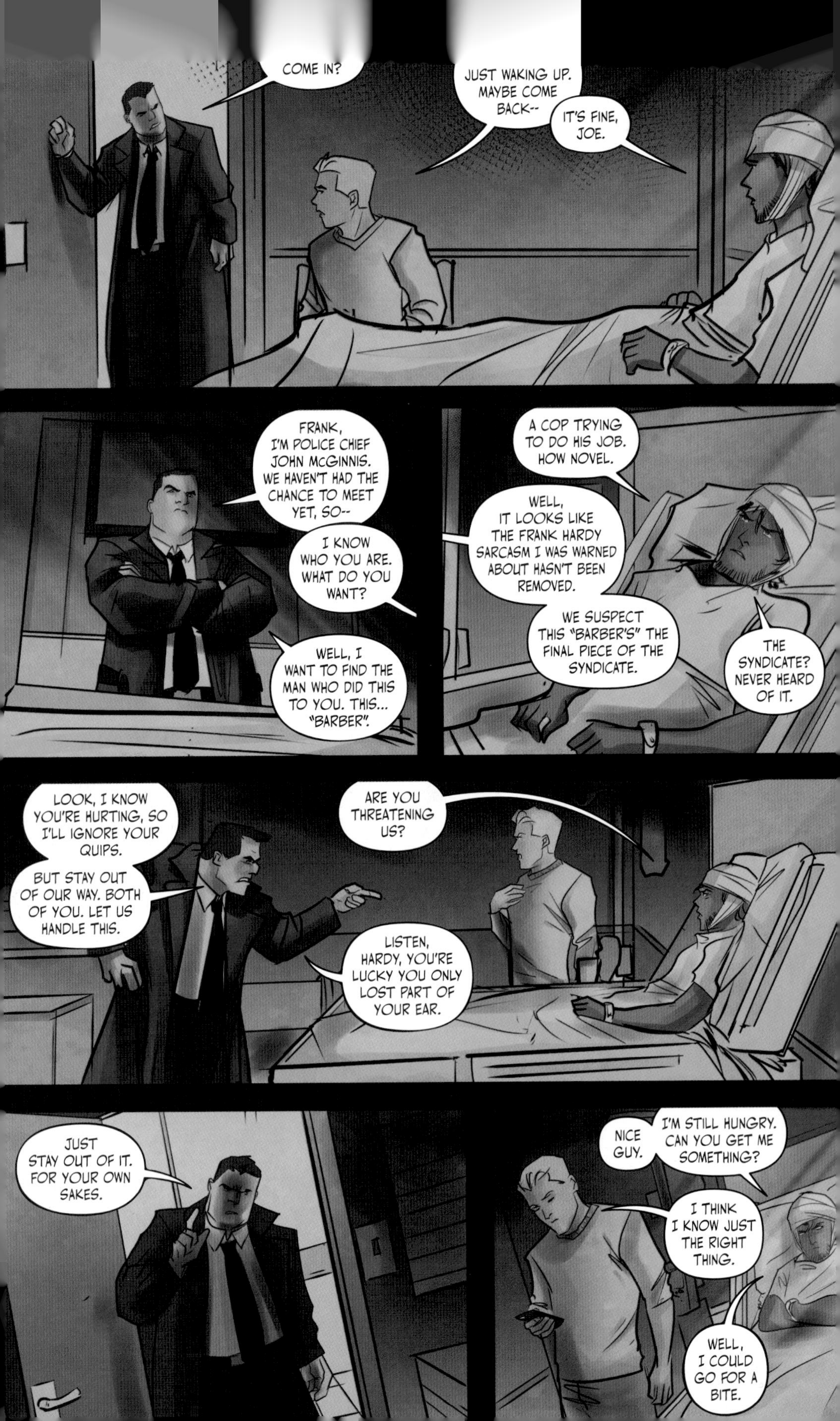
COME IN?
JUST WAKING UP. MAYBE COME BACK--
IT'S FINE, JOE.
FRANK, I'M POLICE CHIEF JOHN McGINNIS. WE HAVEN'T HAD THE CHANCE TO MEET YET, SO--
I KNOW WHO YOU ARE. WHAT DO YOU WANT?
WELL, I WANT TO FIND THE MAN WHO DID THIS TO YOU. THIS... "BARBER".
A COP TRYING TO DO HIS JOB. HOW NOVEL.
WELL, IT LOOKS LIKE THE FRANK HARDY SARCASM I WAS WARNED ABOUT HASN'T BEEN REMOVED.
WE SUSPECT THIS "BARBER'S" THE FINAL PIECE OF THE SYNDICATE.
THE SYNDICATE? NEVER HEARD OF IT.
LOOK, I KNOW YOU'RE HURTING, SO I'LL IGNORE YOUR QUIPS.
BUT STAY OUT OF OUR WAY. BOTH OF YOU. LET US HANDLE THIS.
ARE YOU THREATENING US?
LISTEN, HARDY, YOU'RE LUCKY YOU ONLY LOST PART OF YOUR EAR.
JUST STAY OUT OF IT. FOR YOUR OWN SAKES.
NICE GUY.
I'M STILL HUNGRY. CAN YOU GET ME SOMETHING?
I THINK I KNOW JUST THE RIGHT THING.
WELL, I COULD GO FOR A BITE.

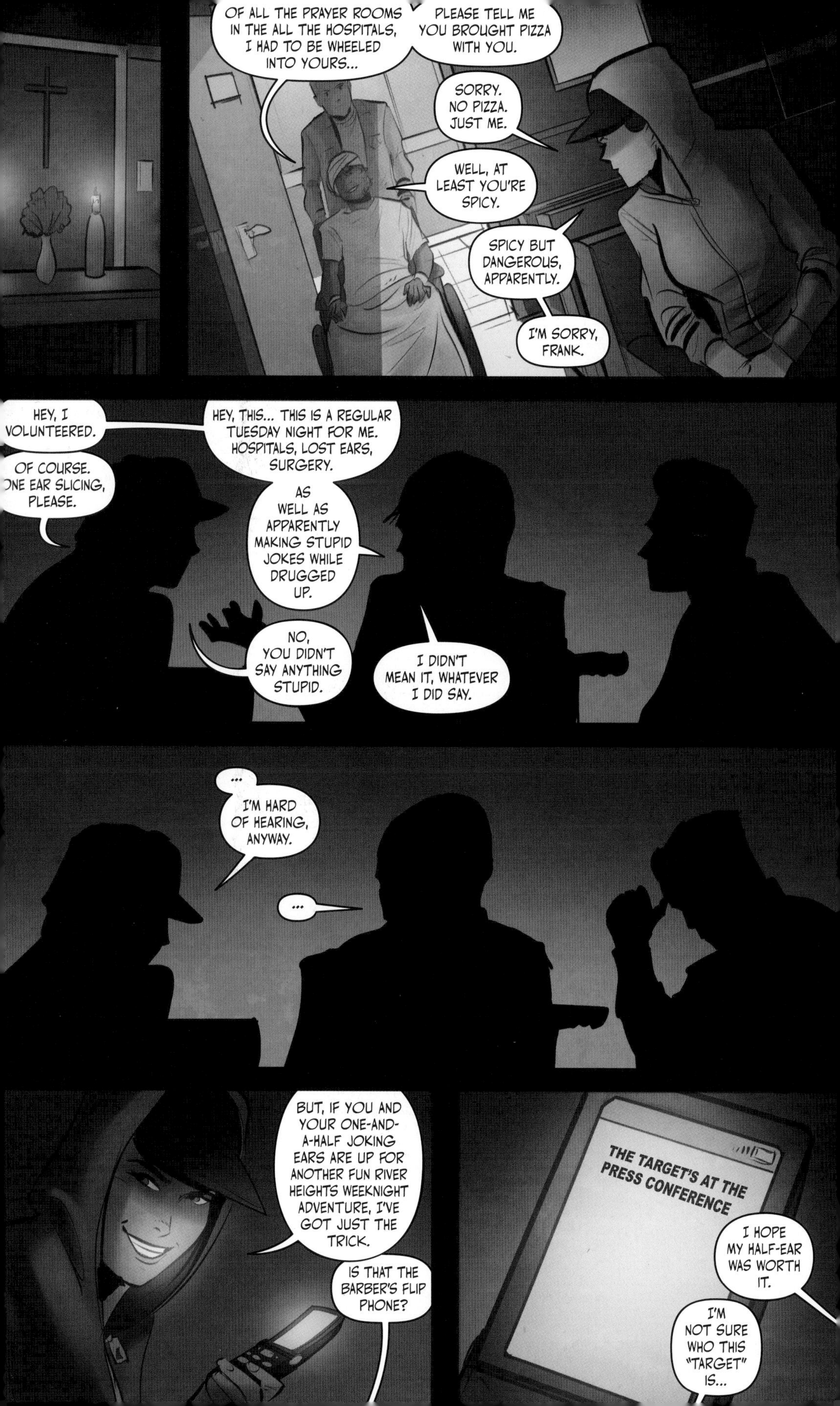
OF ALL THE PRAYER ROOMS IN THE ALL THE HOSPITALS, I HAD TO BE WHEELED INTO YOURS...
PLEASE TELL ME YOU BROUGHT PIZZA WITH YOU.
SORRY. NO PIZZA. JUST ME.
WELL, AT LEAST YOU'RE SPICY.
SPICY BUT DANGEROUS, APPARENTLY.
I'M SORRY, FRANK.
HEY, I VOLUNTEERED.
HEY, THIS... THIS IS A REGULAR TUESDAY NIGHT FOR ME. HOSPITALS, LOST EARS, SURGERY.
OF COURSE. ONE EAR SLICING, PLEASE.
AS WELL AS APPARENTLY MAKING STUPID JOKES WHILE DRUGGED UP.
NO, YOU DIDN'T SAY ANYTHING STUPID.
I DIDN'T MEAN IT, WHATEVER I DID SAY.
...
I'M HARD OF HEARING, ANYWAY.
...
BUT, IF YOU AND YOUR ONE-AND-A-HALF JOKING EARS ARE UP FOR ANOTHER FUN RIVER HEIGHTS WEEKNIGHT ADVENTURE, I'VE GOT JUST THE TRICK.
IS THAT THE BARBER'S FLIP PHONE?
THE TARGET'S AT THE PRESS CONFERENCE
I HOPE MY HALF-EAR WAS WORTH IT.
I'M NOT SURE WHO THIS "TARGET" IS...

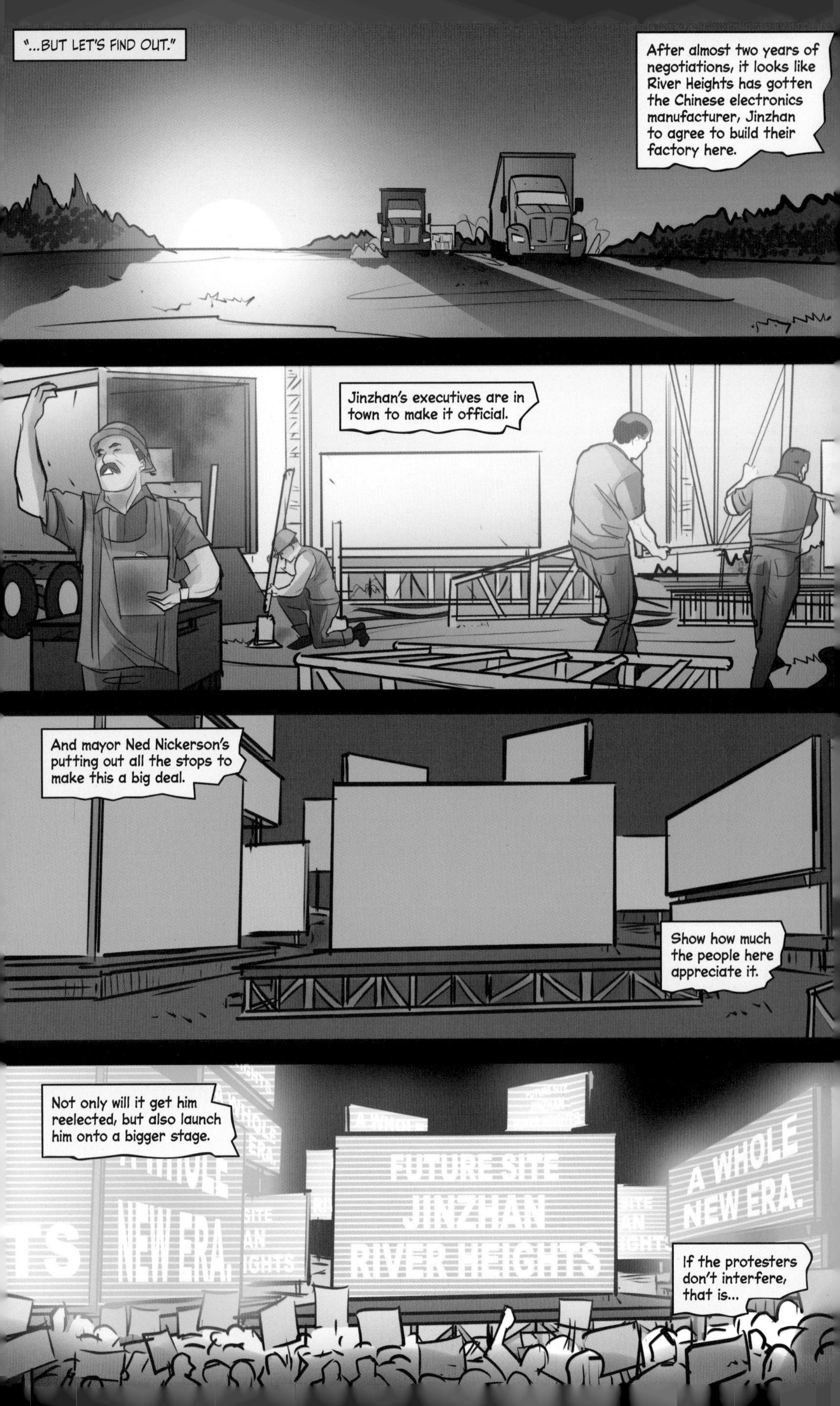
"...BUT LET'S FIND OUT."
After almost two years of negotiations, it looks like River Heights has gotten the Chinese electronics manufacturer, Jinzhan to agree to build their factory here.
Jinzhan's executives are in town to make it official.
And mayor Ned Nickerson's putting out all the stops to make this a big deal.
Show how much the people here appreciate it.
Not only will it get him reelected, but also launch him onto a bigger stage.
FUTURE SITE
JINZHAN
RIVER HEIGHTS
A WHOLE
NEW ERA.
If the protesters don't interfere, that is...

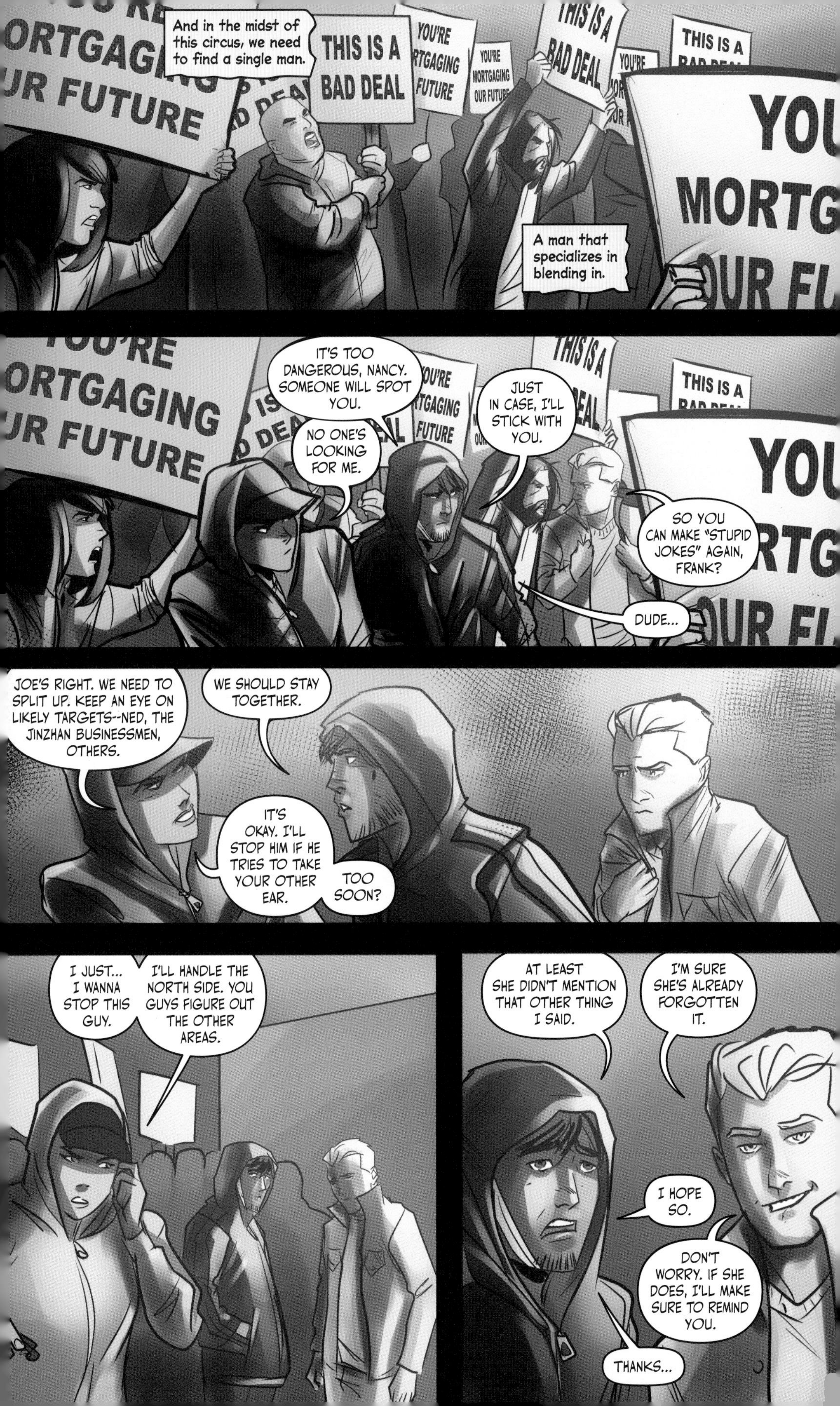

And in the midst of this circus, we need to find a single man.
THIS IS A BAD DEAL
YOU'RE MORTGAGING OUR FUTURE
A man that specializes in blending in.
IT'S TOO DANGEROUS, NANCY. SOMEONE WILL SPOT YOU.
NO ONE'S LOOKING FOR ME.
JUST IN CASE, I'LL STICK WITH YOU.
SO YOU CAN MAKE "STUPID JOKES" AGAIN, FRANK?
DUDE...
JOE'S RIGHT. WE NEED TO SPLIT UP. KEEP AN EYE ON LIKELY TARGETS--NED, THE JINZHAN BUSINESSMEN, OTHERS.
WE SHOULD STAY TOGETHER.
IT'S OKAY. I'LL STOP HIM IF HE TRIES TO TAKE YOUR OTHER EAR.
TOO SOON?
I JUST... I WANNA STOP THIS GUY.
I'LL HANDLE THE NORTH SIDE. YOU GUYS FIGURE OUT THE OTHER AREAS.
AT LEAST SHE DIDN'T MENTION THAT OTHER THING I SAID.
I'M SURE SHE'S ALREADY FORGOTTEN IT.
I HOPE SO.
DON'T WORRY. IF SHE DOES, I'LL MAKE SURE TO REMIND YOU.
THANKS...

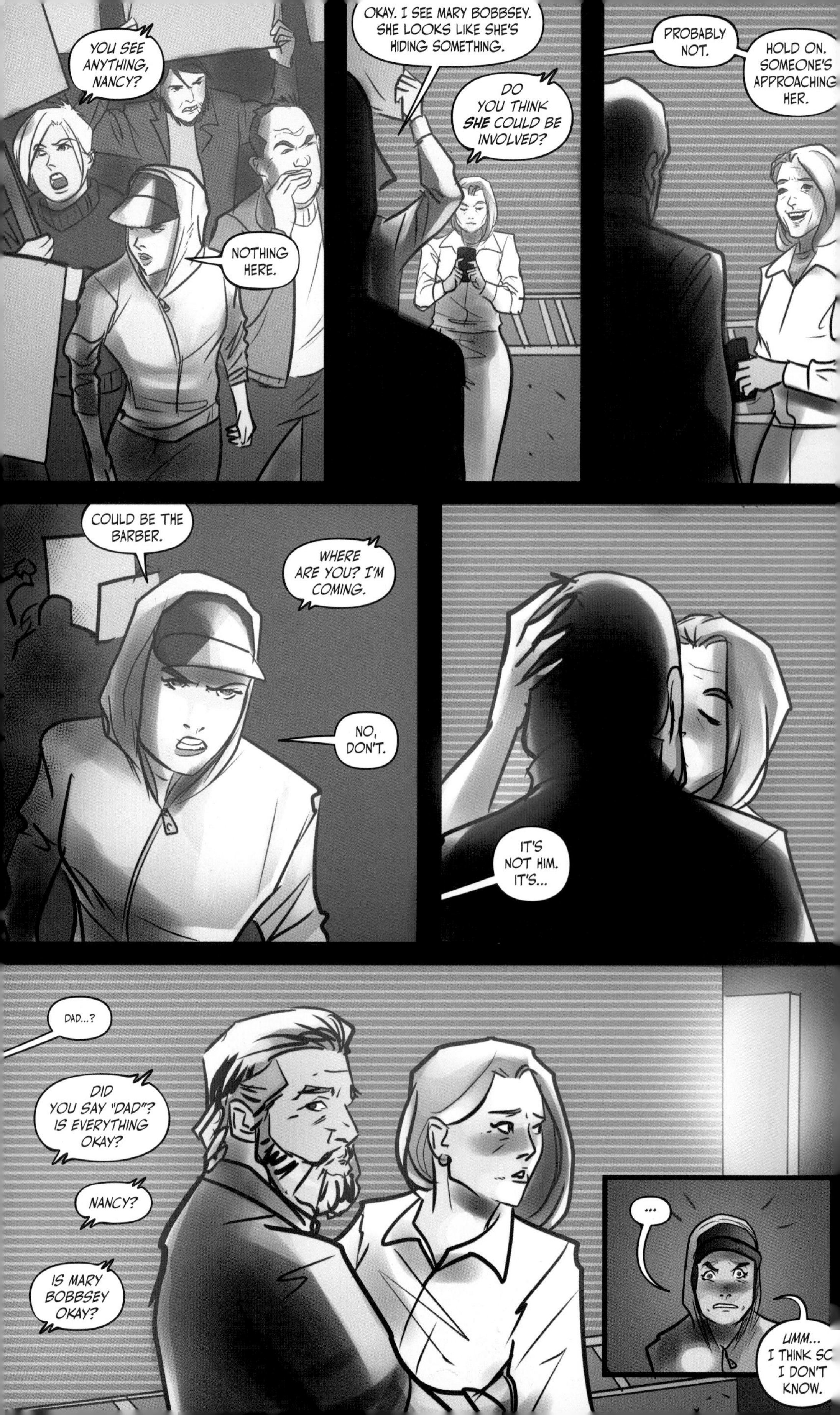
YOU SEE ANYTHING, NANCY?
NOTHING HERE.
OKAY. I SEE MARY BOBBSEY. SHE LOOKS LIKE SHE'S HIDING SOMETHING.
DO YOU THINK SHE COULD BE INVOLVED?
PROBABLY NOT.
HOLD ON. SOMEONE'S APPROACHING HER.
COULD BE THE BARBER.
WHERE ARE YOU? I'M COMING.
NO, DON'T.
IT'S NOT HIM. IT'S...
DAD...?
DID YOU SAY "DAD"? IS EVERYTHING OKAY?
NANCY?
IS MARY BOBBSEY OKAY?
...
UMM... I THINK SO I DON'T KNOW.

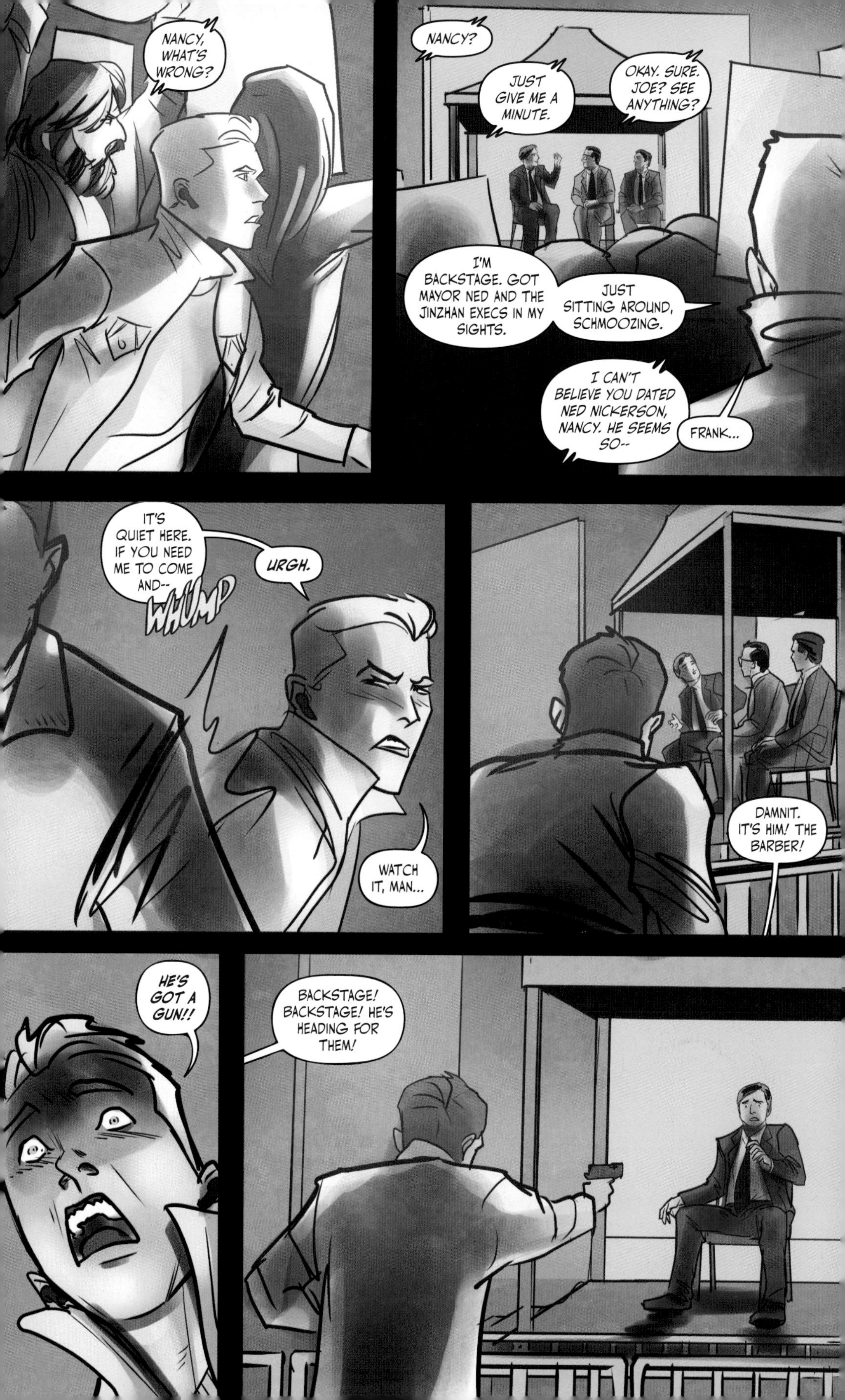
NANCY, WHAT'S WRONG?
NANCY?
JUST GIVE ME A MINUTE.
OKAY. SURE. JOE? SEE ANYTHING?
I'M BACKSTAGE. GOT MAYOR NED AND THE JINZHAN EXECS IN MY SIGHTS.
JUST SITTING AROUND, SCHMOOZING.
I CAN'T BELIEVE YOU DATED NED NICKERSON, NANCY. HE SEEMS SO--
FRANK...
IT'S QUIET HERE. IF YOU NEED ME TO COME AND--
WHUMP
URGH.
WATCH IT, MAN...
DAMNIT. IT'S HIM! THE BARBER!
HE'S GOT A GUN!!
BACKSTAGE! BACKSTAGE! HE'S HEADING FOR THEM!

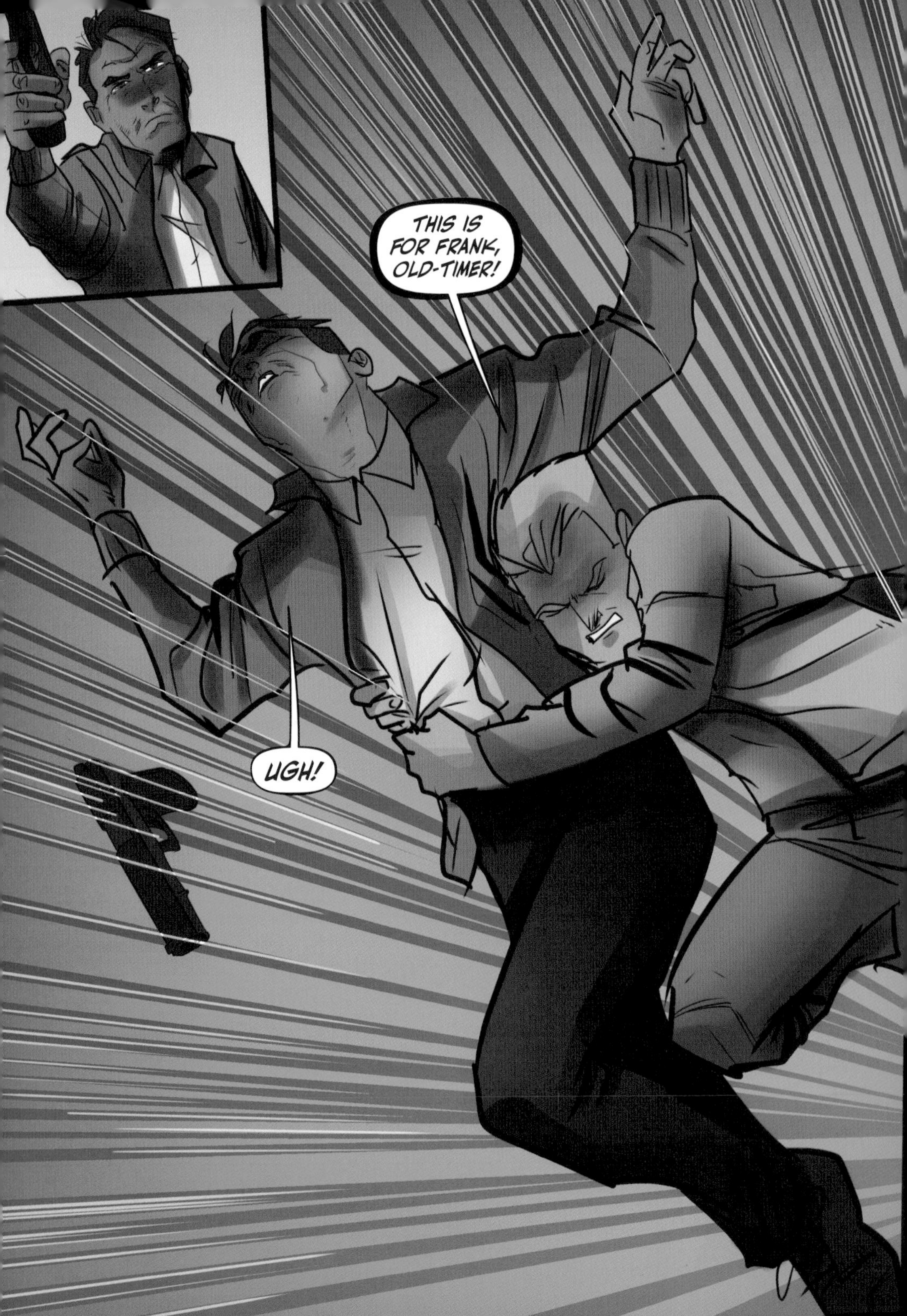
THIS IS FOR FRANK, OLD-TIMER!
UGH!

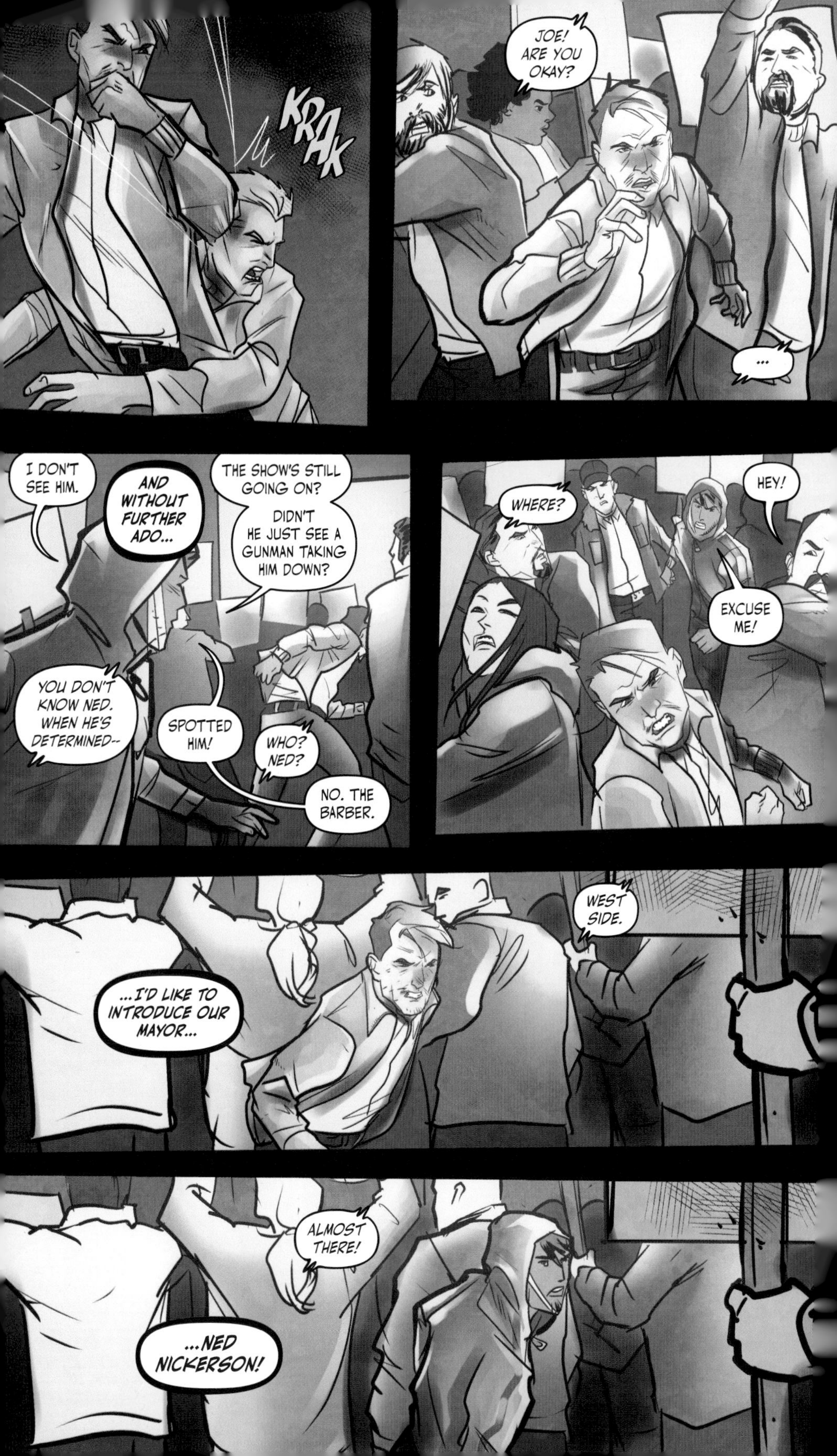
KRAK
JOE! ARE YOU OKAY?
...
I DON'T SEE HIM.
AND WITHOUT FURTHER ADO...
THE SHOW'S STILL GOING ON?
DIDN'T HE JUST SEE A GUNMAN TAKING HIM DOWN?
YOU DON'T KNOW NED. WHEN HE'S DETERMINED--
SPOTTED HIM!
WHO? NED?
NO. THE BARBER.
WHERE?
HEY!
EXCUSE ME!
WEST SIDE.
...I'D LIKE TO INTRODUCE OUR MAYOR...
ALMOST THERE!
...NED NICKERSON!

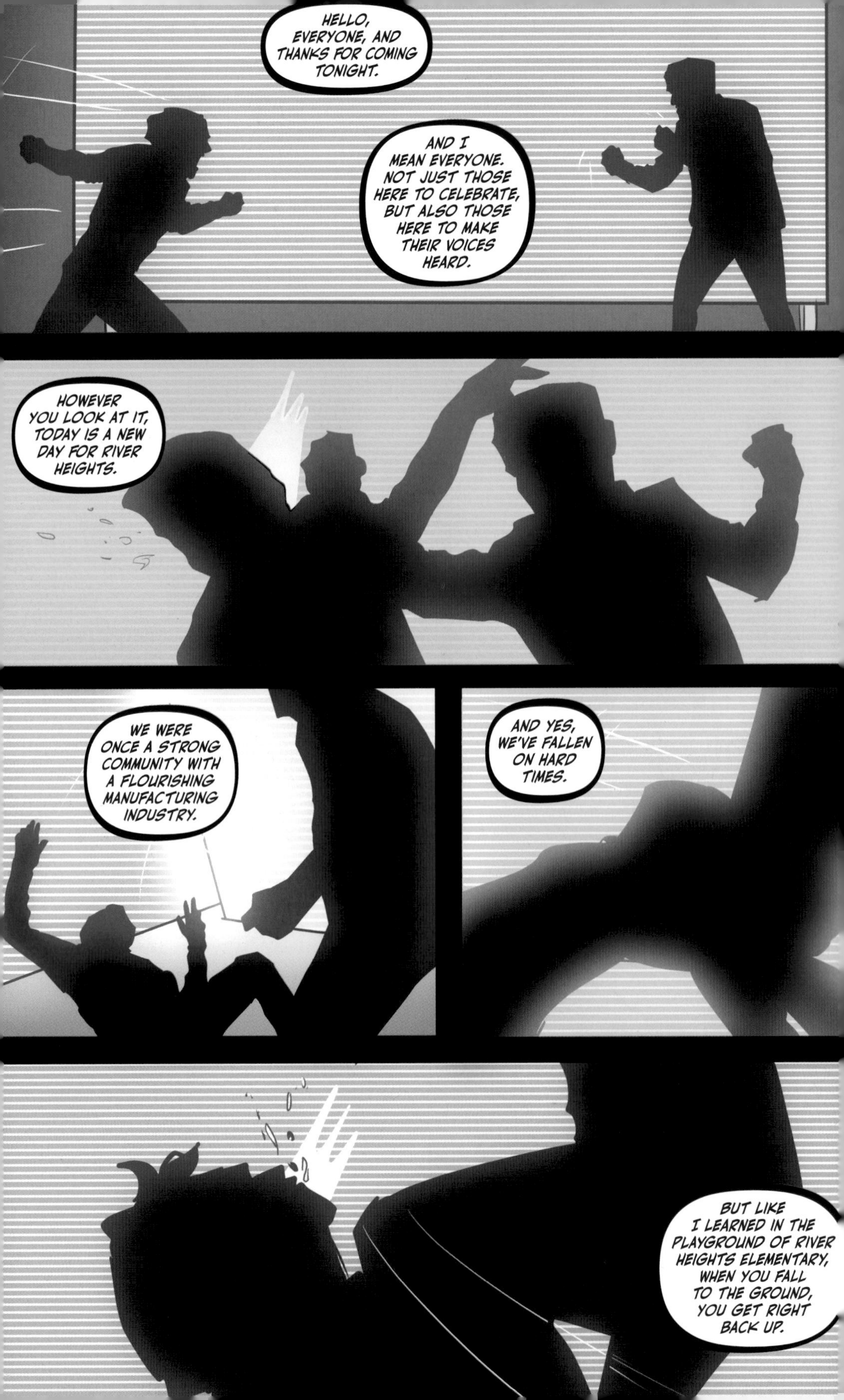
HELLO, EVERYONE, AND THANKS FOR COMING TONIGHT.
AND I MEAN EVERYONE. NOT JUST THOSE HERE TO CELEBRATE, BUT ALSO THOSE HERE TO MAKE THEIR VOICES HEARD.
HOWEVER YOU LOOK AT IT, TODAY IS A NEW DAY FOR RIVER HEIGHTS.
WE WERE ONCE A STRONG COMMUNITY WITH A FLOURISHING MANUFACTURING INDUSTRY.
AND YES, WE'VE FALLEN ON HARD TIMES.
BUT LIKE I LEARNED IN THE PLAYGROUND OF RIVER HEIGHTS ELEMENTARY, WHEN YOU FALL TO THE GROUND, YOU GET RIGHT BACK UP.

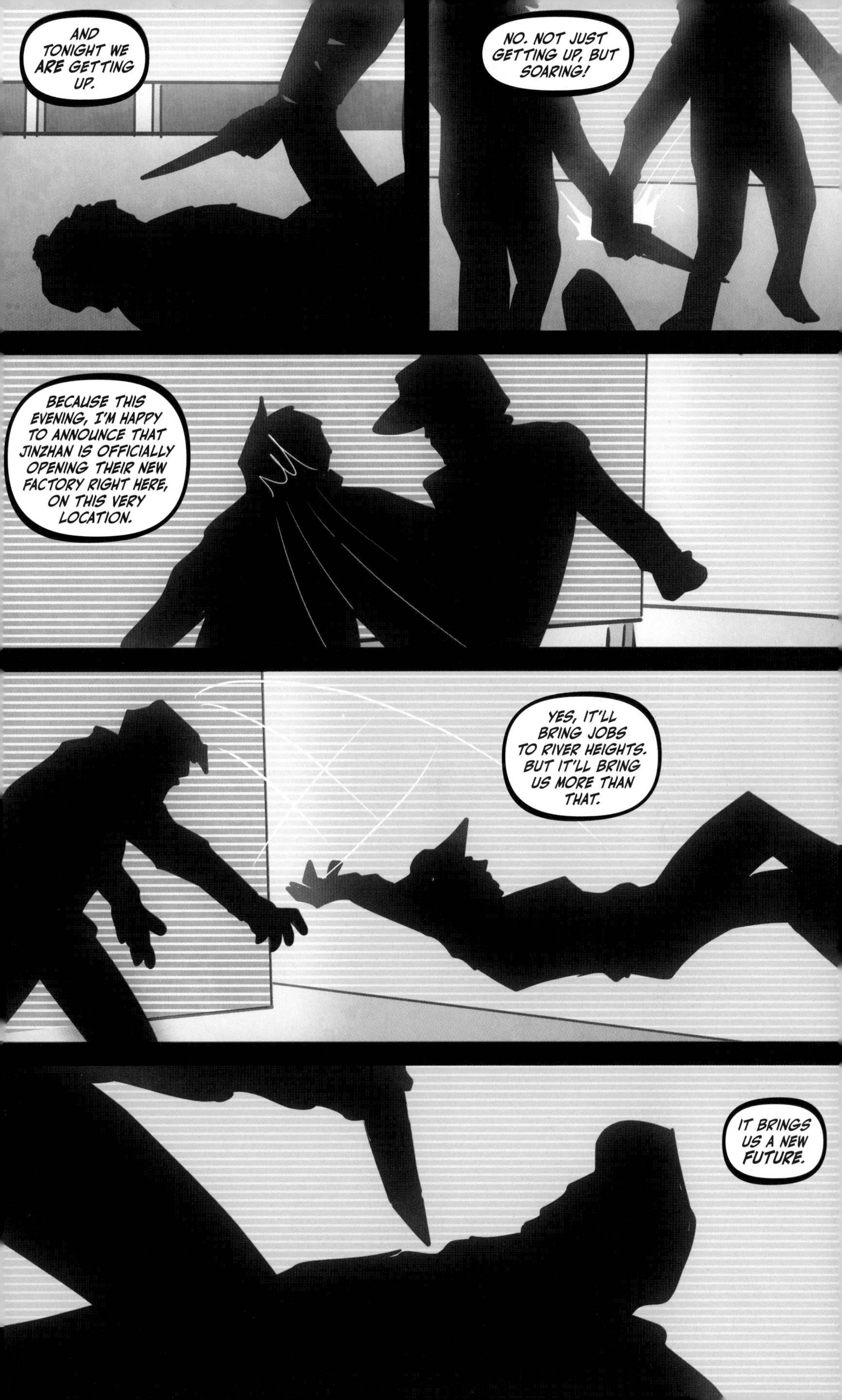
AND TONIGHT WE ARE GETTING UP.
NO. NOT JUST GETTING UP, BUT SOARING!
BECAUSE THIS EVENING, I'M HAPPY TO ANNOUNCE THAT JINZHAN IS OFFICIALLY OPENING THEIR NEW FACTORY RIGHT HERE, ON THIS VERY LOCATION.
YES, IT'LL BRING JOBS TO RIVER HEIGHTS. BUT IT'LL BRING US MORE THAN THAT.
IT BRINGS US A NEW FUTURE.

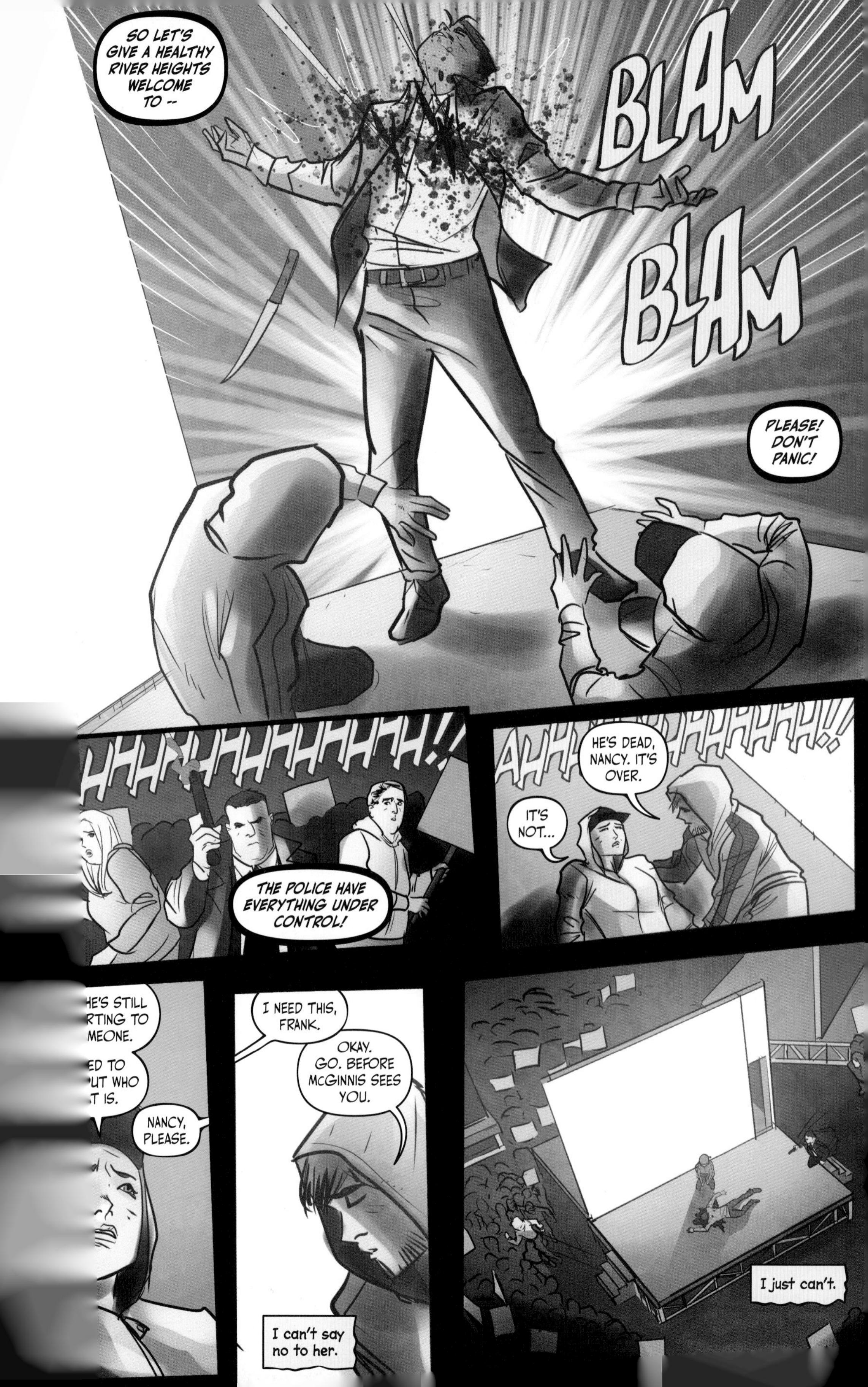
SO LET'S GIVE A HEALTHY RIVER HEIGHTS WELCOME TO --
BLAM
BLAM
PLEASE! DON'T PANIC!
THE POLICE HAVE EVERYTHING UNDER CONTROL!
HE'S DEAD, NANCY. IT'S OVER.
IT'S NOT...
NANCY, PLEASE.
I NEED THIS, FRANK.
OKAY. GO. BEFORE McGINNIS SEES YOU.
I can't say no to her.
I just can't.

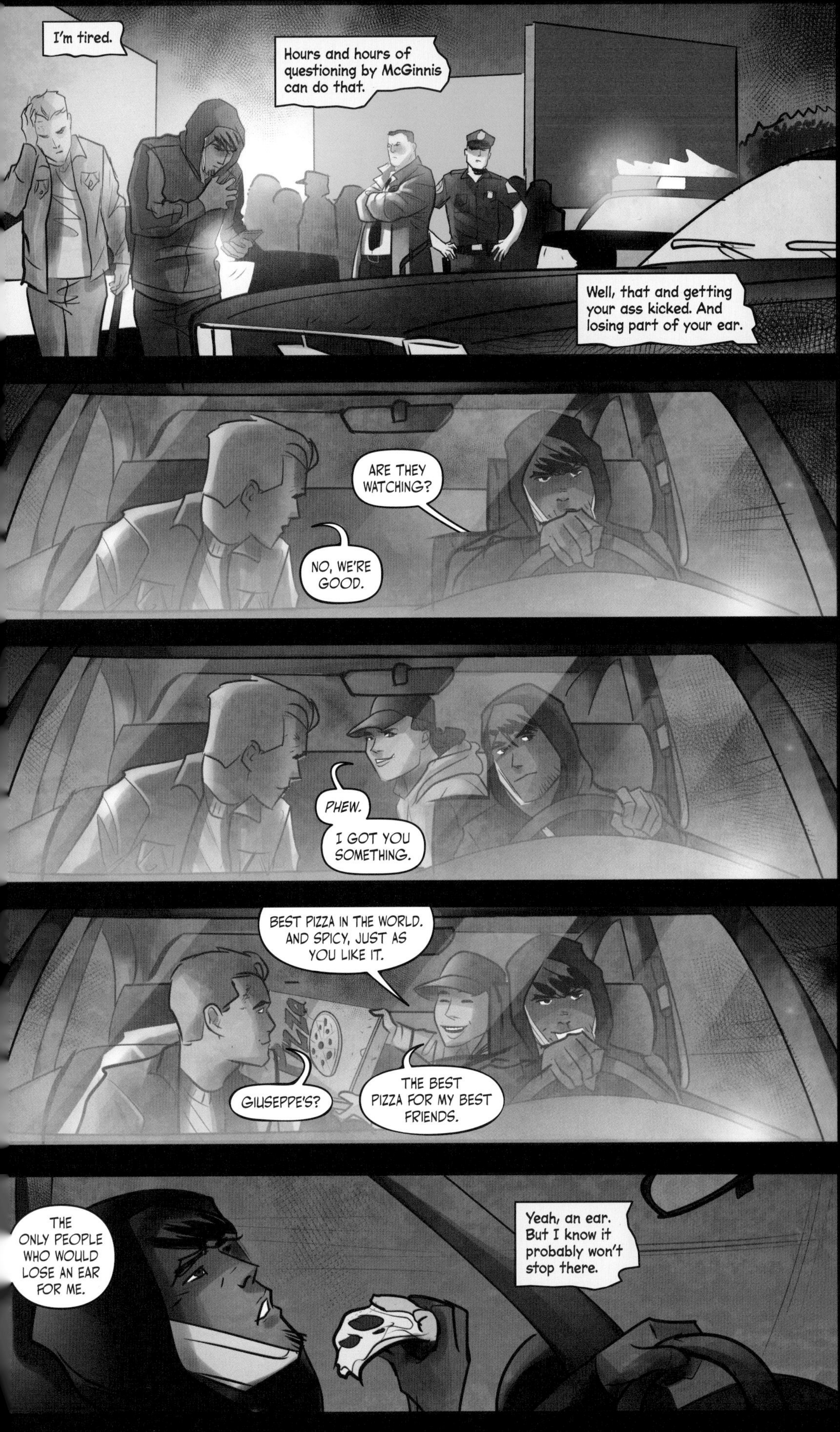
I'm tired.
Hours and hours of questioning by McGinnis can do that.
Well, that and getting your ass kicked. And losing part of your ear.
ARE THEY WATCHING?
NO, WE'RE GOOD.
PHEW.
I GOT YOU SOMETHING.
BEST PIZZA IN THE WORLD. AND SPICY, JUST AS YOU LIKE IT.
GIUSEPPE'S?
THE BEST PIZZA FOR MY BEST FRIENDS.
THE ONLY PEOPLE WHO WOULD LOSE AN EAR FOR ME.
Yeah, an ear. But I know it probably won't stop there.

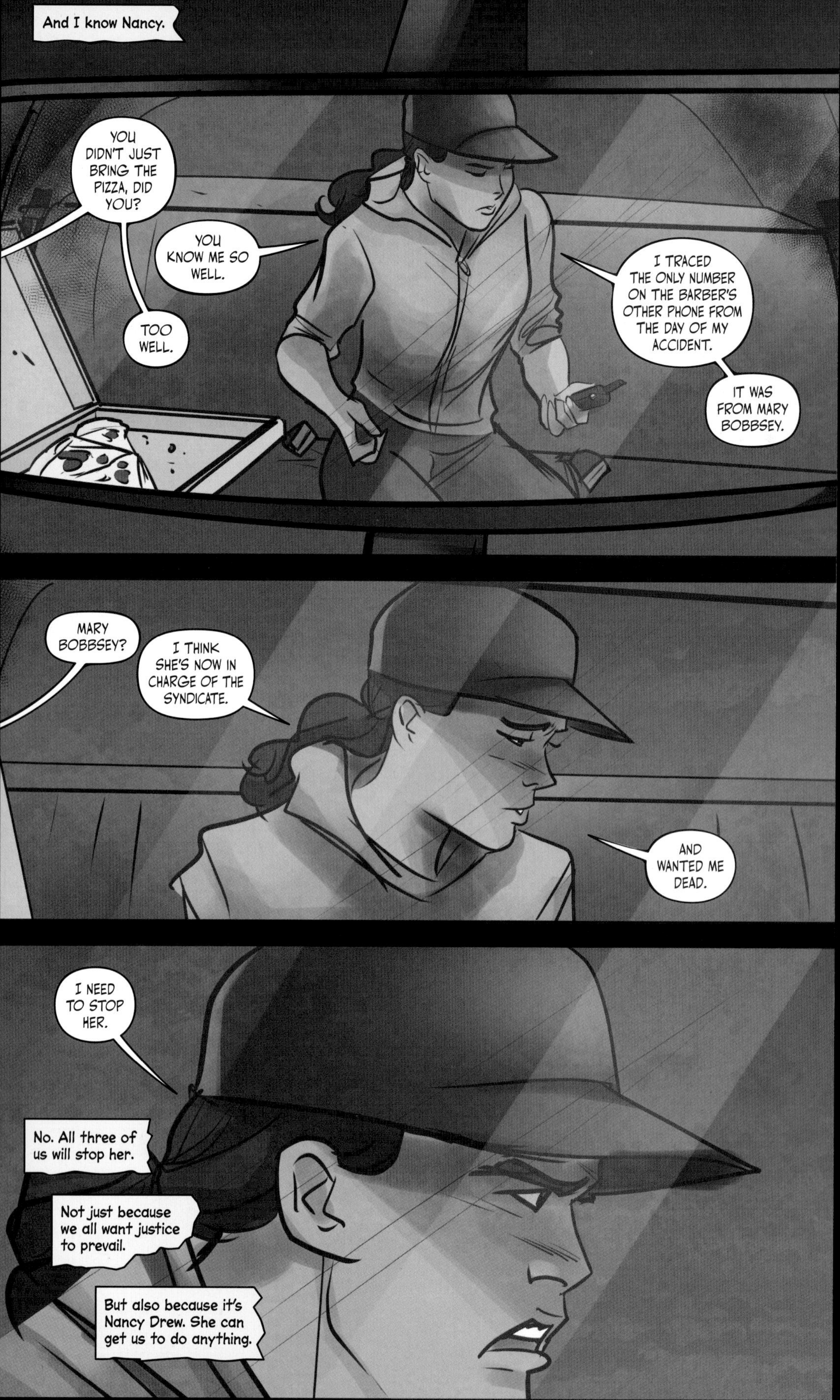

And I know Nancy.
YOU DIDN'T JUST BRING THE PIZZA, DID YOU?
YOU KNOW ME SO WELL.
TOO WELL.
I TRACED THE ONLY NUMBER ON THE BARBER'S OTHER PHONE FROM THE DAY OF MY ACCIDENT.
IT WAS FROM MARY BOBBSEY.
MARY BOBBSEY?
I THINK SHE'S NOW IN CHARGE OF THE SYNDICATE.
AND WANTED ME DEAD.
I NEED TO STOP HER.
No. All three of us will stop her.
Not just because we all want justice to prevail.
But also because it's Nancy Drew. She can get us to do anything.

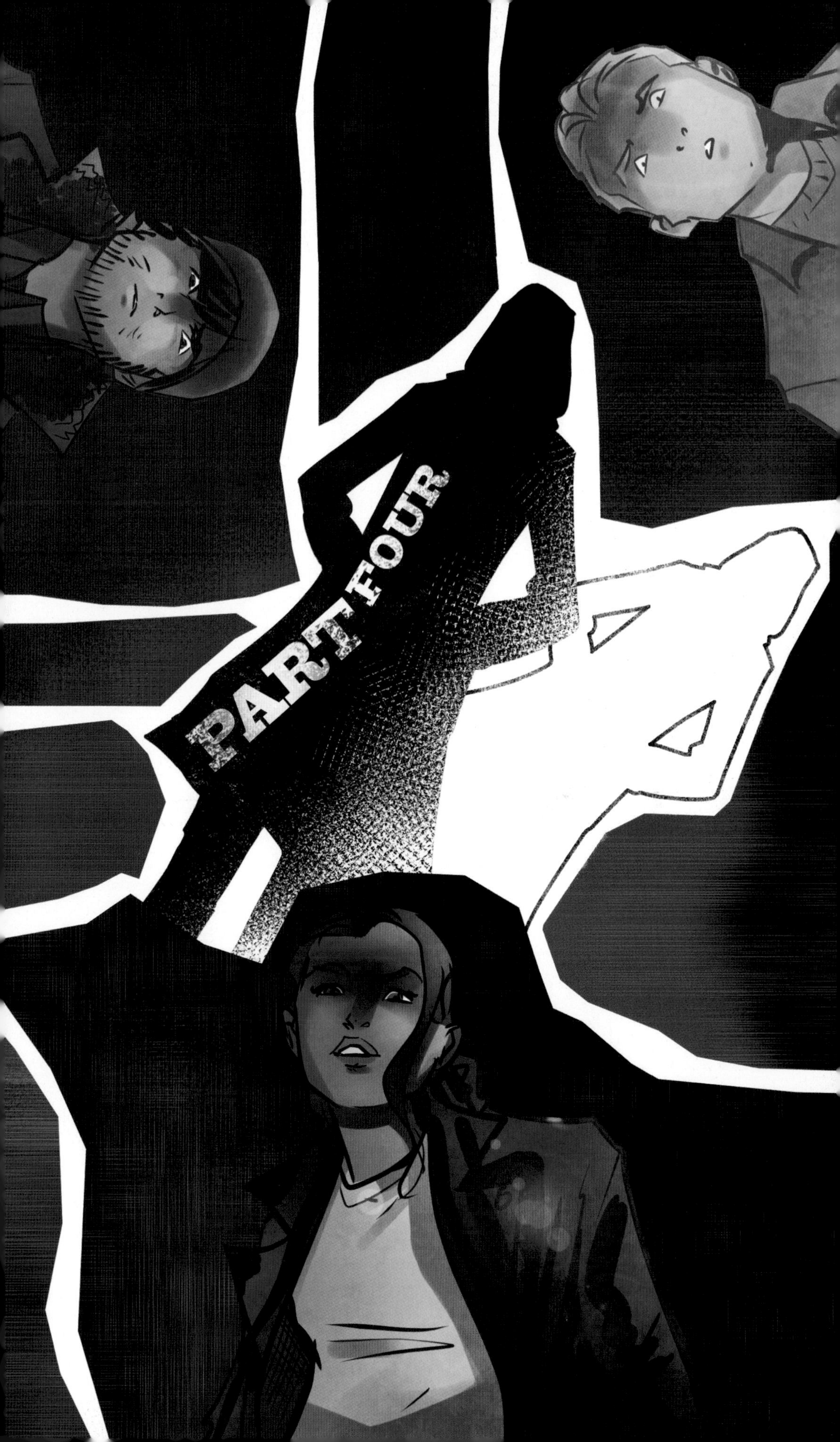
PART FOUR

PART FOUR COVER ART BY **JOE EISMA**

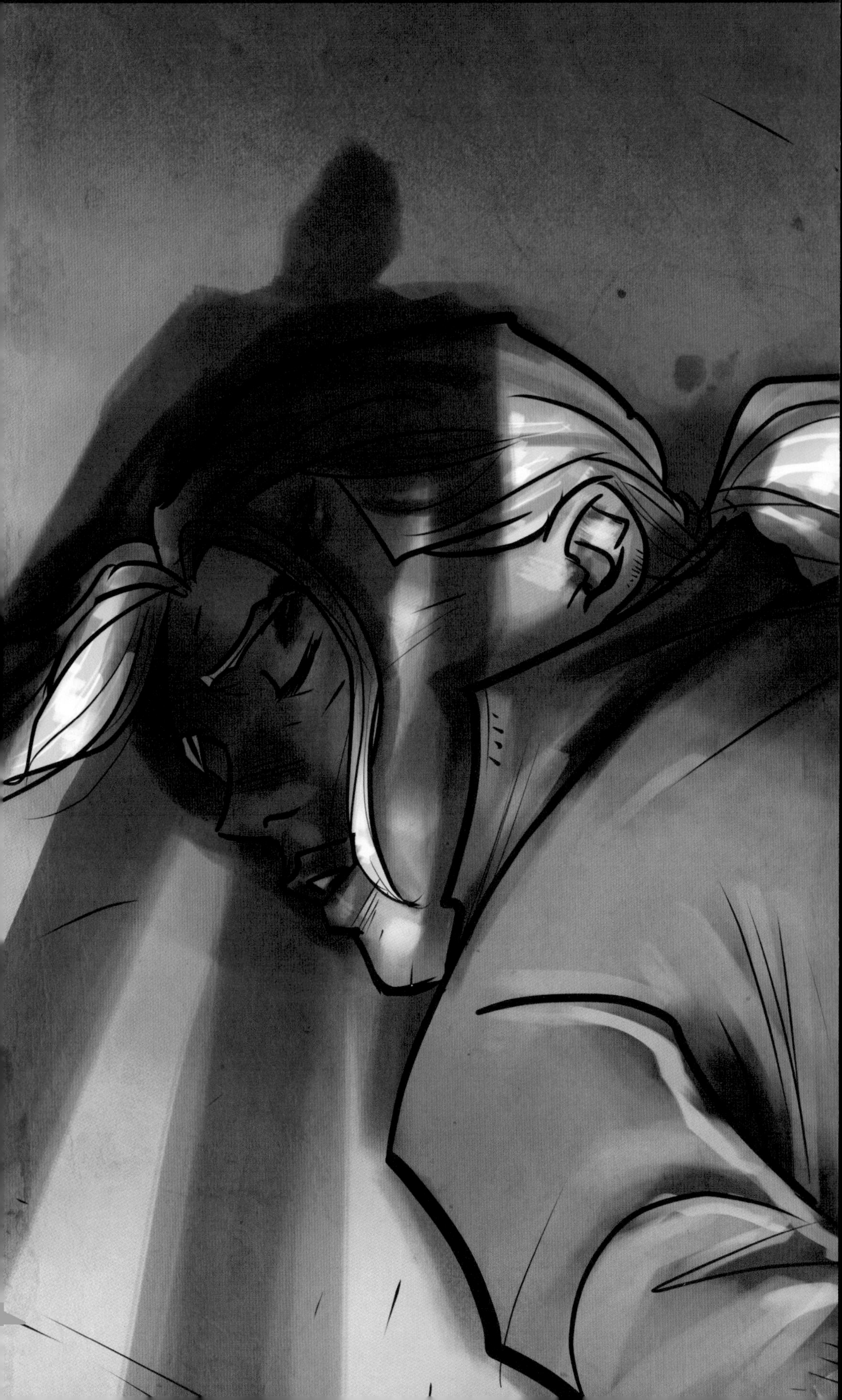

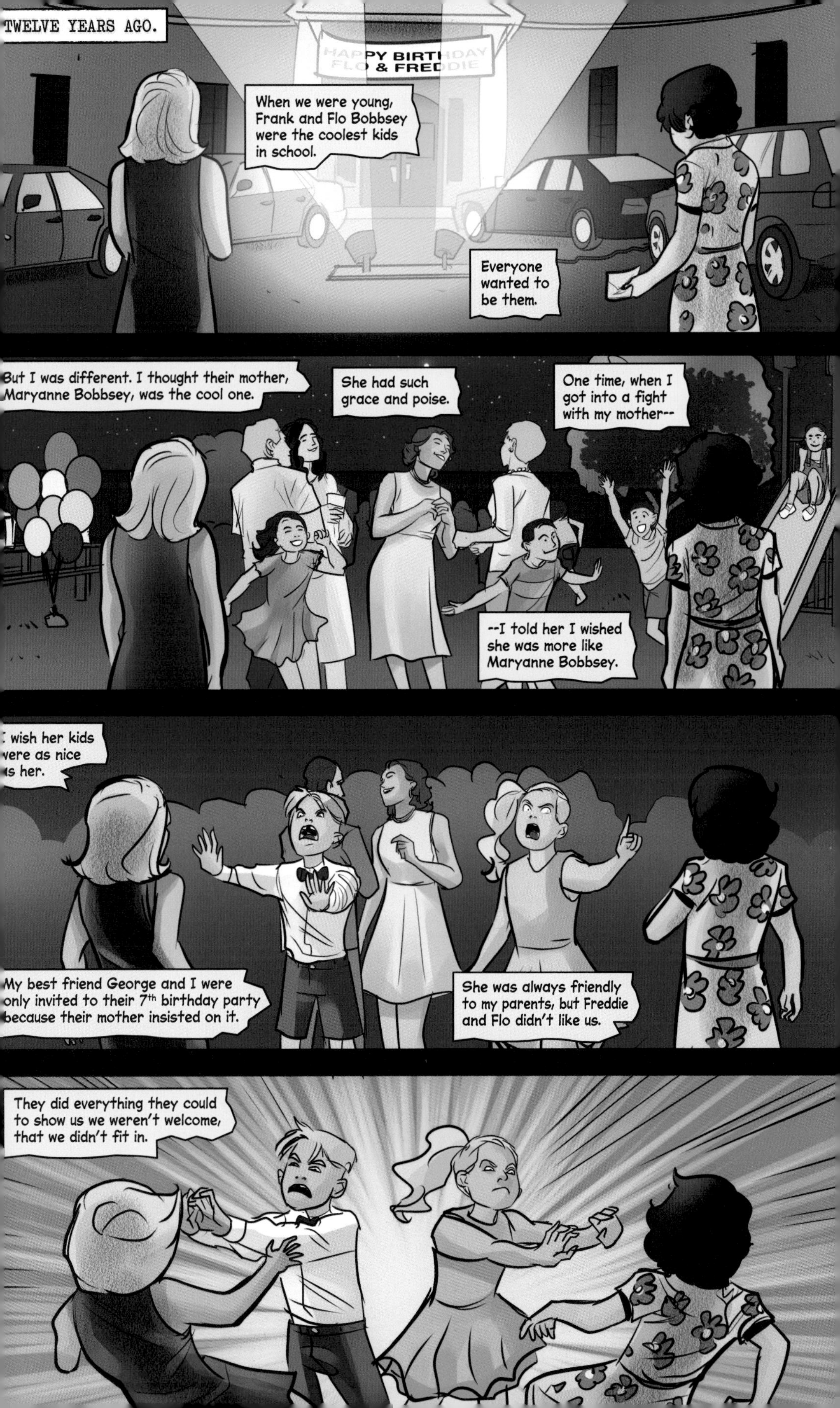
TWELVE YEARS AGO.
HAPPY BIRTHDAY FLO & FREDDIE
When we were young, Frank and Flo Bobbsey were the coolest kids in school.
Everyone wanted to be them.
But I was different. I thought their mother, Maryanne Bobbsey, was the cool one.
She had such grace and poise.
One time, when I got into a fight with my mother--
--I told her I wished she was more like Maryanne Bobbsey.
I wish her kids were as nice as her.
My best friend George and I were only invited to their 7th birthday party because their mother insisted on it.
She was always friendly to my parents, but Freddie and Flo didn't like us.
They did everything they could to show us we weren't welcome, that we didn't fit in.

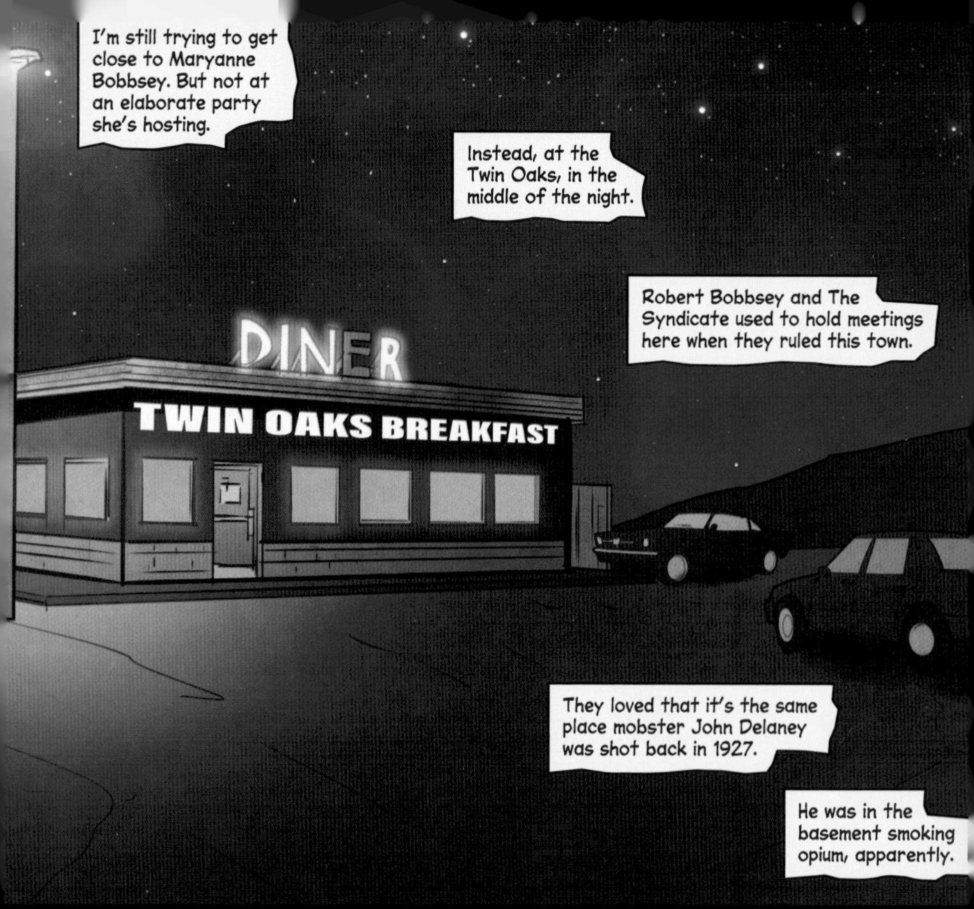
I'm still trying to get close to Maryanne Bobbsey. But not at an elaborate party she's hosting.
Instead, at the Twin Oaks, in the middle of the night.
Robert Bobbsey and The Syndicate used to hold meetings here when they ruled this town.
DINER
TWIN OAKS BREAKFAST
They loved that it's the same place mobster John Delaney was shot back in 1927.
He was in the basement smoking opium, apparently.

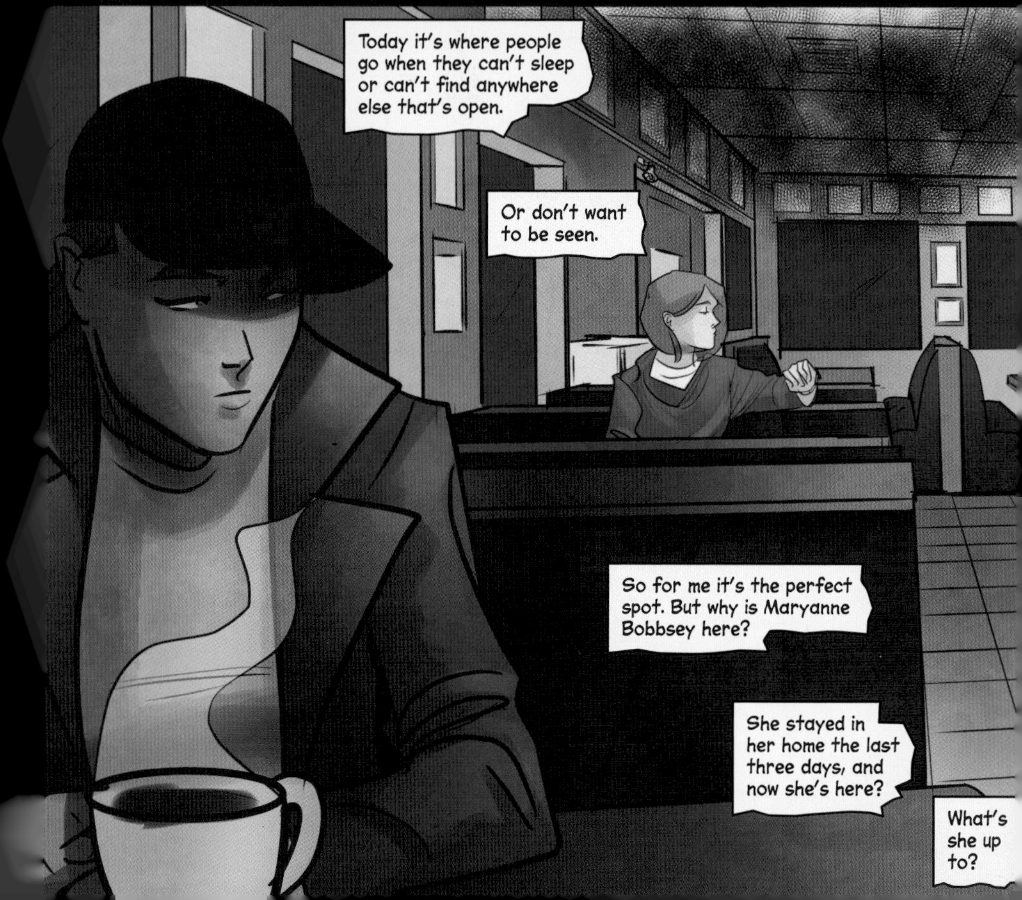
Today it's where people go when they can't sleep or can't find anywhere else that's open.
Or don't want to be seen.
So for me it's the perfect spot. But why is Maryanne Bobbsey here?
She stayed in her home the last three days, and now she's here?
What's she up to?

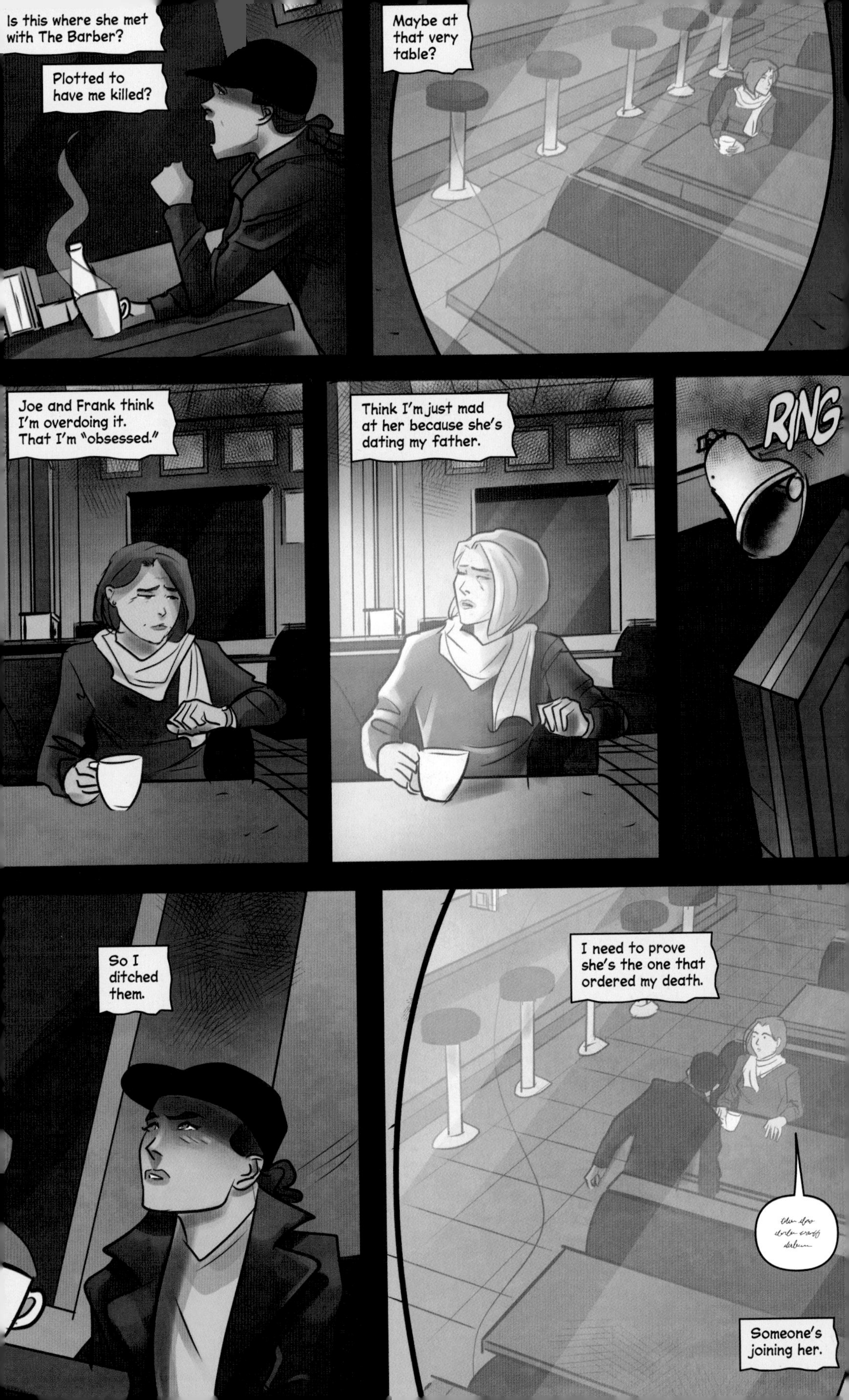
Is this where she met with The Barber?
Plotted to have me killed?
Maybe at that very table?
Joe and Frank think I'm overdoing it. That I'm "obsessed."
Think I'm just mad at her because she's dating my father.
RING
So I ditched them.
I need to prove she's the one that ordered my death.
Someone's joining her.

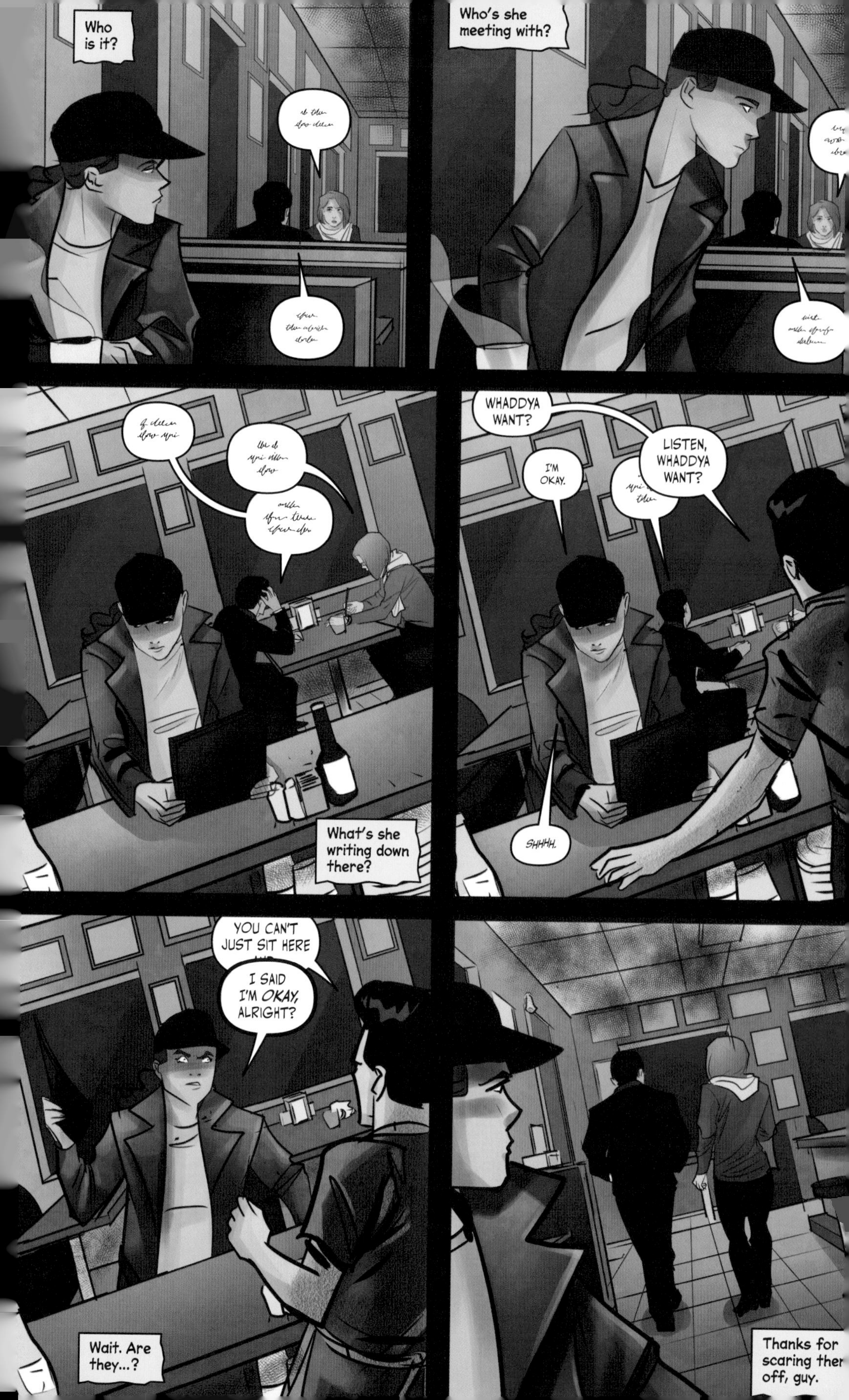
Who is it?
Who's she meeting with?
What's she writing down there?
WHADDYA WANT?
I'M OKAY.
LISTEN, WHADDYA WANT?
SHHHH.
YOU CAN'T JUST SIT HERE
I SAID I'M *OKAY*, ALRIGHT?
Wait. Are they...?
Thanks for scaring ther off, guy.

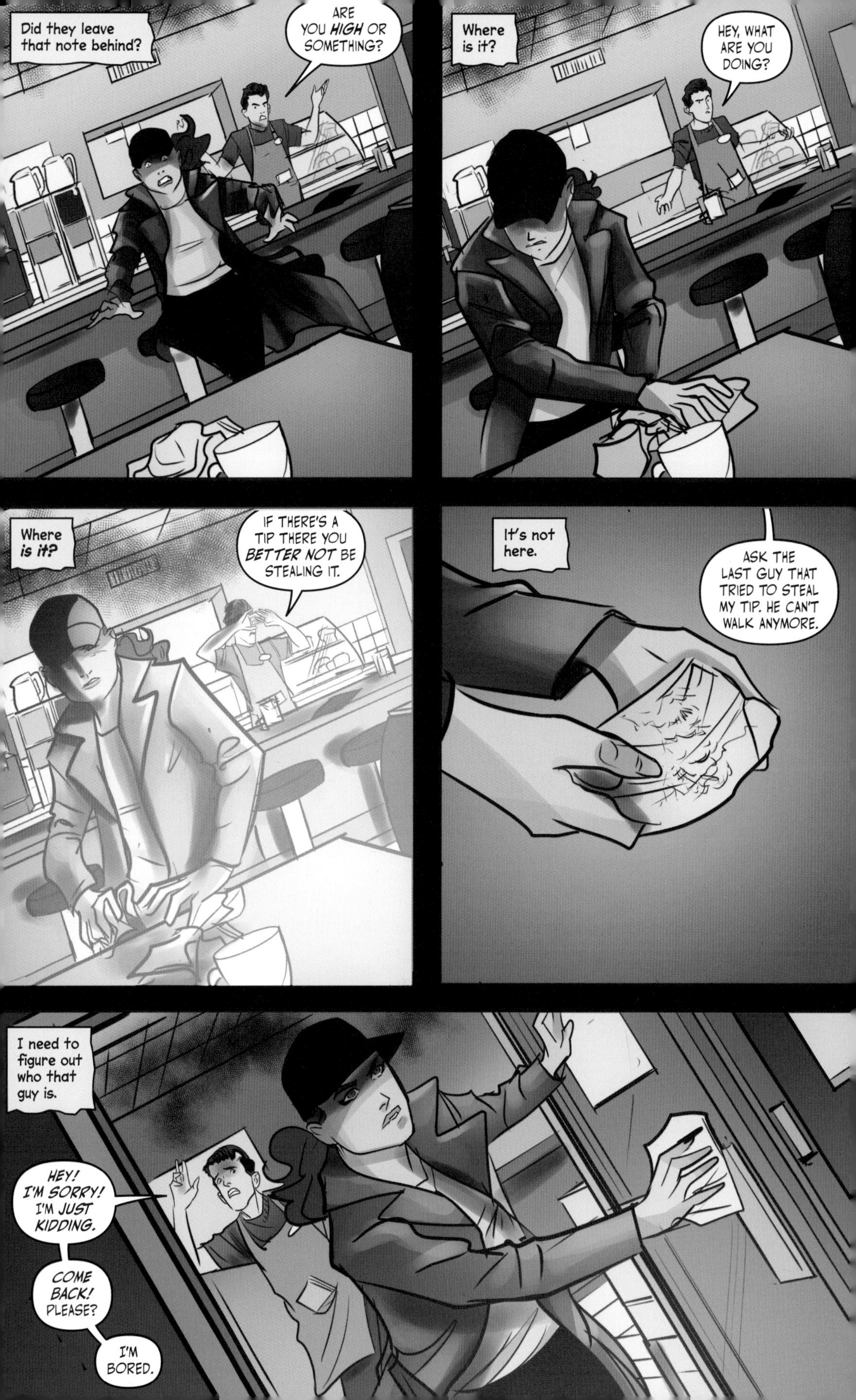
Did they leave that note behind?
ARE YOU HIGH OR SOMETHING?
Where is it?
HEY, WHAT ARE YOU DOING?
Where is it?
IF THERE'S A TIP THERE YOU BETTER NOT BE STEALING IT.
It's not here.
ASK THE LAST GUY THAT TRIED TO STEAL MY TIP. HE CAN'T WALK ANYMORE.
I need to figure out who that guy is.
HEY! I'M SORRY! I'M JUST KIDDING.
COME BACK! PLEASE?
I'M BORED.

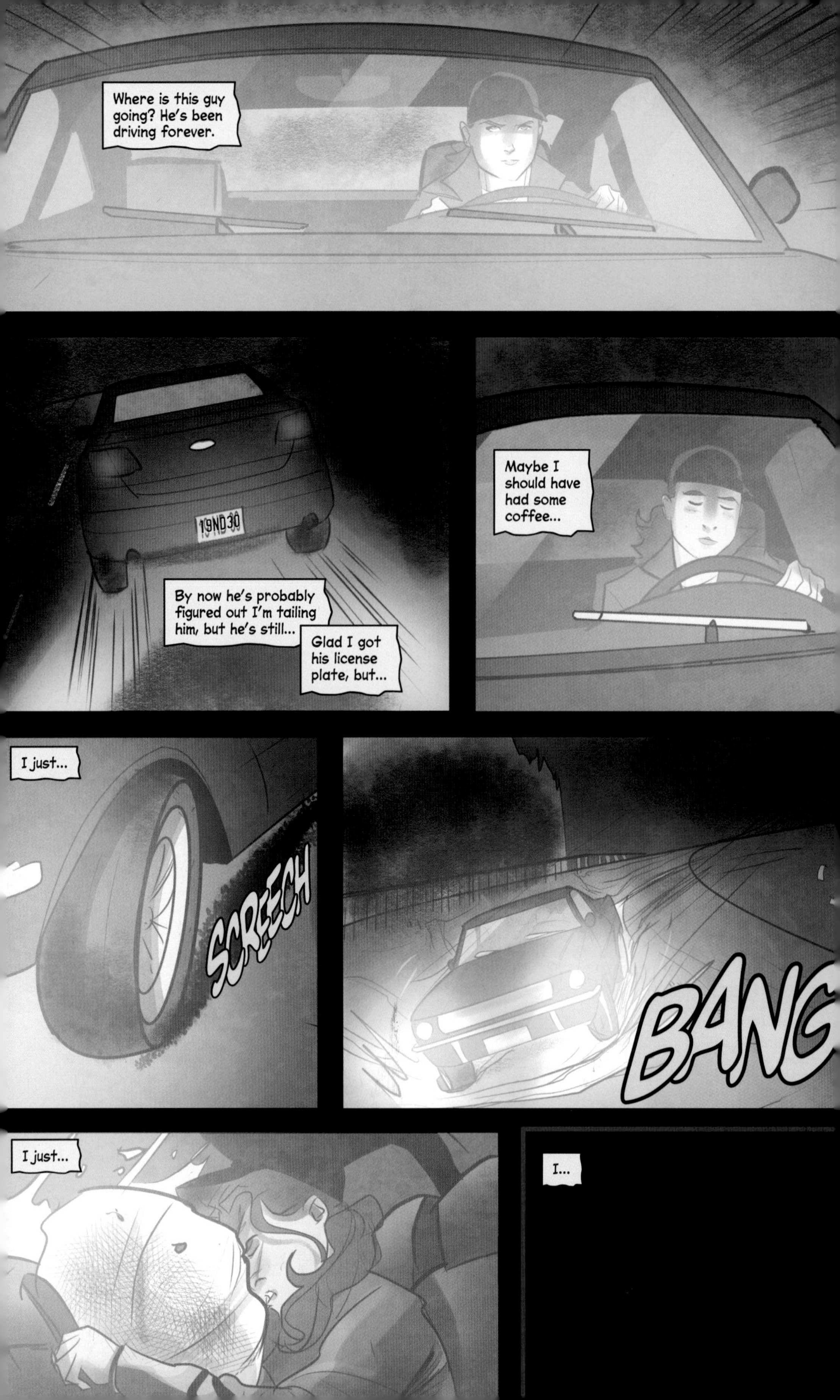

Where is this guy going? He's been driving forever.
19ND30
By now he's probably figured out I'm tailing him, but he's still...
Glad I got his license plate, but...
Maybe I should have had some coffee...
I just...
SCREECH
BANG
I just...
I...

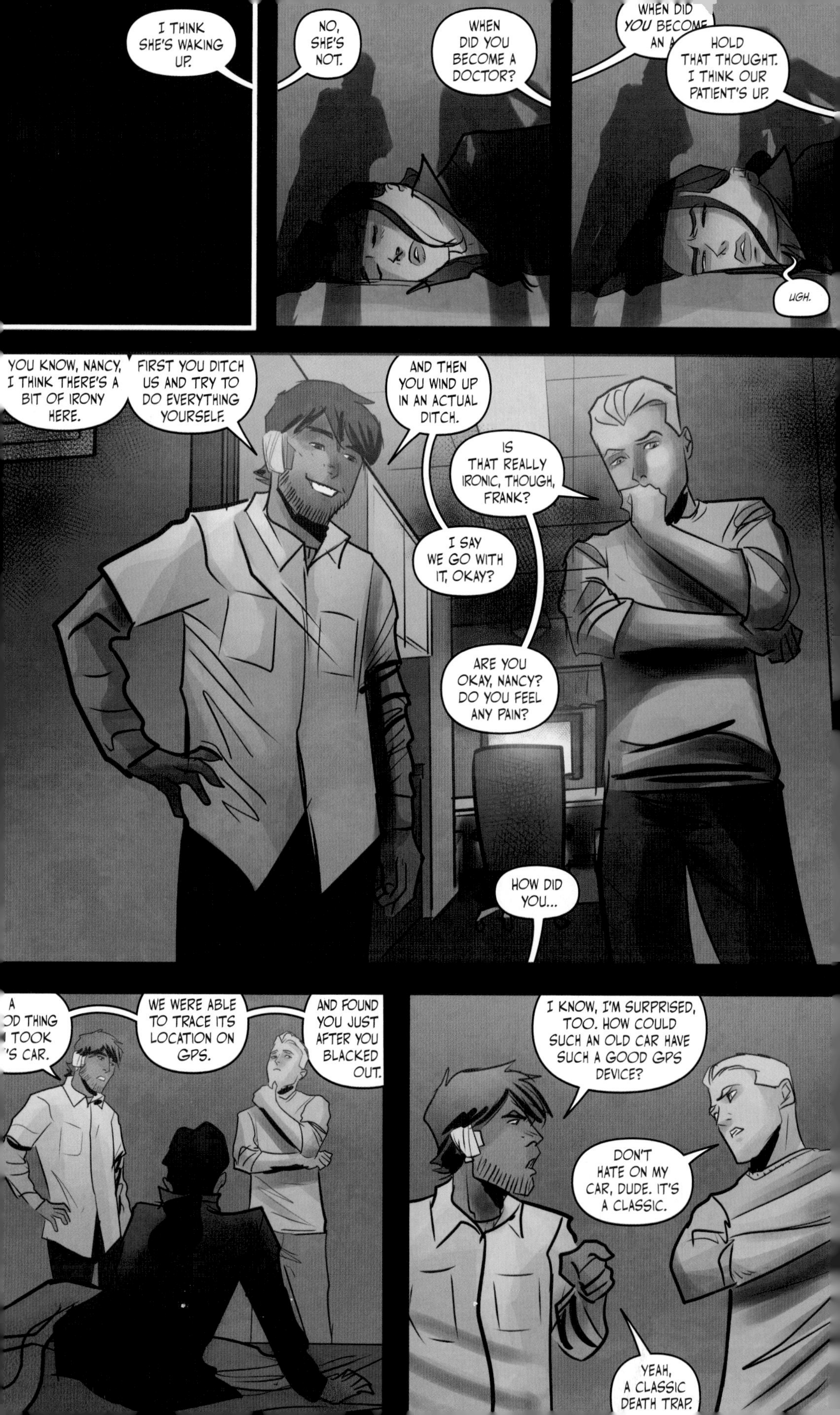
I THINK SHE'S WAKING UP.
NO, SHE'S NOT.
WHEN DID YOU BECOME A DOCTOR?
WHEN DID *YOU* BECOME AN A
HOLD THAT THOUGHT. I THINK OUR PATIENT'S UP.
UGH.
YOU KNOW, NANCY, I THINK THERE'S A BIT OF IRONY HERE.
FIRST YOU DITCH US AND TRY TO DO EVERYTHING YOURSELF.
AND THEN YOU WIND UP IN AN ACTUAL DITCH.
IS THAT REALLY IRONIC, THOUGH, FRANK?
I SAY WE GO WITH IT, OKAY?
ARE YOU OKAY, NANCY? DO YOU FEEL ANY PAIN?
HOW DID YOU...
A
OD THING
TOOK
'S CAR.
WE WERE ABLE TO TRACE ITS LOCATION ON GPS.
AND FOUND YOU JUST AFTER YOU BLACKED OUT.
I KNOW, I'M SURPRISED, TOO. HOW COULD SUCH AN OLD CAR HAVE SUCH A GOOD GPS DEVICE?
DON'T HATE ON MY CAR, DUDE. IT'S A CLASSIC.
YEAH, A CLASSIC DEATH TRAP.

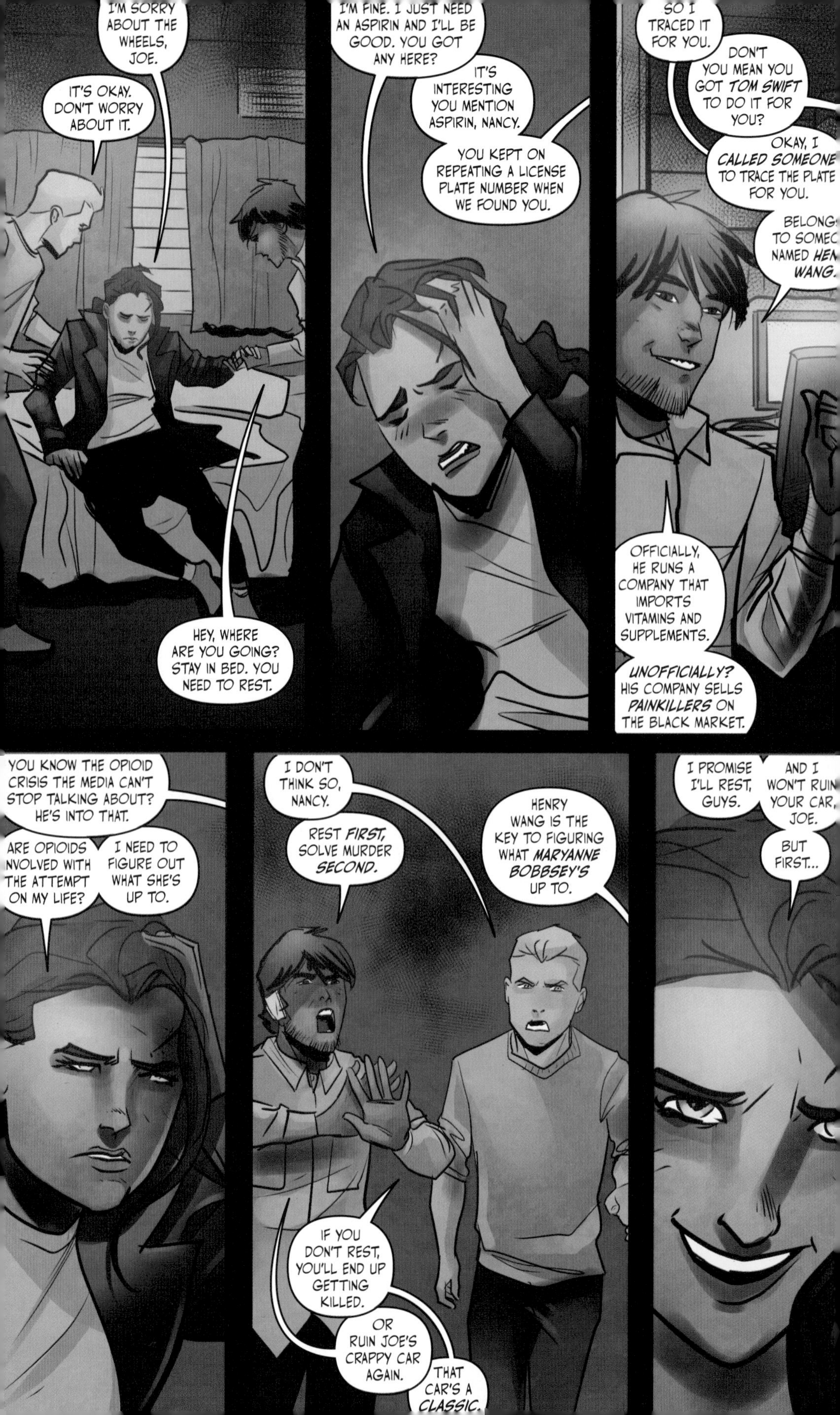
I'M SORRY ABOUT THE WHEELS, JOE.
IT'S OKAY. DON'T WORRY ABOUT IT.
HEY, WHERE ARE YOU GOING? STAY IN BED. YOU NEED TO REST.
I'M FINE. I JUST NEED AN ASPIRIN AND I'LL BE GOOD. YOU GOT ANY HERE?
IT'S INTERESTING YOU MENTION ASPIRIN, NANCY.
YOU KEPT ON REPEATING A LICENSE PLATE NUMBER WHEN WE FOUND YOU.
SO I TRACED IT FOR YOU.
DON'T YOU MEAN YOU GOT *TOM SWIFT* TO DO IT FOR YOU?
OKAY, I *CALLED SOMEONE* TO TRACE THE PLATE FOR YOU.
OFFICIALLY, HE RUNS A COMPANY THAT IMPORTS VITAMINS AND SUPPLEMENTS.
UNOFFICIALLY? HIS COMPANY SELLS *PAINKILLERS* ON THE BLACK MARKET.
YOU KNOW THE OPIOID CRISIS THE MEDIA CAN'T STOP TALKING ABOUT? HE'S INTO THAT.
ARE OPIOIDS INVOLVED WITH THE ATTEMPT ON MY LIFE?
I NEED TO FIGURE OUT WHAT SHE'S UP TO.
I DON'T THINK SO, NANCY.
REST *FIRST,* SOLVE MURDER *SECOND.*
HENRY WANG IS THE KEY TO FIGURING WHAT *MARYANNE BOBBSEY'S* UP TO.
IF YOU DON'T REST, YOU'LL END UP GETTING KILLED.
OR RUIN JOE'S CRAPPY CAR AGAIN.
THAT CAR'S A *CLASSIC.*
I PROMISE I'LL REST, GUYS.
BUT FIRST...

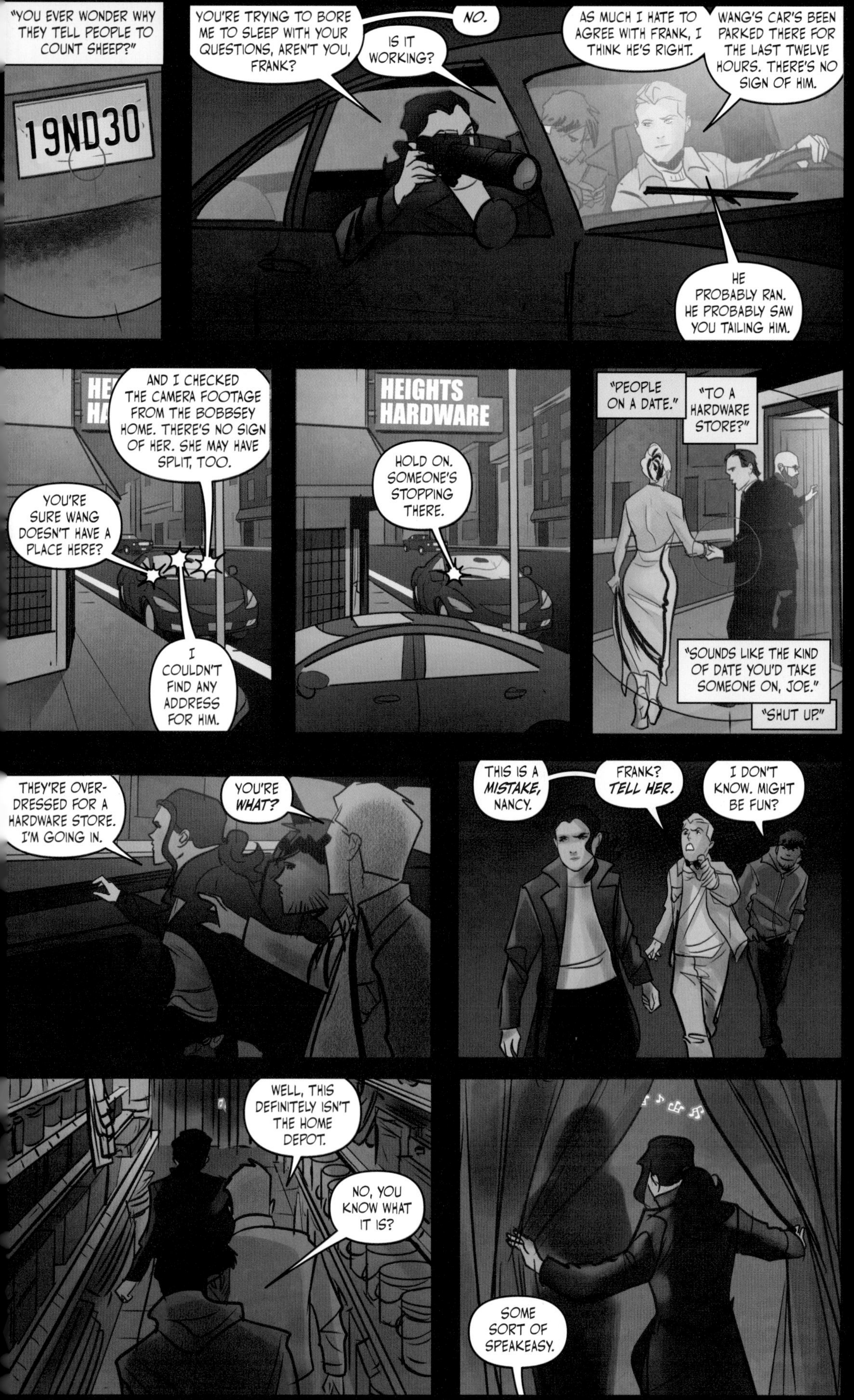

"YOU EVER WONDER WHY THEY TELL PEOPLE TO COUNT SHEEP?"
19ND30
YOU'RE TRYING TO BORE ME TO SLEEP WITH YOUR QUESTIONS, AREN'T YOU, FRANK?
NO.
IS IT WORKING?
AS MUCH I HATE TO AGREE WITH FRANK, I THINK HE'S RIGHT.
WANG'S CAR'S BEEN PARKED THERE FOR THE LAST TWELVE HOURS. THERE'S NO SIGN OF HIM.
HE PROBABLY RAN. HE PROBABLY SAW YOU TAILING HIM.
AND I CHECKED THE CAMERA FOOTAGE FROM THE BOBBSEY HOME. THERE'S NO SIGN OF HER. SHE MAY HAVE SPLIT, TOO.
YOU'RE SURE WANG DOESN'T HAVE A PLACE HERE?
I COULDN'T FIND ANY ADDRESS FOR HIM.
HEIGHTS HARDWARE
HOLD ON. SOMEONE'S STOPPING THERE.
"PEOPLE ON A DATE."
"TO A HARDWARE STORE?"
"SOUNDS LIKE THE KIND OF DATE YOU'D TAKE SOMEONE ON, JOE."
"SHUT UP."
THEY'RE OVER-DRESSED FOR A HARDWARE STORE. I'M GOING IN.
YOU'RE *WHAT?*
THIS IS A *MISTAKE,* NANCY.
FRANK? *TELL HER.*
I DON'T KNOW. MIGHT BE FUN?
WELL, THIS DEFINITELY ISN'T THE HOME DEPOT.
NO, YOU KNOW WHAT IT IS?
SOME SORT OF SPEAKEASY.

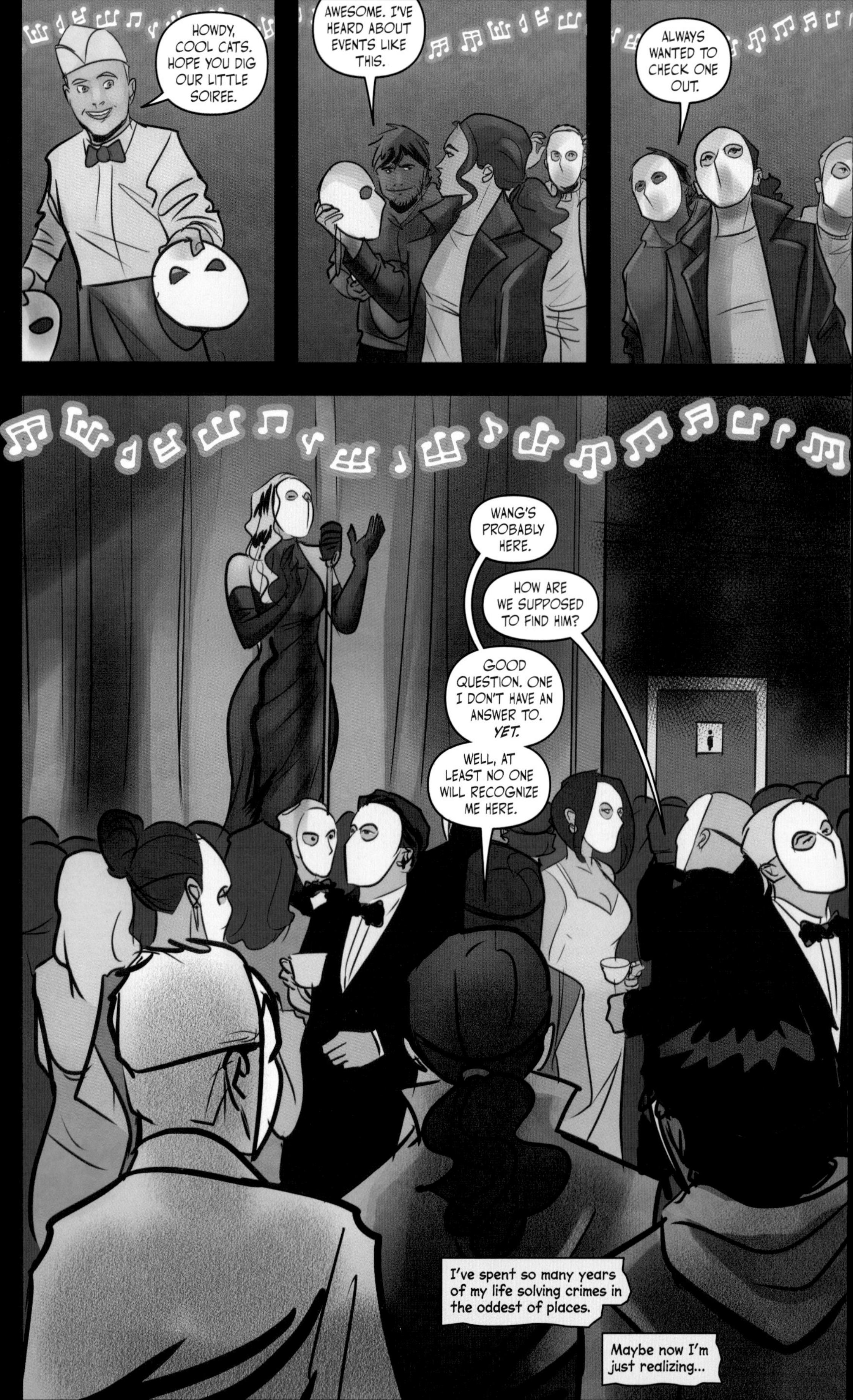
HOWDY, COOL CATS. HOPE YOU DIG OUR LITTLE SOIREE.
AWESOME. I'VE HEARD ABOUT EVENTS LIKE THIS.
ALWAYS WANTED TO CHECK ONE OUT.
WANG'S PROBABLY HERE.
HOW ARE WE SUPPOSED TO FIND HIM?
GOOD QUESTION. ONE I DON'T HAVE AN ANSWER TO. *YET.*
WELL, AT LEAST NO ONE WILL RECOGNIZE ME HERE.
I've spent so many years of my life solving crimes in the oddest of places.
Maybe now I'm just realizing...

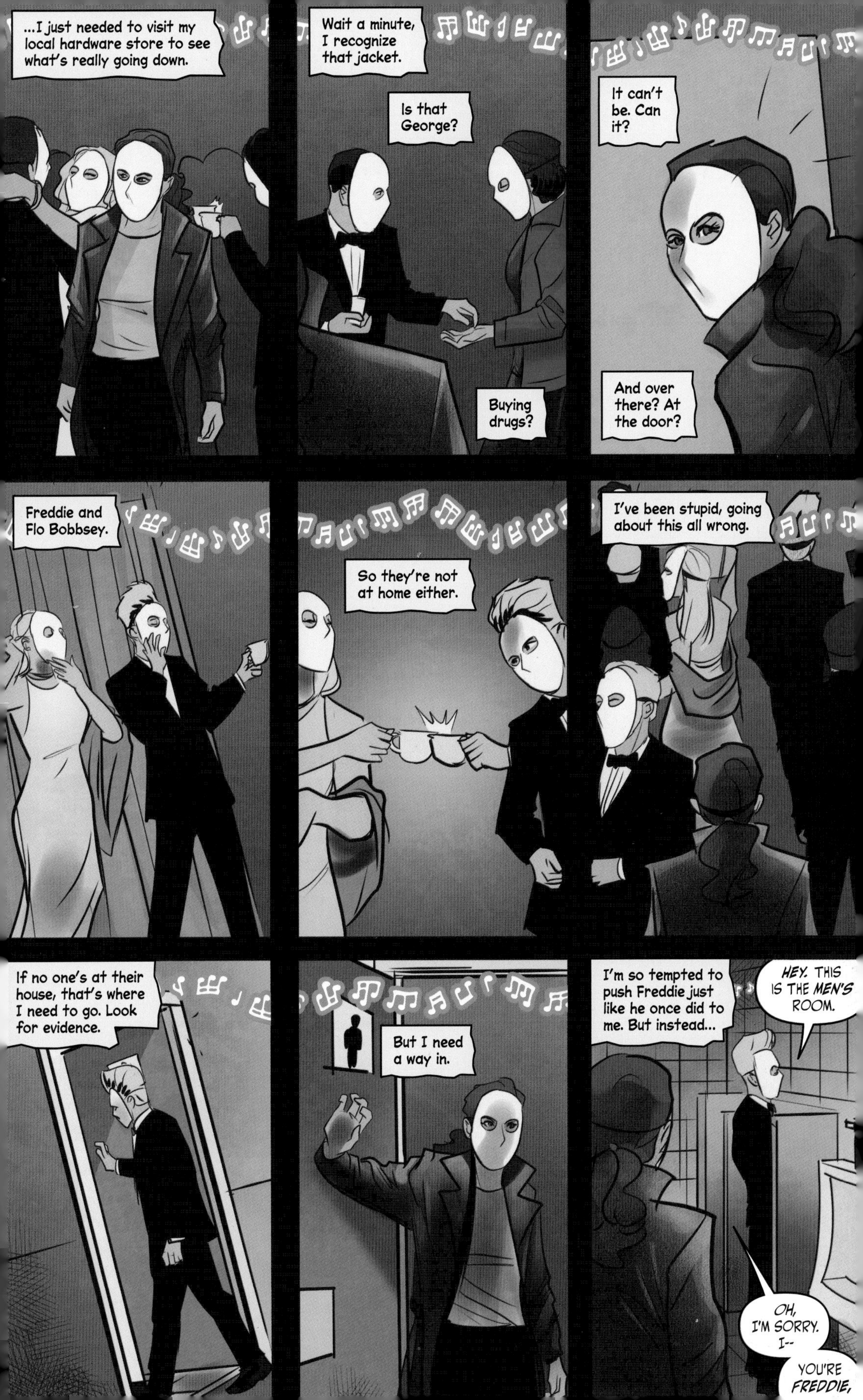
...I just needed to visit my local hardware store to see what's really going down.
Wait a minute, I recognize that jacket.
Is that George?
Buying drugs?
It can't be. Can it?
And over there? At the door?
Freddie and Flo Bobbsey.
So they're not at home either.
I've been stupid, going about this all wrong.
If no one's at their house, that's where I need to go. Look for evidence.
But I need a way in.
I'm so tempted to push Freddie just like he once did to me. But instead...
HEY. THIS IS THE *MEN'S* ROOM.
OH, I'M SORRY. I--
YOU'RE *FREDDIE,*

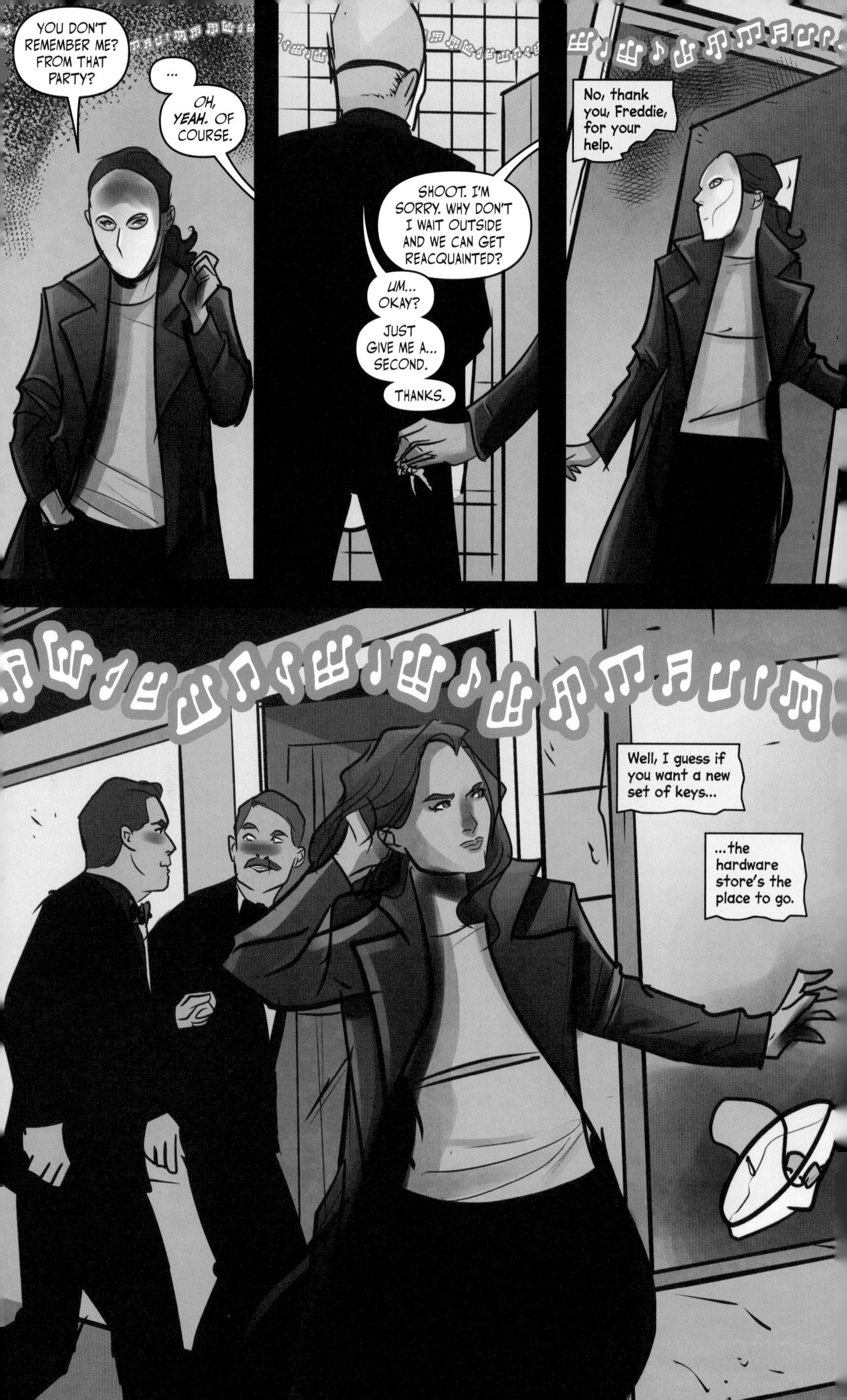
YOU DON'T REMEMBER ME? FROM THAT PARTY?
...
OH, YEAH. OF COURSE.
SHOOT. I'M SORRY. WHY DON'T I WAIT OUTSIDE AND WE CAN GET REACQUAINTED?
UM... OKAY?
JUST GIVE ME A... SECOND.
THANKS.
No, thank you, Freddie, for your help.
Well, I guess if you want a new set of keys...
...the hardware store's the place to go.

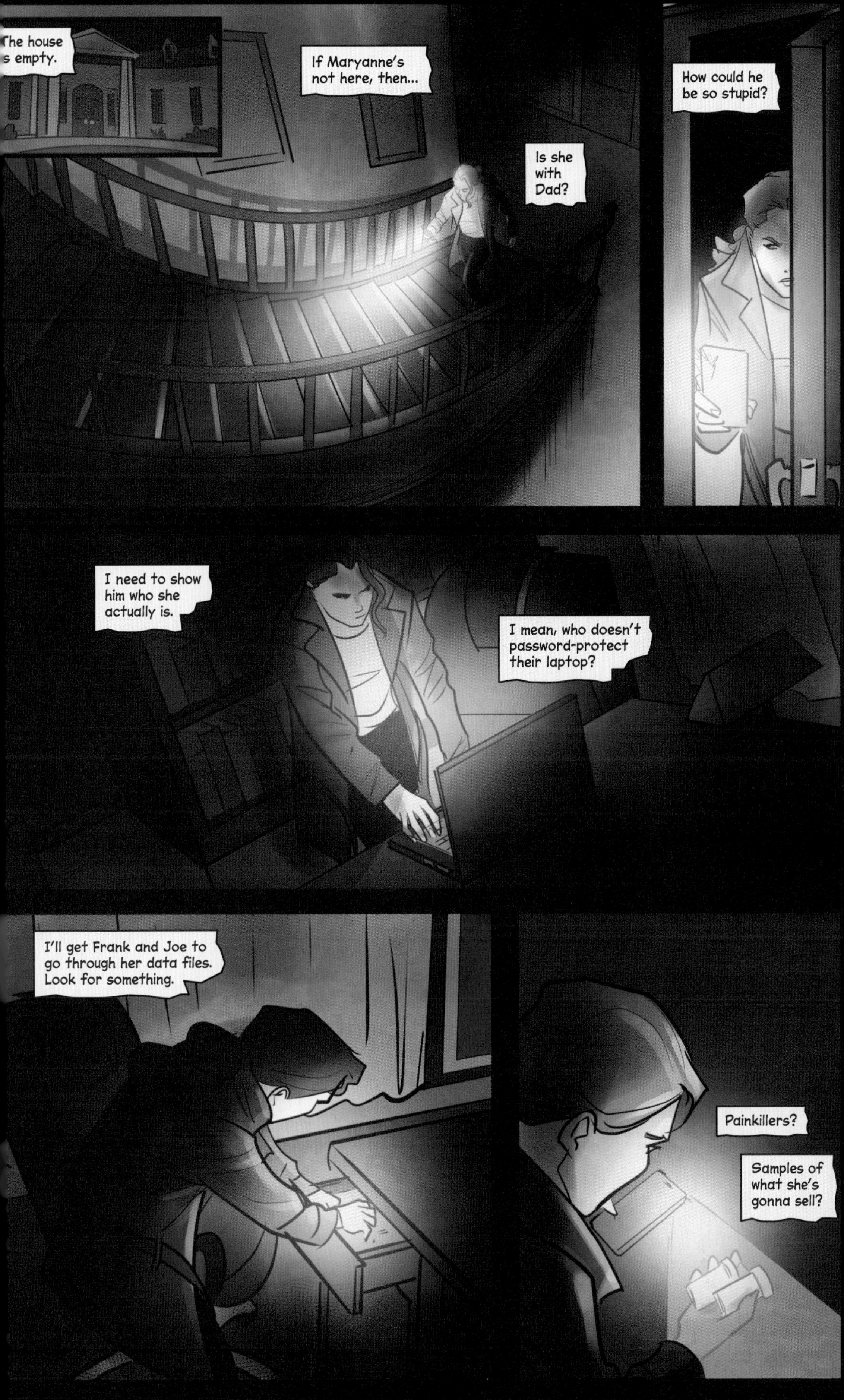
The house
s empty.
If Maryanne's not here, then...
Is she with Dad?
How could he be so stupid?
I need to show him who she actually is.
I mean, who doesn't password-protect their laptop?
I'll get Frank and Joe to go through her data files. Look for something.
Painkillers?
Samples of what she's gonna sell?

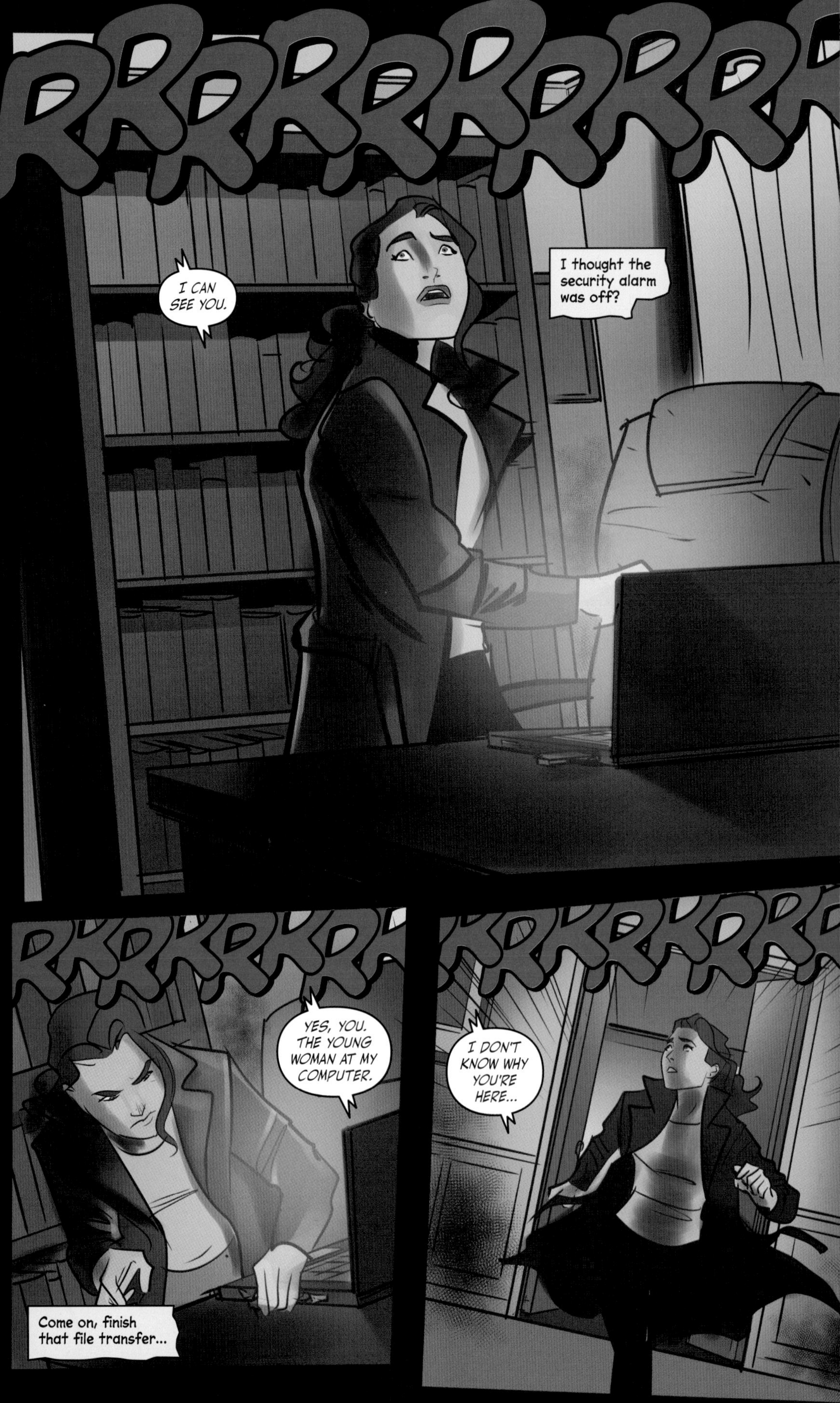
RRRRRRRRRRR
I CAN SEE YOU.
I thought the security alarm was off?
RRRRRRR
YES, YOU. THE YOUNG WOMAN AT MY COMPUTER.
Come on, finish that file transfer...
RRRRRRRR
I DON'T KNOW WHY YOU'RE HERE...

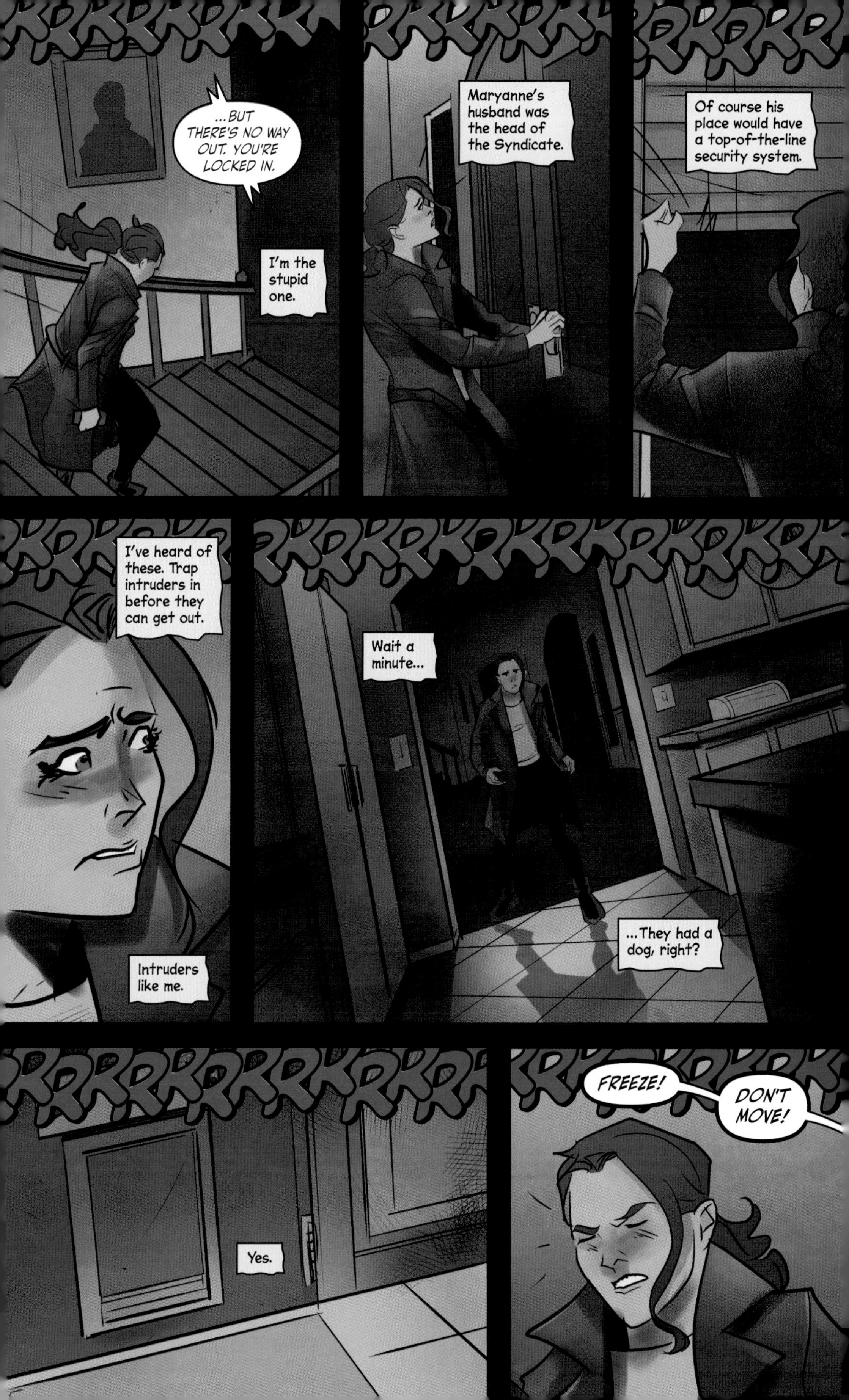
...BUT THERE'S NO WAY OUT. YOU'RE LOCKED IN.
I'm the stupid one.
Maryanne's husband was the head of the Syndicate.
Of course his place would have a top-of-the-line security system.
I've heard of these. Trap intruders in before they can get out.
Intruders like me.
Wait a minute...
...They had a dog, right?
Yes.
FREEZE!
DON'T MOVE!

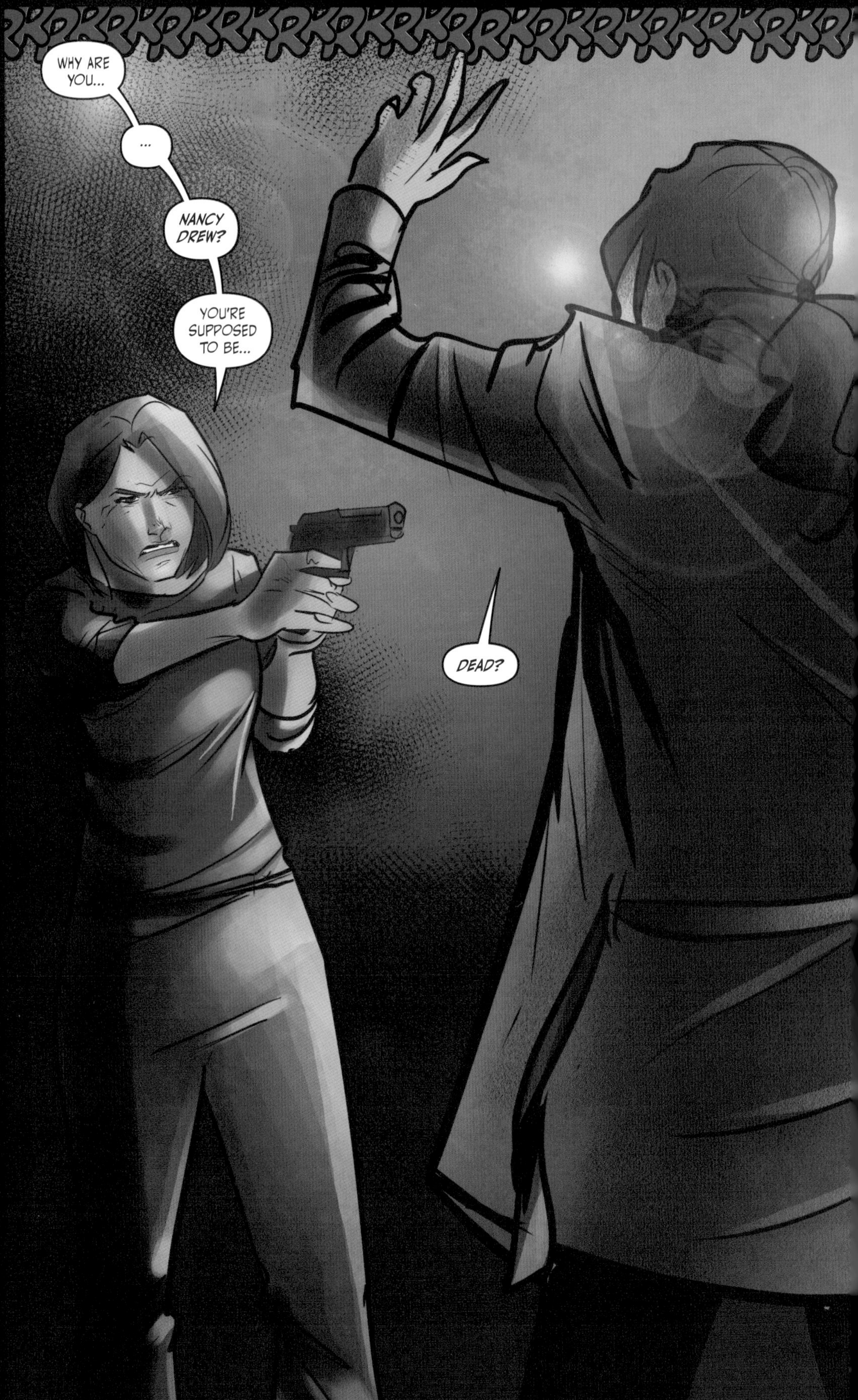
RRRRRRRRRRRRRRRR
WHY ARE YOU...
...
NANCY DREW?
YOU'RE SUPPOSED TO BE...
DEAD?

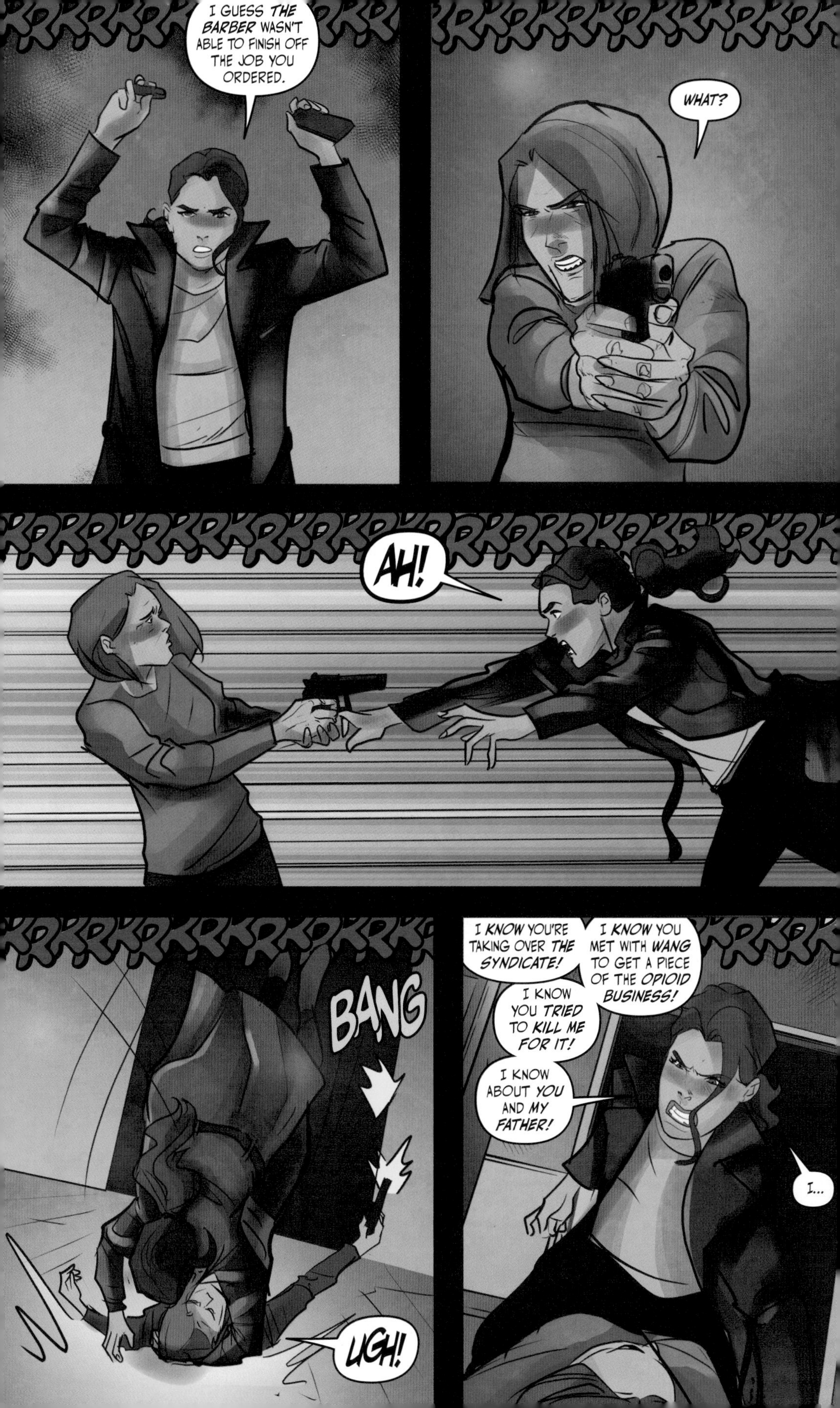

I GUESS THE BARBER WASN'T ABLE TO FINISH OFF THE JOB YOU ORDERED.
WHAT?
AH!
BANG
UGH!
I KNOW YOU'RE TAKING OVER THE SYNDICATE!
I KNOW YOU MET WITH WANG TO GET A PIECE OF THE OPIOID BUSINESS!
I KNOW YOU TRIED TO KILL ME FOR IT!
I KNOW ABOUT YOU AND MY FATHER!
I...

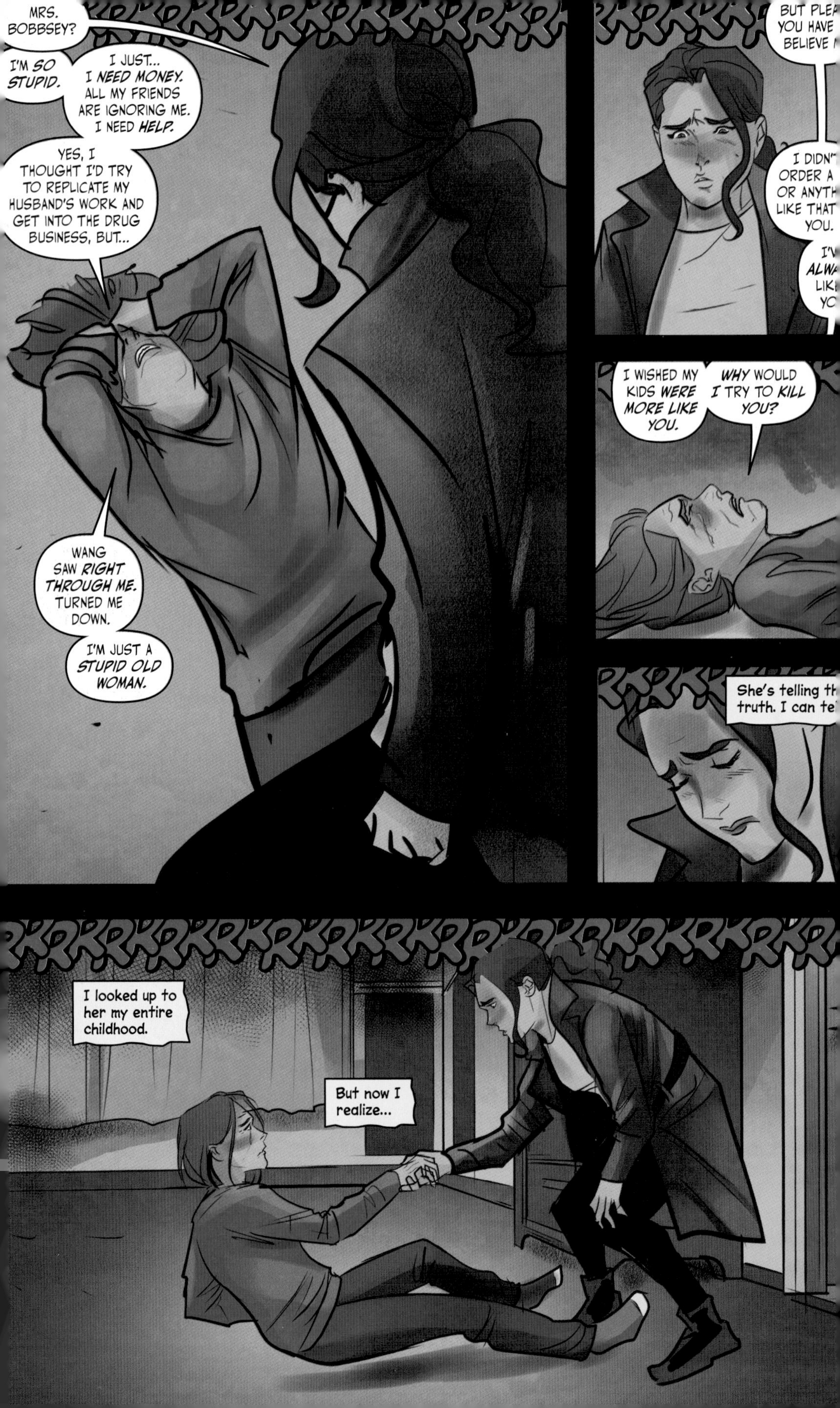
MRS. BOBBSEY?
I'M SO STUPID.
I JUST... I NEED MONEY. ALL MY FRIENDS ARE IGNORING ME. I NEED HELP.
YES, I THOUGHT I'D TRY TO REPLICATE MY HUSBAND'S WORK AND GET INTO THE DRUG BUSINESS, BUT...
WANG SAW RIGHT THROUGH ME. TURNED ME DOWN.
I'M JUST A STUPID OLD WOMAN.
I WISHED MY KIDS WERE MORE LIKE YOU.
WHY WOULD I TRY TO KILL YOU?
I looked up to her my entire childhood.
But now I realize...

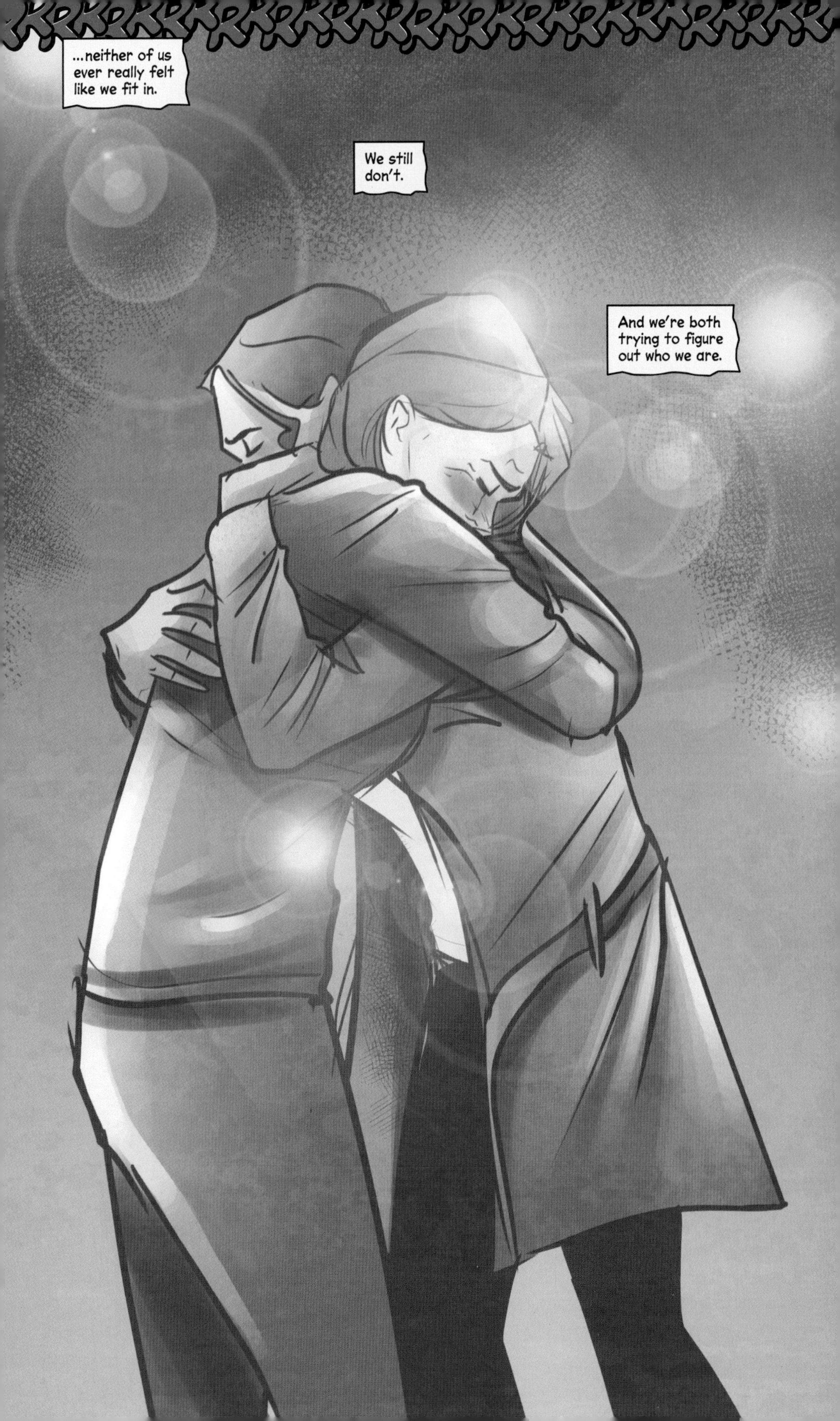
...neither of us ever really felt like we fit in.
We still don't.
And we're both trying to figure out who we are.

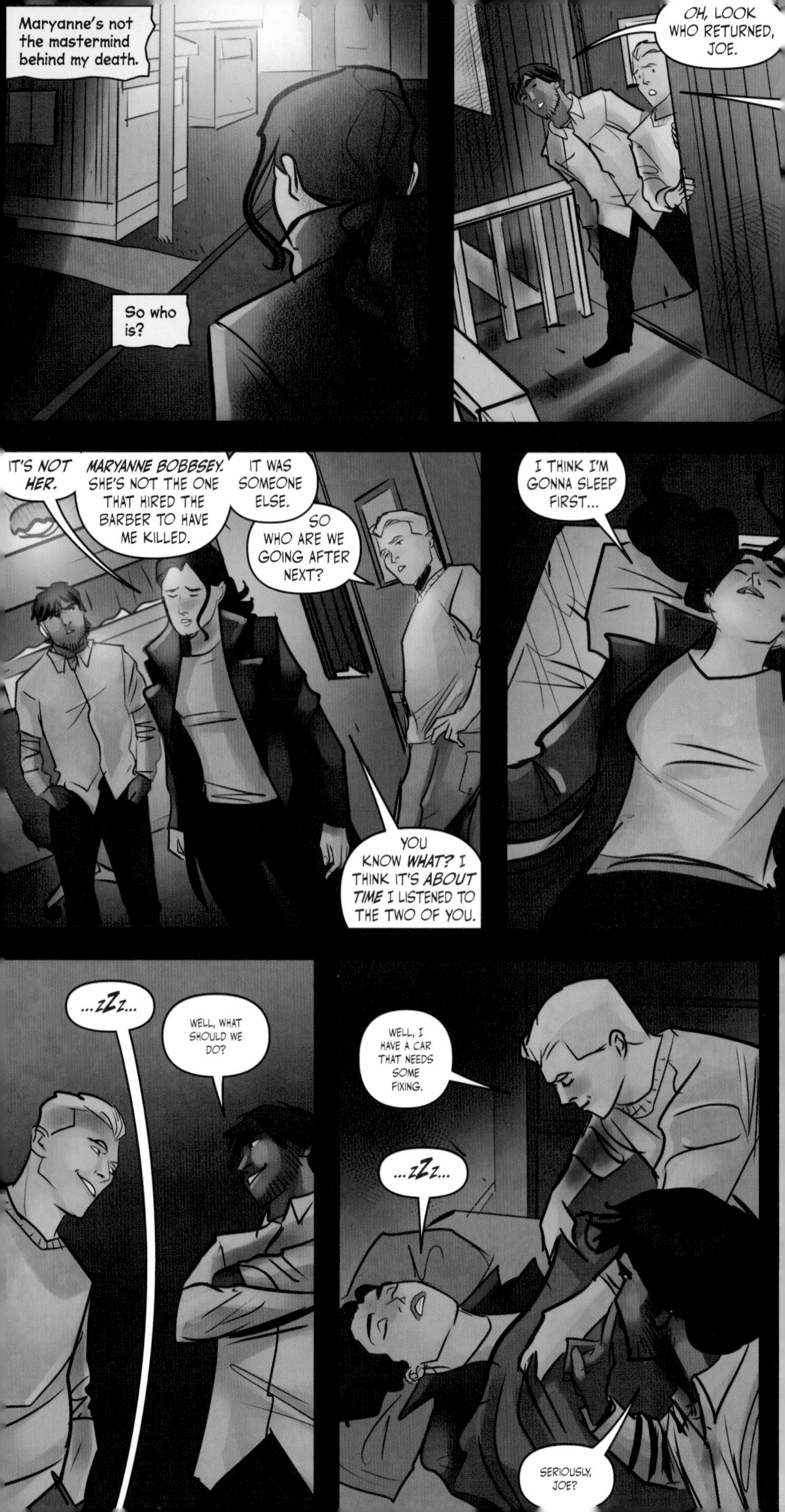

Maryanne's not the mastermind behind my death.
So who is?
OH, LOOK WHO RETURNED, JOE.
IT'S NOT HER.
MARYANNE BOBBSEY. SHE'S NOT THE ONE THAT HIRED THE BARBER TO HAVE ME KILLED.
IT WAS SOMEONE ELSE.
SO WHO ARE WE GOING AFTER NEXT?
YOU KNOW WHAT? I THINK IT'S ABOUT TIME I LISTENED TO THE TWO OF YOU.
I THINK I'M GONNA SLEEP FIRST...
...zZz...
WELL, WHAT SHOULD WE DO?
WELL, I HAVE A CAR THAT NEEDS SOME FIXING.
...zZz...
SERIOUSLY, JOE?

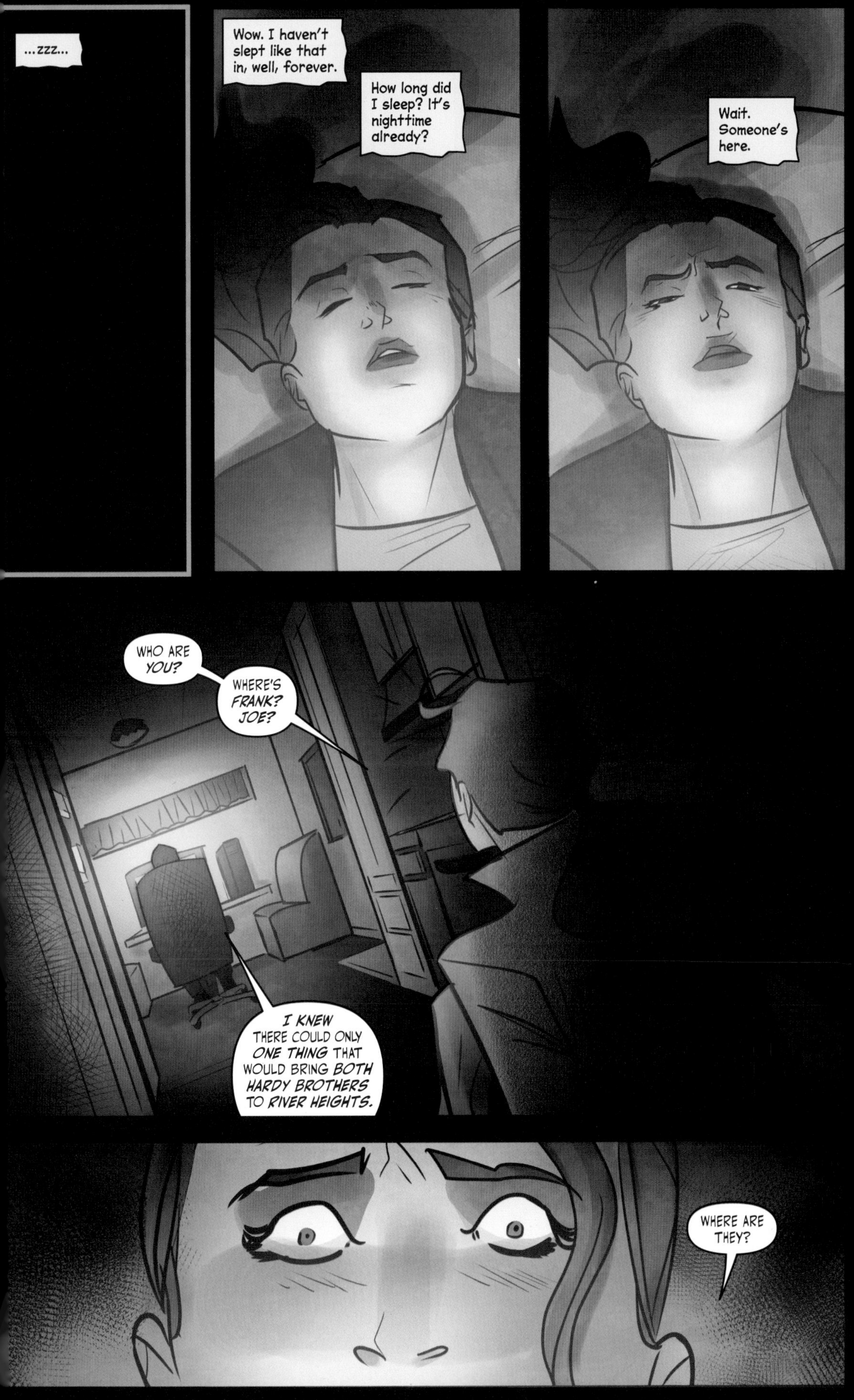
...zzz...
Wow. I haven't slept like that in, well, forever.
How long did I sleep? It's nighttime already?
Wait. Someone's here.
WHO ARE YOU?
WHERE'S FRANK? JOE?
I KNEW THERE COULD ONLY ONE THING THAT WOULD BRING BOTH HARDY BROTHERS TO RIVER HEIGHTS.
WHERE ARE THEY?

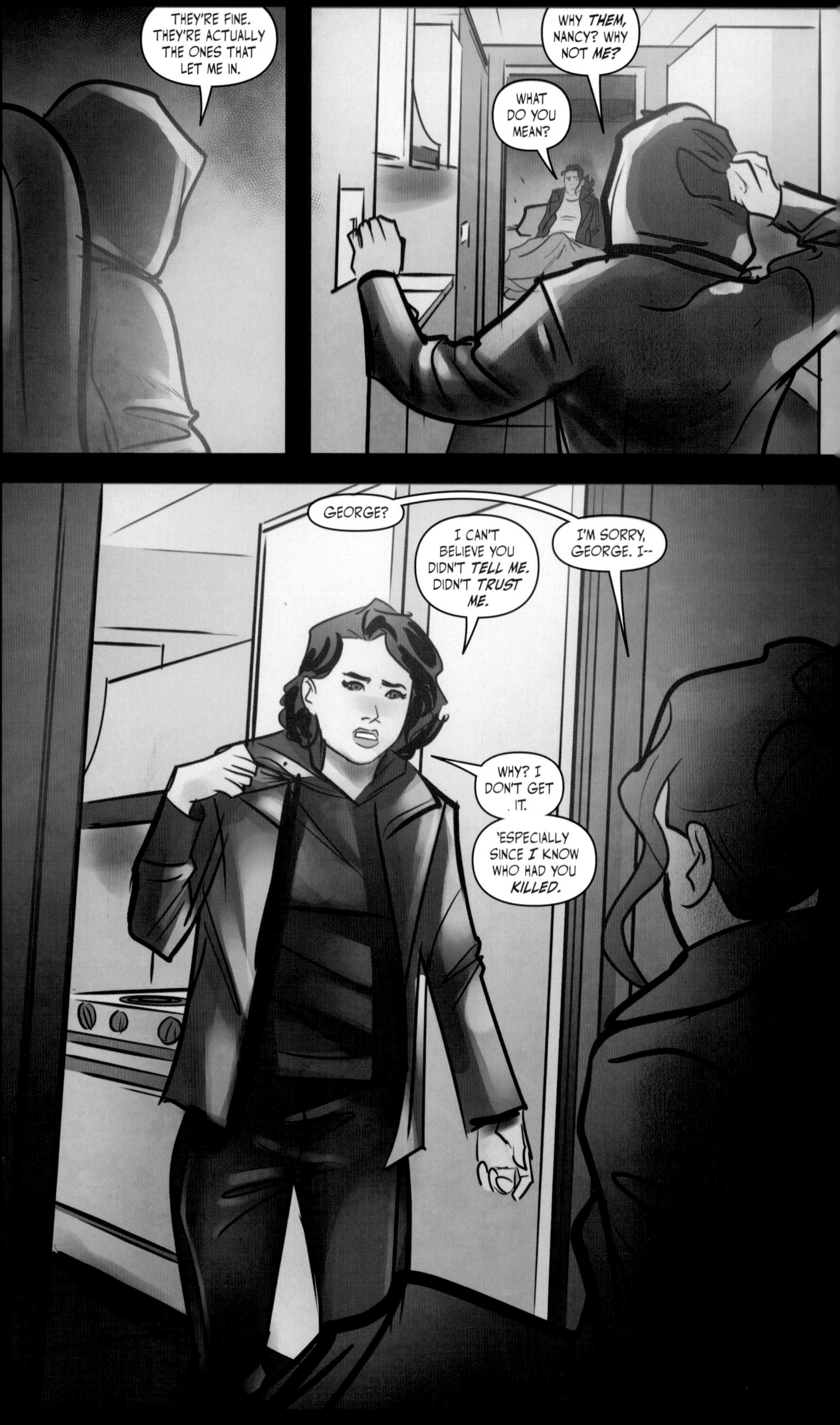
THEY'RE FINE. THEY'RE ACTUALLY THE ONES THAT LET ME IN.
WHY *THEM*, NANCY? WHY NOT *ME?*
WHAT DO YOU MEAN?
GEORGE?
I'M SORRY, GEORGE. I--
I CAN'T BELIEVE YOU DIDN'T *TELL ME.* DIDN'T *TRUST ME.*
WHY? I DON'T GET IT.
'ESPECIALLY SINCE *I* KNOW WHO HAD YOU *KILLED.*

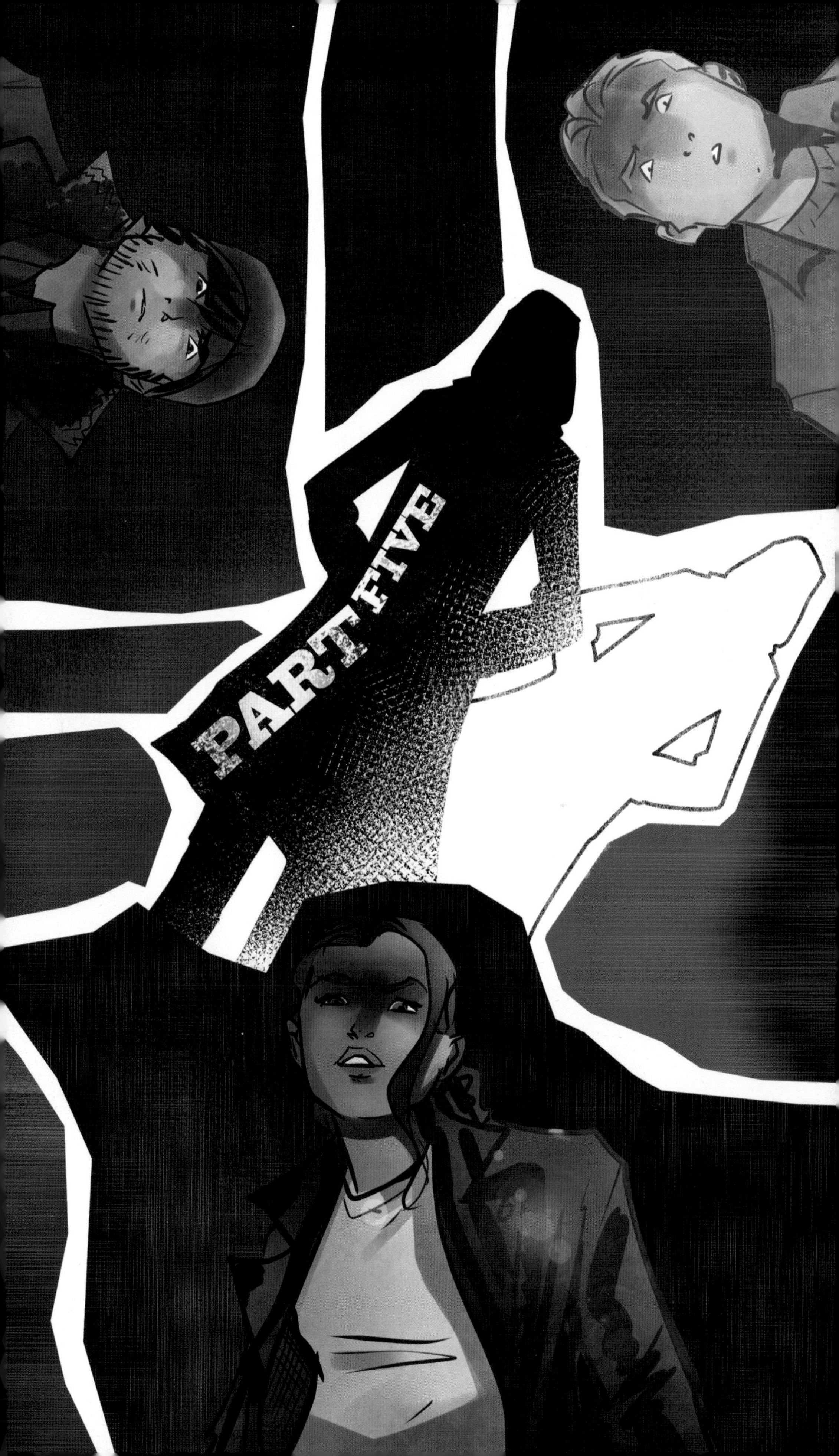
PART FIVE

PART FIVE COVER ART BY **JOE EISMA**

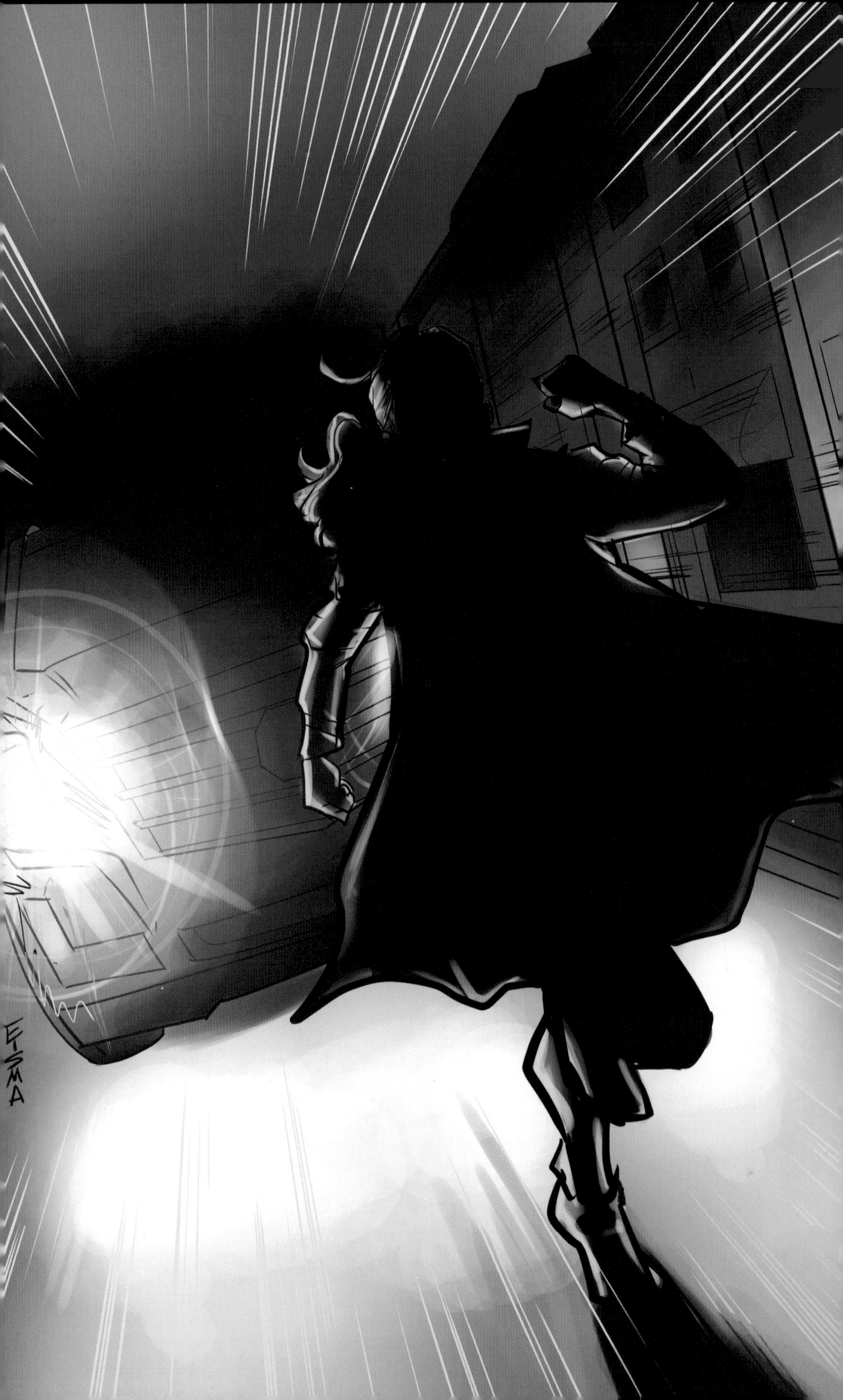
EISMA

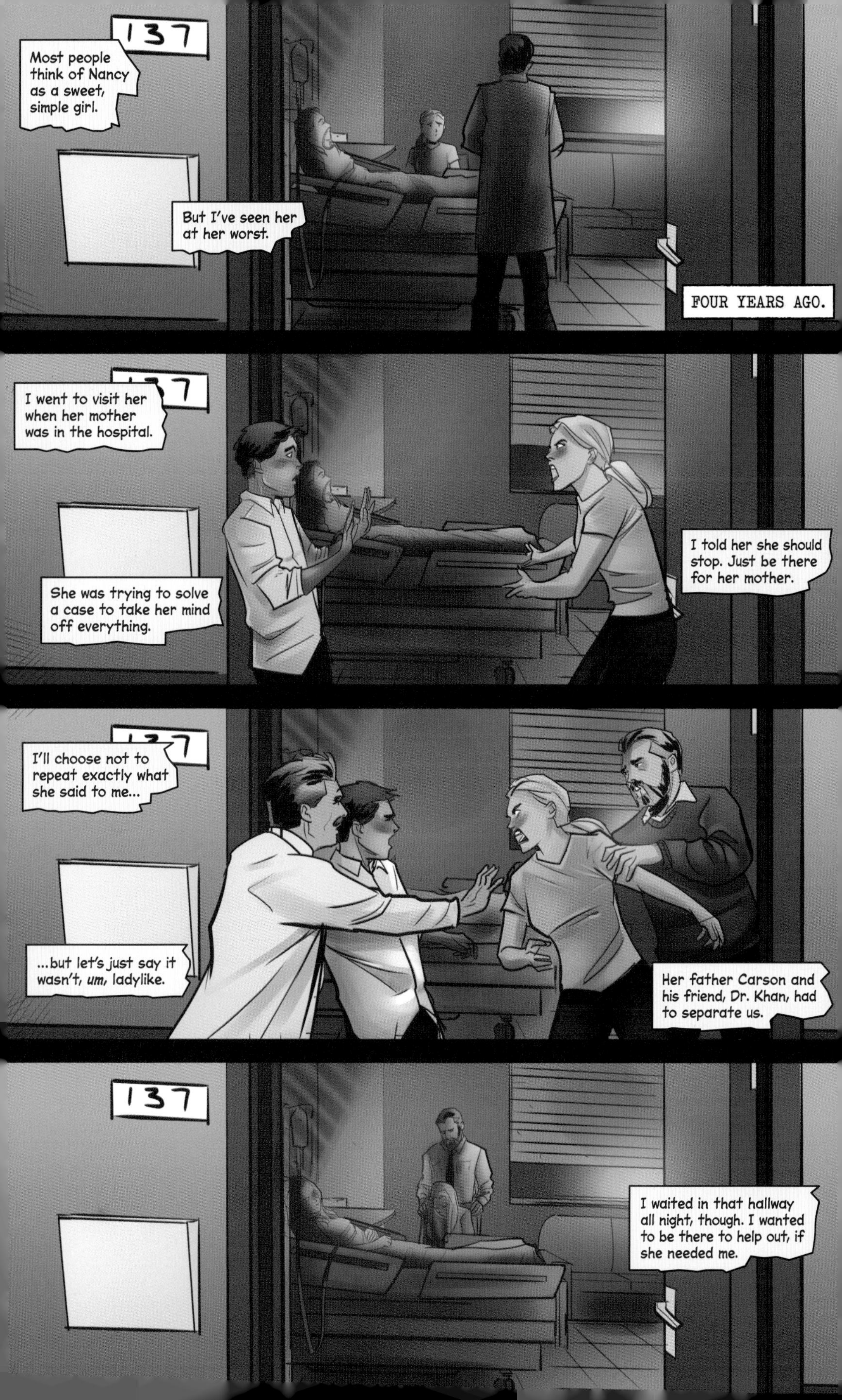
137
Most people think of Nancy as a sweet, simple girl.
But I've seen her at her worst.
FOUR YEARS AGO.
I went to visit her when her mother was in the hospital.
She was trying to solve a case to take her mind off everything.
I told her she should stop. Just be there for her mother.
I'll choose not to repeat exactly what she said to me...
...but let's just say it wasn't, *um*, ladylike.
Her father Carson and his friend, Dr. Khan, had to separate us.
137
I waited in that hallway all night, though. I wanted to be there to help out, if she needed me.

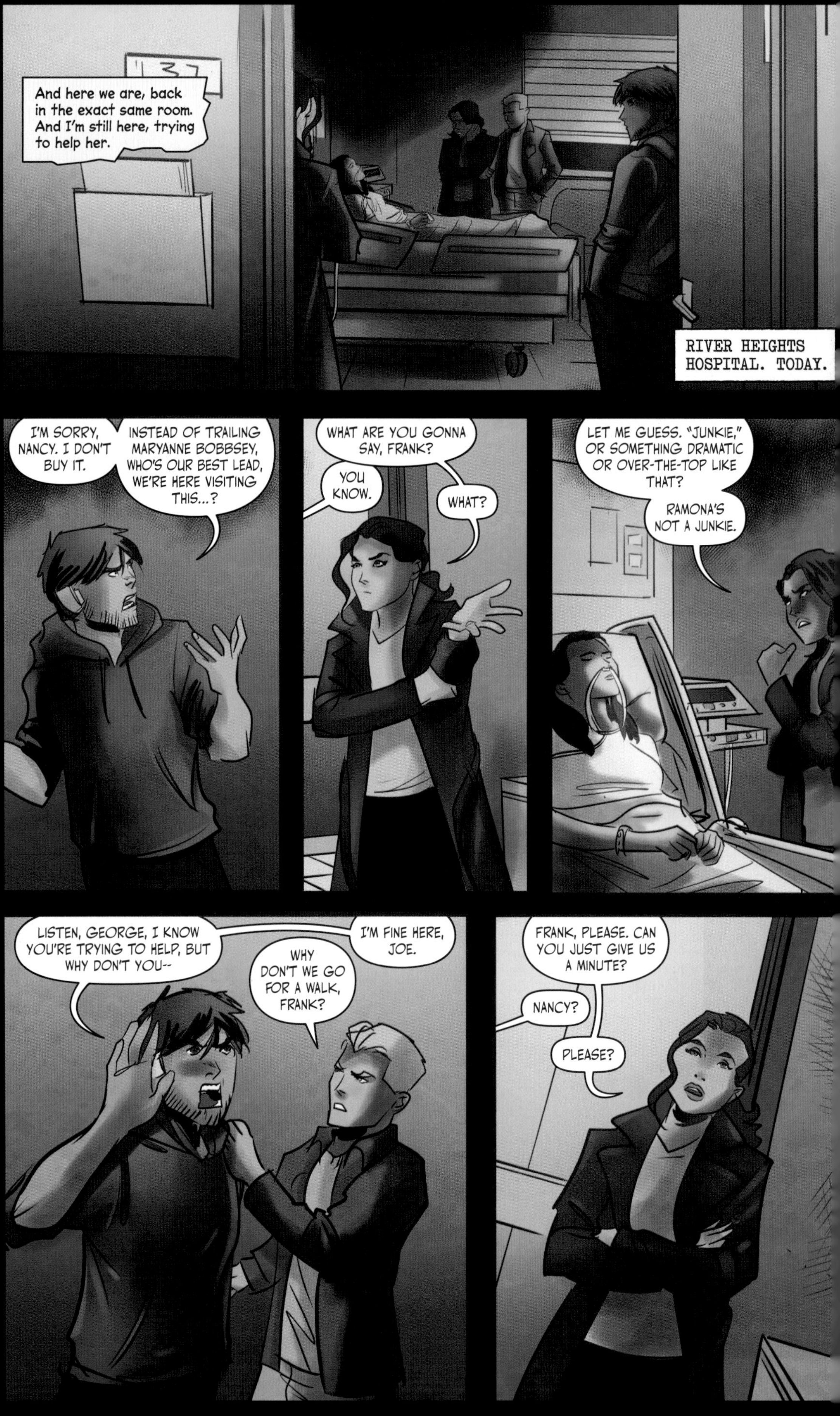

And here we are, back in the exact same room. And I'm still here, trying to help her.
RIVER HEIGHTS HOSPITAL. TODAY.
I'M SORRY, NANCY. I DON'T BUY IT.
INSTEAD OF TRAILING MARYANNE BOBBSEY, WHO'S OUR BEST LEAD, WE'RE HERE VISITING THIS...?
WHAT ARE YOU GONNA SAY, FRANK?
YOU KNOW.
WHAT?
LET ME GUESS. "JUNKIE," OR SOMETHING DRAMATIC OR OVER-THE-TOP LIKE THAT?
RAMONA'S NOT A JUNKIE.
LISTEN, GEORGE, I KNOW YOU'RE TRYING TO HELP, BUT WHY DON'T YOU--
I'M FINE HERE, JOE.
WHY DON'T WE GO FOR A WALK, FRANK?
FRANK, PLEASE. CAN YOU JUST GIVE US A MINUTE?
NANCY?
PLEASE?

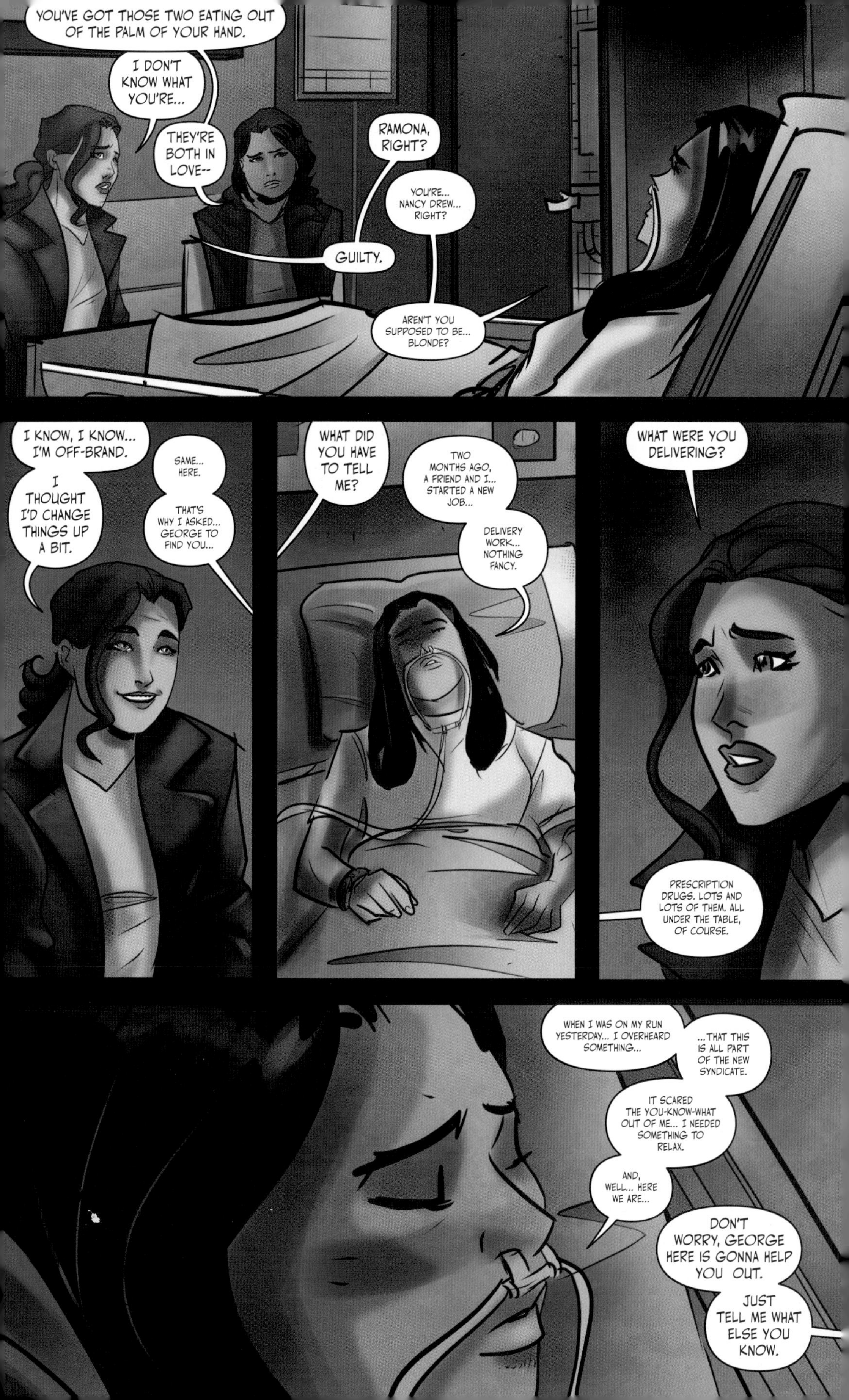
YOU'VE GOT THOSE TWO EATING OUT OF THE PALM OF YOUR HAND.
I DON'T KNOW WHAT YOU'RE...
THEY'RE BOTH IN LOVE--
RAMONA, RIGHT?
GUILTY.
YOU'RE... NANCY DREW... RIGHT?
AREN'T YOU SUPPOSED TO BE... BLONDE?
I KNOW, I KNOW... I'M OFF-BRAND.
I THOUGHT I'D CHANGE THINGS UP A BIT.
SAME... HERE.
THAT'S WHY I ASKED... GEORGE TO FIND YOU...
WHAT DID YOU HAVE TO TELL ME?
TWO MONTHS AGO, A FRIEND AND I... STARTED A NEW JOB...
DELIVERY WORK... NOTHING FANCY.
WHAT WERE YOU DELIVERING?
PRESCRIPTION DRUGS. LOTS AND LOTS OF THEM. ALL UNDER THE TABLE, OF COURSE.
WHEN I WAS ON MY RUN YESTERDAY... I OVERHEARD SOMETHING...
...THAT THIS IS ALL PART OF THE NEW SYNDICATE.
IT SCARED THE YOU-KNOW-WHAT OUT OF ME... I NEEDED SOMETHING TO RELAX.
AND, WELL... HERE WE ARE...
DON'T WORRY, GEORGE HERE IS GONNA HELP YOU OUT.
JUST TELL ME WHAT ELSE YOU KNOW.

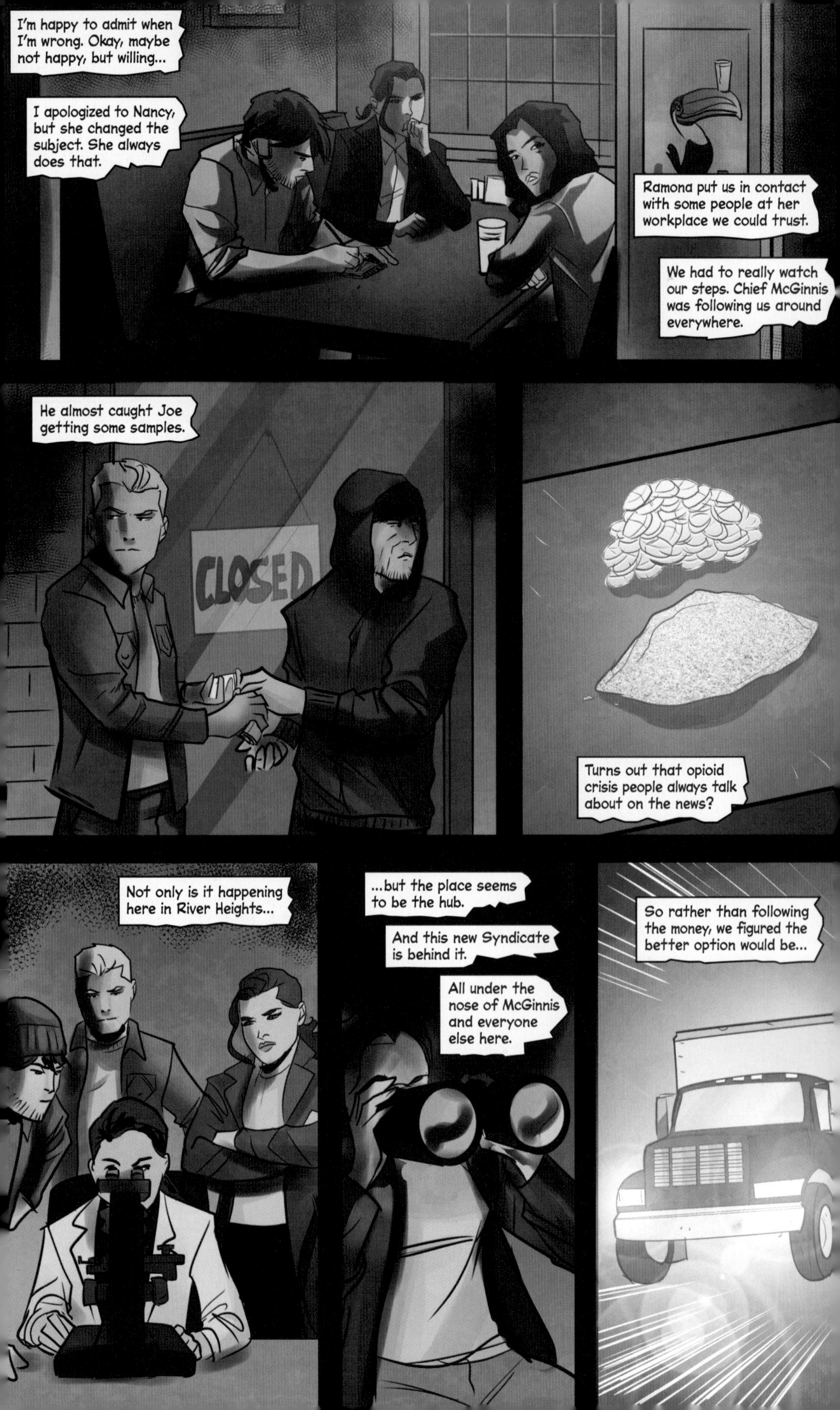
I'm happy to admit when I'm wrong. Okay, maybe not happy, but willing...
I apologized to Nancy, but she changed the subject. She always does that.
Ramona put us in contact with some people at her workplace we could trust.
We had to really watch our steps. Chief McGinnis was following us around everywhere.
He almost caught Joe getting some samples.
CLOSED
Turns out that opioid crisis people always talk about on the news?
Not only is it happening here in River Heights...
...but the place seems to be the hub.
And this new Syndicate is behind it.
All under the nose of McGinnis and everyone else here.
So rather than following the money, we figured the better option would be...

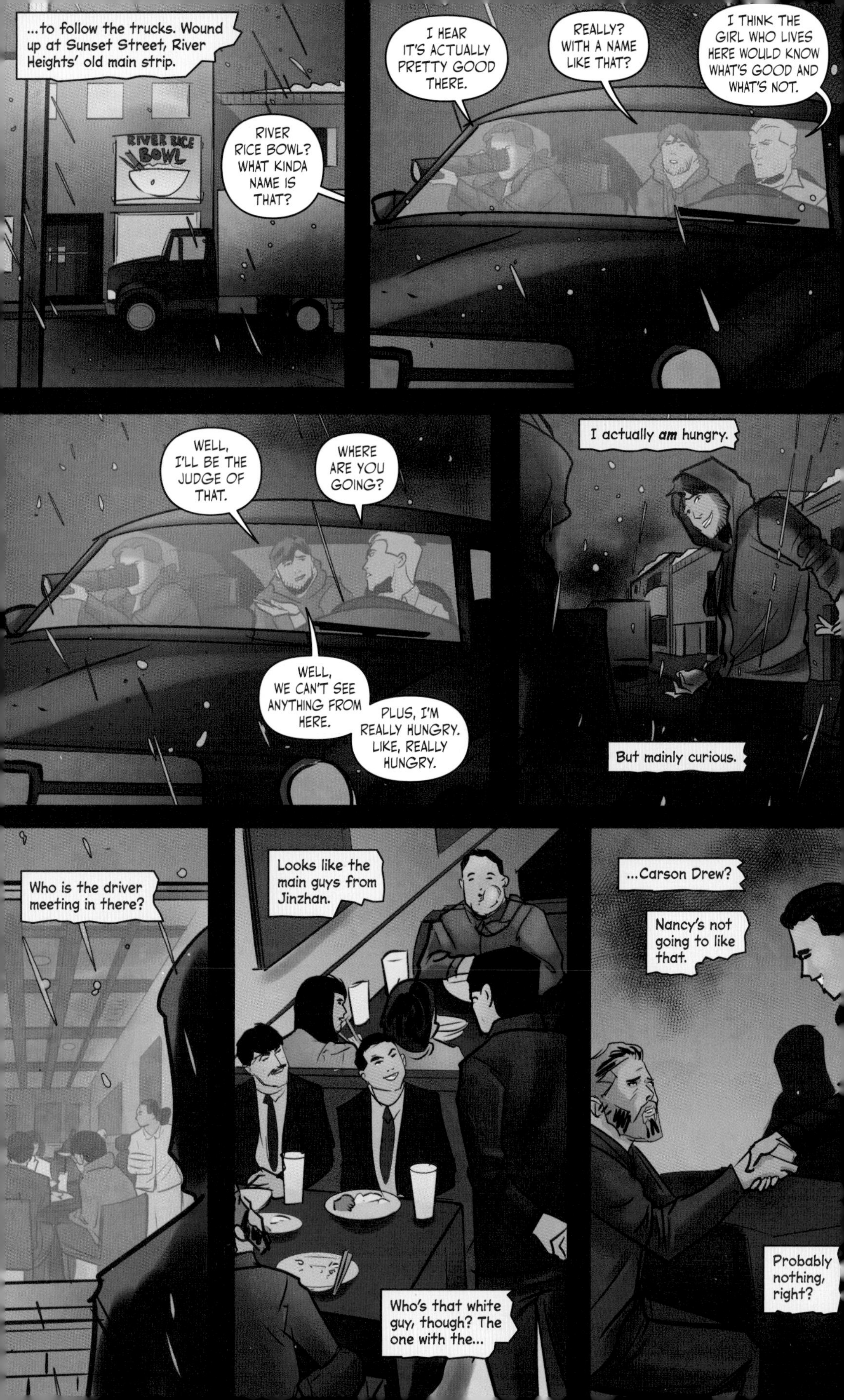
...to follow the trucks. Wound up at Sunset Street, River Heights' old main strip.
RIVER RICE BOWL
RIVER RICE BOWL? WHAT KINDA NAME IS THAT?
I HEAR IT'S ACTUALLY PRETTY GOOD THERE.
REALLY? WITH A NAME LIKE THAT?
I THINK THE GIRL WHO LIVES HERE WOULD KNOW WHAT'S GOOD AND WHAT'S NOT.
WELL, I'LL BE THE JUDGE OF THAT.
WHERE ARE YOU GOING?
WELL, WE CAN'T SEE ANYTHING FROM HERE.
PLUS, I'M REALLY HUNGRY. LIKE, REALLY HUNGRY.
I actually **am** hungry.
But mainly curious.
Who is the driver meeting in there?
Looks like the main guys from Jinzhan.
Who's that white guy, though? The one with the...
...Carson Drew?
Nancy's not going to like that.
Probably nothing, right?

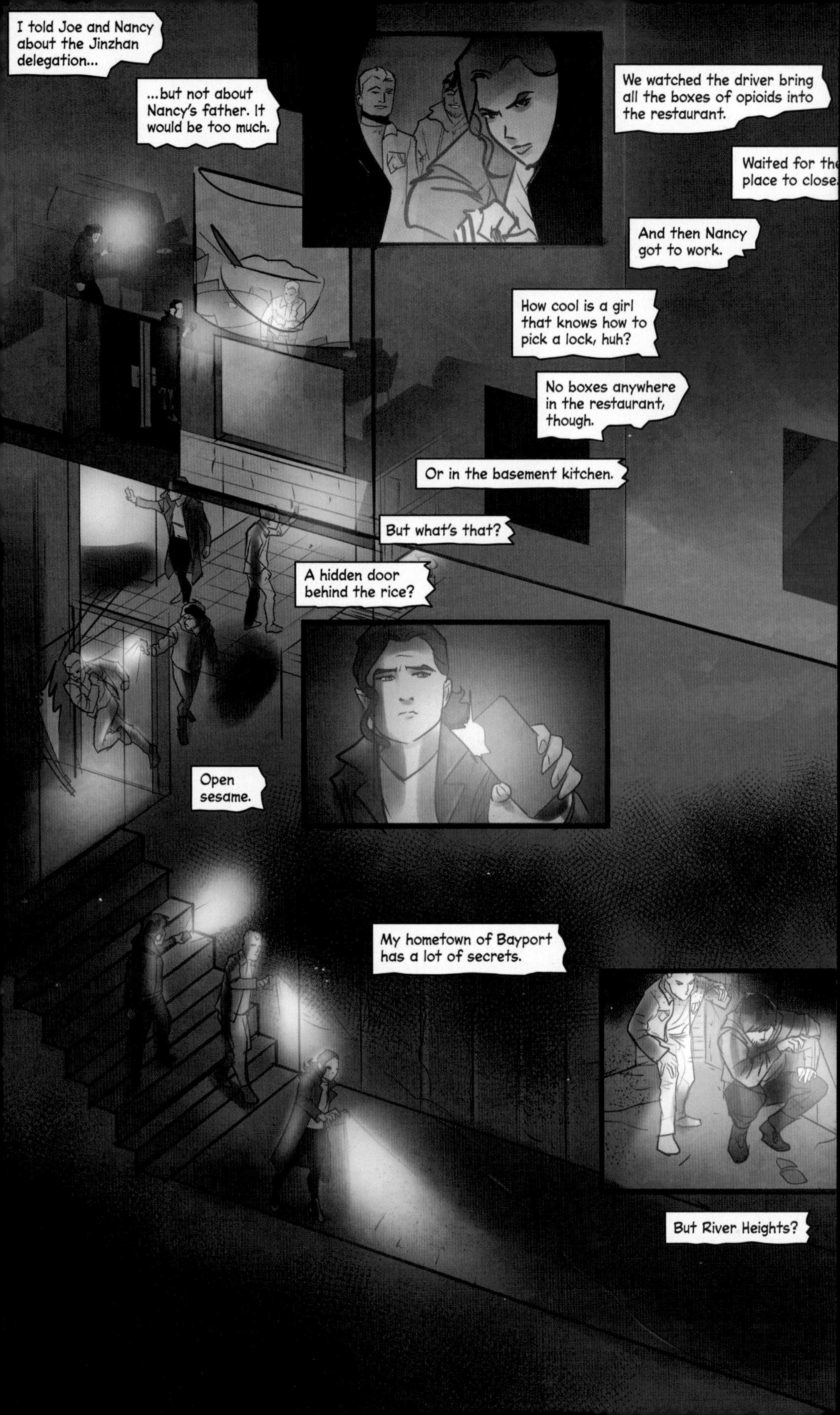
I told Joe and Nancy about the Jinzhan delegation...
...but not about Nancy's father. It would be too much.
We watched the driver bring all the boxes of opioids into the restaurant.
Waited for the place to close.
And then Nancy got to work.
How cool is a girl that knows how to pick a lock, huh?
No boxes anywhere in the restaurant, though.
Or in the basement kitchen.
But what's that?
A hidden door behind the rice?
Open sesame.
My hometown of Bayport has a lot of secrets.
But River Heights?

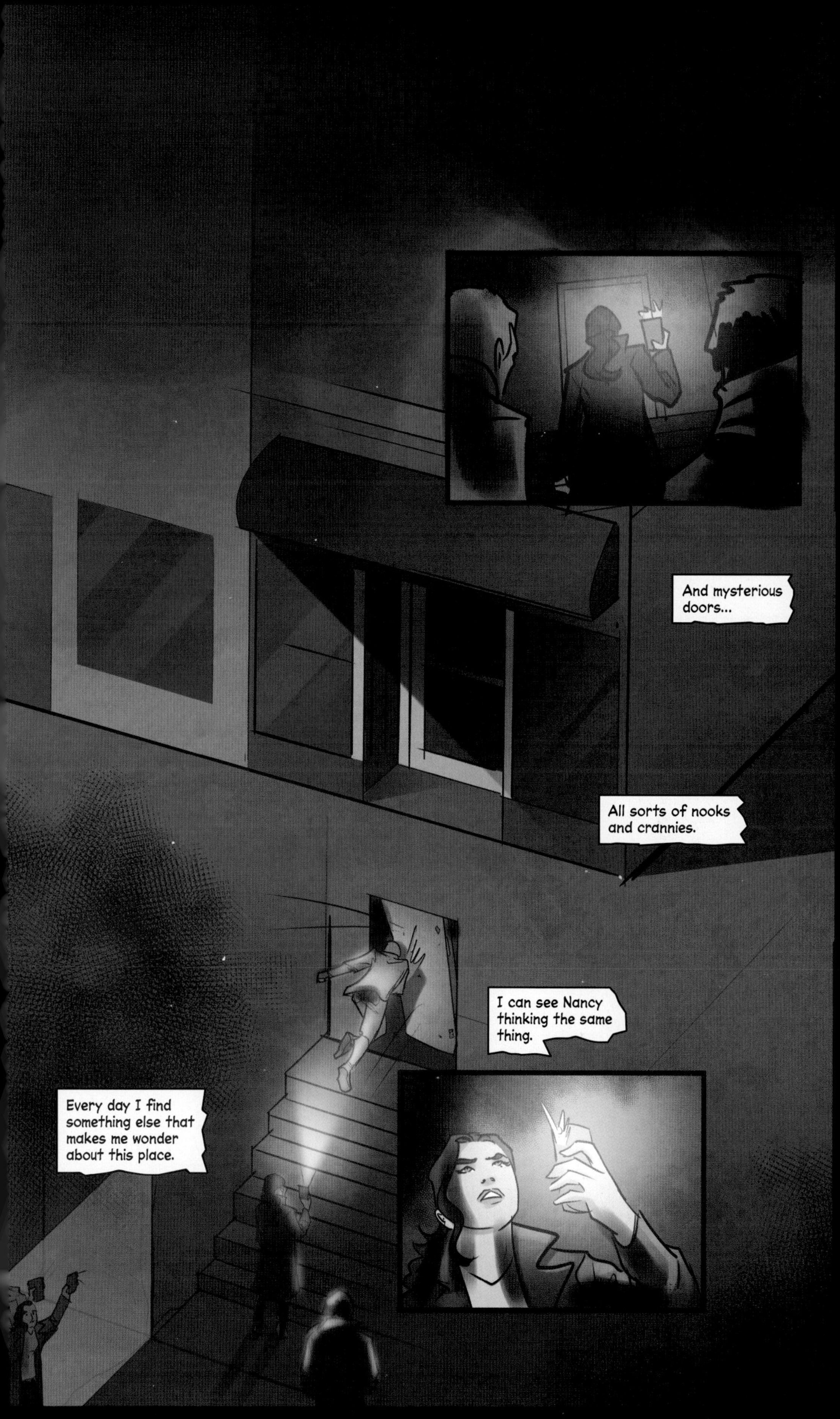
And mysterious doors...
All sorts of nooks and crannies.
I can see Nancy thinking the same thing.
Every day I find something else that makes me wonder about this place.

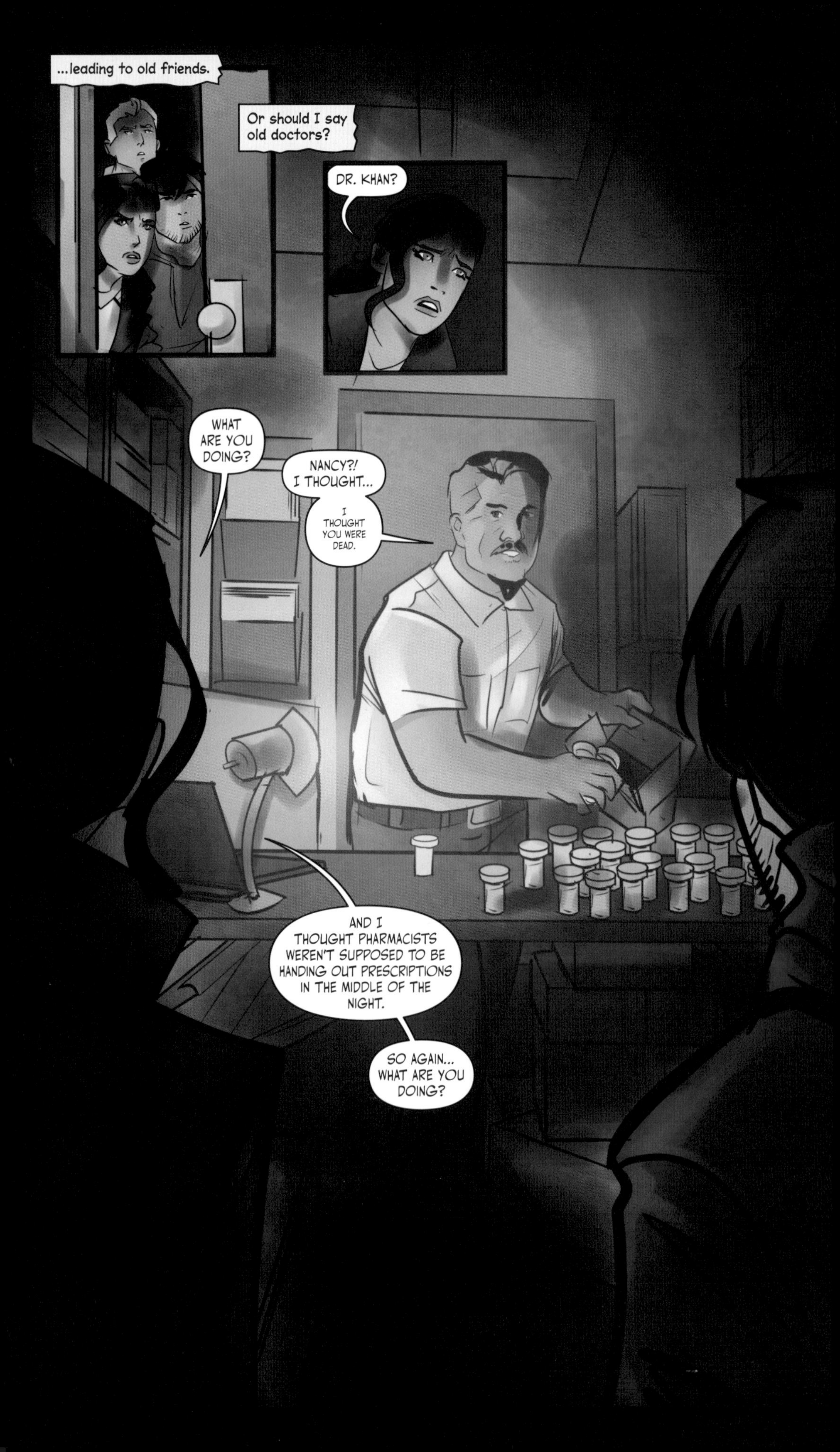
...leading to old friends.
Or should I say old doctors?
DR. KHAN?
WHAT ARE YOU DOING?
NANCY?! I THOUGHT...
I THOUGHT YOU WERE DEAD.
AND I THOUGHT PHARMACISTS WEREN'T SUPPOSED TO BE HANDING OUT PRESCRIPTIONS IN THE MIDDLE OF THE NIGHT.
SO AGAIN... WHAT ARE YOU DOING?

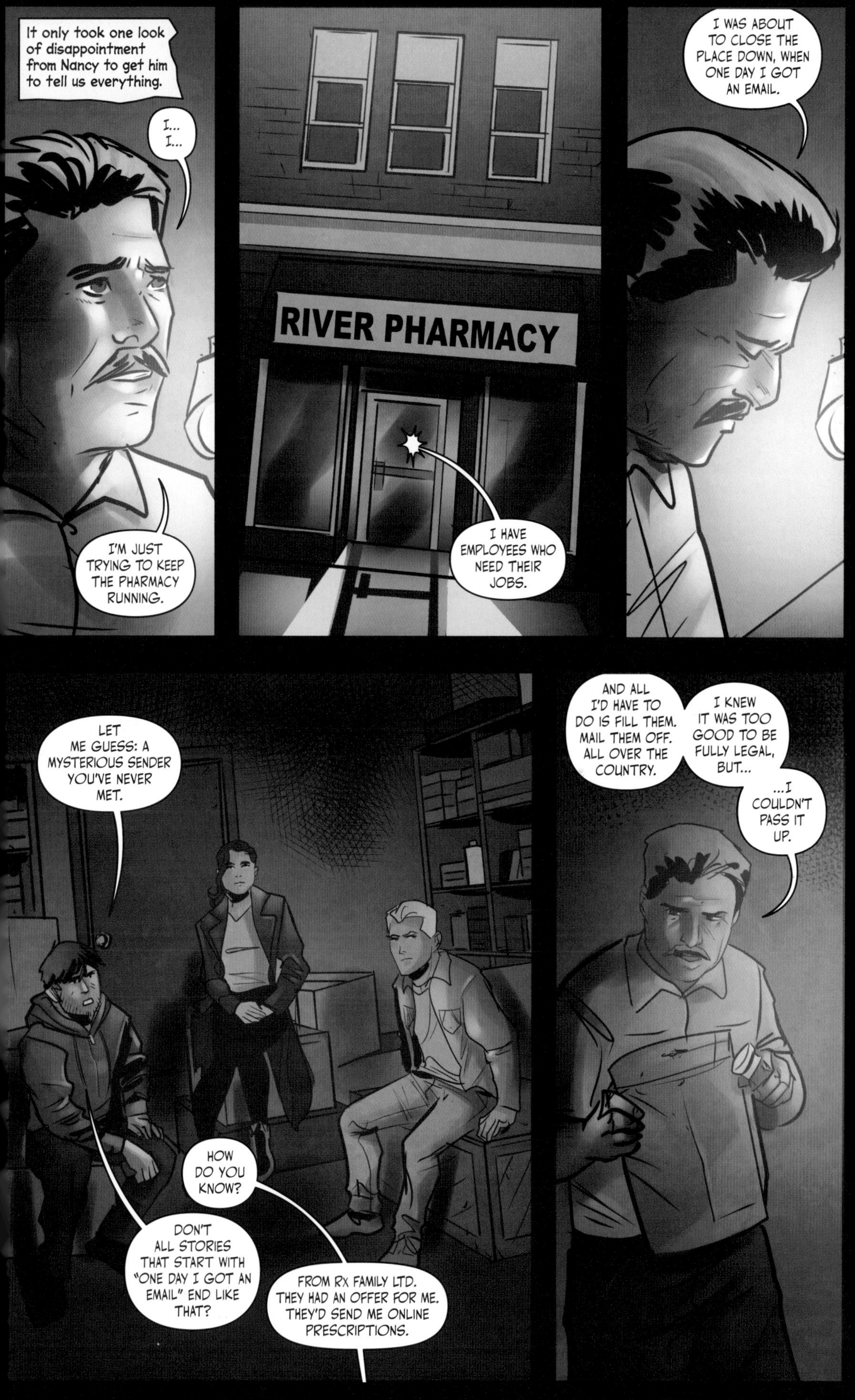
It only took one look of disappointment from Nancy to get him to tell us everything.
I... I...
I'M JUST TRYING TO KEEP THE PHARMACY RUNNING.
RIVER PHARMACY
I HAVE EMPLOYEES WHO NEED THEIR JOBS.
I WAS ABOUT TO CLOSE THE PLACE DOWN, WHEN ONE DAY I GOT AN EMAIL.
LET ME GUESS: A MYSTERIOUS SENDER YOU'VE NEVER MET.
HOW DO YOU KNOW?
DON'T ALL STORIES THAT START WITH "ONE DAY I GOT AN EMAIL" END LIKE THAT?
FROM Rx FAMILY LTD. THEY HAD AN OFFER FOR ME. THEY'D SEND ME ONLINE PRESCRIPTIONS.
AND ALL I'D HAVE TO DO IS FILL THEM. MAIL THEM OFF. ALL OVER THE COUNTRY.
I KNEW IT WAS TOO GOOD TO BE FULLY LEGAL, BUT...
...I COULDN'T PASS IT UP.

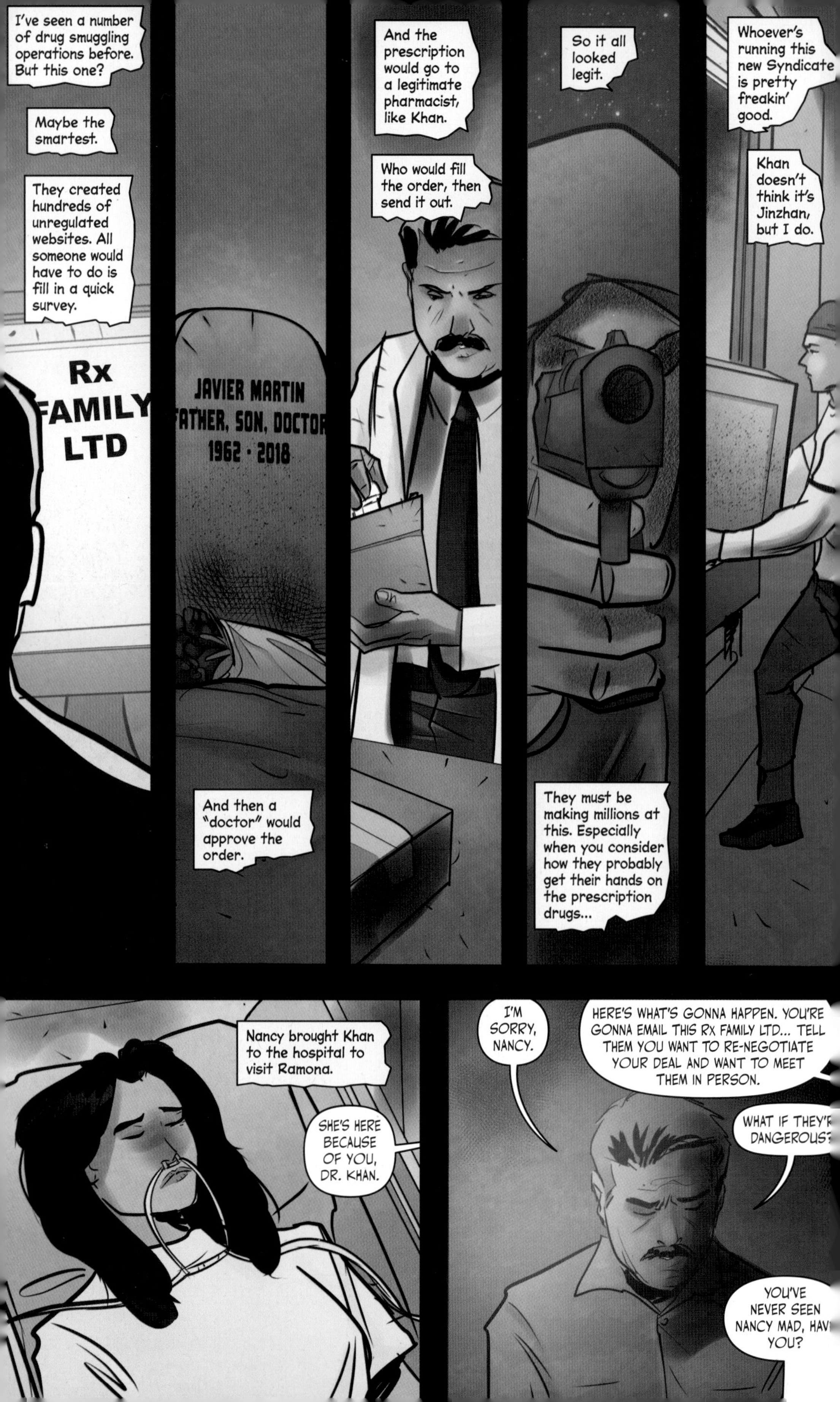
I've seen a number of drug smuggling operations before. But this one?
Maybe the smartest.
They created hundreds of unregulated websites. All someone would have to do is fill in a quick survey.
Rx FAMILY LTD
JAVIER MARTIN
FATHER, SON, DOCTOR
1962 - 2018
And then a "doctor" would approve the order.
And the prescription would go to a legitimate pharmacist, like Khan.
Who would fill the order, then send it out.
So it all looked legit.
They must be making millions at this. Especially when you consider how they probably get their hands on the prescription drugs...
Whoever's running this new Syndicate is pretty freakin' good.
Khan doesn't think it's Jinzhan, but I do.
Nancy brought Khan to the hospital to visit Ramona.
SHE'S HERE BECAUSE OF YOU, DR. KHAN.
I'M SORRY, NANCY.
HERE'S WHAT'S GONNA HAPPEN. YOU'RE GONNA EMAIL THIS Rx FAMILY LTD... TELL THEM YOU WANT TO RE-NEGOTIATE YOUR DEAL AND WANT TO MEET THEM IN PERSON.
YOU'VE NEVER SEEN NANCY MAD, HAV YOU?

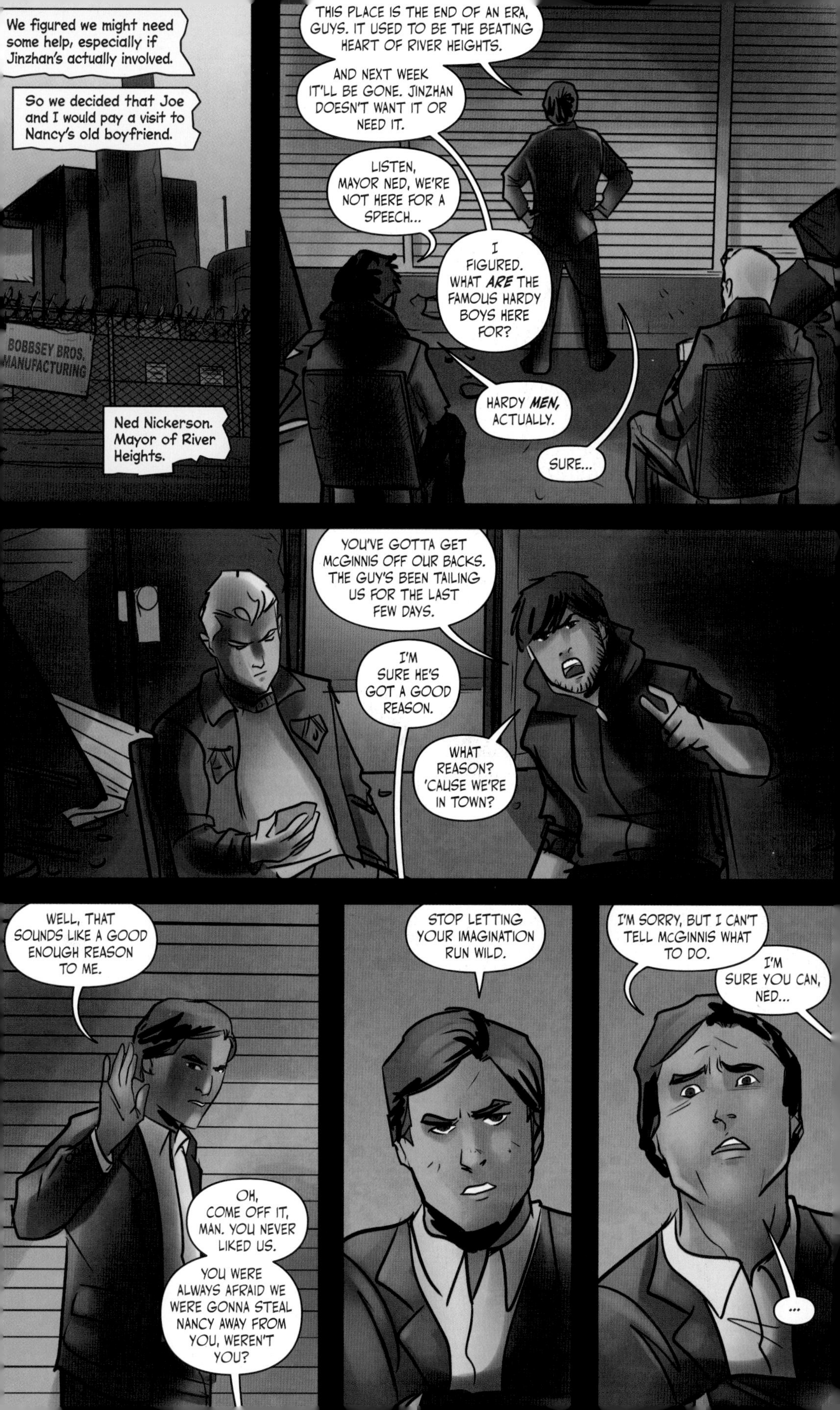

We figured we might need some help, especially if Jinzhan's actually involved.
So we decided that Joe and I would pay a visit to Nancy's old boyfriend.
BOBBSEY BROS. MANUFACTURING
Ned Nickerson. Mayor of River Heights.
THIS PLACE IS THE END OF AN ERA, GUYS. IT USED TO BE THE BEATING HEART OF RIVER HEIGHTS.
AND NEXT WEEK IT'LL BE GONE. JINZHAN DOESN'T WANT IT OR NEED IT.
LISTEN, MAYOR NED, WE'RE NOT HERE FOR A SPEECH...
I FIGURED. WHAT ARE THE FAMOUS HARDY BOYS HERE FOR?
HARDY MEN, ACTUALLY.
SURE...
YOU'VE GOTTA GET McGINNIS OFF OUR BACKS. THE GUY'S BEEN TAILING US FOR THE LAST FEW DAYS.
I'M SURE HE'S GOT A GOOD REASON.
WHAT REASON? 'CAUSE WE'RE IN TOWN?
WELL, THAT SOUNDS LIKE A GOOD ENOUGH REASON TO ME.
OH, COME OFF IT, MAN. YOU NEVER LIKED US.
YOU WERE ALWAYS AFRAID WE WERE GONNA STEAL NANCY AWAY FROM YOU, WEREN'T YOU?
STOP LETTING YOUR IMAGINATION RUN WILD.
I'M SORRY, BUT I CAN'T TELL McGINNIS WHAT TO DO.
I'M SURE YOU CAN, NED...
...

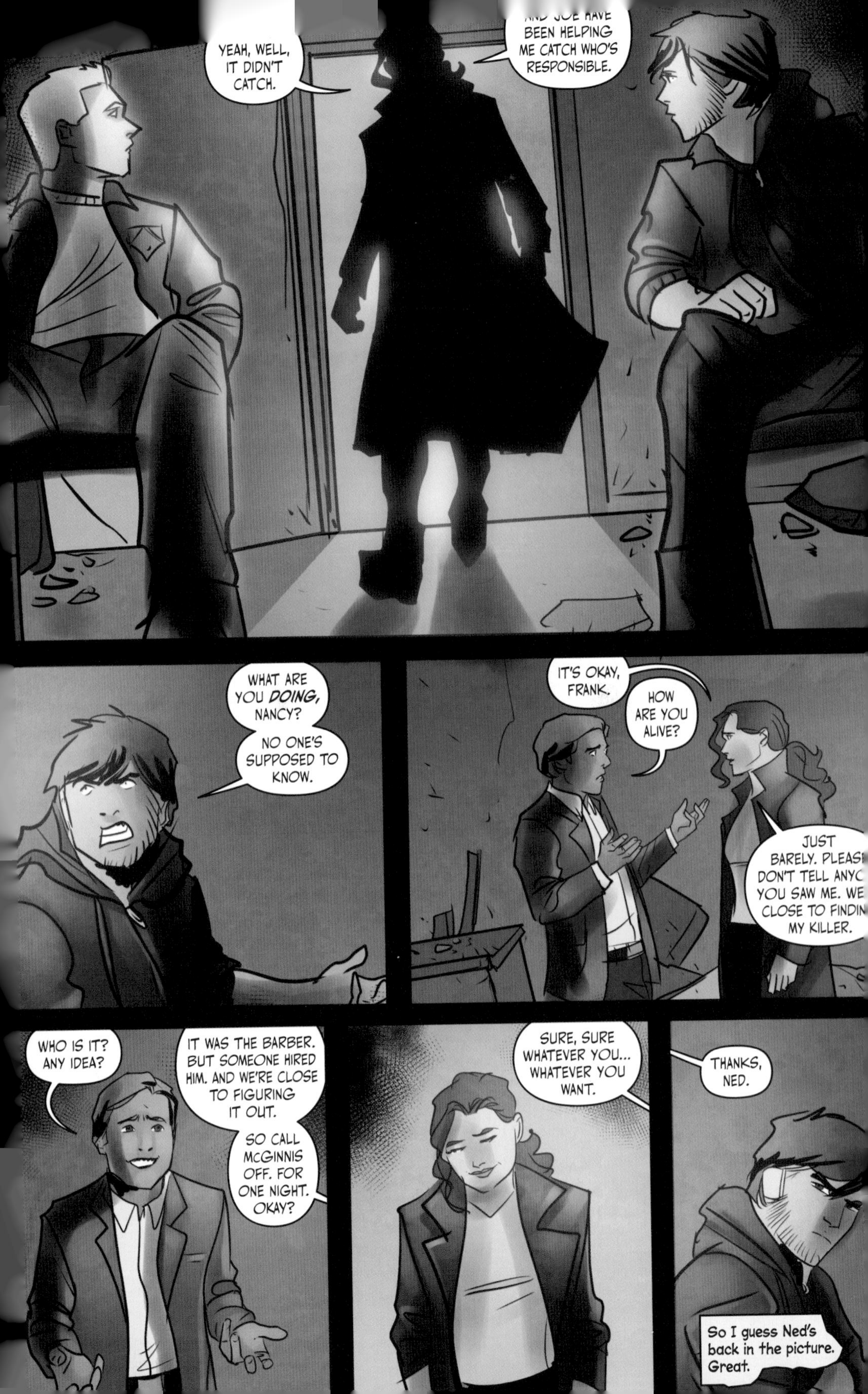
YEAH, WELL, IT DIDN'T CATCH.
BEEN HELPING ME CATCH WHO'S RESPONSIBLE.
WHAT ARE YOU *DOING*, NANCY?
NO ONE'S SUPPOSED TO KNOW.
IT'S OKAY, FRANK.
HOW ARE YOU ALIVE?
JUST BARELY. PLEAS
DON'T TELL ANYC
YOU SAW ME. WE
CLOSE TO FINDIN
MY KILLER.
WHO IS IT? ANY IDEA?
IT WAS THE BARBER. BUT SOMEONE HIRED HIM. AND WE'RE CLOSE TO FIGURING IT OUT.
SO CALL MCGINNIS OFF. FOR ONE NIGHT. OKAY?
SURE, SURE WHATEVER YOU... WHATEVER YOU WANT.
THANKS, NED.
So I guess Ned's back in the picture. Great.

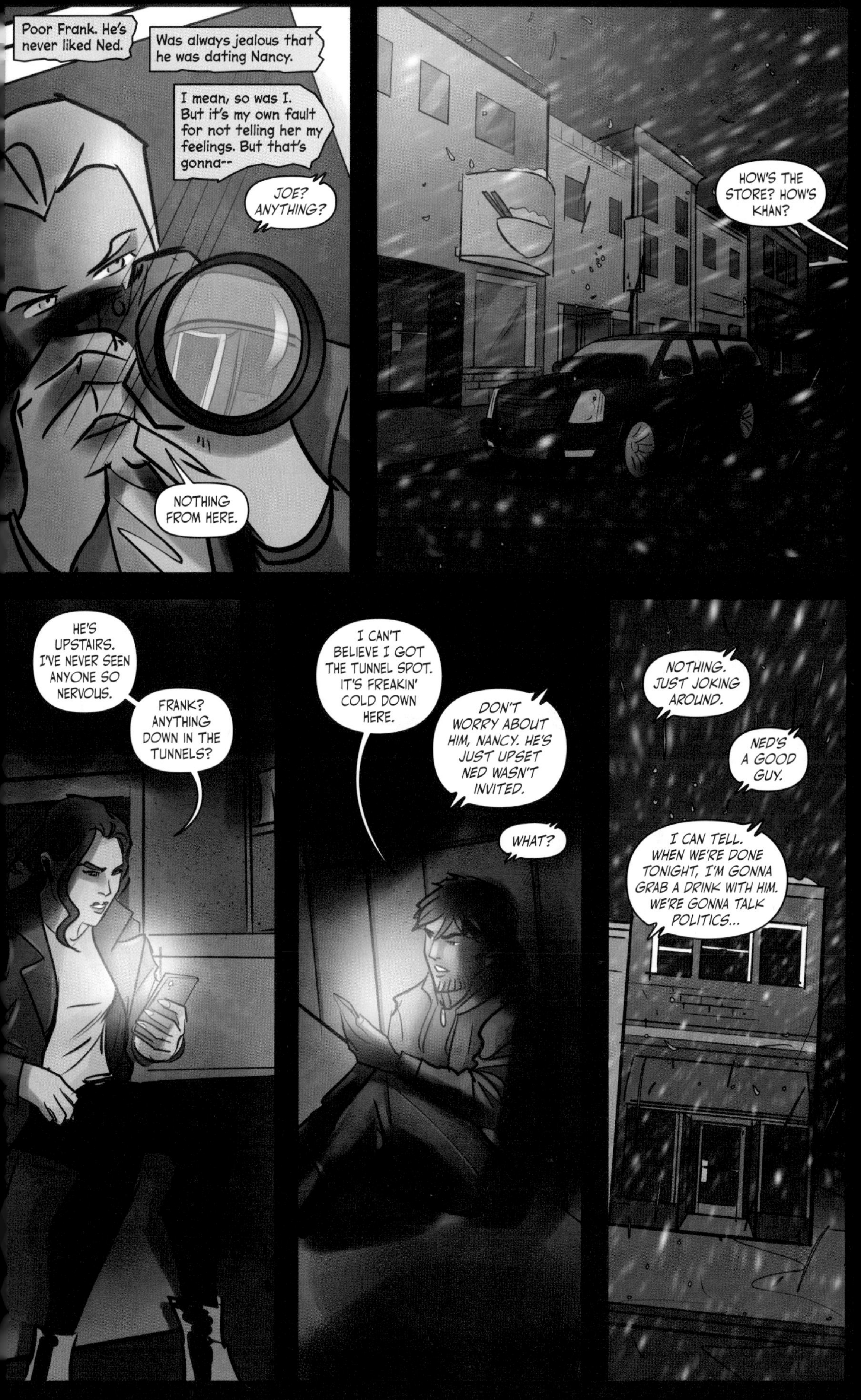
Poor Frank. He's never liked Ned.
Was always jealous that he was dating Nancy.
I mean, so was I. But it's my own fault for not telling her my feelings. But that's gonna--
JOE? ANYTHING?
NOTHING FROM HERE.
HOW'S THE STORE? HOW'S KHAN?
HE'S UPSTAIRS. I'VE NEVER SEEN ANYONE SO NERVOUS.
FRANK? ANYTHING DOWN IN THE TUNNELS?
I CAN'T BELIEVE I GOT THE TUNNEL SPOT. IT'S FREAKIN' COLD DOWN HERE.
DON'T WORRY ABOUT HIM, NANCY. HE'S JUST UPSET NED WASN'T INVITED.
WHAT?
NOTHING. JUST JOKING AROUND.
NED'S A GOOD GUY.
I CAN TELL. WHEN WE'RE DONE TONIGHT, I'M GONNA GRAB A DRINK WITH HIM. WE'RE GONNA TALK POLITICS...

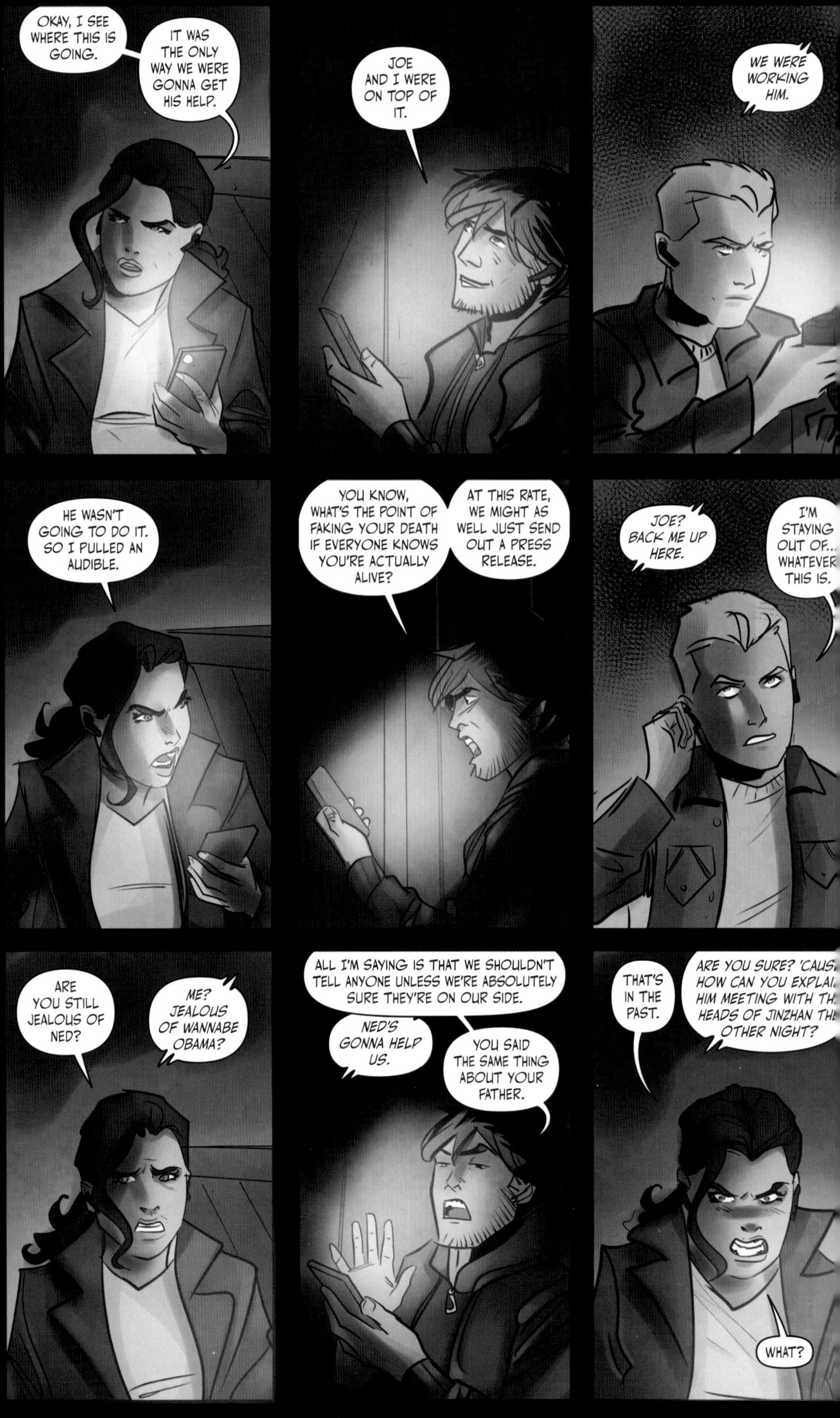

OKAY, I SEE WHERE THIS IS GOING.
IT WAS THE ONLY WAY WE WERE GONNA GET HIS HELP.
JOE AND I WERE ON TOP OF IT.
WE WERE WORKING HIM.
HE WASN'T GOING TO DO IT. SO I PULLED AN AUDIBLE.
YOU KNOW, WHAT'S THE POINT OF FAKING YOUR DEATH IF EVERYONE KNOWS YOU'RE ACTUALLY ALIVE?
AT THIS RATE, WE MIGHT AS WELL JUST SEND OUT A PRESS RELEASE.
JOE? BACK ME UP HERE.
I'M STAYING OUT OF... WHATEVER THIS IS.
ARE YOU STILL JEALOUS OF NED?
ME? JEALOUS OF WANNABE OBAMA?
ALL I'M SAYING IS THAT WE SHOULDN'T TELL ANYONE UNLESS WE'RE ABSOLUTELY SURE THEY'RE ON OUR SIDE.
NED'S GONNA HELP US.
YOU SAID THE SAME THING ABOUT YOUR FATHER.
THAT'S IN THE PAST.
ARE YOU SURE? 'CAUS HOW CAN YOU EXPLAI HIM MEETING WITH TH HEADS OF JINZHAN TH OTHER NIGHT?
WHAT?

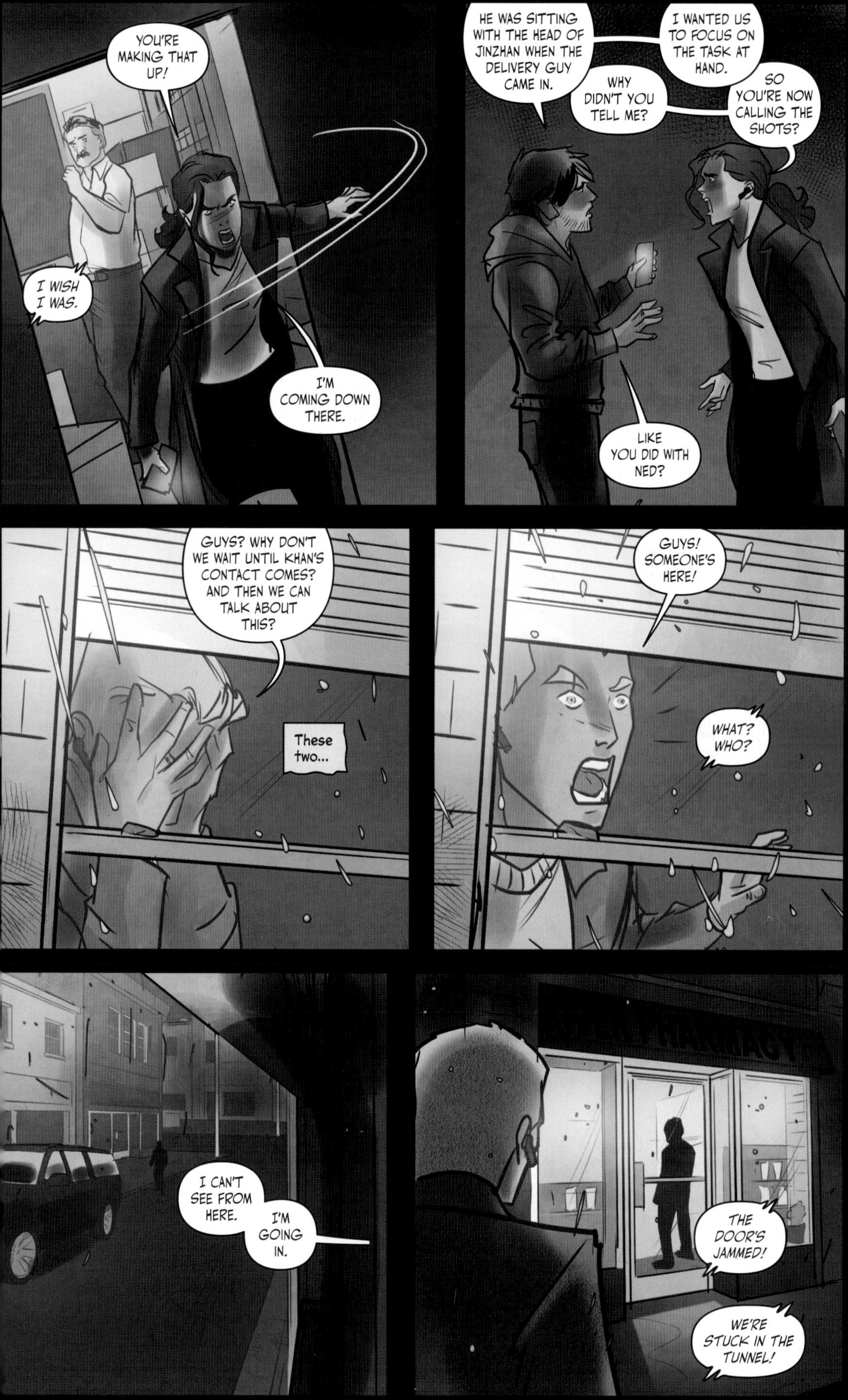

YOU'RE MAKING THAT UP!
I WISH I WAS.
I'M COMING DOWN THERE.
HE WAS SITTING WITH THE HEAD OF JINZHAN WHEN THE DELIVERY GUY CAME IN.
WHY DIDN'T YOU TELL ME?
I WANTED US TO FOCUS ON THE TASK AT HAND.
SO YOU'RE NOW CALLING THE SHOTS?
LIKE YOU DID WITH NED?
GUYS? WHY DON'T WE WAIT UNTIL KHAN'S CONTACT COMES? AND THEN WE CAN TALK ABOUT THIS?
These two...
GUYS! SOMEONE'S HERE!
WHAT? WHO?
I CAN'T SEE FROM HERE.
I'M GOING IN.
THE DOOR'S JAMMED!
WE'RE STUCK IN THE TUNNEL!

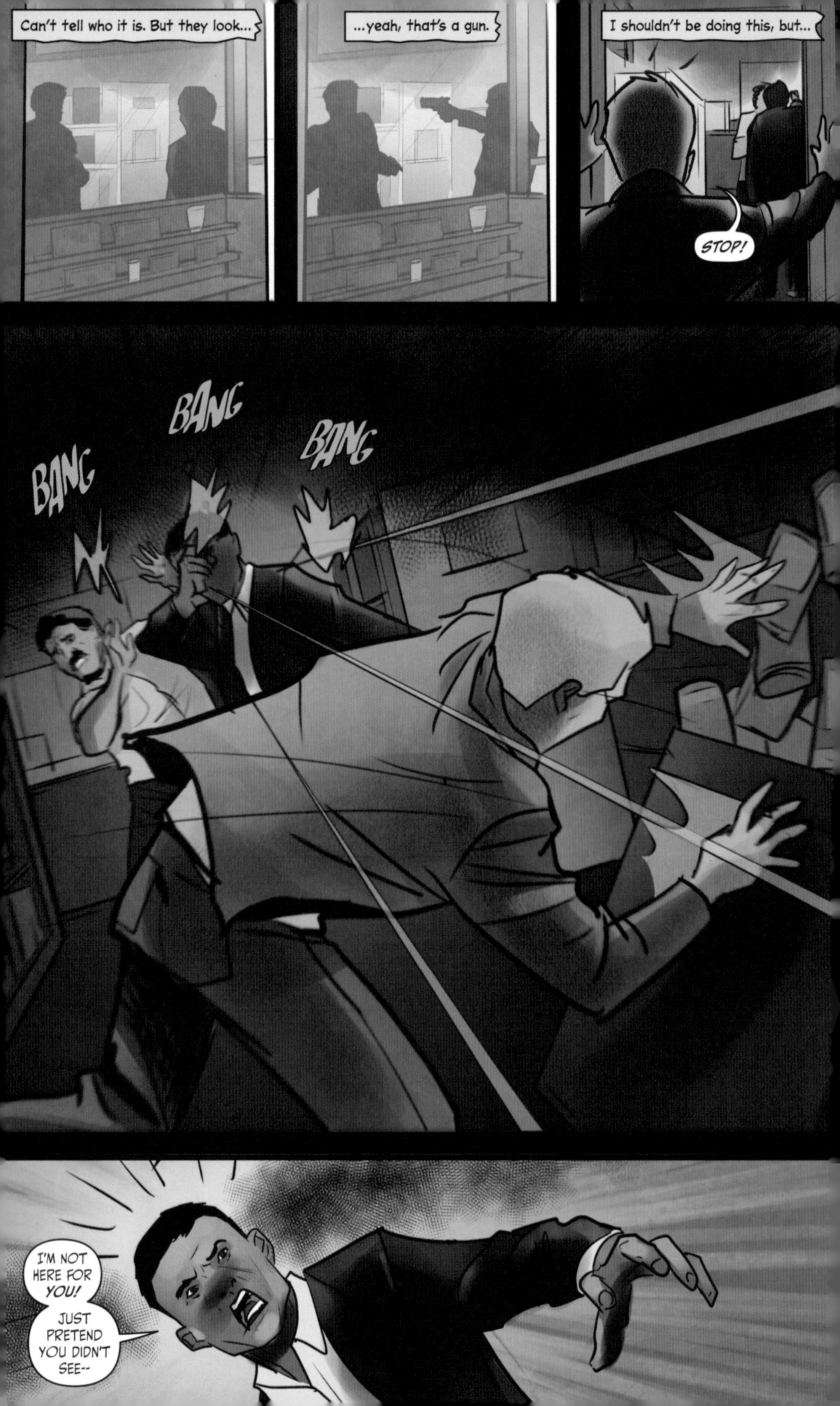

Can't tell who it is. But they look...
...yeah, that's a gun.
I shouldn't be doing this, but...
STOP!
BANG
BANG
BANG
I'M NOT HERE FOR YOU!
JUST PRETEND YOU DIDN'T SEE--

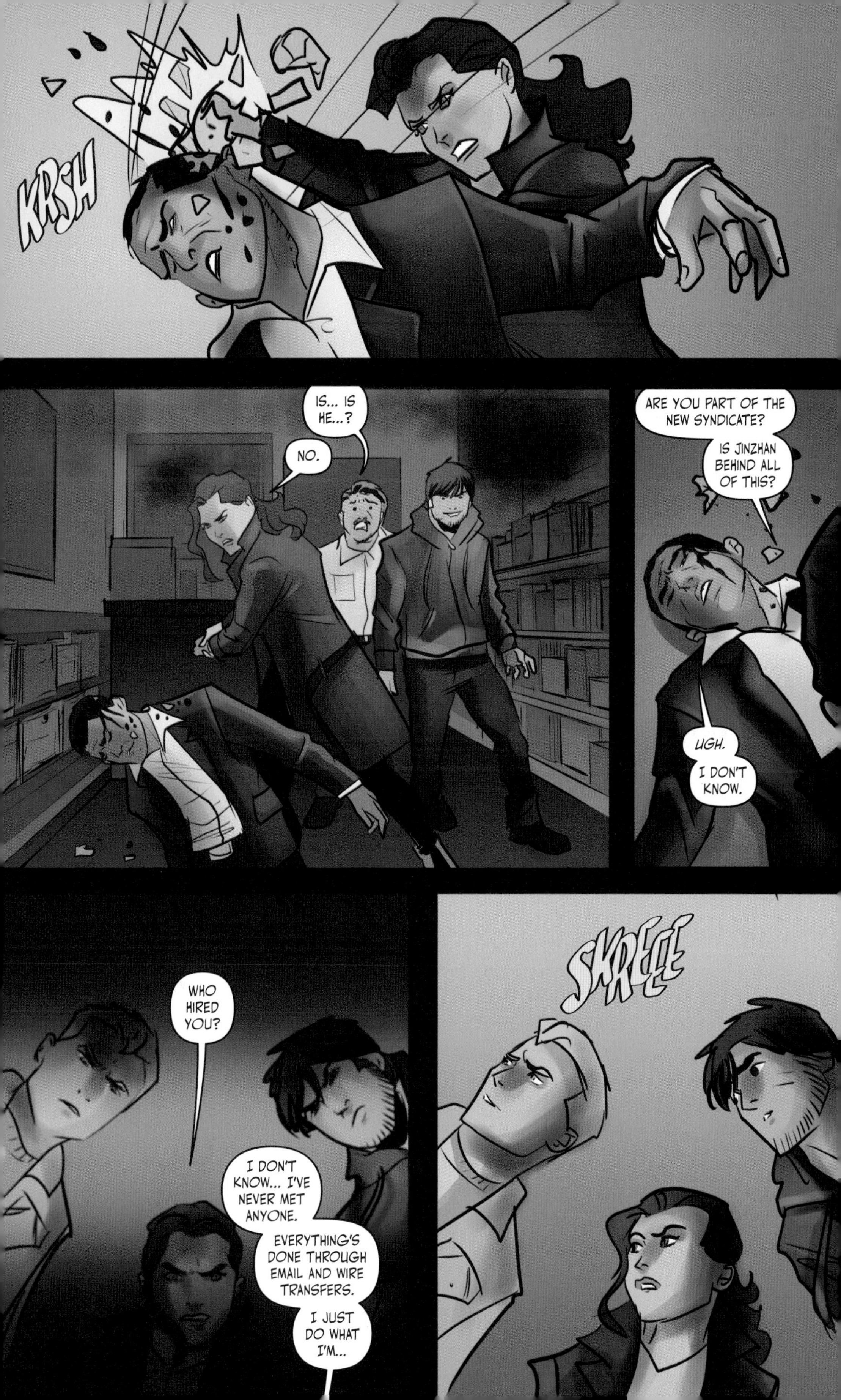
KRSH
IS... IS HE...?
NO.
ARE YOU PART OF THE NEW SYNDICATE?
IS JINZHAN BEHIND ALL OF THIS?
UGH.
I DON'T KNOW.
WHO HIRED YOU?
I DON'T KNOW... I'VE NEVER MET ANYONE.
EVERYTHING'S DONE THROUGH EMAIL AND WIRE TRANSFERS.
I JUST DO WHAT I'M...
SKREEEE

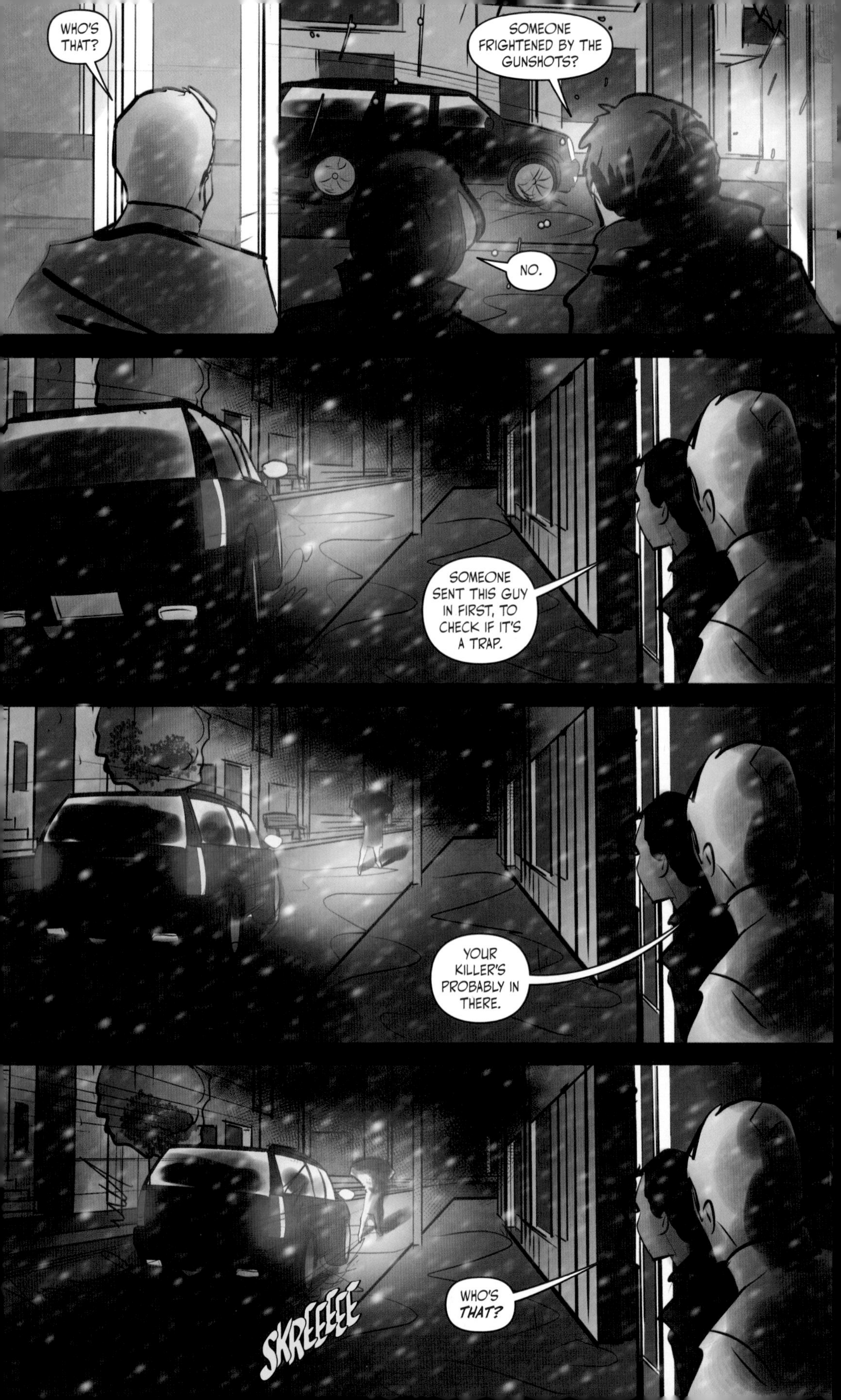
WHO'S THAT?
SOMEONE FRIGHTENED BY THE GUNSHOTS?
NO.
SOMEONE SENT THIS GUY IN FIRST, TO CHECK IF IT'S A TRAP.
YOUR KILLER'S PROBABLY IN THERE.
WHO'S *THAT?*
SKREEEEEE

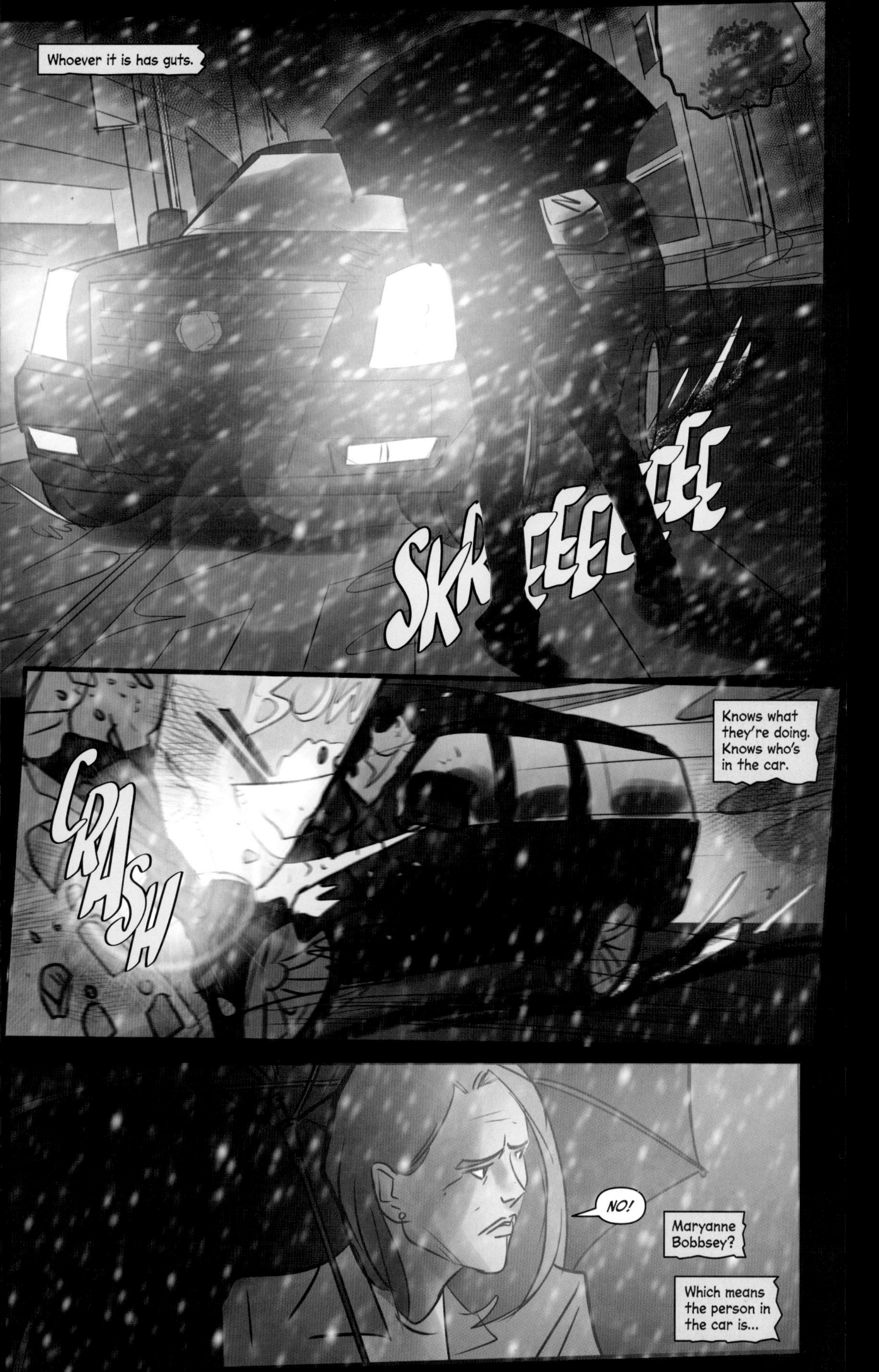
Whoever it is has guts.
SKREEEEEEE
CRASH
Knows what they're doing. Knows who's in the car.
NO!
Maryanne Bobbsey?
Which means the person in the car is...

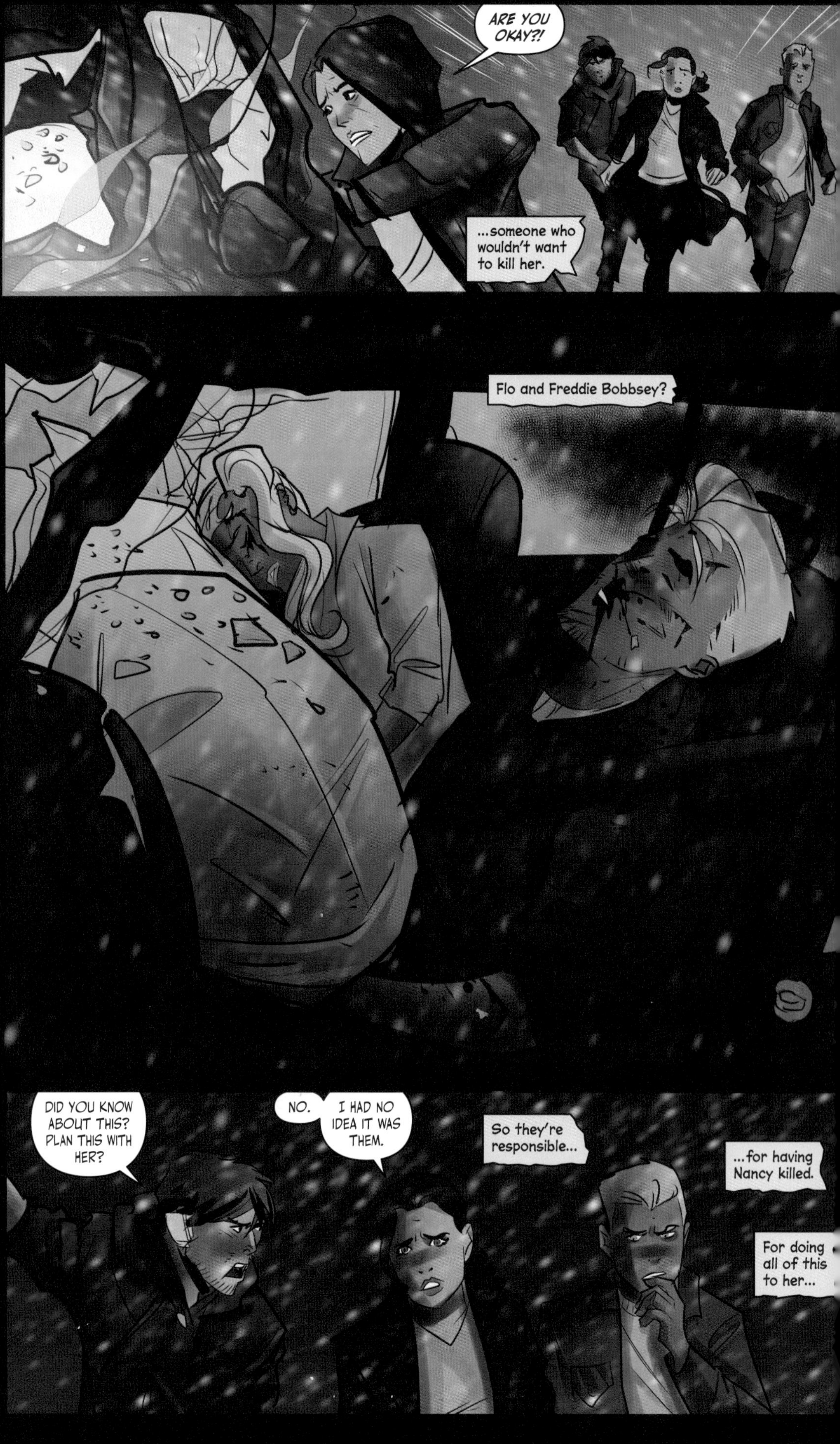
ARE YOU OKAY?!
...someone who wouldn't want to kill her.
Flo and Freddie Bobbsey?
DID YOU KNOW ABOUT THIS? PLAN THIS WITH HER?
NO.
I HAD NO IDEA IT WAS THEM.
So they're responsible...
...for having Nancy killed.
For doing all of this to her...

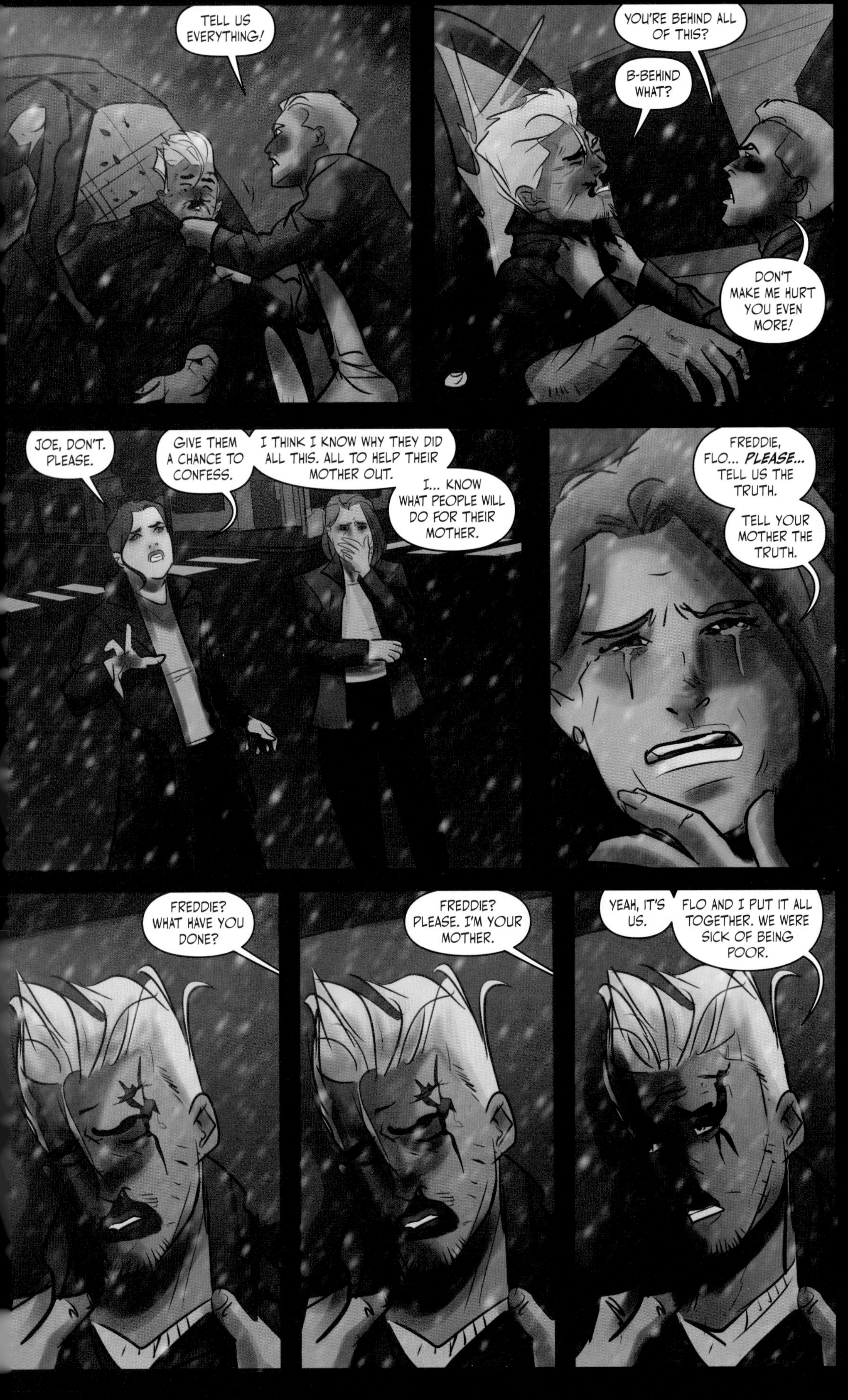
TELL US EVERYTHING!
YOU'RE BEHIND ALL OF THIS?
B-BEHIND WHAT?
DON'T MAKE ME HURT YOU EVEN MORE!
JOE, DON'T. PLEASE.
GIVE THEM A CHANCE TO CONFESS.
I THINK I KNOW WHY THEY DID ALL THIS. ALL TO HELP THEIR MOTHER OUT.
I... KNOW WHAT PEOPLE WILL DO FOR THEIR MOTHER.
FREDDIE, FLO... PLEASE... TELL US THE TRUTH.
TELL YOUR MOTHER THE TRUTH.
FREDDIE? WHAT HAVE YOU DONE?
FREDDIE? PLEASE. I'M YOUR MOTHER.
YEAH, IT'S US.
FLO AND I PUT IT ALL TOGETHER. WE WERE SICK OF BEING POOR.

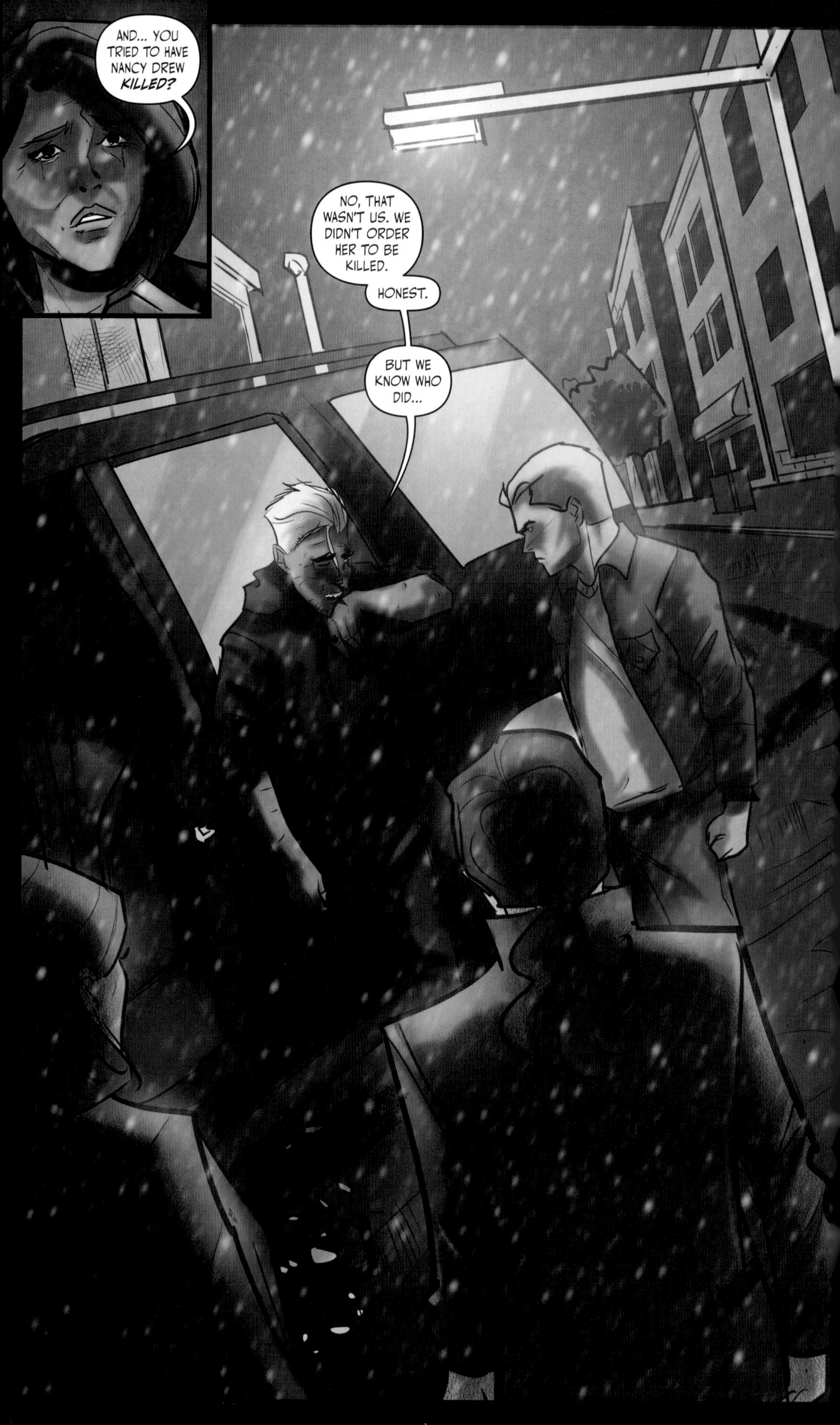
AND... YOU TRIED TO HAVE NANCY DREW KILLED?
NO, THAT WASN'T US. WE DIDN'T ORDER HER TO BE KILLED.
HONEST.
BUT WE KNOW WHO DID...

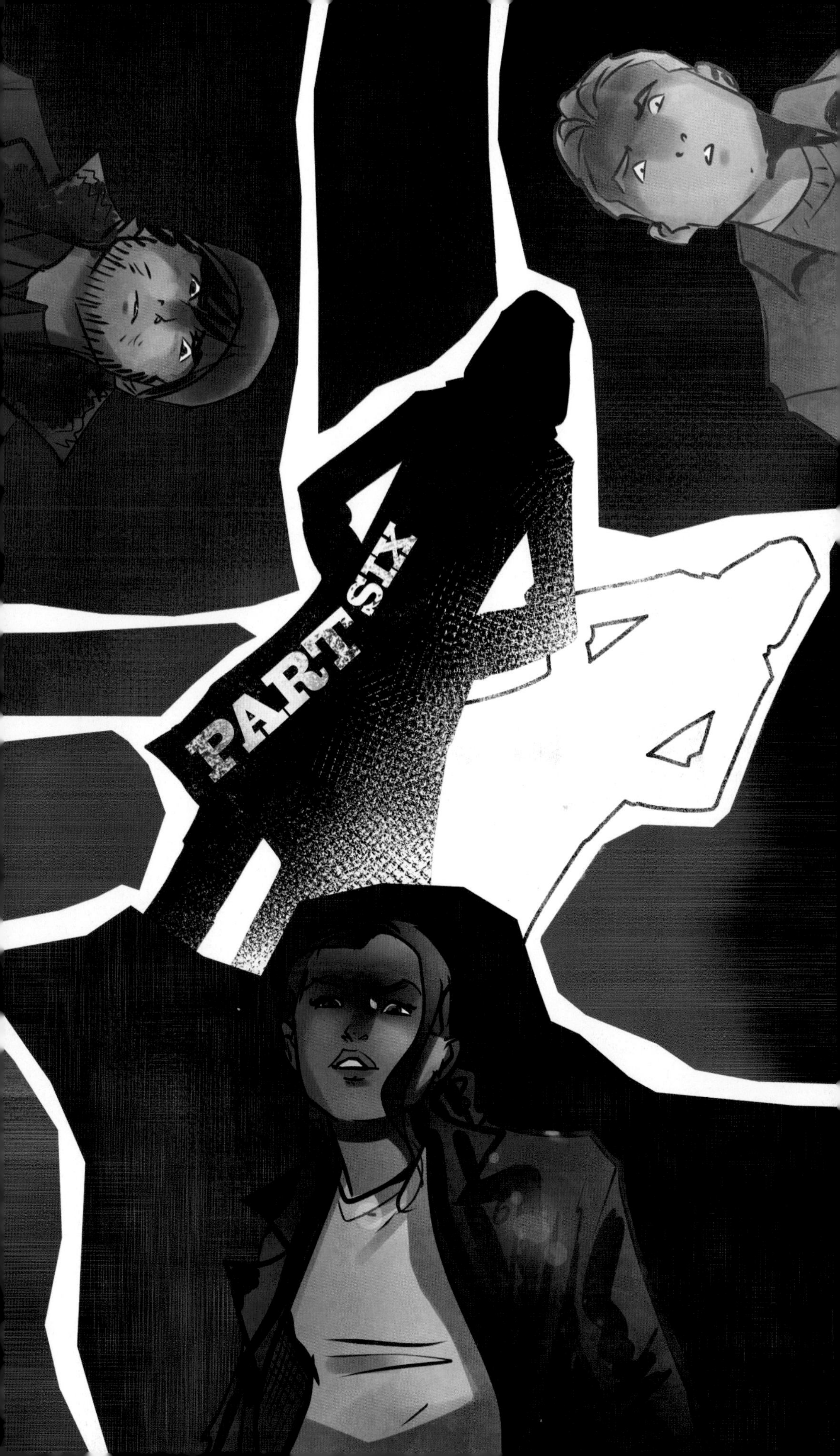
PART SIX

PART SIX COVER ART BY **JOE EISMA**

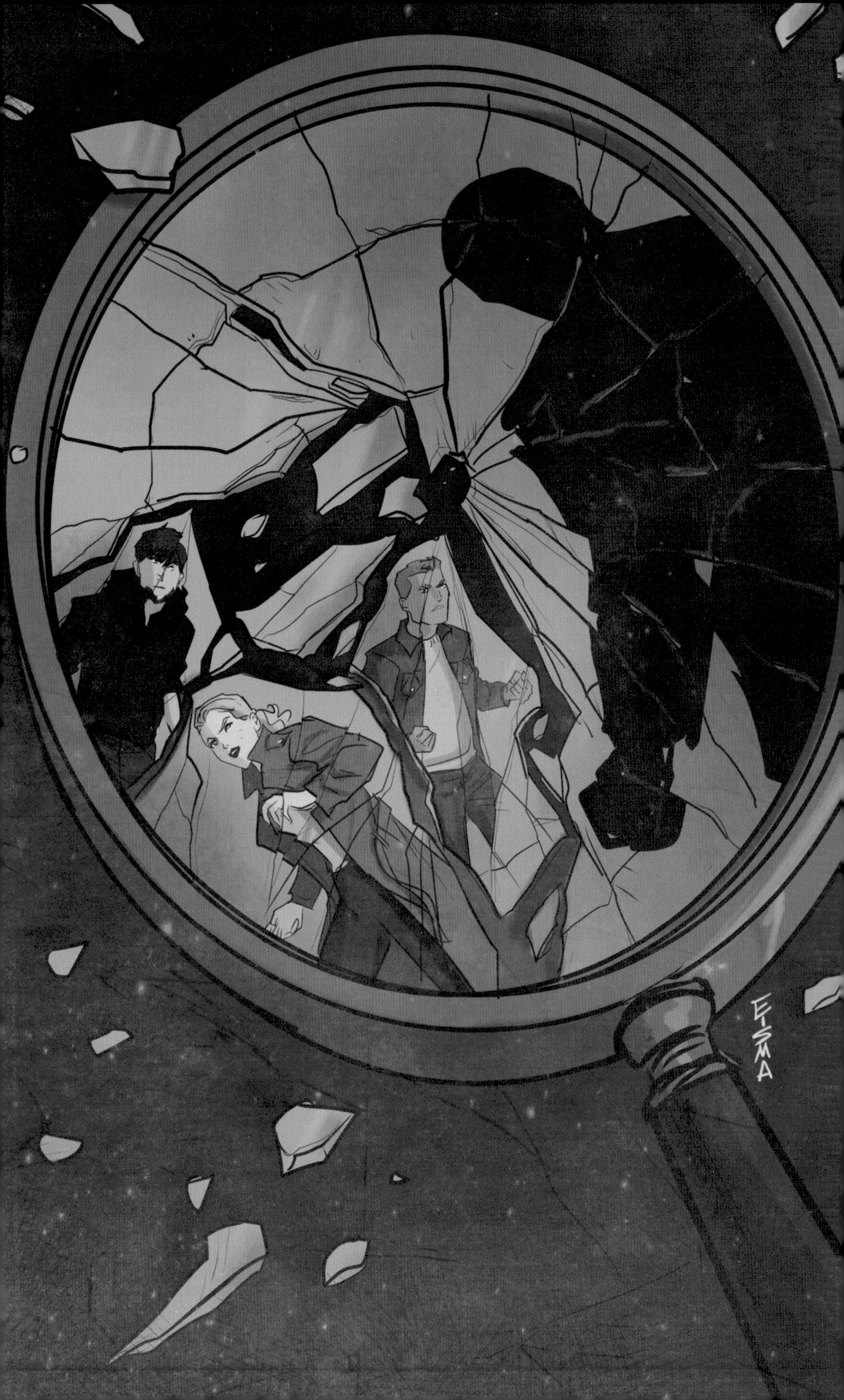
EISMA

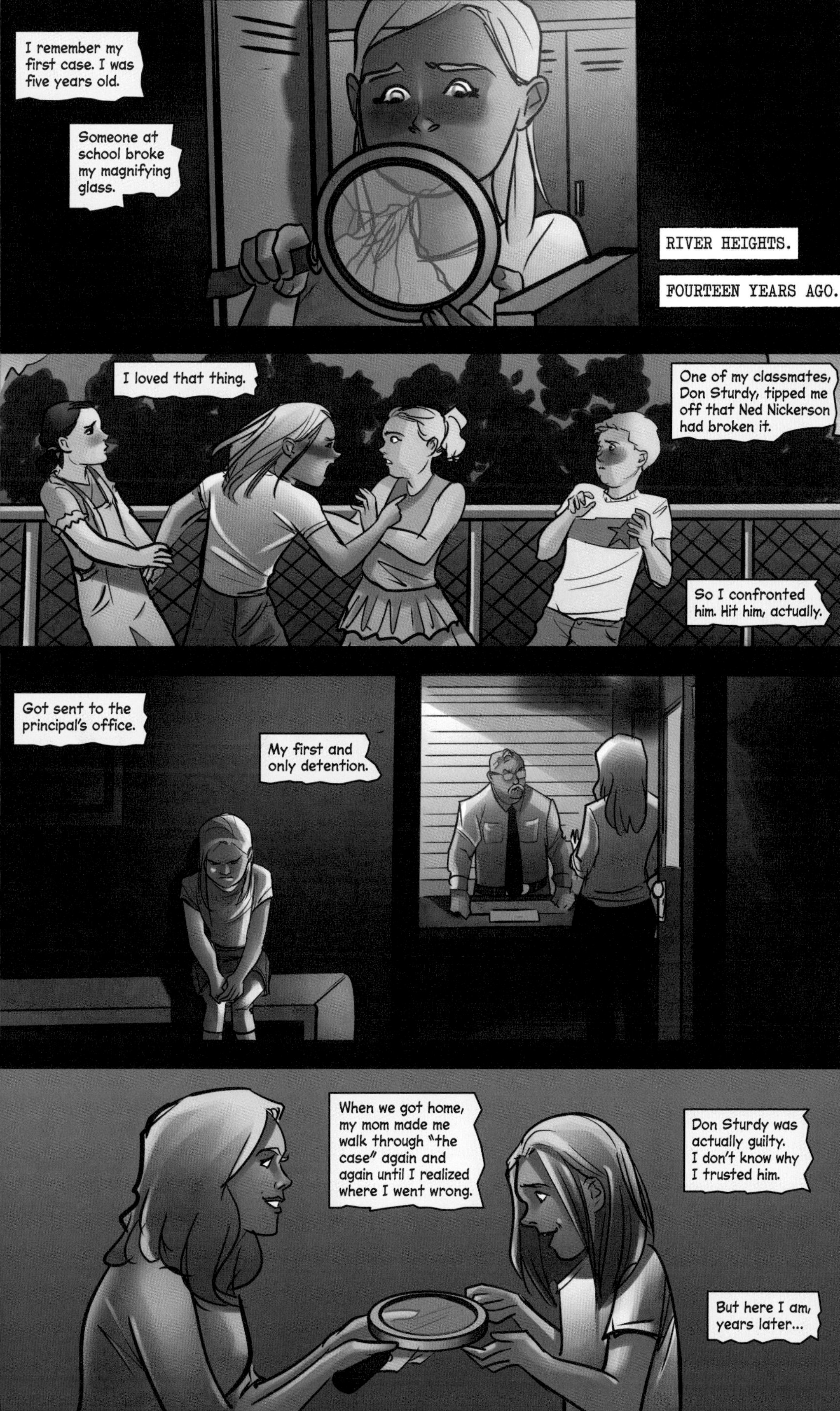
I remember my first case. I was five years old.
Someone at school broke my magnifying glass.
RIVER HEIGHTS.
FOURTEEN YEARS AGO.
I loved that thing.
One of my classmates, Don Sturdy, tipped me off that Ned Nickerson had broken it.
So I confronted him. Hit him, actually.
Got sent to the principal's office.
My first and only detention.
When we got home, my mom made me walk through "the case" again and again until I realized where I went wrong.
Don Sturdy was actually guilty. I don't know why I trusted him.
But here I am, years later...

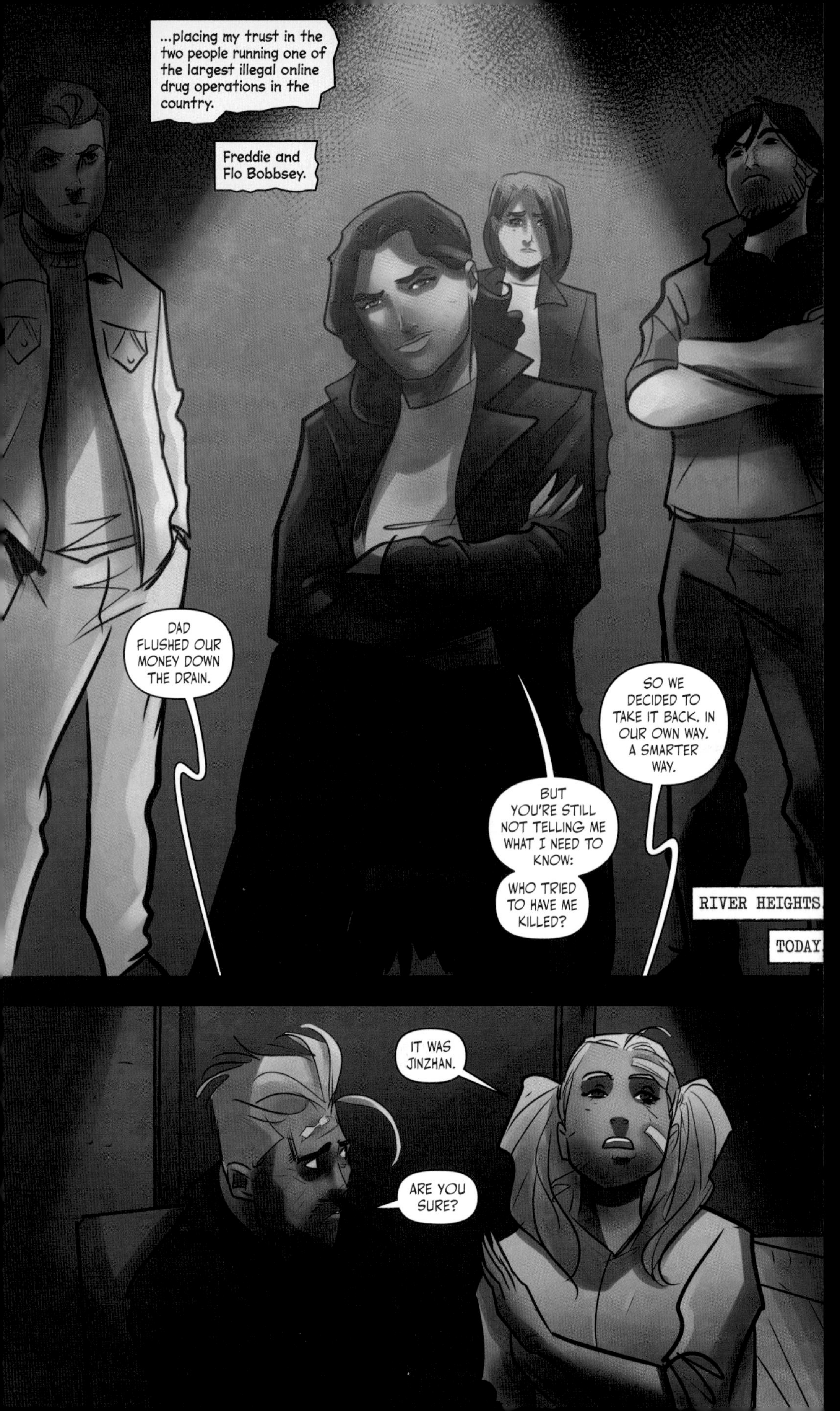
...placing my trust in the two people running one of the largest illegal online drug operations in the country.
Freddie and Flo Bobbsey.
DAD FLUSHED OUR MONEY DOWN THE DRAIN.
SO WE DECIDED TO TAKE IT BACK. IN OUR OWN WAY. A SMARTER WAY.
BUT YOU'RE STILL NOT TELLING ME WHAT I NEED TO KNOW:
WHO TRIED TO HAVE ME KILLED?
RIVER HEIGHTS.
TODAY
IT WAS JINZHAN.
ARE YOU SURE?

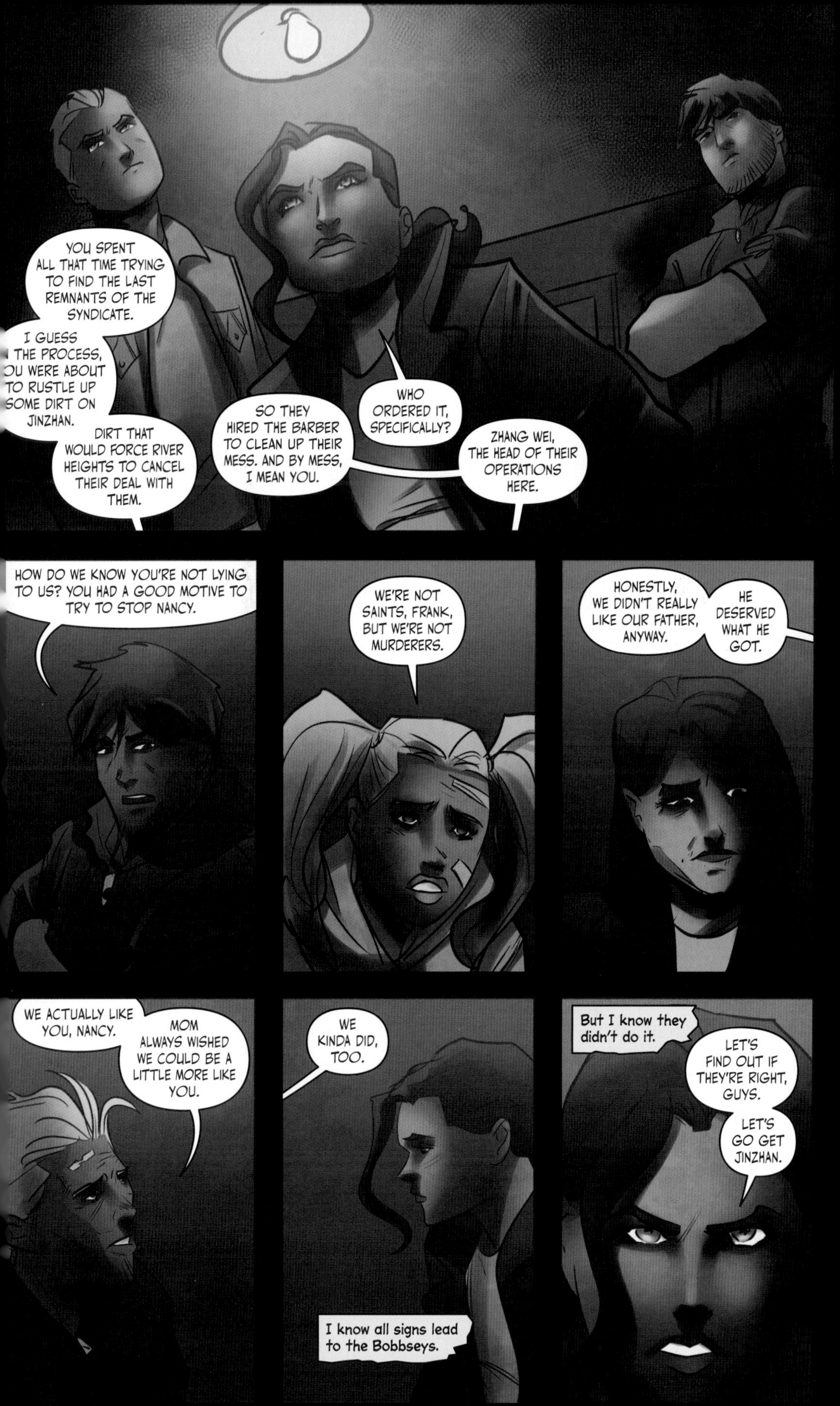

YOU SPENT ALL THAT TIME TRYING TO FIND THE LAST REMNANTS OF THE SYNDICATE.
I GUESS THE PROCESS, YOU WERE ABOUT TO RUSTLE UP SOME DIRT ON JINZHAN.
DIRT THAT WOULD FORCE RIVER HEIGHTS TO CANCEL THEIR DEAL WITH THEM.
SO THEY HIRED THE BARBER TO CLEAN UP THEIR MESS. AND BY MESS, I MEAN YOU.
WHO ORDERED IT, SPECIFICALLY?
ZHANG WEI, THE HEAD OF THEIR OPERATIONS HERE.
HOW DO WE KNOW YOU'RE NOT LYING TO US? YOU HAD A GOOD MOTIVE TO TRY TO STOP NANCY.
WE'RE NOT SAINTS, FRANK, BUT WE'RE NOT MURDERERS.
HONESTLY, WE DIDN'T REALLY LIKE OUR FATHER, ANYWAY.
HE DESERVED WHAT HE GOT.
WE ACTUALLY LIKE YOU, NANCY.
MOM ALWAYS WISHED WE COULD BE A LITTLE MORE LIKE YOU.
WE KINDA DID, TOO.
I know all signs lead to the Bobbseys.
But I know they didn't do it.
LET'S FIND OUT IF THEY'RE RIGHT, GUYS.
LET'S GO GET JINZHAN.

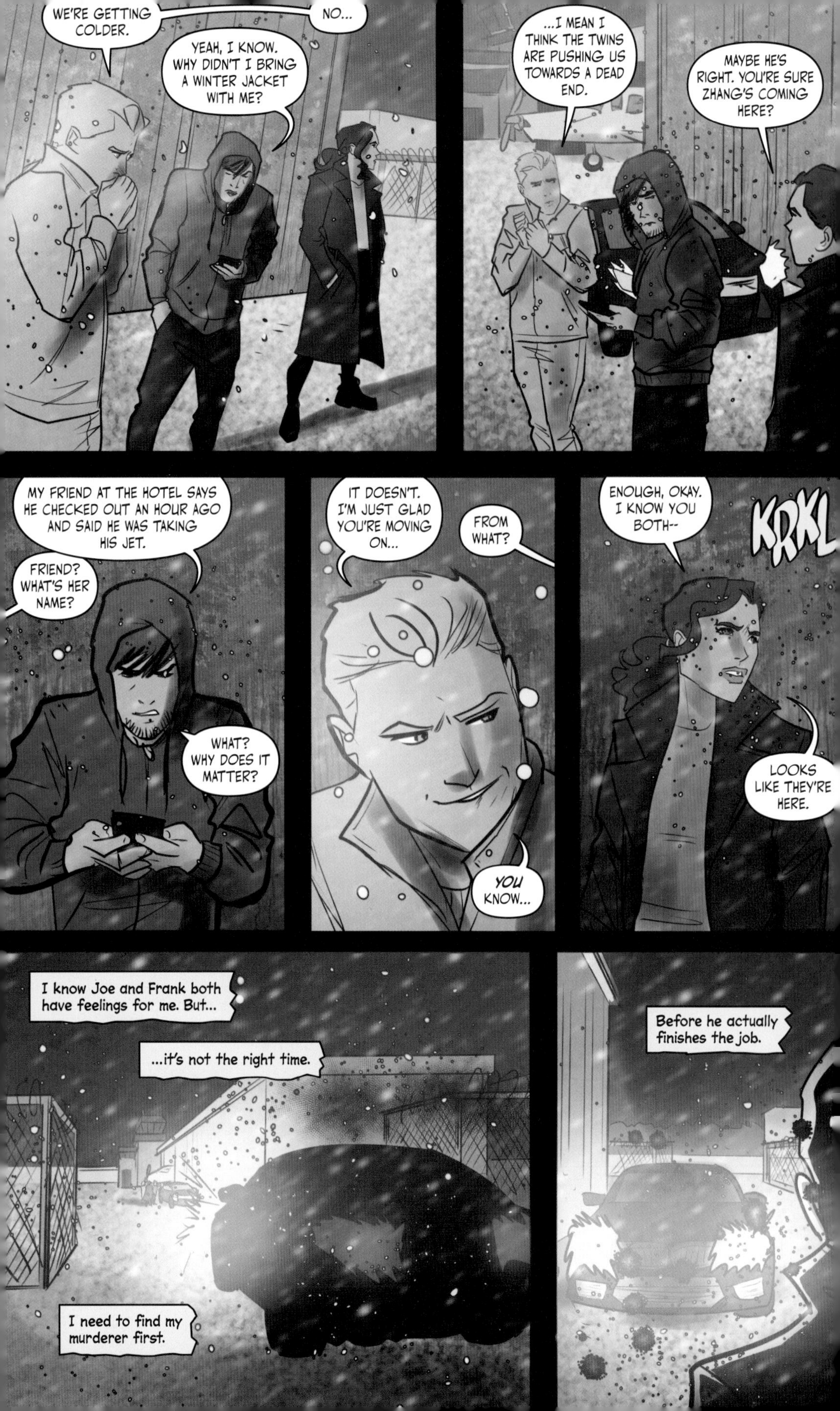
WE'RE GETTING COLDER.
NO...
YEAH, I KNOW. WHY DIDN'T I BRING A WINTER JACKET WITH ME?
...I MEAN I THINK THE TWINS ARE PUSHING US TOWARDS A DEAD END.
MAYBE HE'S RIGHT. YOU'RE SURE ZHANG'S COMING HERE?
MY FRIEND AT THE HOTEL SAYS HE CHECKED OUT AN HOUR AGO AND SAID HE WAS TAKING HIS JET.
FRIEND? WHAT'S HER NAME?
WHAT? WHY DOES IT MATTER?
IT DOESN'T. I'M JUST GLAD YOU'RE MOVING ON...
FROM WHAT?
YOU KNOW...
ENOUGH, OKAY. I KNOW YOU BOTH--
KRKL
LOOKS LIKE THEY'RE HERE.
I know Joe and Frank both have feelings for me. But...
...it's not the right time.
I need to find my murderer first.
Before he actually finishes the job.

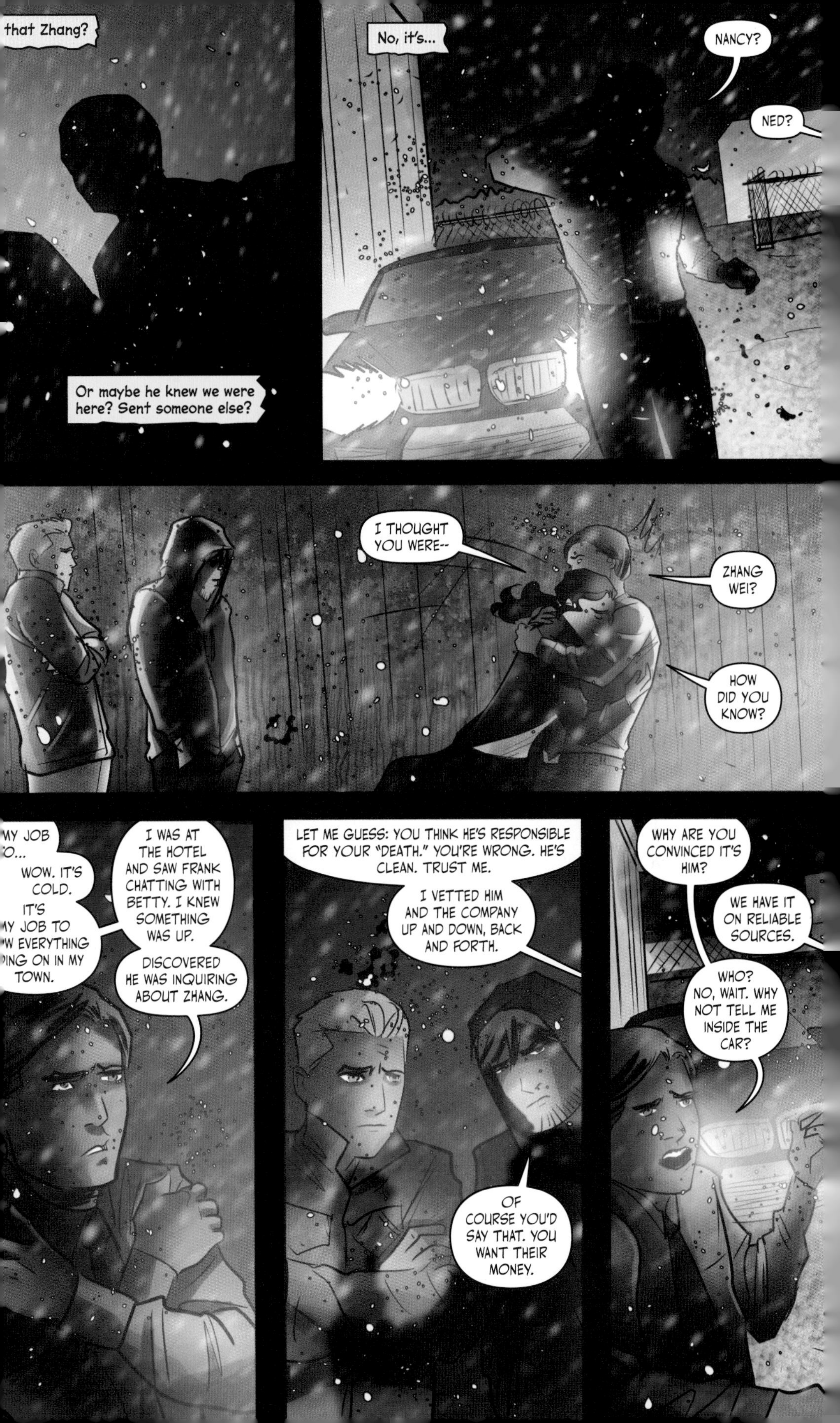
that Zhang?
Or maybe he knew we were here? Sent someone else?
No, it's...
NANCY?
NED?
I THOUGHT YOU WERE--
ZHANG WEI?
HOW DID YOU KNOW?
MY JOB
O...
WOW. IT'S COLD.
IT'S
MY JOB TO
W EVERYTHING
ING ON IN MY
TOWN.
I WAS AT THE HOTEL AND SAW FRANK CHATTING WITH BETTY. I KNEW SOMETHING WAS UP.
DISCOVERED HE WAS INQUIRING ABOUT ZHANG.
LET ME GUESS: YOU THINK HE'S RESPONSIBLE FOR YOUR "DEATH." YOU'RE WRONG. HE'S CLEAN. TRUST ME.
I VETTED HIM AND THE COMPANY UP AND DOWN, BACK AND FORTH.
OF COURSE YOU'D SAY THAT. YOU WANT THEIR MONEY.
WHY ARE YOU CONVINCED IT'S HIM?
WE HAVE IT ON RELIABLE SOURCES.
WHO? NO, WAIT. WHY NOT TELL ME INSIDE THE CAR?

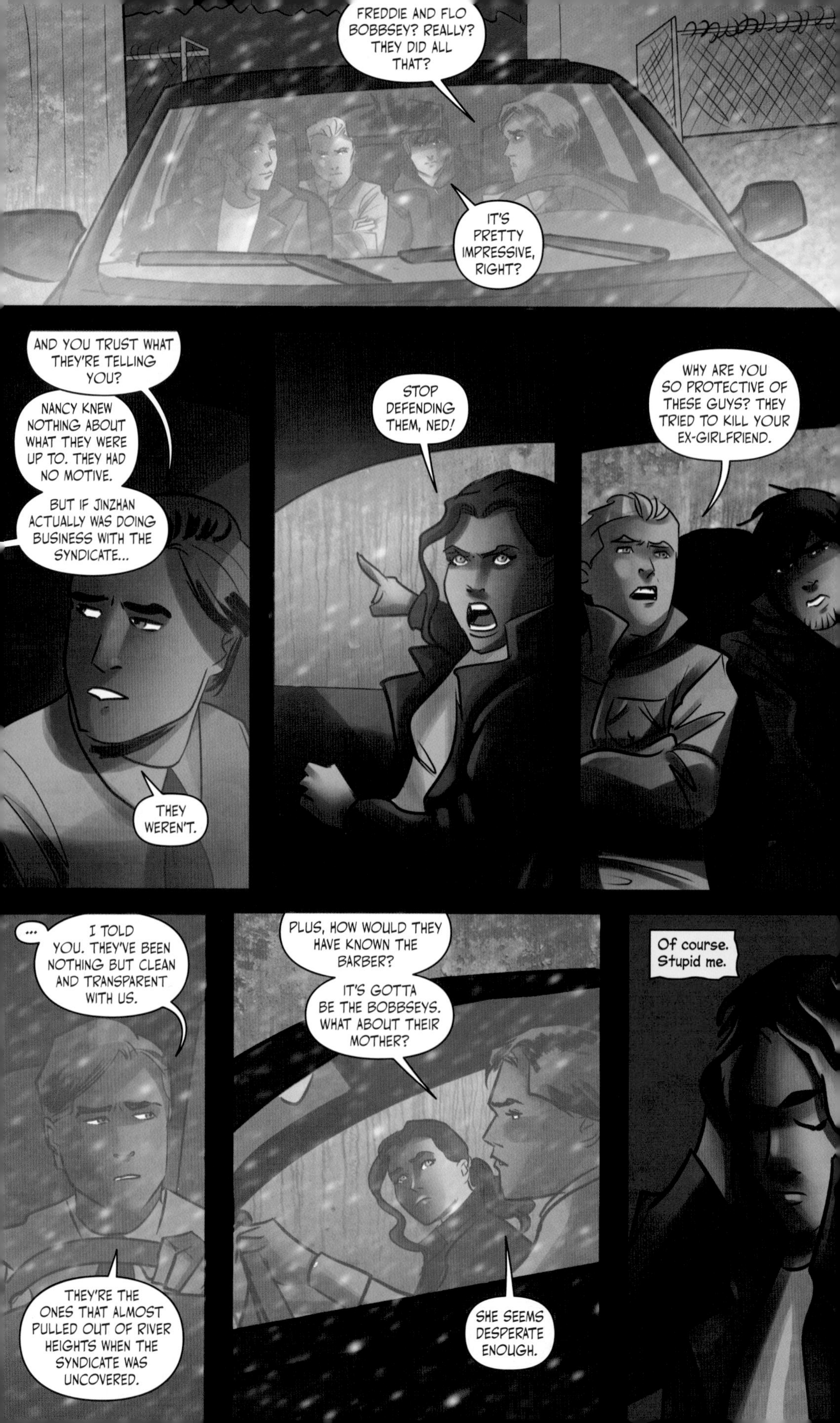
FREDDIE AND FLO BOBBSEY? REALLY? THEY DID ALL THAT?
IT'S PRETTY IMPRESSIVE, RIGHT?
AND YOU TRUST WHAT THEY'RE TELLING YOU?
NANCY KNEW NOTHING ABOUT WHAT THEY WERE UP TO. THEY HAD NO MOTIVE.
BUT IF JINZHAN ACTUALLY WAS DOING BUSINESS WITH THE SYNDICATE...
THEY WEREN'T.
STOP DEFENDING THEM, NED!
WHY ARE YOU SO PROTECTIVE OF THESE GUYS? THEY TRIED TO KILL YOUR EX-GIRLFRIEND.
...
I TOLD YOU. THEY'VE BEEN NOTHING BUT CLEAN AND TRANSPARENT WITH US.
THEY'RE THE ONES THAT ALMOST PULLED OUT OF RIVER HEIGHTS WHEN THE SYNDICATE WAS UNCOVERED.
PLUS, HOW WOULD THEY HAVE KNOWN THE BARBER?
IT'S GOTTA BE THE BOBBSEYS. WHAT ABOUT THEIR MOTHER?
SHE SEEMS DESPERATE ENOUGH.
Of course. Stupid me.

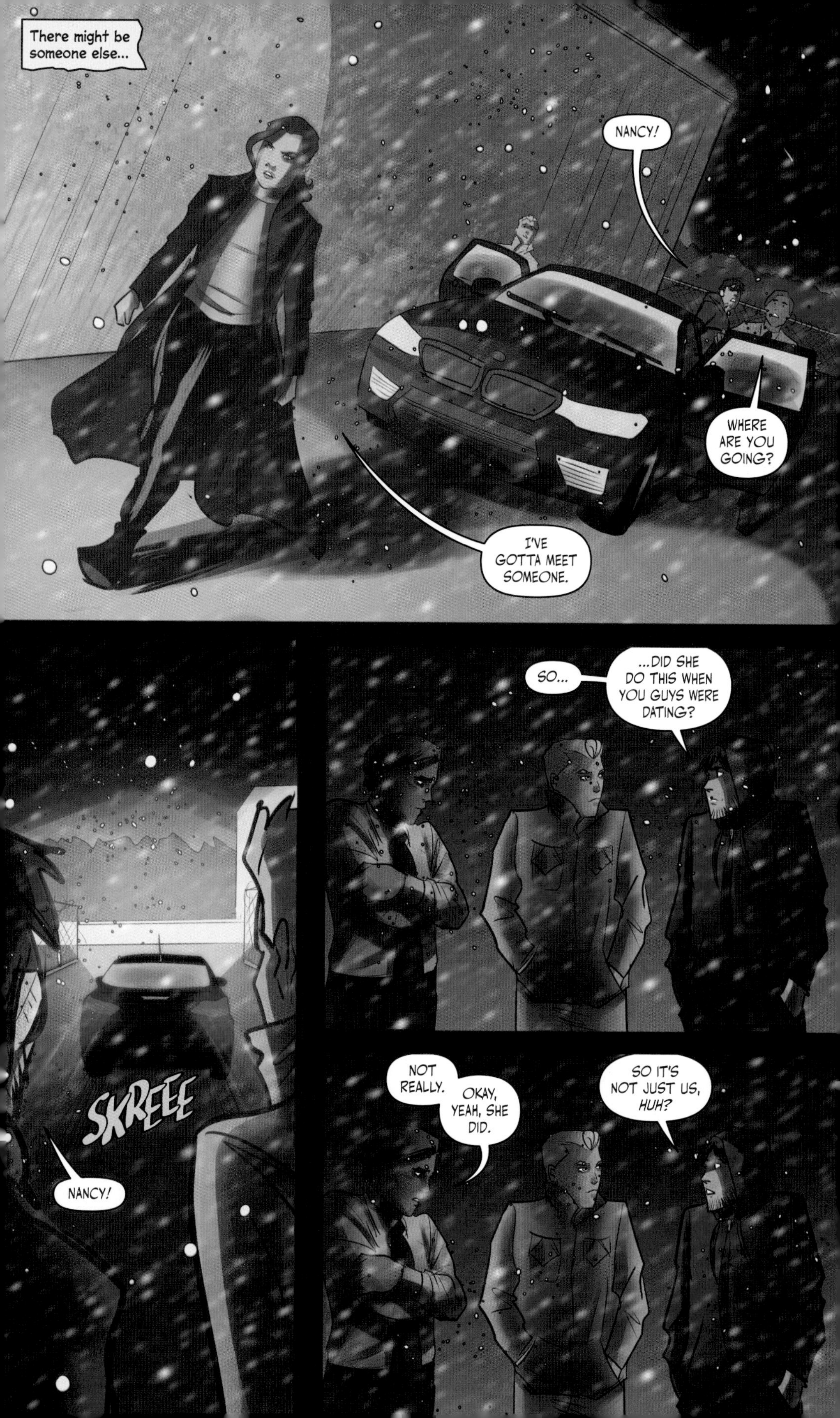
There might be someone else...
NANCY!
WHERE ARE YOU GOING?
I'VE GOTTA MEET SOMEONE.
SKREEE
NANCY!
SO...
...DID SHE DO THIS WHEN YOU GUYS WERE DATING?
NOT REALLY.
OKAY, YEAH, SHE DID.
SO IT'S NOT JUST US, HUH?

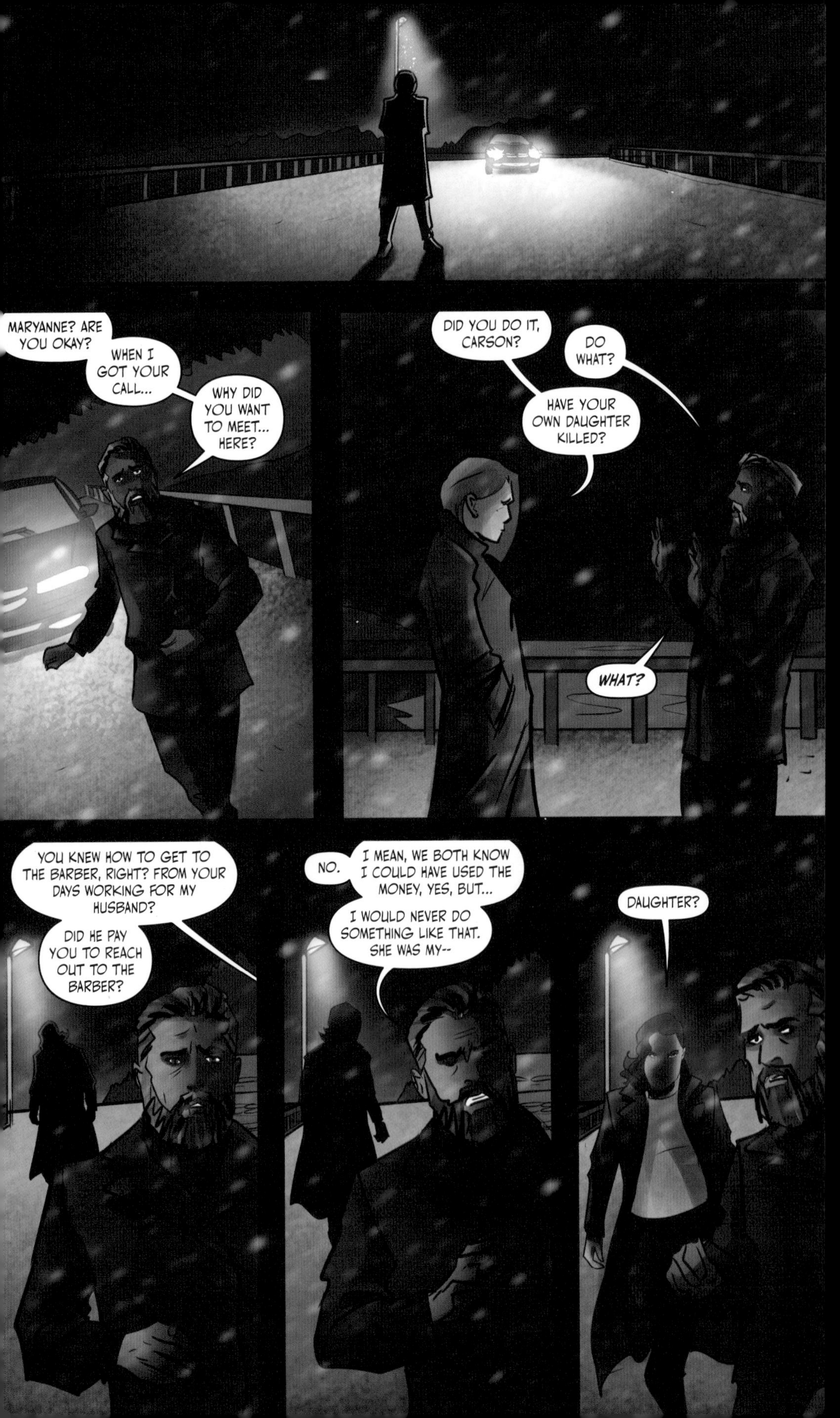
MARYANNE? ARE YOU OKAY?
WHEN I GOT YOUR CALL...
WHY DID YOU WANT TO MEET... HERE?
DID YOU DO IT, CARSON?
DO WHAT?
HAVE YOUR OWN DAUGHTER KILLED?
WHAT?
YOU KNEW HOW TO GET TO THE BARBER, RIGHT? FROM YOUR DAYS WORKING FOR MY HUSBAND?
DID HE PAY YOU TO REACH OUT TO THE BARBER?
NO.
I MEAN, WE BOTH KNOW I COULD HAVE USED THE MONEY, YES, BUT...
I WOULD NEVER DO SOMETHING LIKE THAT. SHE WAS MY--
DAUGHTER?

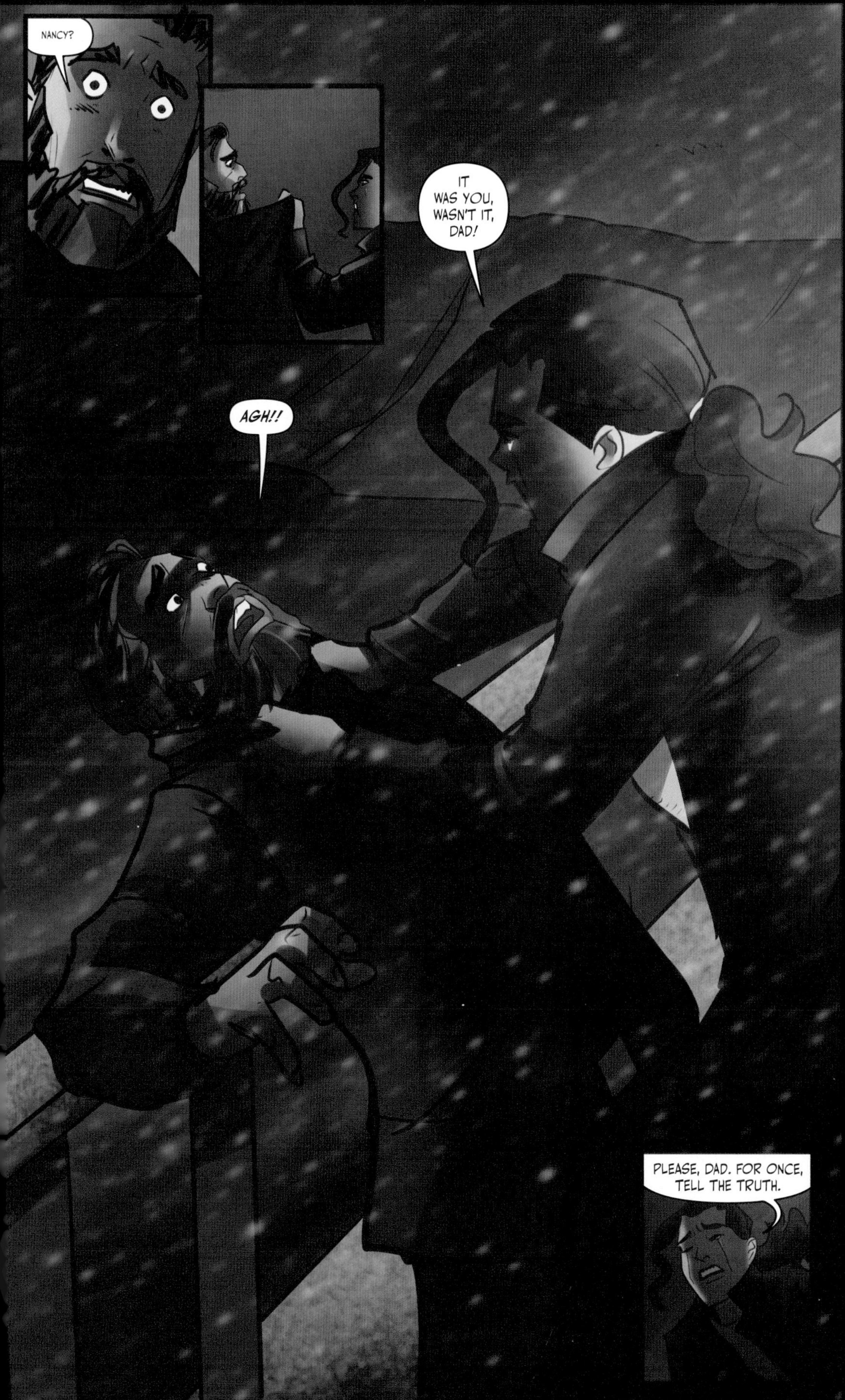
NANCY?
IT WAS YOU, WASN'T IT, DAD!
AGH!!
PLEASE, DAD. FOR ONCE, TELL THE TRUTH.

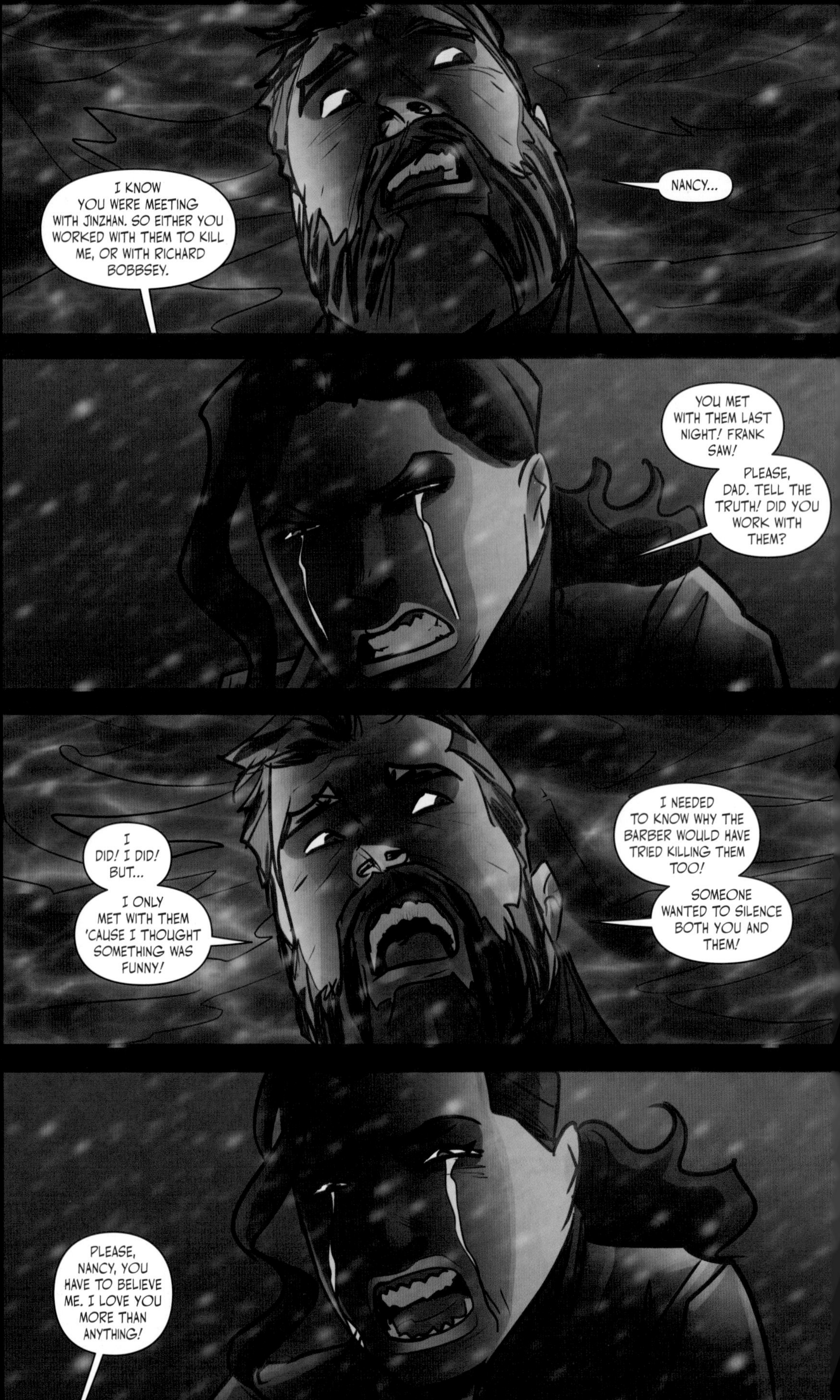
NANCY...
I KNOW YOU WERE MEETING WITH JINZHAN. SO EITHER YOU WORKED WITH THEM TO KILL ME, OR WITH RICHARD BOBBSEY.
YOU MET WITH THEM LAST NIGHT! FRANK SAW!
PLEASE, DAD. TELL THE TRUTH! DID YOU WORK WITH THEM?
I DID! I DID! BUT...
I ONLY MET WITH THEM 'CAUSE I THOUGHT SOMETHING WAS FUNNY!
I NEEDED TO KNOW WHY THE BARBER WOULD HAVE TRIED KILLING THEM TOO!
SOMEONE WANTED TO SILENCE BOTH YOU AND THEM!
PLEASE, NANCY, YOU HAVE TO BELIEVE ME. I LOVE YOU MORE THAN ANYTHING!

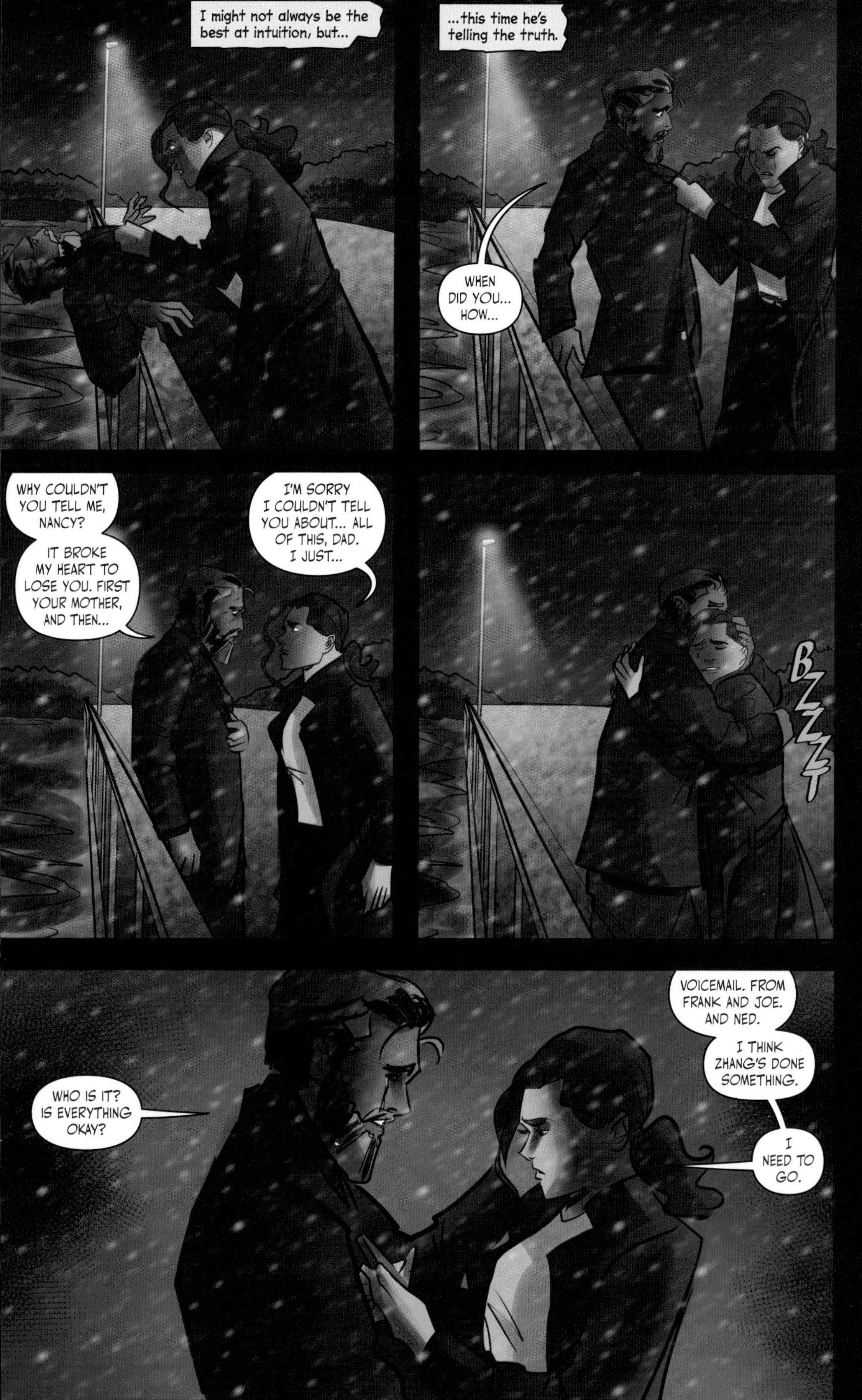
I might not always be the best at intuition, but...
...this time he's telling the truth.
WHEN DID YOU... HOW...
WHY COULDN'T YOU TELL ME, NANCY?
IT BROKE MY HEART TO LOSE YOU. FIRST YOUR MOTHER, AND THEN...
I'M SORRY I COULDN'T TELL YOU ABOUT... ALL OF THIS, DAD. I JUST...
BZZZT
WHO IS IT? IS EVERYTHING OKAY?
VOICEMAIL. FROM FRANK AND JOE. AND NED.
I THINK ZHANG'S DONE SOMETHING.
I NEED TO GO.

There's scuffling in the background of the voicemail.

Some blood on the ground. A fight.

Whoever came here was pretty good at hiding.

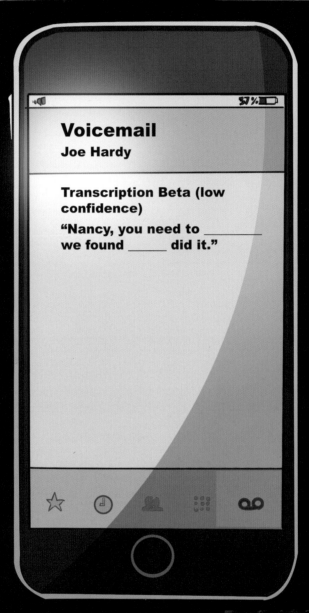

Voicemail
Joe Hardy

Transcription Beta (low confidence)

"Nancy, you need to _____ we found _____ did it."

Dad was right. Someone wanted Zhang dead.

And I think I finally know who. And where to find them.

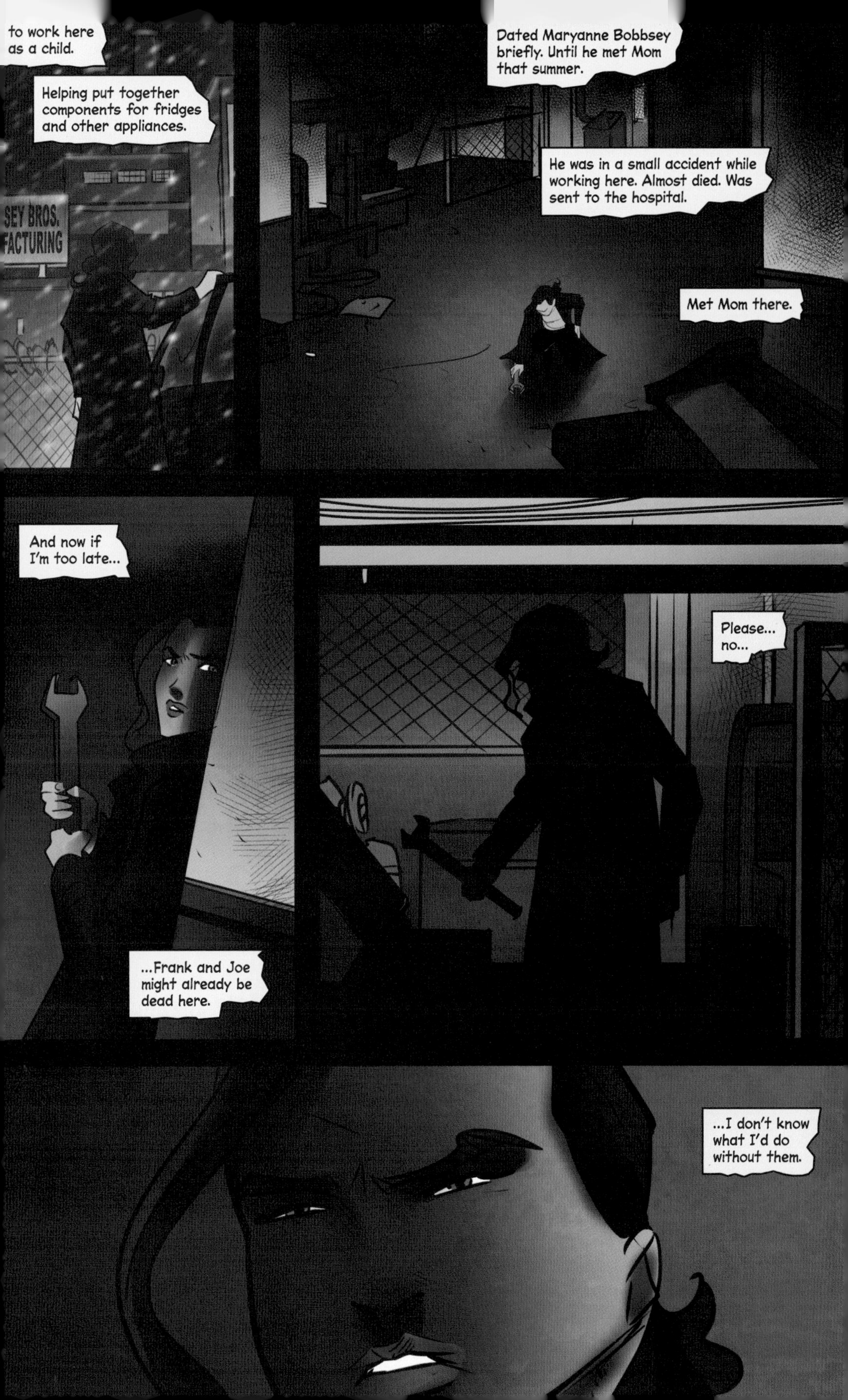

to work here as a child.
Helping put together components for fridges and other appliances.
SEY BROS.
FACTURING
Dated Maryanne Bobbsey briefly. Until he met Mom that summer.
He was in a small accident while working here. Almost died. Was sent to the hospital.
Met Mom there.
And now if I'm too late...
...Frank and Joe might already be dead here.
Please... no...
...I don't know what I'd do without them.

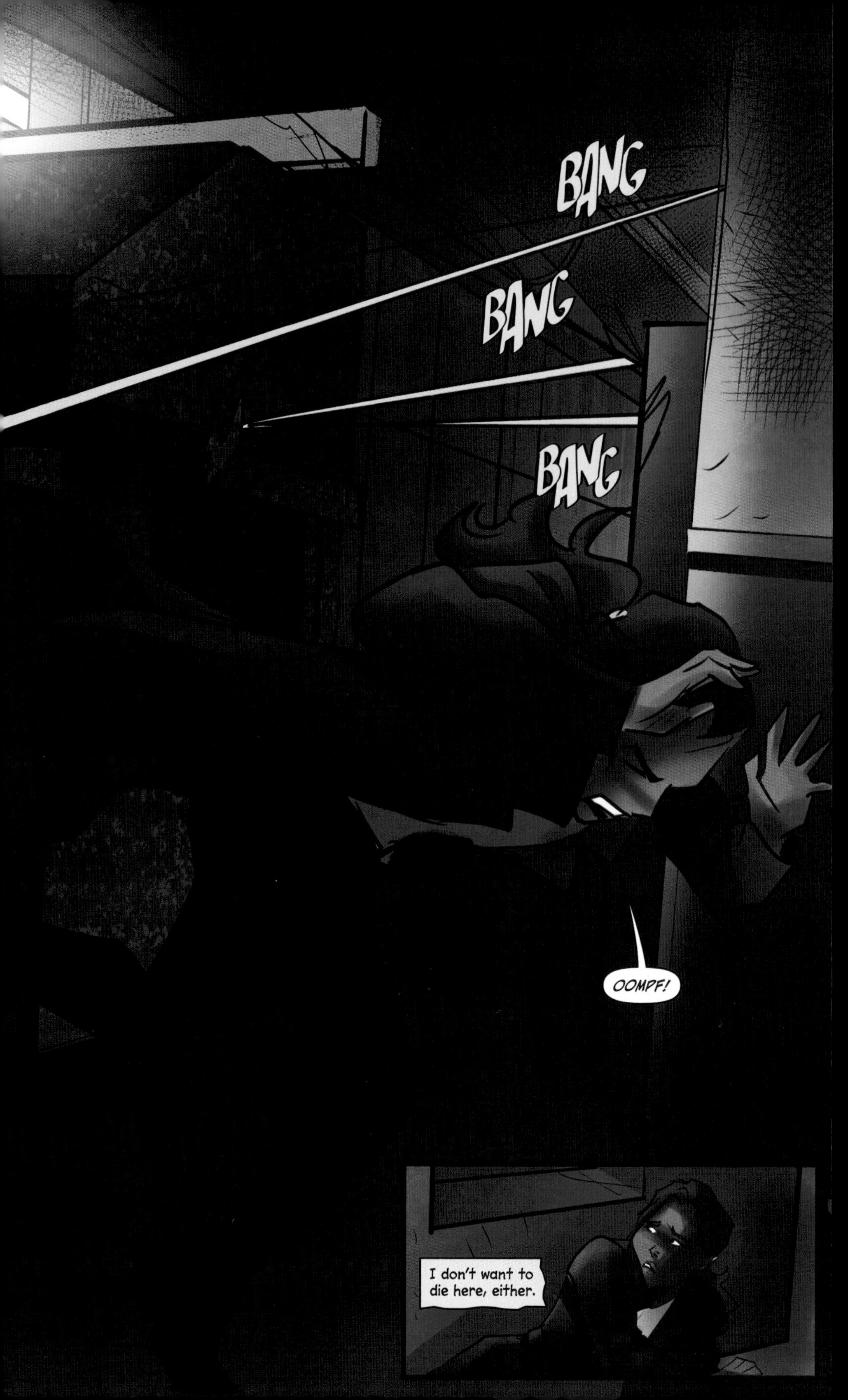
BANG
BANG
BANG
OOMPF!
I don't want to die here, either.

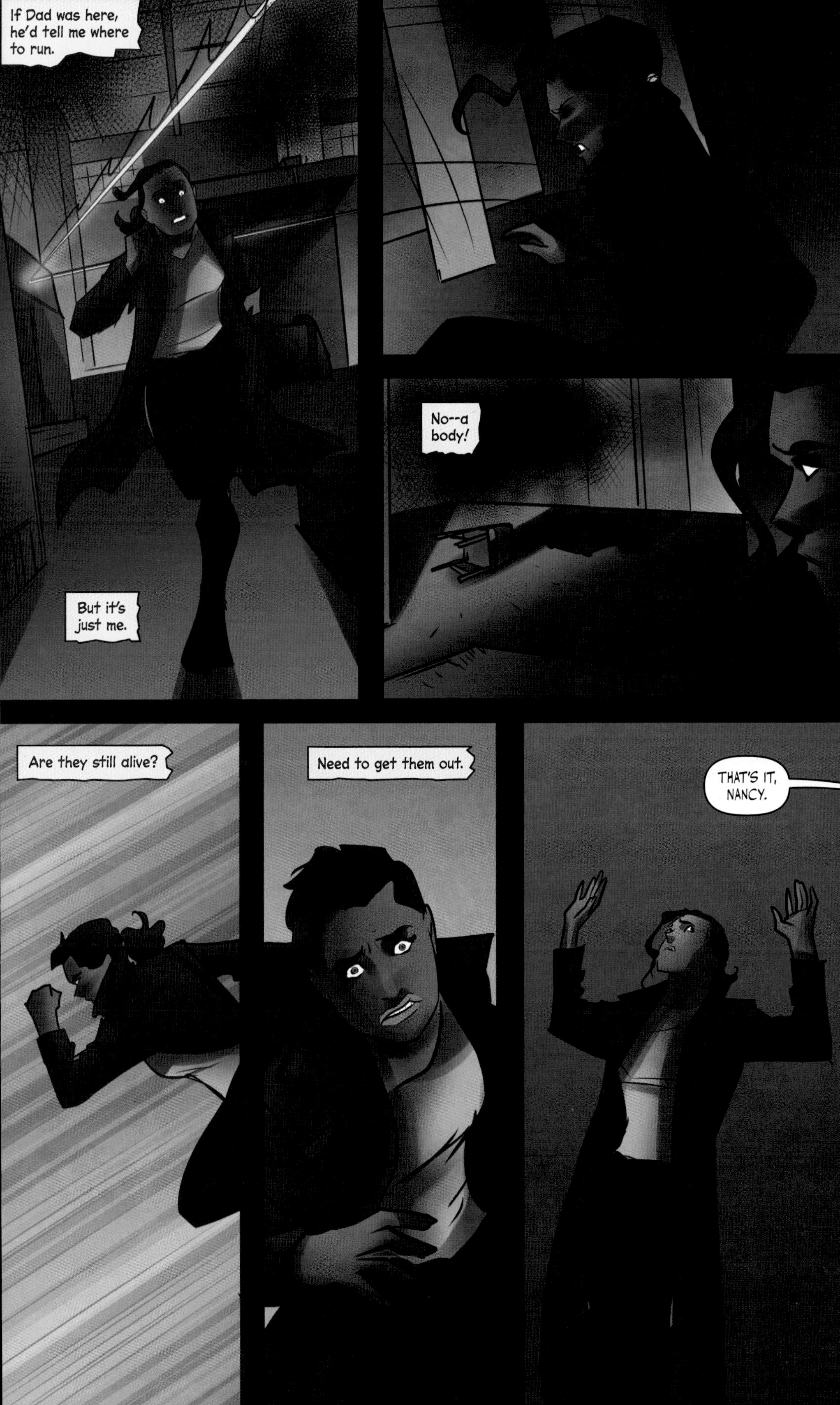
If Dad was here, he'd tell me where to run.
But it's just me.
No--a body!
Are they still alive?
Need to get them out.
THAT'S IT, NANCY.

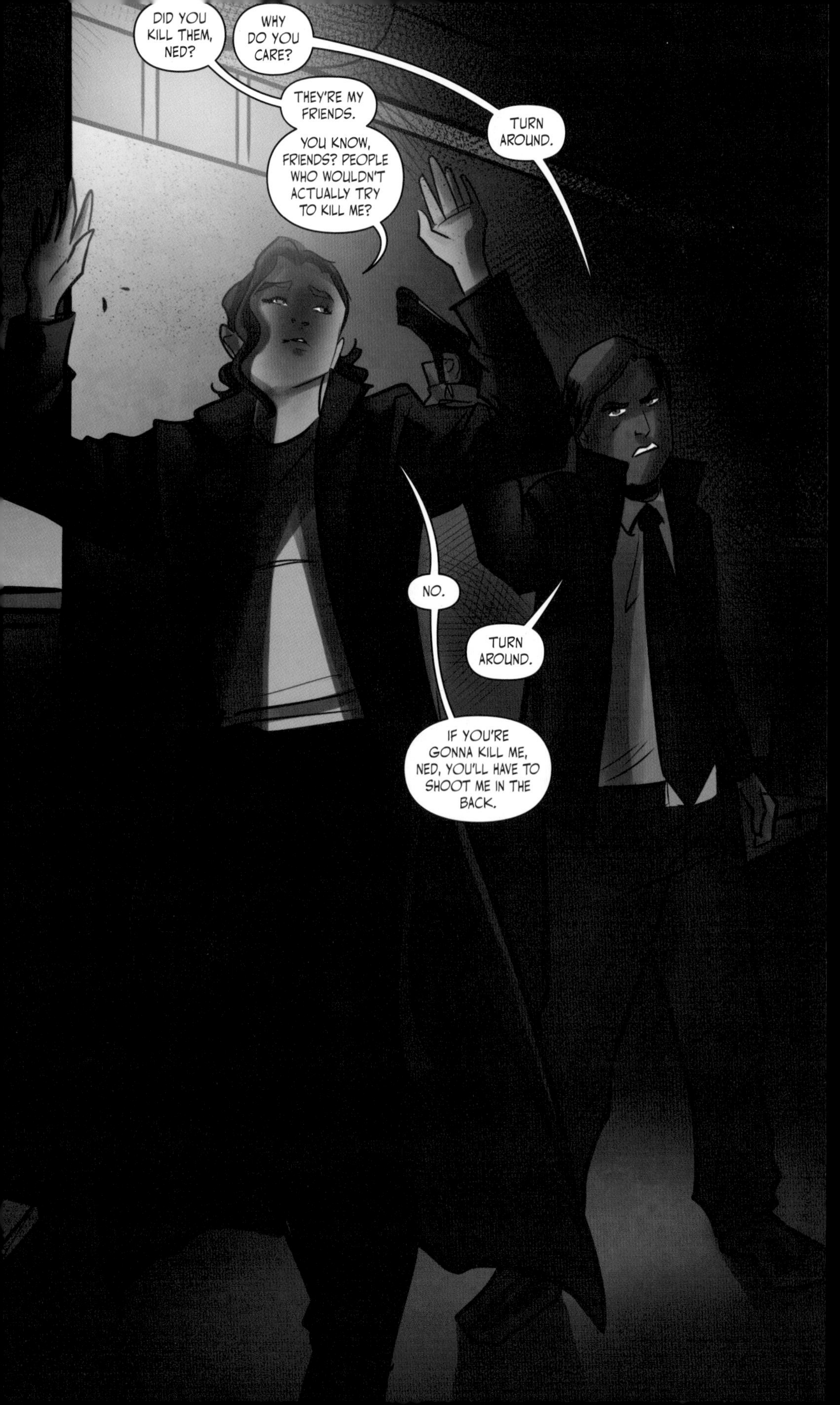
DID YOU KILL THEM, NED?
WHY DO YOU CARE?
THEY'RE MY FRIENDS.
YOU KNOW, FRIENDS? PEOPLE WHO WOULDN'T ACTUALLY TRY TO KILL ME?
TURN AROUND.
NO.
TURN AROUND.
IF YOU'RE GONNA KILL ME, NED, YOU'LL HAVE TO SHOOT ME IN THE BACK.

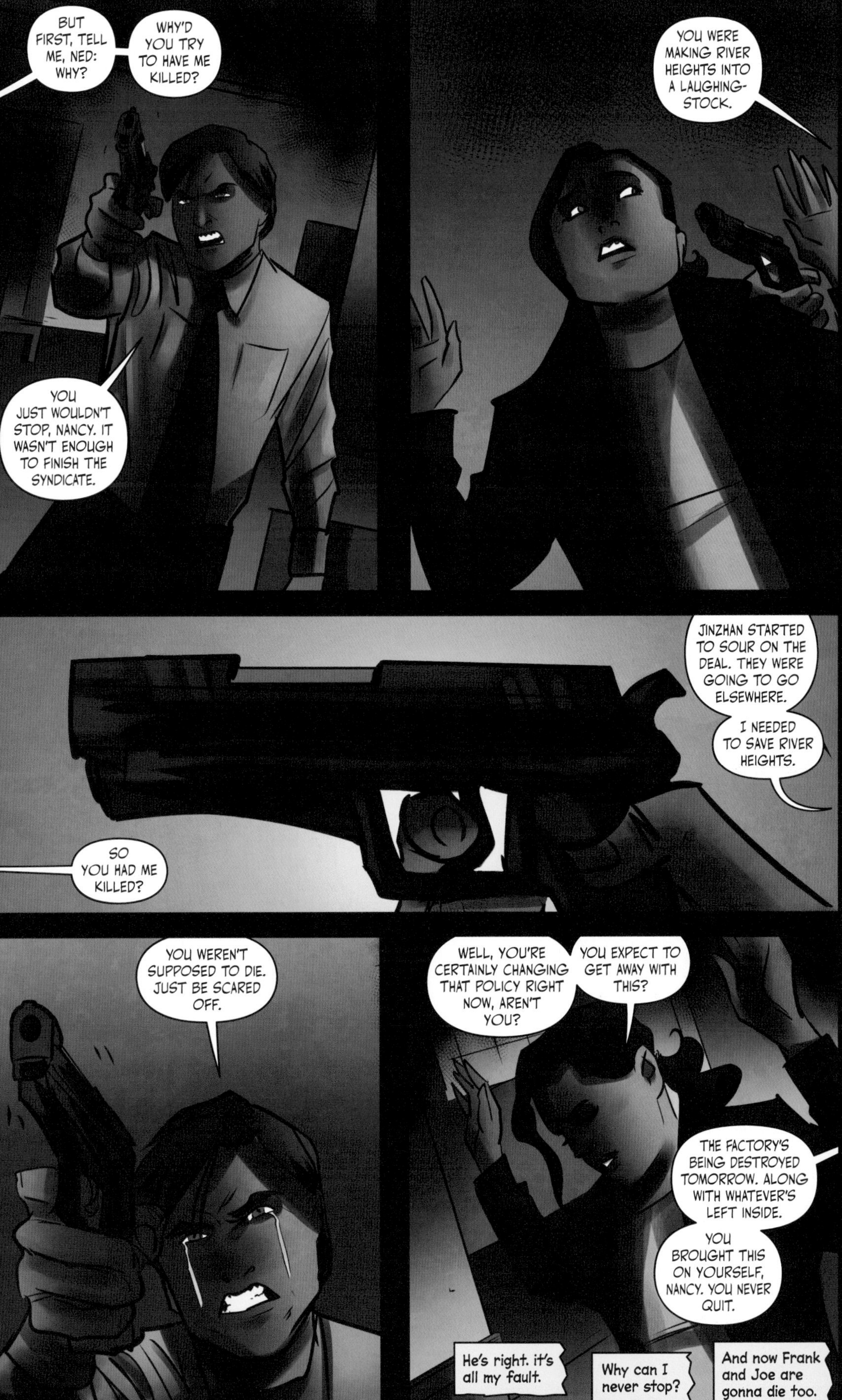
BUT FIRST, TELL ME, NED: WHY?
WHY'D YOU TRY TO HAVE ME KILLED?
YOU JUST WOULDN'T STOP, NANCY. IT WASN'T ENOUGH TO FINISH THE SYNDICATE.
YOU WERE MAKING RIVER HEIGHTS INTO A LAUGHING-STOCK.
JINZHAN STARTED TO SOUR ON THE DEAL. THEY WERE GOING TO GO ELSEWHERE.
I NEEDED TO SAVE RIVER HEIGHTS.
SO YOU HAD ME KILLED?
YOU WEREN'T SUPPOSED TO DIE. JUST BE SCARED OFF.
WELL, YOU'RE CERTAINLY CHANGING THAT POLICY RIGHT NOW, AREN'T YOU?
YOU EXPECT TO GET AWAY WITH THIS?
THE FACTORY'S BEING DESTROYED TOMORROW. ALONG WITH WHATEVER'S LEFT INSIDE.
YOU BROUGHT THIS ON YOURSELF, NANCY. YOU NEVER QUIT.
He's right. it's all my fault.
Why can I never stop?
And now Frank and Joe are gonna die too.

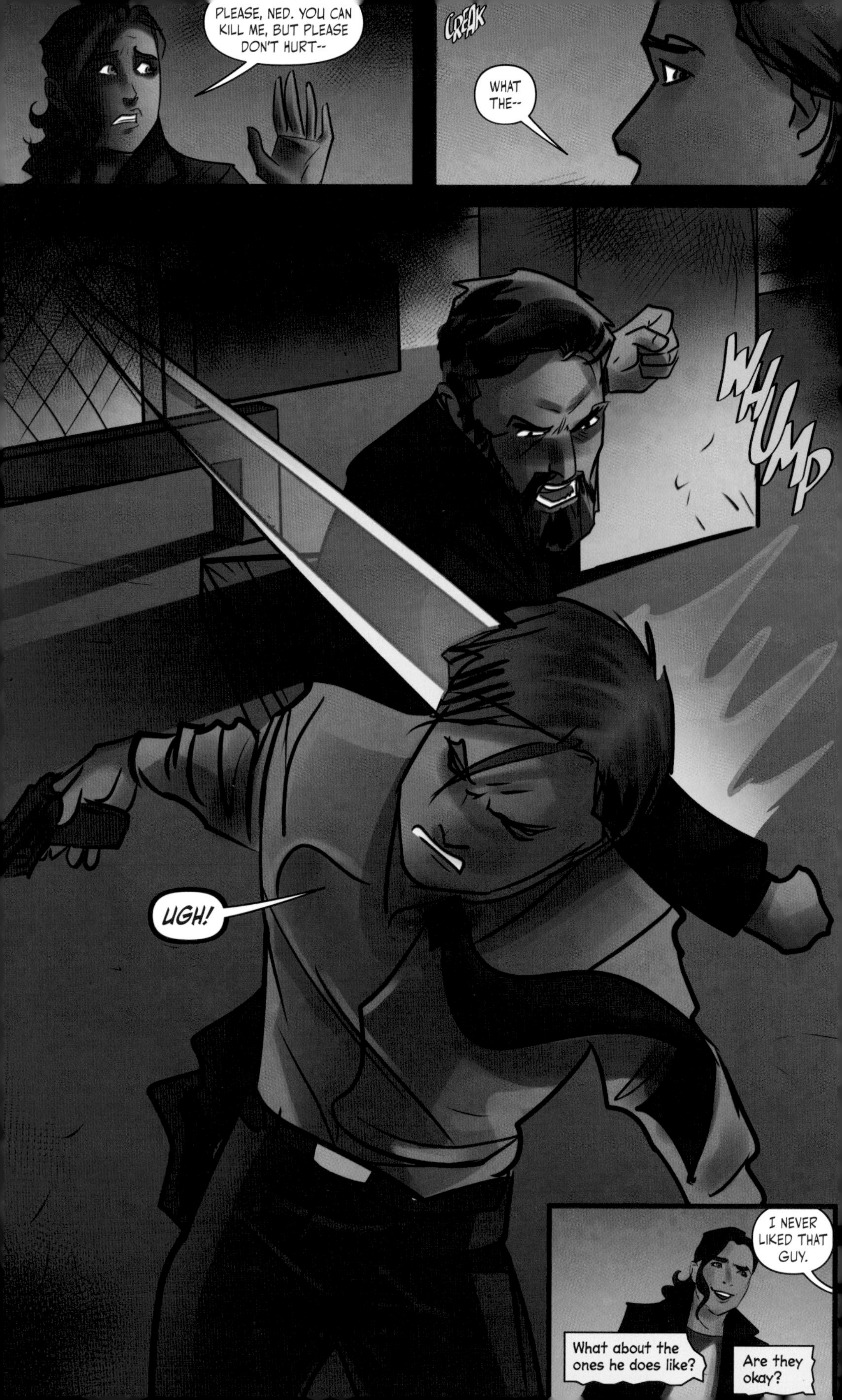
PLEASE, NED. YOU CAN KILL ME, BUT PLEASE DON'T HURT--
CREAK
WHAT THE--
WHUMP
UGH!
I NEVER LIKED THAT GUY.
What about the ones he does like?
Are they okay?

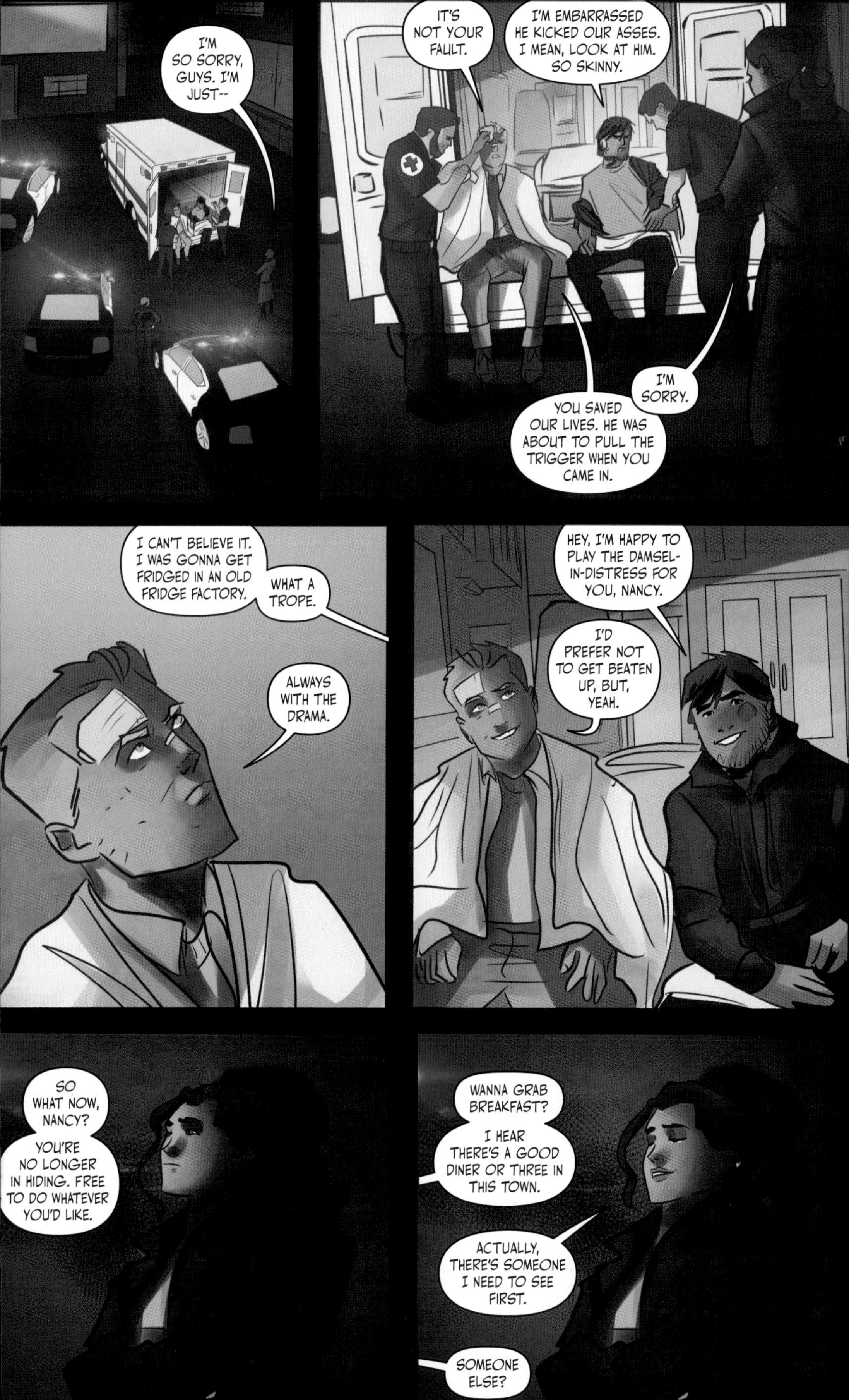
I'M SO SORRY, GUYS. I'M JUST--
IT'S NOT YOUR FAULT.
I'M EMBARRASSED HE KICKED OUR ASSES. I MEAN, LOOK AT HIM. SO SKINNY.
I'M SORRY.
YOU SAVED OUR LIVES. HE WAS ABOUT TO PULL THE TRIGGER WHEN YOU CAME IN.
I CAN'T BELIEVE IT. I WAS GONNA GET FRIDGED IN AN OLD FRIDGE FACTORY.
WHAT A TROPE.
ALWAYS WITH THE DRAMA.
HEY, I'M HAPPY TO PLAY THE DAMSEL-IN-DISTRESS FOR YOU, NANCY.
I'D PREFER NOT TO GET BEATEN UP, BUT, YEAH.
SO WHAT NOW, NANCY?
YOU'RE NO LONGER IN HIDING. FREE TO DO WHATEVER YOU'D LIKE.
WANNA GRAB BREAKFAST?
I HEAR THERE'S A GOOD DINER OR THREE IN THIS TOWN.
ACTUALLY, THERE'S SOMEONE I NEED TO SEE FIRST.
SOMEONE ELSE?

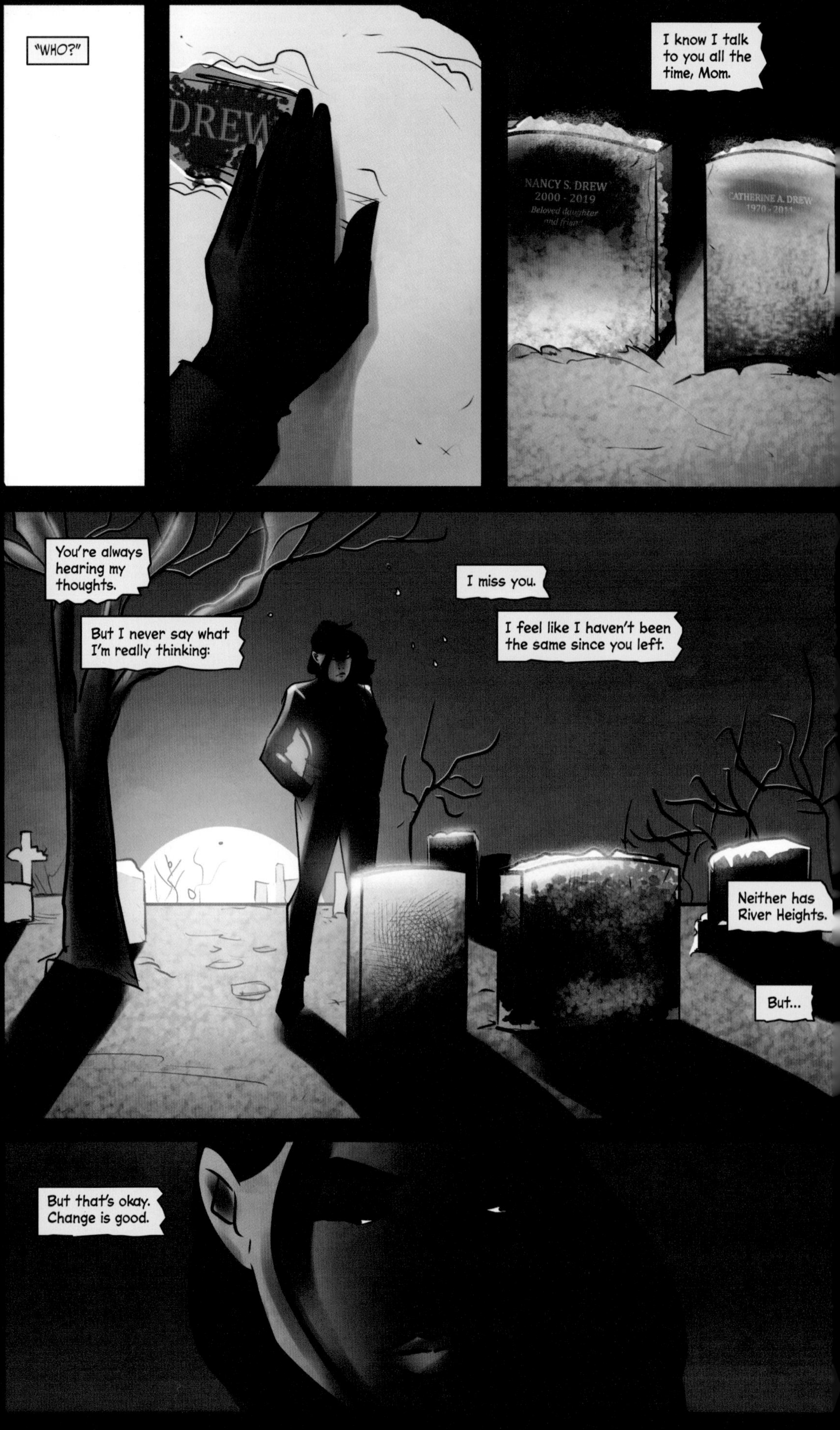
"WHO?"
DREW
I know I talk to you all the time, Mom.
NANCY S. DREW
2000 - 2019
Beloved daughter
CATHERINE A. DREW
You're always hearing my thoughts.
But I never say what I'm really thinking:
I miss you.
I feel like I haven't been the same since you left.
Neither has River Heights.
But...
But that's okay. Change is good.

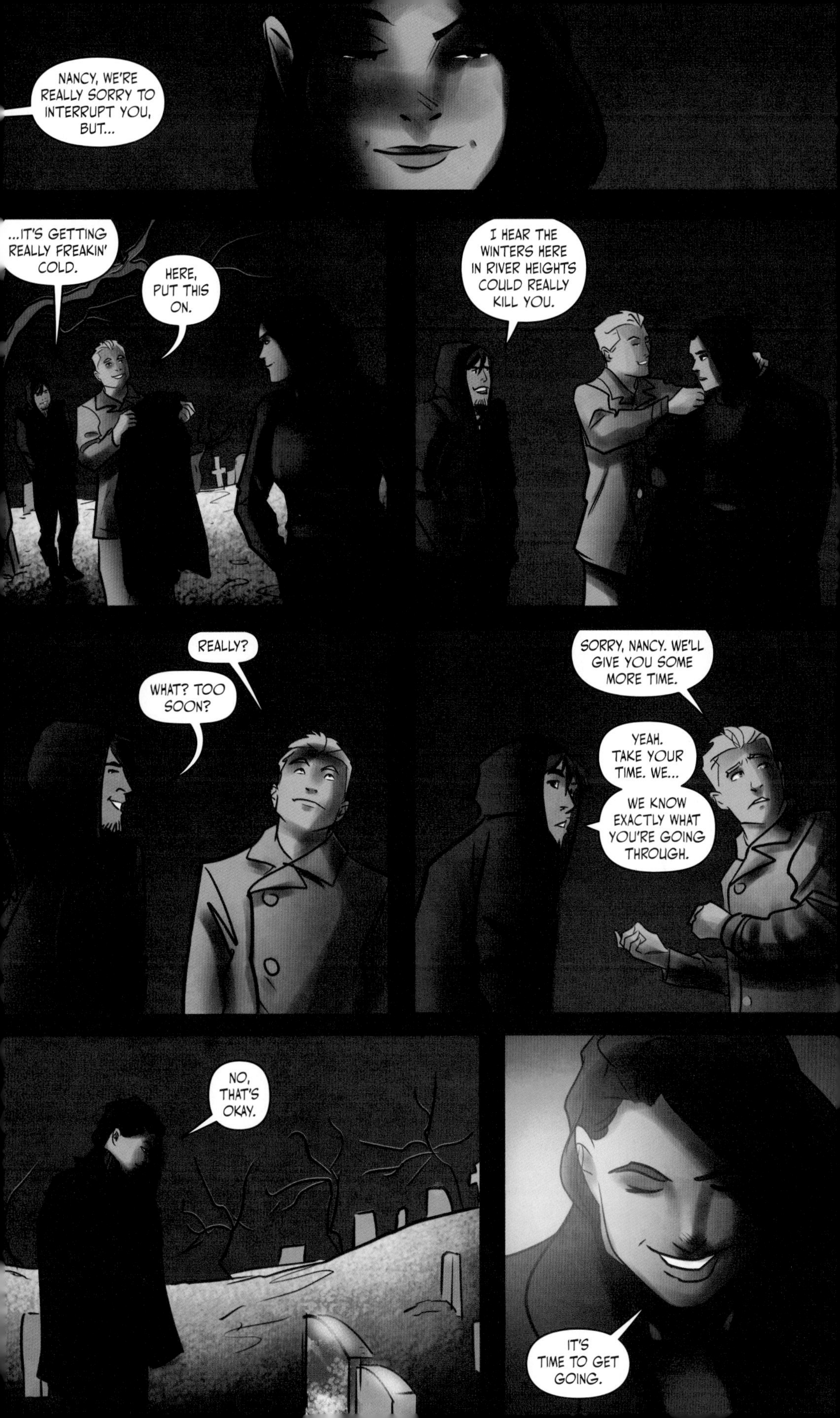

NANCY, WE'RE REALLY SORRY TO INTERRUPT YOU, BUT...
...IT'S GETTING REALLY FREAKIN' COLD.
HERE, PUT THIS ON.
I HEAR THE WINTERS HERE IN RIVER HEIGHTS COULD REALLY KILL YOU.
REALLY?
WHAT? TOO SOON?
SORRY, NANCY. WE'LL GIVE YOU SOME MORE TIME.
YEAH. TAKE YOUR TIME. WE...
WE KNOW EXACTLY WHAT YOU'RE GOING THROUGH.
NO, THAT'S OKAY.
IT'S TIME TO GET GOING.

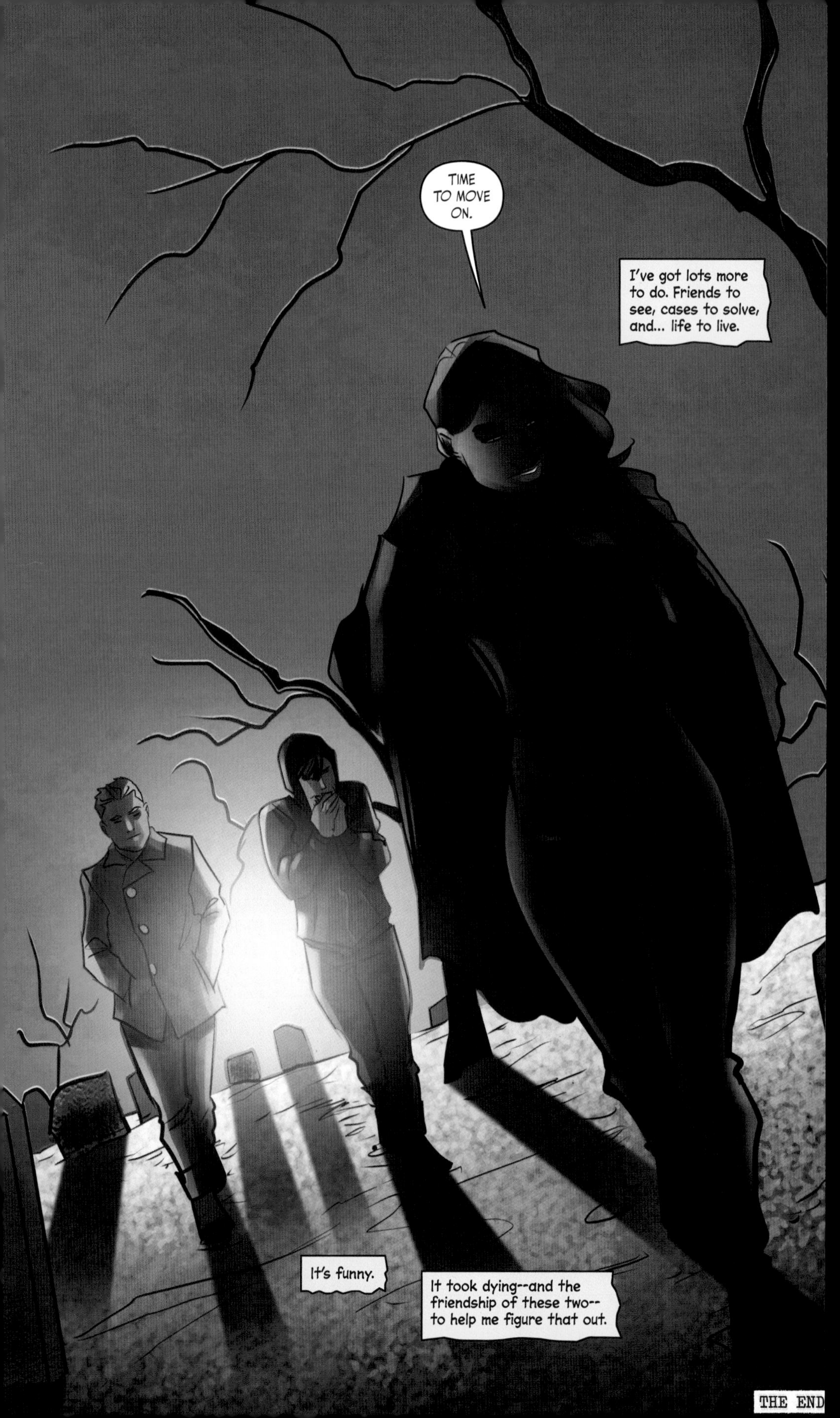
TIME TO MOVE ON.
I've got lots more to do. Friends to see, cases to solve, and... life to live.
It's funny.
It took dying--and the friendship of these two--to help me figure that out.
THE END

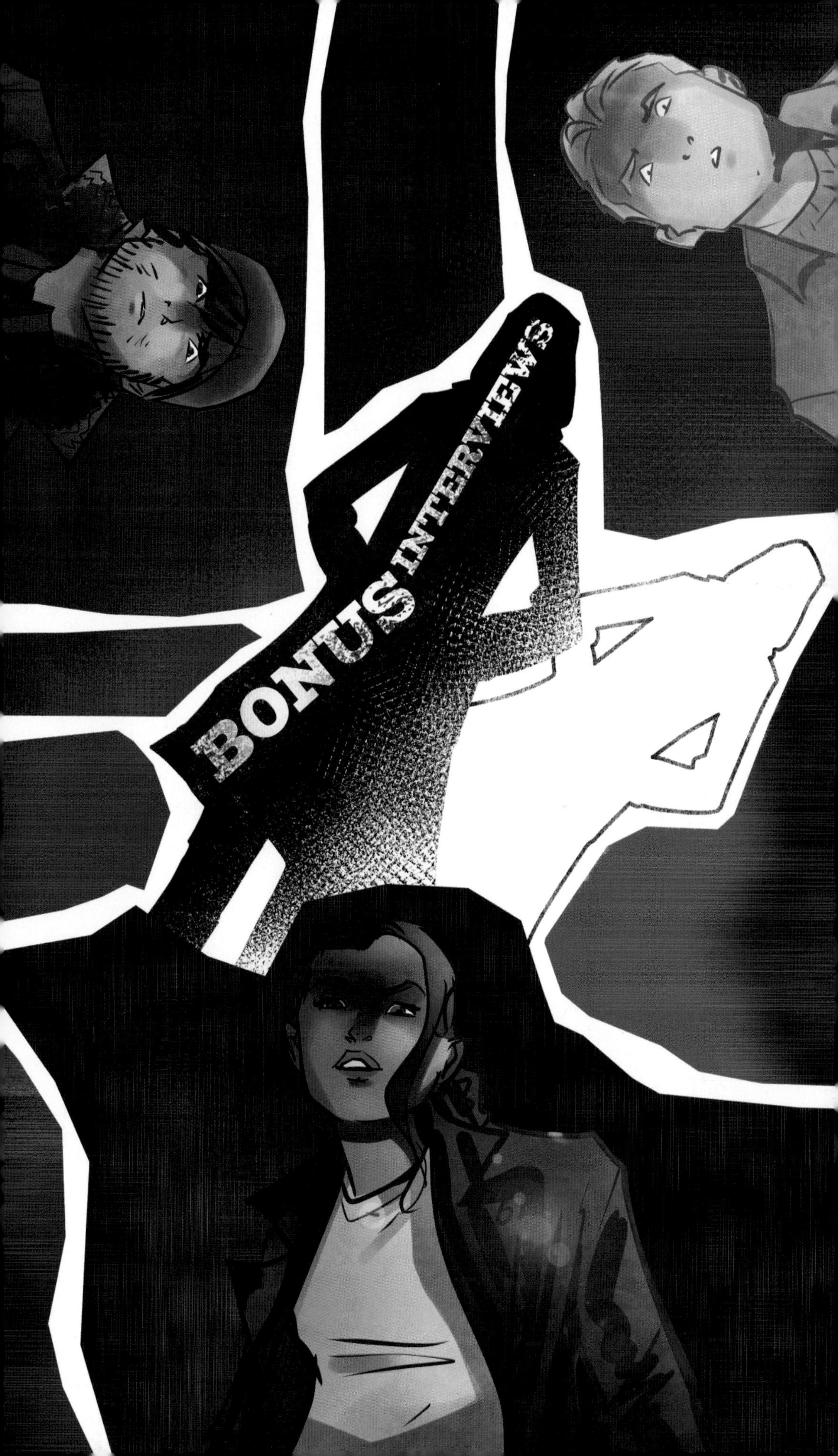
BONUS INTERVIEWS

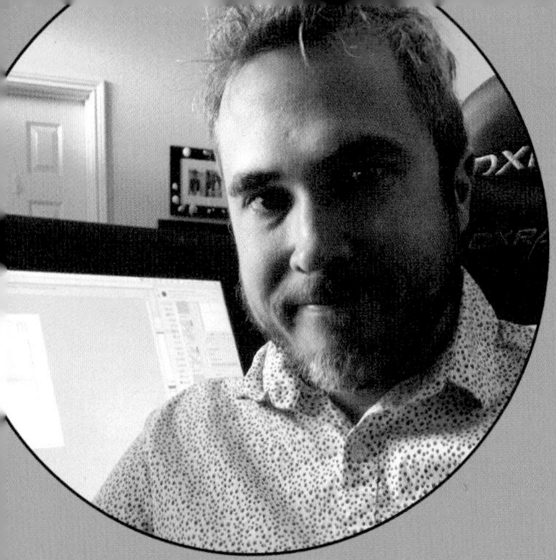
DXR

^ **Artist Joe Eisma**

APRIL 2020

Q&A with Writer ANTHONY DEL COL and Artist JOE EISMA

Anthony: Joe! Well, first of all, I think we shou state that we're doing this Q&A in the midst the Coronavirus pandemic. Where are you current and how are you feeling about the state of t world?

Joe: I'm in the Dallas/Fort Worth area, and r family and I are doing pretty good, all thin considered. My sons took a bit to get used doing their school online, but we're all into o routines now. As for how I feel about the state the world—concerned is the overbearing feelir I try not to live on social media, consuming nev but I do keep my eyes on things.

Anthony: Yeah, I know! Things here in Brookl are still kinda surreal. But moving on, I just wa to say it's been so great working with you on t series. I've been a fan of yours for years now a as soon as I saw that we could work together this, I got so excited! Okay, enough gushing let's go with a generic-but-still-kinda-f question: how did you get your start in the con book industry? What was your first big break?

Joe: Aw, thanks! I was really flattered a surprised when you first contacted me about t series way back when. I really enjoyed Kill Shak speare and was excited to get started. I got r start in comics around 2008, doing a miniser for a local publisher here in Dallas. The wri and I clicked and continued to work on proje for various publishers, and all the while I w posting my art online at Brian Michael Benc message board, Jinxworld. Nick Spencer lik what he saw, and contacted me about drawi a new idea of his, a book called Morning Glori That was my big break, and it's been a crazy ri ever since!

Anthony: Morning Glories? Never heard of it [Editor's note: Anthony's kidding... or is he.. Okay, I'm always curious about the process of illustrator. What hours do you work? Where you work (a studio at home, a studio with oth artists)?

Joe: I work from home out of my home offi These days my process is pretty much all digita I use Clip Studio Paint for my line art, and Pho op for my color and painting work. I'm a morning person, so I generally get up ound 7 am and work through the morning, then take a break for lunch and ercise, and then back at it til 5.

thony: That's a pretty good schedule. I'm so glad you fit in time for ercise. I find so many people forget that part of the process. As a writer, I also to make time to go for walks and recharge my creative batteries. I also try consume as much as possible. I find my influences all over the place – books, mics, tv, film, etc. Where do you find yourself turning to most for inspiration?

e: I'm big into film as well. It was my major in college, and I love the works of lley Scott, Stanley Kubrick, Alfred Hitchcock and Akira Kurosawa. Anime and nga are a huge influence on me as well—my favorite creators are Satoshi n, Into Asano, Naoki Urasawa and Katsuhiro Otomo.

thony: I didn't know you were a film major! That's awesome. I always nted to be a film major but decided to take the safe path and went to siness school. Not sure how I ended up in comics… Okay, our last question l be a hard-hitting one: Which of the three main characters do you enjoy awing most? Nancy? Frank? Joe? None of them?

e: Nancy's my favorite, for sure. She has an intensity to her that is really pealing to draw. I would say Frank is a close runner up—I see him kind of as e comic relief in the book, and comedy has always been one of my top things draw.

thony: Okay, I lied – I have one more hard-hitting question: Do you have y embarrassing stories about our editor Matt Idelson? I could really use some t on him…

e: There was the time I had to bail him out of jail during one particular wild nvention weekend, but I promised I'd never elaborate. Needless to say, Matt panned from the state of Kansas for life.

thony: I knew it! [Editor's Note: These two are idiots and I will never hire em again…]

^ Colorist Salvatore Aiala

JULY 2020

Q&A with Writer ANTHONY DEL COL and Colorist SALVATORE AIALA

aka "WE FINALLY MEET!"

Anthony: Salvatore! I'm sure some will be surpri
when they hear this: this is the first time we're ac
ally chatting! Yes, I know… but that's the state of
comics industry these days, especially in the time
coronavirus...

Anyways, I'd love to take this opportunity to THA
YOU for all the incredible work you've been doing
this series. I've really been impressed with the co
you've created for this issue and the entire series t
far. You've really helped add to the very noir fe
ing that Joe Eisma and I have been aiming to cre
throughout.

And since we're now chatting, I (along with the re
ers) would love to find out more about you. I'll st
with an easy question: Where are you currently, a
how have you been coping during this pandemic?

Salvatore: Anthony! good to hear you. Thanks
Nancy Drew! I am Brazilian and I live in São Pau
and I am at my home, which has also been my pl
of work for many years. I think I am dealing with t
pandemic like everyone else, quarantining it at ho
away from family and friends and trying to do wh
can online. These are strange times.

Anthony: So glad to hear. I've been in Brook
with my family and we really miss our family up
Canada (long story short, there's a travel ban
Canada that's preventing us from going up to vi
I'd love to know how you do your work. Where
you work? At home? In a studio with other artis
And what hours do you work?

Salvatore: I hope you can visit your family
Canada soon! I made a space in my house fo
studio with the equipment we need. I work in pa
nership with my wife, she does all the flats and I fir
the pages. I always try to stick to business hours,
sometimes I work late if necessary.

Anthony: How did you get into comics in the f
place? What was the first moment you thought y
could make yourself a career in this industry?

Salvatore: This happened in 1998 in a Brazil
edition, Spirit of the Amazon." After that, I wor
on small publications here. I wanted to go furth
and in 2000 I colored material for The Egmont Grou
"Disney Pixar" for 5 years.

2009, I started working with Dynamite on many things and eventually became the
[reg]ular colorist for *Red Sonja* and *Queen Sonja*.

[al]so did other works including *A Train Called Love* (I never had so much fun color-
[ing] a series), *James Bond: Felix Leiter*, *Turok* (fantastic) and *White Sand*. And now,
[Na]ncy Drew!!

[An]thony: Pardon my ignorance, but what's the comic industry like where you are?
[Wh]at are the comics that you're enjoying reading at the moment? And what are some
[of] your all-time favorites?

[Sa]lvatore: I think that the comic book industry in Brazil is getting stronger. Although
[ma]ny artists here work for the international market, there are many artists here who do
[no]t have this opportunity ... and I wish there was a publisher here to invest in these talents.

[I h]aven't been regularly reading comics for a while ... but I'm a big Batman fan (I
[thi]nk everyone is, hee hee). The ones I liked the most are Frank Miller's *Dark Knight*,
[Da]redevil: The Man Without Fear, *Watchmen*, *Batman: Year One*, *Kingdom Come*,
[Sp]awn, *Marvel 1602*, *Logan: Origin* ... among others.

[An]thony: Okay, my last question will be a tough one: What's the favorite project
[yo]u've worked on thus far in your career? Don't worry, you don't have to say *The Death
[of] Nancy Drew*...

[Sal]vatore: *Nancy Drew* has given me the opportunity to explore the noir universe,
[an]d I'm really enjoying it. The story is very engaging. But the title that is my favorite is
[Re]d Sonja, I really like this character.

[An]thony: Okay, I lied – I have one more hard-hitting question: Do you have any em-
[ba]rrassing stories about our editor Matt Idelson? I could really use some dirt on him...

[Sa]lvatore: Haha! Matt has been a good friend since *Turok* (our first job together).
[Al]ways in a good mood in the mails (You are a rock and roll god, sir!). One time he
[dis]appeared, but then he appeared, he had a problem with his cat's health, so I thought
[his] cat is as crazy as the cat I have here.

[Th]anks, Anthony, for the opportunity to have this conversation, thanks to you and Joe
[Ei]sma for *Nancy Drew*. Thanks, Matt, for the partnership in the works.

^ Crank

Q&A WITH WRITER ANTHONY DEL COL AND LETTERER CRANK!

Anthony: Crank!! First off, I love that your prof[es]sional name ends with an exclamation point. I f[eel] like that's the most "on brand" a letterer can be[.]

Secondly, I just wanted to commend you on h[ow] great a job you've been doing on this series. [Se]riously, you've been hitting it out of the pa[rk] every single issue you've done and I'm happy [to] have you on the team. Every time I get a pro[of] back I'm wowed by how much better it is tha[n I] thought it would be.

Anyways, I think readers are more interested [in] hearing some answers from you than reading [me] sending kudo after kudo in your direction. So[.] Since we don't know each other very well, wh[ere] are you currently reading this? And how ha[ve] you been coping with the pandemic and how t[he] world's been changed in the last six months?

Crank: I'm in the Cincinnati area; a city in sou[th]west Ohio. Given that I barely left the house [in] 2019, you'd think the pandemic wouldn't ha[ve] affected me much, but it's a different thing wh[en] you can't go much of anywhere. I rather li[ke] wearing a mask, though; I feel like a ninja.

Anthony: Aw, man, I love your outlook on [all] of it! I can't believe despite living in Brookl[yn,] I haven't actually stepped foot in Manhattan [in] the last six months! Speaking of environmen[t,] please tell me (and the readers) where you [do] your work? Is there a studio you work out of? [An] office? The kitchen table?

Crank: I have a Cape Cod-style place where t[he] upper floor is all one room so that's my stud[io.] It's comfortably cluttered.

Anthony: I can just picture it – and again, [I'm] jealous. When did you realize you could be [a] comic book letterer? Was it something you [al]ways had an eye for, or something that just kin[d of] fell into your lap?

Crank: I started lettering comics when the pu[b]lisher I worked for laid most of us off. I want[ed] to stay in comics so I took up lettering. It wa[s a] "right place at the right time" kind of thing.

thony: I find that lettering is an underappreciated art, yet so incredibly ıl. What are the worst mistakes you see new letterers make?

ank: Consistency, I think. Balloons and word stacking that are all over the ce with spacing, shape, tails, etc.

thony: Okay, here's the controversial / emotional part of the interview. What your favorite fonts outside of comics? I personally go with Garamond in every ument I write (as you can tell in this Word doc)*. Tell me if that's good or bad.

ank: Albertus! It's a classic, elegant font used in a bunch of movie titles and ewhere. Garamond is fine. Just not as good as Albertus.

thony: Wow. Now you're shaming me, aren't you? Albertus isn't even avail- e on my laptop. And though you won't admit it, you probably did lose re- ct for me... How can I salvage this? Oh, I know! What's your favorite project u've worked on thus far in your career? Don't worry, you don't have to say Death of Nancy Drew...

ank: Like children, I don't like to have favorites. I will say that I've been rking on a book called Grumble that's a lot of fun. It's got a great team: ke Norton, Rafer Roberts, and Marissa Louise. It's about a ne'er-do-well con- n magically changed into a sort of pug, on the run from cosmic hitmen.

thony: What? I've never heard of that, but I want to read it. Now! Oh, okay, ed – I have one more hard-hitting question: Do you have any embarrassing ries about our editor, Matt Idelson? For those that actually read these inter- ws, they'll know that I'm always trying to find ways to embarrass him, but one ever wants to help me out...

att: Well... there was that one time on camel back in the desert when— ıh, I'll leave it there.

thony: I knew Matt had a camel story to share! How much is he paying eryone to be quiet...? Well, Crank!, thanks so much for taking the time to swer these little questions. And keep up the great work on this series – I nk you're the star of the entire run!

hile Anthony may have used Garamond in the rd Doc, we here in the production department are using iger for this interview.

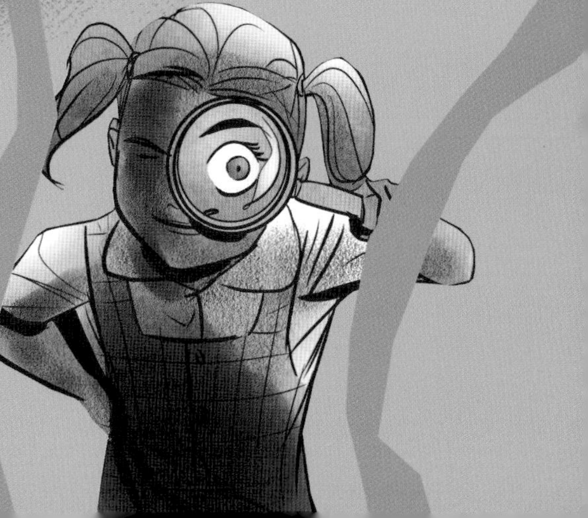

^ Matt on a good day.

SEPTEMBER 2020

Q&A WITH WRITER ANTHONY DEL COL AND EDITOR MATT IDELSON

Anthony: Matt! In our first Nancy Drew se[ries] together (The Big Lie), I did Q&As with every[one] on the creative team (artist, colorist, letterer, c[o] artist, etc.)... but I didn't do one with you. [And] thus far in this series I've sat down (virtually [at] least) with Joe and Salvatore (Crank! will b[e] the next issue)... and now I finally get to d[o] with you!

Yay!

First off, I want to THANK YOU for the great [work] you've done shepherding this series over the [past] few years. It's been an absolute treat work[ing] with you and I've learned a great deal from y[ou.]

Now that I've gotten that cheesy stuff out of [the] way, I'd love to ask a few questions I'm sure re[ad]ers are interested in getting to answer to.

First off, am I your favorite creator you've e[ver] worked with?

Matt: Most likely no...

Anthony: Second-favorite?

Matt: Negatory.

Anthony: Top ten?

Matt: Do I have to answer that?

Anthony: Wow. My heart is crushed... B[ut I] know you've worked with some of the bes[t in] the industry, so I guess that's a consolation[.] In all seriousness, what part of working on [this] book have you enjoyed the most? Feel free to [say] anything other than working with me...

Matt: It's hard to pick one thing, to be hon[est.] Your take on the principal characters has b[een] terrific, but that's just one aspect of what yo[u've] brought to the table, let alone everyone else [on] the two series.

.thony: What are some noir stories that you like the most (either in comics, :rature, film, etc.)?

tt: Oh man... Devil in a Blue Dress, The Big Sleep, L.A. Confidential for oks, Double Indemnity, The Third Man, Sunset Boulevard for films. I won't . into comics—wouldn't want to offend anyone I might omit.

thony: What's your favorite part of working with creators?

att: Seeing how they bring the ideas to life versus what their respective ers do on other projects, sometimes involving the same characters. The nradery's often fun, too.

thony: And your least favorite? You're not allowed to say "doing Q&As :h annoying creators"...

att: Well besides that, everything is else is awesome.

thony: For those aspiring to become top editors like you, what sort of vice would you give them?

att: Have a point of view for each series or run of a series and hire people o agree with it, don't make the work about you, and remember you're in ge part there to facilitate the vision of the creators to the extent possible.

thony: And finally... Are you sure I'm not your most favorite creator you've rked with?

att: You're definitely second after Ed McGuinness.

thony: I guess I'll settle for that. Thanks so much, Matthieu!

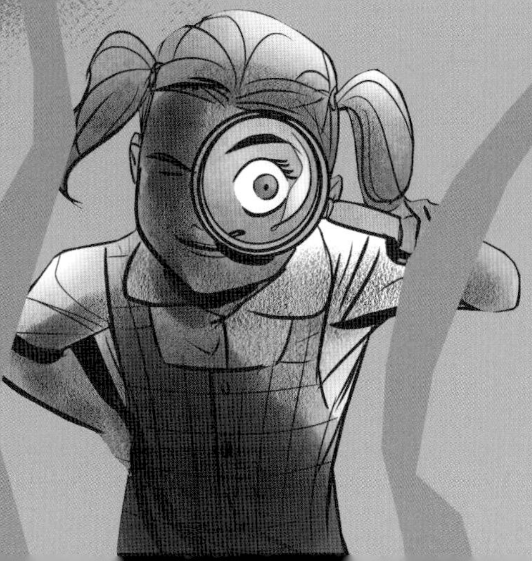

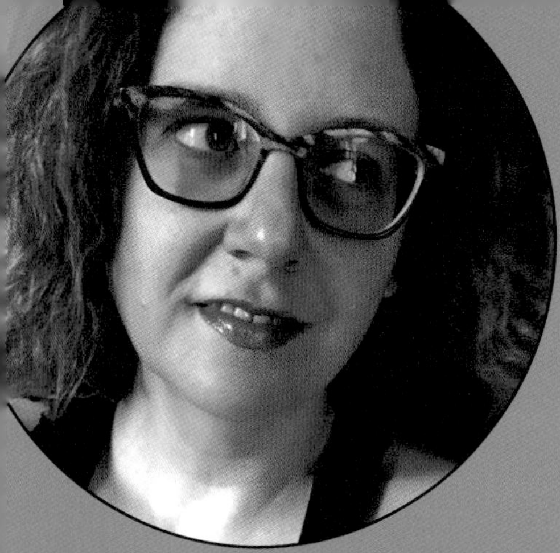

^ Cathy Heard

OCTOBER 2020

Q&A WITH WRITER ANTHONY DEL COL AND DESIGNER CATHY HEARD

Anthony: Cathy! Well, this is a first for me, a I'm excited about this. For the last 12 issues of Nancy Drew run I've interviewed a key member the team, ranging from the artist to colorist to l terer to cover artist to editor. But I haven't had opportunity to interview the designer of the lo and book!

So, I'm really happy to be sitting down with y (well, over email, to be precise...) and chat abo what you've done for this series and in general.

So, I'll start it off easy. I'm currently writing t while quarantining up in Canada (visiting my fa ily up here). Where are you at the moment? Wh do you normally work from (pre-pandemic), a where are you working these days? Do you ha an office setup or working from a kitchen table

Cathy: Hi, Anthony! So happy to be included the interviews! I was in the Dynamite office in t Before Times but am now situated in our ho office/library/place where our plants and all so of junk live and our cats aren't allowed. It's kin sorta close to an actual office! With a nice vie Meanwhile, my husband is downstairs at the d ing room table. Haha...

Anthony: What attracted you to design wo When did you realize this is what you wanted to d And when did you get started designing comics?

Cathy: Oof... this is a long answer. I sort of into it, to be honest, and moving to comics was at all a straight line. I actually didn't go to sch for art (communications major!), but from a you age was always very into art, specifically photo raphy, and eventually – relevant to my work comics – very, very into the look of pop cultur poster designs, album cover designs, movie ti sequences and so forth.

I was in web design a long time before jump back to print when I joined the Dynamite staff 2016.

The Art Director then, Jason Ullmeyer, wanted hire someone outside of the comics world to bri in a fresh aesthetic, and I was just coming of stint doing web design in the music business.

Anthony: Okay, let's increase the challenge in th questions... I know that design is a very difficult a

...e-consuming process. Can you walk ... reader through everything that you ... at the publisher?

...thy: There's a lot! The production ...partment is small, and we have to ... everything. I'll just focus on the cre-...on of logo and dress. And a lot of the ...me steps also come into play when ... collect issues into a trade and need ... entire book design.

...en you start with nothing, there's ...dialogue with the editor. You learn ... direction. Frequently I look at titles ...dmire, often outside of comics, and ...ate a mood board on Pinterest. Ba-...lly, for me, a mood board is a col-...tion of images related to the history ... the property (and, obviously, Nancy ...ew has a very rich and long history), ... history of the genre (mystery) and ...at's going on with the genre now. ...o sketches. Play with font possibili-...s and customizing those fonts so they ...n't feel too directly out of the box. If ... lucky, I get to test logos over future ...ver art to really see what I'm doing. ...e whole time I have to make sure I'm ...nking of how it will work in a comic ...re – meaning if at all possible, the ...o must be very visible on a shelf.

...addition to the logo, I have to think ...out where the Dynamite logo will go, ...ere creator credits will go, the price ...o, issue number, etc. I have to think ...out how far I'm going to deviate from ... standard logo/price/rating box. I ...ve to go back to my collected ideas ... see what type works with the logo ...d reads clearly. Once I'm really getting ...mewhere, I submit what I've got to ... editor and wait for critiques.

...thony: Walk us through your de-...n for The Death of Nancy Drew. It's ...ry unconventional, with the logo ...anging locations every issue (and ... some completely blending into the ...age). What were you looking to do ...th this logo?

Cathy: Actually, I had a starting point by going back to Nancy Drew & The Hardy Boys: The Big Lie. Early in the process with that series you were very specific about its narrative tone and look drawing inspiration from the film Brick. I knew this series was going to be similarly dark, so I decided to go back to the type we used for The Big Lie por-tion of the logo and play with it more. I liked the idea of really integrating the logo into the art rather than having a standalone title over top of the art. I wanted it to blend in with the action or have it emerge from the shadows. I wanted it to have a gritty texture like The Big Lie.

Anthony: Okay, now for the hardest question of all: Do you have any embar-rassing stories about our editor, Matt Idelson? Readers of these Q&As will know that I've been trying for twelve issues to get embarrassing stories or dirt on the man, but I'm always failing. Please, please, please... do you have anything?

Cathy: This is more sweet than em-barrassing, but when I first became Art Director it was a very stressful transi-tion. After some running jokes about Garfield between us and a couple other co-workers, he bought a Garfield phone from the 80s for me at a flea market and shipped it to the Dynamite offices to cheer me up. At one point our IT person hooked it up and set up Garfield voice mail greetings downloaded from the interwebs. Now Garfield's just staring at me on my desk - forever hating Mondays and dying for lasagna.

Anthony: Thanks for taking the time to walk us through your role not only in this book but the entire process. It takes an entire team to create a comic book series and I'm glad to have been able to highlight your role in the process.

Cathy: My pleasure!

Thank You!

Murder is hard (so we're told...), and staging the death of one of literature's favorite characters takes a lot of time and help. Anthony and Joe would love to thank the following for aiding and abetting this story...

Laura Becker for signing off on this project before anyone else did and continuing to be its biggest champion; the team at Simon & Schuster for letting us kill one of their darlings; Jenn Fischer for her Nancy Drew know-how and guidance; Werther Dell'Edera and Stefano Simeone for their artistic contribution in the original series, THE BIG LIE; Keith Morris, Sasha Fraze and Toyin Oluwole for their work in the early stages of the story; the entire team at Dynamite but specifically Alan Payne and Vincent Faust who were there to help us out when word of our series blew up and people on Twitter hated us; Ryan Nord for helping out with legal discussions with Dynamite.

Joe would like to thank his wife, Sherryl, for being his number 1 cheerleader and supporter; his sister, Lorell, for letting him steal her Nancy Drew books when they were kids, and Matt and Anthony for going to hell and back for this book!

Anthony would like to thank his own creative team at home – Lisa, Dash and Siena.

Most importantly, a HUGE thanks to editor Matt Idelson, perhaps the most patient person in the industry, for not only guiding this project but putting up with Anthony's constant and unending questions and requests... You are truly the hero of this story.

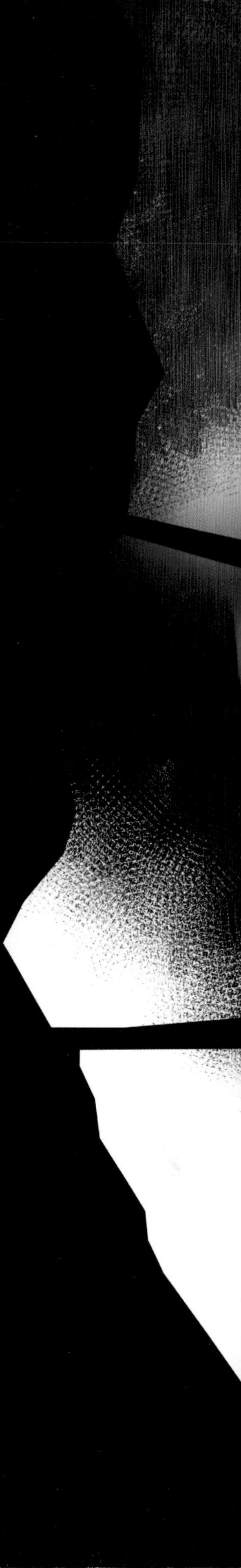